The Criminal Justice System

THEORY, RESEARCH, AND PRACTICE

2nd Edition

Kendall Hunt
publishing company

Melchor C. de Guzman | **Maryann S. White**

Cover © Shutterstock.com

www.kendallhunt.com
Send all inquiries to:
4050 Westmark Drive
Dubuque, IA 52004-1840

Copyright © 2018, 2020 by Kendall Hunt Publishing Company

ISBN: 978-1-7924-5055-6

Published in the United States of America

CONTENTS

An introduction to criminal justice exposes the student to the whole gamut of the business of administering justice in society. This book intends to serve as a comprehensive introduction to criminal justice. It is comprehensive on the breadth of the topics covered, but not so much in depth. The objective is simply to provide an awareness of the issues of crime and justice without overwhelming a novice learner. To accomplish these tasks, the authors designed the book as a survey of a typical criminal justice curriculum to give the readers exposure to the variety of courses that students might encounter throughout their academic careers. The chapters are carefully selected to fit most criminal justice curriculum in the United States. The intent of the authors is to develop a book that serves as a foundational reference to students as they progress in their academic careers. Thus, it is not designed as a buyback or a throwaway book at the end of the semester.

Likewise, the book exposes the reader to the variety of careers that are available in criminal justice. We provide information that would inspire and guide prospective practitioners in any field. Criminal justice majors will be informed about the many possibilities and innovations in the administration of justice. Students who are not majors of criminal justice, but intended to take the course as an elective, should find the textbook beneficial and related to their specific disciplines. For example, a practicing nurse might learn about how to deal with the offending population if he or she happens to work in criminal justice facilities such as correctional institutions or even as a nurse for uniformed personnel or victims of crime. Science students will also get glimpses into how they can venture into the criminal justice world by examining the workings and opportunities in forensics, cybercrime, and even careers as forensic medical examiners. Indeed, it is not only a book of information, but a book of opportunities.

The content of the book first touches on both criminology and the criminal justice system in the United States. Chapter 1 begins with the objectives of expounding the meaning of justice and the dynamics that criminal justice actors exhibit within the criminal justice system. Behavioral tendencies and factors that precipitate these behaviors are also discussed.

As an introduction to criminology, three major chapters have been prepared. We include a chapter on theories and explanations of crime, as well as a chapter on victimology. These chapters should complement each other because they provide snapshots of how both offenders and victims are enmeshed in crime. Additionally, we provide a foundational chapter on the nature and operations of criminal law, which provides insights to the legal restrictions and legal tools upon which the justice system operates.

In Chapter 5, students are exposed to the different criminal justice data that they may be able to utilize if they want to further examine some of these theories and principles of criminology and criminal justice. This chapter on measures of crime departs from other criminal justice textbooks, however. It exposes students not only to the databases and sources that are aimed at examining the phenomenon of crime and criminal justice in the United States, but also includes discussions about databases and information sources that they could examine if they want to expand on their knowledge about international crime and criminal justice. Thus, students are led to some major sources for both US data and international crime data.

Necessarily, the book discusses the different agencies of the criminal justice system—police, courts, and corrections. The approach used in these chapters is what is known as the descriptive approach, using the actors/systems strategy and the functions/operations strategy. In these regards, the agencies are discussed first as organizations, including some aspects of their management. Moving on, each agency is discussed as to how it performs its specific functions in this system. Thus, chapters about the system and the processes are equally discussed throughout the segments pertaining to the main agencies of the criminal justice system.

After the discussions of each agency, the book becomes more exciting as we examine the hottest topics in criminal justice. The third section of the book begins with implications of policing in the world of accommodations. Chapter 12 discusses the processing of juveniles in the criminal justice system. This chapter stresses the various ways by which the criminal justice actors adjust their roles to serve this special population. The characteristics and challenges involved with administering justice to these populations will also be discussed. The chapter will note several innovative initiatives or normative solutions for addressing the needs of the special population of juveniles and expounds on the differences between the criminal justice system and the juvenile justice system.

Drug offenses, terrorism, organized crime, and cybercrime are some of the crimes that present major challenges to the criminal justice system. The unique characteristics of these crimes as dynamic and transnational are discussed in Chapter 13. We examine some of the measures that have been adopted, but left out judgments on the effectiveness of these measures against these crimes. We took caution in presenting normative solutions, as these crimes seem to manifest themselves as wicked problems. Criminal justice agencies have tried multiple approaches to address these specific crimes, yet they continue to persist, grow, and spread. The very nature of these crimes makes it difficult to adopt more lasting and effective solutions. Within criminal justice, drugs, terrorism, organized crime, and cybercrime are topics that are most relevant to today's globalized world. Students will understand the transnational characteristics of these crimes and the significant challenges that the nexus of groups involved in the commission of these offenses could present to the criminal justice system. Sometimes, solutions to these problems are not INTER-national, but INTERNATIONAL, in scope. This chapter presents interesting developments in the control and prosecution of international crimes.

The book closes with the issue of community justice. Chapter 14 discusses the implications of community participation as related to the administration of justice. It is stressed that communities are key to the effectiveness and efficiency of the criminal justice system. Citizens can effectively participate in the administration of justice and provisions of safety. At the same time, students will come to realize that community justice is nothing revolutionary, but is a traditional function of citizens. Indeed, in some countries, community is declared the fourth pillar of the criminal justice system. The authors believe that community is not a pillar, but actually the foundation that holds the justice system together. Despite such advantages of having community participation, there are challenges for enticing citizens to participate. The chapter provides some insights into these challenges. Likewise, we have to be cautious of any unintended consequences of the establishment of a community justice system.

In the second edition, you will find new content intended to supplement and enhance the subject matter from the previous edition. Notably, chapters 10, 11, and 12 were newly written for this edition.

Also, at the end of each chapter, there is a comprehension check, or a set of questions that can be used to examine understanding of some of the important concepts within the chapter. In addition, several Career Highlights boxes have been added throughout the book to provide more information about various career opportunities in criminal justice and criminology. Finally, we have added ancillary materials for instructors to aid in using this book to teach introductory courses in criminal justice, which are available online.

This book will likely continue to evolve in the future as criminal justice continues its quest for effective, efficient, and fair justice system administration. This book is not intended to "box in" students to the information presented. Instead, we encourage students and professors to enhance the learning experience by providing the depth and breadth necessary for the learning objectives of their individual classrooms. Certainly, it is the hope of the authors that this book inspires criminal justice students to move forward with their careers, armed with the foundational tools provided by this textbook, and to become successful in their chosen fields.

Melchor C. de Guzman, PhD
Maryann S. White, PhD

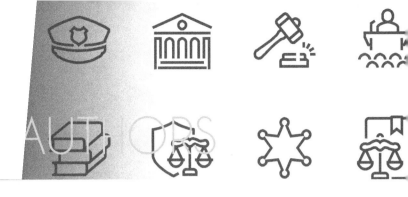

Melchor C. de Guzman received his Ph.D. in criminal justice from the University of Cincinnati. His professional career has traversed both the academe and professional practice. He is a full professor at Georgia Gwinnett College. He was also a former managing editor for *Police Practice & Research: An International Journal* and a book editor for the International Police Executive Symposium. He is currently the immediate past president of the Criminal Justice Association of Georgia (CJAG) after serving as the association's president for two years. He has published over 20 journal articles and book chapters and authored and co-edited 4 books.

Maryann S. White received her Ph.D. in criminology and criminal justice from Old Dominion University. She is currently an assistant professor at Georgia Gwinnett College. Prior to teaching in higher education, she worked as a freelance editor, subject matter expert, and as an independent research consultant. She has presented her research at several national conferences as well as authored and co-authored multiple peer-reviewed articles. Her current research focuses on serial murderers, violent crime, victimology and victimization, and psychological aspects of criminal behavior.

This book is dedicated to the students.

May you find the path that is right for you. It may not be the easiest path to take, and it will certainly require hard work, but it will all be worth it to discover what ignites your passion.

SECTION 1
CRIMINAL JUSTICE, LAW, AND CRIMINOLOGY

Chapter 4
Victimology

Chapter 5
Crime Measurement Tools and Other Criminal Justice Databases

©AVNphotolab/Shutterstock.com

The Dynamics of Criminal Justice

LEARNING OBJECTIVES

After reading this chapter, the student should be able to

1 Explain the different conceptualizations of justice and the specific goals of the criminal justice system in the administration of justice

2 Explain the different views about the operation of the criminal justice system in the United States

3 Discuss the key characteristics of the criminal justice system in the United States

4 Identify the behaviors of the criminal justice system and the factors that shape these behaviors

5 Outline the challenges that the justice system faces in the modern world

Introduction

The criminal justice system is a prominent feature of the American daily life. The roles that the criminal justice system perform in society are complexed and dynamic. The complexity of the justice system's roles emanates from several sources. The first reason involves the problem with conceptualizing the meaning of justice. The meanings of justice abound (Hunter, Barker, & de Guzman, 2018), with some defining the term as the reparation of harm (restorative justice), the maintenance of an equilibrium disturbed by crime (retributive justice), or the pursuit of the utilitarian purpose of protecting the status quo (distributive justice and social justice). Additionally, the criminal justice system does not have the bestowed power to set its own conception of justice. The definition of safety and its provisions are now shared with various entities (Bayley & Shearing, 2001). The legislatures implicitly define what justice means and its provisions by means of enacting statutes. Equally, the community has the ability to provide inputs on the meanings of justice. In an age of a community justice model, this power to shape the meaning of justice is sometimes reposed to the community (see Chapter 14).

The second reason for the complexity of administering justice lies in the governmental structure and the basic principles of government. The United States is a federated government. This means that criminal justice powers are sometimes administered in an uncoordinated and multilevel system (Bayley, 1985, 1992). To the uninitiated, trying to conform one's conduct to the laws of the state and the federal government can become challenging and confusing. Likewise, someone has to understand the specific agencies and their procedures at every level and jurisdiction. For example, the sheriff and the county police might exist as separate entities in one county, but in some counties both offices are merged. The state police and the investigation units are unified in some states but divided in others (Worrall & Schmalleger, 2018). Two types of prosecutors might exist in one state, the federal district attorneys and the state prosecutors. In this milieu of justice agencies, one can get easily confused.

The third reason for the complexity of the criminal justice system is due to its dynamic nature. The primary source of this dynamism is the nature of its legal system—the common law legal system. Indeed, this legal system makes it easy to adapt to the needs and sentiments of the time. This process, however, brings about a perpetual contest in the supremacy of whose views of justice should prevail. The debate over due process or crime control is an ongoing political struggle even within the justice system.

This political struggle brings about the next source of dynamism. The criminal justice system is not totally devoid of politics. The law enforcement, prosecution, courts, and correctional personnel are intimately wedded with politicians. In fact, several justice personnel (e.g., sheriffs, prosecutors, and judges) are directly elected by the people. Hence, the winds of justice sometimes swing different ways depending on the political culture that is prevailing.

In light of these dynamics, the justice system develops some behavioral patterns to effectively and officially carry out its functions and make sense of its roles in the administration of justice (Maguire & Katz, 2002). This chapter lays out the different conceptualizations of justice in US society and the competing views about the structure of the criminal justice system in the United States. Also, the interconnectedness of the agencies and the actors within the justice system will be outlined to highlight the challenges of the justice system and how these challenges influence the behaviors of the criminal justice system and its actors.

The Meanings of Justice

Despite the claim that justice is objective, the term justice is really a socially constructed term. This implies that its conceptualization is something that emerges as a product of a consensus on what it means. In most cases, an adjective is appended to the word to describe the form of justice being conveyed. A cursory search of the meaning of justice would result in several dimensions and appendages attached to the word. Some of these meanings are presented here.

Moral Justice versus Legal Justice

Moral justice is the resolution of conflict and the attainment of an outcome based on the current morals. On the other hand, legal justice is the faithful adherence to the law in resolving a conflict (Miltner, 1931). Observers of the criminal justice system are sometimes confused and aghast at the lack of morality and fairness in the system's actions and decisions. For example, a person who might be factually or believed to be guilty is sometimes allowed to walk free. As a specific example, there was an informal consensus that O. J. Simpson was guilty of murder, but he was declared as not guilty by the jury. In yet another instance, the police officers who beat Rodney King were found by the court to have justifiably used necessary force when they were beating him. These cases illustrate the disjunctions that can occur between moral justice and legal justice. The ideal situation is that the application of the law would produce a moral outcome—the guilty ones are punished and the victims are given justice. Yet, the reality is that the US justice system is bound by legal justice more than by moral justice principles. Most often, the letter of the law is given weight over the arrival at a morally just outcome. This is a reality about the operation of our justice system. Hence, it is not surprising that those that have moralist perspectives will have disagreements with those that adhere to the legalist perspective. It cannot be denied, however, that most laws, when applied skillfully, would most likely produce a morally acceptable outcome.

Different Types of Justice

To further understand the complexities of justice administration, let us discuss some of the meanings of justice. As we said earlier, a descriptive word is sometimes appended to justice to declare its objective and intent. These objectives are sometimes tied to some ideologies and perspectives that can at times become contradictory when simultaneously pursued. There are four types of justice that people can seek when they have been wronged (Maiese, 2003).

Distributive Justice

Distributive justice has been conceptualized as economic justice; that is, fairness in what people receive, from goods to attention. Its foundation is socialism where equality is a fundamental principle. Under this system, law and justice are merely instruments to arrive at equality. The system is not to protect the right or status of a person, but to bring about equilibrium on people's economic statuses.

Procedural Justice

The principle of fairness is also found in the idea of fair play (as opposed to the fair share of distributive justice). If people believe that a fair process was used in deciding what is to be distributed, then they may well accept an imbalance in what they receive in comparison to others (Leventhal, 1980; Thibaut & Walker, 1975). Tyler (2017) suggests that procedural justice can be achieved by providing two avenues for citizens. First is the availability to have a voice and be heard. The other dimension is being treated with fairness and dignity. These two components are actually embodied as ideals of due process and, therefore, must be practiced in the criminal justice system (Thibaut, Walker, LaTour, & Houlden, 1974; Thibaut, Walker, & Lind, 1972).

Restorative Justice

The first thing that the betrayed person may seek from the betrayer is some form of restitution, putting things back as they should be. The simplest form of restitution is a straightforward apology. Restoration means putting things back as they were, so it may include some act of contrition to demonstrate one is truly sorry. This may include action and even extra payment to the offended party. Restorative justice is also known as corrective justice or peacemaking (Fuller, 2003). Under this conceptualization, justice is characterized by compassion for both the offenders and victims of crime. The ideals of restoration can only happen if there is a repair of the relationships broken by crime (Braithwaite, 1989). The process normally observed involved arbitration and mediation (Van Ness & Strong, 2006).

Retributive Justice

Retributive justice works on the principle of punishment and appeasement for a wrong done. This form of justice works on proportionality (an eye for an eye doctrine). Although the intent may be to dissuade the perpetrator or others from future wrongdoing, the reoffending rate of many criminals indicates the limited success of this approach. Punishment in practice is more about the satisfaction of victims and those who care about them. This form of justice sometimes strays into the realm of revenge, which can be many times more severe than the reparation needed. In such cases, justice is typically subjective and emotional rather than that with intent for fairness or prevention.

Social Justice

Social justice is rendering to everyone that which is his or her due as a human being. Social justice goes beyond emphasizing equity and fairness in the application of law. This form of justice extends all the way to regulating how a society's resources are allocated (Crank, 2003). Wealth equality by the use of progressive tax systems, strict regulation of business, including reparations, and extensive use of social interventions by government are principles embodied within social justice.

Criminal Justice Defined

Various definitions of criminal justice are presented. Rush (2004) defines the criminal justice system as the "process of adjudication by which the legal rights of private parties are vindicated and the guilt or innocence of accused persons are established." Hunter et al. (2018) noted that "the criminal justice system is concerned not only with the enforcement of laws but with the protection of legal rights as well." Thus, Davis (2016) defines the criminal justice system as "the entire governmental apparatus that formally processes crime, including but not limited to law enforcement, prosecution, defense, the courts and corrections." Mentor (2013) and Belshaw and Deboer (2013) noted that criminal justice is the business of government in the enforcement of laws, affirming social norms, and the administration of justice. In all of these definitions, the notions of process, actors, and the administration of justice come into play. These elements of the various definitions, indeed, encompass what the criminal justice system is all about. Thus, the discussion of this chapter defines the goals of the criminal justice system, the structure of the US justice system, the behaviors of the criminal justice system, and the factors that influence these behaviors.

For purposes of this book, we present a definition of **criminal justice** as "the accordance of legal due process by various independent agencies of government and citizens to bring about safety and equilibrium in a society that has been disrupted by crime." This definition encompasses all the various conceptualization of justice from the utilitarian perspective of providing law and order in society to the attainment of equality under the law as envisioned by social justice. This process has the distinct characteristics of the rule of law and fairness (due process and procedural justice). This definition also realizes that crime creates a disruption of social life and, therefore, the social life disturbed by crime needs to be repaired and restored (Braithwaite, 1989). Finally, the definition stresses that justice administration is not solely a governmental business, but also a community endeavor where citizens are enjoined to contribute as part of a democratic society. Thus, in this book, we allotted a chapter on community justice and highlighted the various ways that community members can contribute to the administration of criminal justice.

The Goals of Criminal Justice

Doing Justice

The notion of justice here is legal justice, meaning that the conduct or behavior falls within the legal definition of the criminal law. Being factually guilty is different from being legally guilty. For example, if you actually fired the gun and killed a person, the facts show that you did the killing. However, if you fired a gun against someone due to the imminent threat to your life, then you are excused from the killing and did not violate a criminal law. In this case, justice demands that your case be dismissed because you did not meet the requirement for committing the act of homicide. This goal is supreme, but also the most complex. As stated earlier, the meanings of justice abound and they have tendencies to clash.

Controlling Crime

The notion of controlling crime involves the intervention of the criminal justice system in order for the crime rate to remain within a tolerable limit. At this juncture, the courts might place an offender under state supervision in order for that offender to desist from committing an offense. Likewise, the police might use their force and restraint options in order to stop ongoing crimes. Finally, the correctional institutions might not release an individual back into the community. Most often, this goal is conceptualized as where a crime is already happening but something has to be done to stop it from spreading. For example, an active shooter will be immediately attended to by the police to stop the shooter from continuing with his or her crime.

Preventing Crime

The other goal of the criminal justice system is to prevent crime. Lab (2004) defines crime prevention as one that "entails any action designed to reduce the actual level of crime and/or the perceived fear of crime." This definition is outcome based rather than action based. Other definitions, however, are action based, such as the definition of crime prevention as "the anticipation, recognition and appraisal of a crime risk and the initiation of some action to remove or reduce it" (Catholic University of America, 2018). For this definition, crime prevention means using your instinct, common sense, and action to reduce a potential criminal's opportunity (Cohen & Felson, 1979). Plainly speaking, **crime prevention** is recognizing that a crime risk exists and the criminal justice system takes some corrective action to eliminate or reduce that risk. Crime prevention means risk reduction. Reporting suspicious persons and/or activities, locking unoccupied rooms, securing doors and windows at the end of the day, securing university and personal property, and being aware of your surroundings are all important risk reduction strategies.

Goal Satisfaction and Prioritization

There is a view that these criminal justice goals should be equally and minimally, if not maximally, satisfied (Travis & Langworthy, 2008). This form of goal satisfaction means that criminal justice serves these three goals simultaneously and equally. This view could be illustrated in Figure 1.1. The figure indicates that it does not matter what goal you pursue. All the goals complement each other and they will all be served by pursuing any of them.

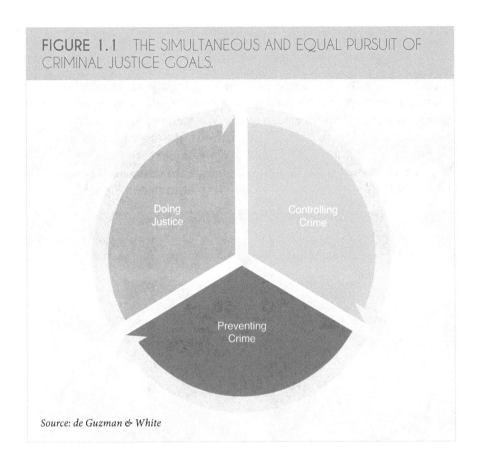

FIGURE 1.1 THE SIMULTANEOUS AND EQUAL PURSUIT OF CRIMINAL JUSTICE GOALS.

Doing Justice

Controlling Crime

Preventing Crime

Source: de Guzman & White

However, the alternative view is that one takes precedence over the other. The alternative view suggests that administering justice is the fount and primary goal as portrayed in Figure 1.2. When justice is served, citizens will respect the law and thereby control and prevent crime (Tyler, 2017). Likewise, the fair administration of justice will inspire citizens to participate in the administration of justice and become more effective in controlling crime or become more proactive in the prevention of crime (Lambertus & Yakimchuk, 2007).

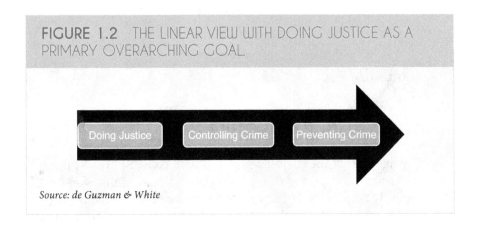

FIGURE 1.2 THE LINEAR VIEW WITH DOING JUSTICE AS A PRIMARY OVERARCHING GOAL.

Doing Justice   Controlling Crime   Preventing Crime

Source: de Guzman & White

The final view is that these goals are independent of each other and can therefore be pursued in a parallel manner. This view also means that such goals can be pursued at different times and at varying degrees. In contrast to the first view, the justice system is pursuing these goals equally but without necessarily being concerned with minimally satisfying all of them or giving priority to any of them. In fact, it is sometimes necessary to achieve more than one of these goals. In other words, the justice system can simply pursue doing justice without controlling or preventing crimes. In contrast, it can pursue crime control and crime prevention without necessarily achieving justice (Packer, 1968). This view is illustrated in Figure 1.3.

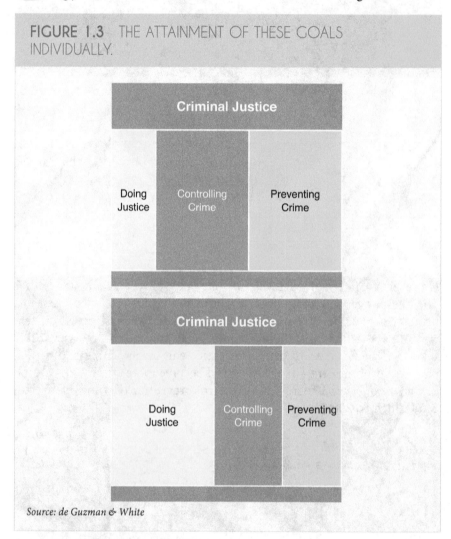

FIGURE 1.3 THE ATTAINMENT OF THESE GOALS INDIVIDUALLY.

Source: de Guzman & White

Criminal Justice Structure

The main agencies of the criminal justice system consist of the legislature, law enforcement, courts, and corrections (Hunter et al., 2018). The legislature primarily decides the criminalization of a conduct. In fact, the legislature provides the foundational policies and actions toward crime in society.

They are responsible for creating executive agencies and the allocation of funding for programs and interventions. Due to these functions, the legislatures in the federal and state levels breathe life to the criminal justice system. In one of the major legislations, the US Congress created the Department of Homeland Security, which also precipitated the creation of antiterrorism units in the state levels. Very recently, the US Congress extended and refined the surveillance operations of the criminal justice system against those that threaten the security of the nation. In other words, legislative acts have major implications on the behaviors, structures, and activities of the criminal justice system.

The law enforcement agency is considered as the face of criminal justice (Hunter et al., 2018; Worrall & Schmalleger, 2018). The law enforcement units of this country consist of both the federal and local enforcement units that make up the entire apparatus of the law enforcement executive. The local police are particularly important as they deal with the day-to-day activities of policing that have direct impact on people's lives (Travis & Langworthy, 2008). The law enforcement units include even those that enforce border security and those that gather intelligence for prevention of terrorist attacks. There are also the law enforcement units that police the tribal lands. Special purpose police are also considered law enforcers that address crimes in specific jurisdictions such the transportation police, the park police, and the university police (Travis & Langworthy, 2008). Public police have become more involved in the school setting with the deployment of School Resource Officers (SROs).

The court system consists of the different judges and prosecutors. The prosecutors decide who needs to be brought to the court for adjudication. The prosecutors are sometimes aided by community members in this decision-making through their participation in the grand jury deliberations. In turn, the judges test these decisions by the prosecutor through the ceremonial processes of the court from bail hearing, pretrial detention hearing, and finally, the trial and sentencing phases of the court proceedings. The court actors also include the defense attorneys who represent defendants in criminal cases.

The correctional agencies include both the institutional correctional agencies, private and public, that work in detention facilities like prisons and jails. Probation and parole staff are also considered as part of the correctional apparatus. Finally, other inmate intervention professionals such as counsellors, medical and mental health staff, among others, are also part of this component of the criminal justice system.

The criminal justice structure is a vast array of these institutions and personnel. Hagan (2018) estimates that about $214 billion annually are spent on average in the national budget for criminal justice expenditures. This monetary figure does not take into account the other expenditures that are spent by private institutions for the provisions of inmate services as well as victim services needed for their safety and recovery from crime. Criminal justice is, thus, personnel heavy and an expensive government business.

Conceptualizing the Relationships of the Criminal Justice Agencies

The relationships of these criminal justice agencies have been conceptualized in a variety of ways. The primary criteria for some of these observations are due to their structural characteristics and their functional differentiations. The justice system in the United States has been described in three different ways—a fragmented system, a coordinated system, and a loosely coupled system.

The Fragmented System

This view suggests that the criminal justice agencies do not properly coordinate with each other. Since each agency has been given its own domain, the agents within each agency do not necessarily have to consider the actions and reactions of the other agencies. The agencies are perceived sometimes to be working at cross-purposes of each other. Sometimes, they are characterized as undermining or questioning each other's works. Conceivably under this fragmented arrangement, the wheels of justice would stop if the police would not do their job of apprehending offenders. Likewise, the courts could hinder the work of the police through the questioning of the processes that the police use against offenders. As noted above, the court can question even the prosecution's decisions. Similarly, the different actors of the criminal justice system can question the decisions handed by courts by filing appeals and assailing its jurisdiction. Finally, the correctional institutions can undermine the work of the other agencies if they fail to rehabilitate the offender or they release an offender to the community early. In other words, there is a potential for each agency to hinder one another's work without any formal obligation to coordinate.

Likewise, the agencies' goals are seen as contrary to each other. The police are seen as anticriminals by aggressively catching offenders and punishing them for their behaviors. The courts are sometimes perceived as favoring the offenders by providing them with all the protection against abuses by the system and other units of government. Some citizens are even questioning why obviously guilty individuals are still given the right to trial and presumed as innocent. Similarly, the roles and activities of the correctional agencies are seen as contrary to the implicit goals of the system (i.e., punishing offenders). An offender committed a harm and was supposedly being punished, but the offender is afforded rehabilitation services and amenities that include education, housing, counseling, and other amenities that law-abiding citizens can barely afford for themselves. Due to these observations, the criminal justice system has been viewed as fragmented.

The Coordinated System

The coordinated system suggests that all the agencies are working together like an assembly plant with unified goals. To illustrate the argument for the coordinated system, let us examine the twin goals of offender control and citizen safety. The criminal justice system seems to have twin goals under this view. The first is the promotion of safety though the control of the individual and the second is the enhancement of safety though the reformation of the individuals who committed an offense. Under this goal of reformation, the police produce the main product to the system by catching the criminal offender. In other words, they decide the proper target for the intervention. The courts maintain quality control of the product (the offender) by making sure that they are appropriate to be processed by the criminal justice system. This has the equivalence of determining the risks and needs of the offender in order for him or her to be given effective interventions. Finally, the correctional system polishes the product in their facilities so that the offender can return to the community as a reformed individual. The safety of society is pursued alongside this process of apprehending and reformatting the individuals. However, the justice system makes sure that some who may not respond to rehabilitation are effectively restrained either by charging them with the most severe forms of crime, assigning them the harshest penalties, and denying them of pathways back to the community by not giving parole or probation. In this view, the processes for achieving these twin goals are adopted by each agency of the system. For the system to achieve these assembly line characteristics, the agency should be seen as being coopted and cooperative with each other. We shall see later how these values are reflected in the behaviors of the criminal justice system.

The Loosely Coupled System

"Coupling is the degree to which organizational elements are linked, connected, related or interdependent (Maguire & Katz, 2002, p. 504)." By implication, loose coupling means that organizations are loosely or minimally connected. A loosely coupled system is characterized by independence in operation and administration but is connected by several lynchpins. With respect to the criminal justice system, the lynchpins that make the agencies connected are the ideals that are enshrined in the constitution. The Bill of Rights in the Constitution demands that each action of the agencies in the system is within the rule of law. The different actors are also connected to each other by their clients (victims and offenders) whose control and welfare they have to decide. Therefore, even if they belong to separate branches of government, their relationships are more of collaboration rather than competition.

Whose View Is Correct?

Valid arguments seem to exist for each of the views. Since the agencies of the criminal justice system are independently funded, managed, and controlled, then we can say that they might be a fragmented system. Despite the organizational isolation of each agency it cannot be denied that there is a high degree of dependency on each other for the processing of clients. The system must perform their jobs well in order to produce a viable outcome. More importantly, they deal with the same client all throughout the process. This means that the criminal justice may resemble an assembly line that passes on the product for completion at each level. These features are semblances for a coordinated system. However, it cannot be denied that sometimes the system lacks the essential feature of coordination in terms of the unity of purpose and nonantagonistic relationships. In this regard, the loose coupling perspective seems to be the more accurate view to depict the relationships that exist within the criminal justice. The agencies operate independently with seeming disregard for the other actors' input in the process. At the same time, each of the actor's decisions are motivated by justice and their actions are vetted against their observances of the mandates of the Constitution through the Bill of Rights and the due process clause of the Constitution. In addition, the processes at each level are additive rather than diminutive in the attainment of the ideals of justice. This means that all the rights and protections are accorded to every client of the system at every stage of the proceedings and the final outcome is a product of the different contributions of each actor. To illustrate these points further, let us examine the working attributes of the criminal justice system.

The Key Characteristics of the US Justice System

The key characteristics of the criminal justice system are bound by the legal system under which they operate and the organizational culture and working arrangements that have been developed by the criminal justice system in their administration of justice. These characteristics have been developed in response to the social and legal contexts of the operational environment of the criminal justice system.

The Common Law System

The United States is under the common law legal tradition, but some of its principles are influenced by the civil law system (Reichel, 2018). As a common law system, the characteristics of liberal interpretation of laws to arrive at fairness and the resort to customs in resolving some unchartered territories are allowed. There is also the ability for the decisions of the Supreme Court as having the force and effect of law. For example, the court determines the consequences or criminal responsibility for aborting a fetus at a certain stage of pregnancy without the legal statute covering such action. In a civil law system, strict legal construction and the absence of law would preclude the judge from using logic or analogy to resolve a dispute. In addition, to maintain consistency and legal stability of the decisions, the courts observe the principle of **stare decisis**.[1] One of the basic features of the common law system is the ability of the courts to make decisions that have the equivalence of law. In a strict civil law system, judges cannot infer rights based on traditions but they have to rely on the law and its spirit in deciding disputes. Aside from this basic characteristic of the US legal system, there are other unique characteristics of the US criminal justice system.

Dual Justice System

The federated nature of the United States provides for a dual system of justice. The federal government operates to handle violations of federal laws. At the same time, the states have their own criminal justice structures to process offenders of the state laws. Thus, there might be times when an offense traverses both jurisdictions and an offender might be processed by both systems without violating the principle of double jeopardy.[2] The dual system can be advantageous as there are multiple jurisdictions that can make an offender accountable before the law. At the same time, the offender might be unduly disadvantaged due to the multiplicity of jurisdictions that may jeopardize his or her rights as an accused.

The Sequential Process

The criminal justice system works in a sequential process. This means that an offender has to go through all the ceremonies or processes that are observed in each agency. The nonobservance of these sequences will redound to a faulty system whereby an offender is not accorded due process resulting in an unfair outcome.

The Filtering/Sifting Process

The criminal justice system has limited resources, but there is an over-abundance of complaints and offenders that go through its system. In this regard, the criminal justice system has to engage in a filtering process. In the case of the police, they tend to focus on more serious crimes, serious offenders, or the protection of more vulnerable victims. The prosecutor also engages in screening the offenses that they bring to trial. It is estimated that only about 5 percent of cases are brought to trial while the rest are dismissed, dropped, or plea bargained (Cole, Smith, & DeJong, 2018). To accomplish this enormous task of sifting through the cases, the prosecutor uses criteria such as resource demands, ability to gain conviction, or the political impact of the case. Despite these initial filters, offenders are further narrowed down at the correctional level. Even when defendants are found guilty, most of them are placed on probation or given intermediate sanctions. Only those that are serious and repeat offenders tend to be sentenced to prison. Because of this filtering process, the criminal justice system is sometimes perceived to be discriminatory or soft on crime. Likewise, it is also considered to be "all bark no bite" in its punishment because of the early releases of convicted persons (Cole et al., 2018).

Adversarial System

The criminal justice system has been described as adopting the adversarial system. The gladiatorial process is dramatized primarily in the courtroom where the prosecutor and the defense are expected to argue two different sides. The prosecutor will try to prove the guilt of the accused, whereas the defense will argue for the innocence of the defendant. This process has been described as a "storytelling" contest (Meyer, 2018). Each side will try to present its own version of the case (i.e., story). The one that tells the most believable story wins the contest. This adversarial process can extend beyond these actors. For example, the defense counsel can also question the process and motives of the law enforcement in order to sow doubt and acquit the accused. The judges are not also spared in this adversarial process because the defense can question the jurisdiction of the court as well as attack the competence and impartiality of the judge during appeals. These contests are sometimes participated in by victims and witnesses including the general public by protesting the outcomes of the process. Thus, the appearance of viciousness and antagonisms among the courtroom actors sometimes portrays the courtroom as a battleground of advocacies (Neubauer & Fradella, 2011).

Discretion

Discretion has been defined as the authority to choose between two courses of action. (Worrall & Schmalleger, 2016) At every stage of the criminal justice intervention, actors use their discretion. Discretion, as Black (1980) suggests, could be good or bad depending on the basis for the use of that discretion. According to Black (1980), the use of legal factors in order to make a discretionary determination of action is a good base for the exercise of discretion. For example, the seriousness of the offense is a good basis for exercising discretion. On the other hand, the use of extra-legal factors (i.e., factors that have nothing to do with the case) is a bad base for the decision to use discretion. For example, the use of such demographic factors such as race, class, or even gender produces a disparate form of administration of justice. The bad form of discretion violates one of the characteristics of law, which is the uniform application or enforcement of law (Reichel, 2018). Davis (2016) considers the use of discretion by the criminal justice system as circumvention of the legislative intent. Thus, the use of extra-legal factors would result in such circumvention.

Resource Dependence and Mutual Assistance

The justice system follows the primary principle of separation of powers. The criminalization of a conduct is reposed in the legislative assemblies. The enforcement of criminal laws and punishments of offenders are reposed within the domain of the police, prosecutors, and correctional officers who are within the supervision and control of the executive branch. The determination of guilt and sentencing are reposed in the judges. They operate independently with specific mandates and different administrative structures. Yet, they all deal with the same clients. For effective processing to happen, they rely on their own expertise, education, and work production. As a result, the police must arrest individuals before the prosecutor can have someone to charge. Likewise, the prosecutor must decide on whether to involve the court in the process. Even then, the skill of the prosecutor in proving a case is needed for conviction to happen and punishments to be imposed. Finally, the correctional institution will receive a client depending on the judgments of the courts. In this regard, a system of dependency occurs. For example, the court only relies on the evidence collected by the police and presented by the prosecutor. The courts do not have the resources nor the expertise to perform these functions. Correctional agencies must be effective in their rehabilitation or correctional efforts; otherwise, the same clients will become a burden again for the entire system. Therefore, it is imperative that the actors in each agency assist effectively in the processing of cases. We will see in Chapter 8 how the interconnectedness and collaborations among the various actors are becoming a trend in the operations of the criminal justice system. To give a quick example, the drug courts in the country promote a collaborative effort in the processing of offenders with substance use disorders by tapping the collective wisdom of the police, prosecutors, and treatment providers in the process of rehabilitating the person with the substance use disorder.

Behaviors of the Justice System

Over the years, several behavioral patterns by the criminal justice system have emerged. Understanding the behaviors of the criminal justice system is essential to decipher the decision-making processes by the actors in the system and make predictions about the system.

The Dynamics of Ideology in Justice Administration

The dilemma of the criminal justice system is how to balance the interest of the society for safety from crime and the protection of the rights of the individual who is facing the entire resources of the state when accused of the crime. The behavior of the criminal justice system along this dimension is the ideology that the justice system embraces. Packer's (1968) dichotomized models of behavior has been labeled as either the crime control model (CCM) or due process model (DPM).

Packer particularly traces the source of ideological leanings from the operations of the courts. Specifically, he attributes the emergence of a particular justice model based on the ideological leanings of those that interpret the law (i.e., judges). He argues that when the composition of the court is more conservative whereby common good is subjugated to the individual welfare, there is a tendency to embrace the CCM. On the contrary, when there is a more liberal ideology that dominates the composition of the court, there is the tendency to place the welfare of the individual accused over the will of the majority of citizens. He sums up the characteristics of these justice models by means of an analogy. He compares the CCM to an assembly line process of delivering justice where the value of the system is the quick processing of an offender but with low control. The DPM is compared to an obstacle course where each agency must overcome the hurdle (standards of the law) in order to process an offender.

The Dynamics of Balancing Freedom and Order

The criminal justice system is torn between two competing interests. The first interest is the need of citizens to enjoy the freedoms guaranteed by law as well as the principle embodied in the declaration of independence; that is, the guarantee of life, liberty, and the pursuit of happiness. However, the freedom is bounded by the rights of others to exercise their individual freedoms. The other interest is the right to have a peaceful life which might be encroached upon by others in the exercise of their freedoms. Maintaining this balance is essential for the peaceful coexistence of the members of society. Under the social contract theory, citizens give up some of their freedoms in exchange for the protection of the state (Taylor & Auerhan, 2015). However, such contract on the surrender of some of these freedoms for the common good are not easily calibrated. These competing interests are what sometimes put the criminal justice system in a lot of criticisms (Figure 1.4).

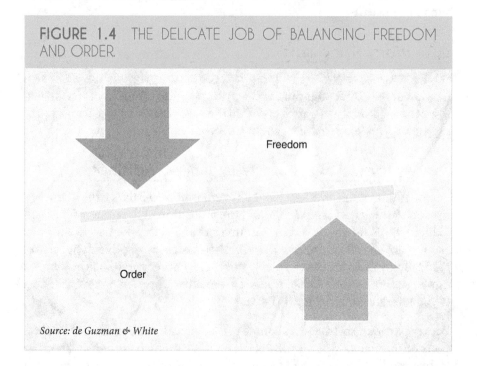

FIGURE 1.4 THE DELICATE JOB OF BALANCING FREEDOM AND ORDER.

Freedom

Order

Source: de Guzman & White

The Dynamics of Priorities

Walker (2011) describes the behavior of the criminal justice system as analogous to a wedding cake. Each layer of the wedding cake represents the nature and seriousness of the offenses involved at each layer. At the top of the wedding cake layer are the celebrated cases. These cases are few and far between, but it is also where the resources and major focus of the criminal justice system are mostly expended. Cases become celebrated cases due to the heinous character of the offense, the status of the offender, or the characteristics of the victim. The recent case of the Ohio sexual offender, Ariel Castro, could exemplify such case where he sexually enslaved several teens for several years. A case can also become a celebrated case due to the celebrity status of the offender and the victim. Again, O. J. is a good example of this type of celebrated case and we have seen several others that have come up over the years, such as the case of football player Aaron Hernandez. Lately, the case of Dr. Larry Nassar was prominently covered due to the celebrity status of the victims, many of whom are Olympic gold medal gymnasts.

The second layer of the wedding cake consists of the more serious offenses, such as murder or sex crimes. Special circumstances such as issues of racial discrimination can also become more prominent in the public consciousness. For example, the case of George Zimmerman who was accused of shooting a young African American was featured prominently in the media when such a crime would have been just a normal crime of homicide. The third layer of the wedding cake consists of the less serious felony offenses. These offenses receive some attention, but they are more expeditiously resolved, primarily though plea bargaining. At the bottom layer are the misdemeanor cases. This last layer makes up the bulk of the cases, but they are also processed mechanically, mostly with plea bargaining and guilty pleas, with very minimal resources and attention being paid to these cases. However, these are also the cases that tend to have the most repeat offenders and these offenders have the tendency to become more serious offenders. Less attention is paid to the intervention with these offenders that there might be some suspicion that this is the reason we are not making a dent in our more serious crimes because of this neglect.

As Figure 1.5 depicts, the scant resources that are allocated for misdemeanors result in a lot of the systems' clients being underserved. The offenders are treated with such generality and impersonality that this population might be receiving more harsh sentences when they should not (false positives). Likewise, some offenders receive no service at all when they would have needed it most (false negatives). They become either neglected or abused by the system in the process. This situation is illustrated in Figure 1.5 where about a fourth of the clients are not within the blue shade (i.e., given less resources). The upper layer cases are being showered upon with humongous amounts of time and effort when these resources are not necessary. These cases end up wasting these resources, as indicated by the excess in the resources that these cases get (see the blue shade in Figure 1.5).

The Dynamics of Social Contexts

Cultural shifts in society produce certain effects in the behaviors of the criminal justice system. The media, particularly popular media, have influenced the expectations and behaviors of actors in the administration of justice (Hayes-Smith & Levitt, 2011; Maeder & Corbett, 2015; Stevens, 2008). The presence of cameras and mobile technologies have influenced criminal justice behaviors. The concerns about these portrayals of justice administration on the media are the potential for biasing decision in the

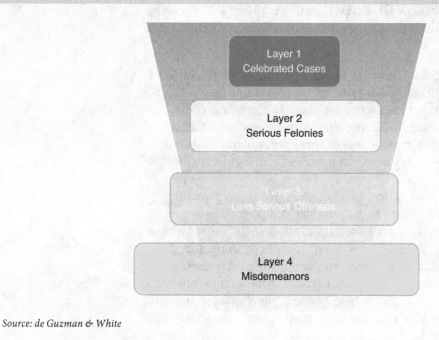

Source: de Guzman & White

adjudication of cases. The viewing of justice media shows might align their beliefs and attitudes with the shows that they are watching (Hayes-Smith & Levitt, 2011). This is known as the cultivation theory (Bilandzic, Busselle, Spitzner, Kalch, & Reich, 2009).

The first of this effect of technology in the administration of justice is the CNN effect. This phenomenon involves the ability of ordinary citizens to comment and pass judgments on cases. The audience also passes upon judgments as well on criminal justice actors and behaviors. The extensive media analyses of the theories and behaviors of the court actors have become the main draw for watching these shows. Criminal justice actors come under stricter scrutiny because of the proliferation of video cameras during their actual performance of their duties. These doses of real-life criminal justice dramas were in full display during the murder trial of O. J. Simpson. Another dramatic real-life criminal justice event was the beating of Rodney King by the Los Angeles Police Department (LAPD) and the ensuing riots that occurred as a consequence of the acquittal of the police officers in that case. The mass media have captured several incidents where the workings of the criminal justice actors are in full display and subjected to intense debates both in the media, the academe, and in the streets.

The other phenomenon has been called as the Crime Scene Investigation (CSI) effect (Pozzulo, Dempsey, Maeder, & Allen, 2010; Pozzulo, Lemieux, Wilson, Crescini, & Girardi, 2009; Tyler, 2006). Due to the popular portrayal by some television shows depicting crime solution and prosecution of crimes on TV, there is now a misconception that justice is a swift process that can be resolved more efficiently through the use of forensic technology (Tyler, 2006). Consequently, trials have been inundated sometimes with forensic evidence and jurors are likewise expecting some form of scientific evidence to be presented during trials. Punishments and execution of offenders have also been affected due to these expectations that science can bring out exonerations of offenders who are wrongfully convicted. Indeed, there seems to be evidence that these shows have influence on the decision-making of jurors (Schweitzer & Saks, 2007; Hawkins & Scherr, 2017). However, a combination of forensic evidence and eyewitness evidence increases the confidence of the jurors on their decisions (Hawkins & Scherr, 2017). Again, the lesson from the O. J. Simpson case is illustrative of this phenomenon. The Simpson trial was inundated with forensic evidence. In the end, the key evidence was the demonstration of the glove not fitting O. J. Simpson. Similarly, the Zimmerman case was also replete with forensic evidence, including voice analysis. In the end, the eyewitness testimonies regarding the circumstances of the case tipped the balance for the defense and exonerated the accused, Zimmerman. Hawkins and Scherr (2017) indicated that TV drama viewing's effect on juror verdicts is more complex than currently hypothesized. They claim that TV viewing has increased their confidence in their verdicts particularly when forensic evidence and other real and oral evidence are presented during trials.

The Dynamics of Control and Rehabilitation

This dynamic involves a dimension distinct from Packer's models mentioned earlier. In this dynamic, the dilemma involves the consideration about the treatment of an individual offender. The criminal justice system can decide to become more punitive and exercise its discretion to control the offender. Under this mind-set, the criminal justice system is expected to be retributive and prefers the deterrence and incapacitation of an individual. Alternatively, the criminal justice system can elect to seek for the best interest of the offender. In this mind-set, the objective is to pursue a restorative justice model in order to reform the individual.

The pendulum swings regarding the determinate and indeterminate sentencing models illustrates this dynamic. The criminal justice system has long established an indeterminate sentencing model in order to fit the offender's needs. Several quarters lamented the early release of offenders and the associated abuse of the system in the disparate grant of probation and parole. In order to control these abuses, several jurisdictions have provided for determinate sentencing. The laws took away judges and correctional discretions. Similarly, the determinate sentencing model became disadvantageous for some inmates who were eligible for early release. The process also placed a tremendous stress on the correctional resources because of the net widening and net strengthening effects of determinate sentencing that some states eventually came up with a hybrid form of sentencing model. This is how the dynamics of control and welfare impact the behaviors of the criminal justice system.

The Criminal Justice Thermodynamics

The criminal justice thermodynamics was described by Walker (2011) as the criminal justice system having an informal understanding about the goals and processes involved. This principle means that for every action, there is a corresponding reaction. As a system, the criminal justice system sets up certain sanctions for nonconformity for expected behaviors of each agency within the criminal justice system. They develop the so-called courtroom work group (Eisenstein & Jacob, 1970). The courtroom work group consists of the prosecutors, defense attorneys, judges, and police officers who establish the "going rate" (predictable outcomes of cases based on the seriousness of the offense and the defendant's prior record).

The workflow is normally observed through the observance of the system's "going rate" both in the number of cases and punishments for offenders. The agencies of the systems react to the violations of these workplace norms by adjusting their own operations. For example, when courts become overwhelmed by the police with more arrests, there is a tendency to dismiss cases or indirectly censure police officers for making "bad" arrests. Likewise, defense attorneys who violate these norms would tend to experience more difficulty dealing with the prosecutors or the judges. Even agencies outside of this group can potentially participate in this relationship. For example, when correctional agencies are being inundated with inmates due to the punitiveness of the judge, they might engage in early or discretionary releases of inmates. Thus, for every action, there is a corresponding reaction—the principle of thermodynamics (Walker, 2011). Under this system, the prosecutor acts as the conductor who can effectively impose rewards and sanctions for all the actors in the work group (Lynch, 2003).

Comprehension Check

1. What is the meaning of criminal justice and differentiate this definition from the different conceptualizations of justice?
2. What are the different views about the relationships of the different components of the criminal justice system?
3. Explain the essential characteristics of the criminal justice system.
4. How does the criminal justice wedding cake influence the workings of the criminal justice system?
5. Explain the differences between the due process model and the crime control mode of the justice system.

References

Bayley, D. H. (1985). *Patterns of policing: An international comparative analysis.* New Brunswick, NJ: Rutgers University Press.

Bayley, D. H. (1992). Comparative organization of the police in English speaking countries. In M. Tonry & N. Morris (Eds.). *Crime and justice: A review of research* (Vol. 2, pp. 509–545). Chicago, IL: University of Chicago Press.

Bayley, D. H., & Shearing, C. D. (2001). *The new structure of policing: Description, conceptualization, and research agenda.* Washington, DC: National Institute of Justice.

Belshaw, S. H., & Deboer, L. H. (2013). *Criminal justice* (2nd ed.). Dubuque, IA: Kendall Hunt.

Black, D. J. (1980). *Manners and customs of the police.* New York, NY: Academic Publishing.

Bilandzic, H., Busselle, R., Spitzner, F., Kalch, A., & Reich, S. (2009). *The CSI cultivation effect. Exploring the influence of need for closure and the disposition for narrative engagement* (pp. 8–36). Conference papers—International Communication Association, Chicago, IL.

Braithwaite, J. (1989). *Crime, shame and reintegration.* New York, NY: Cambridge University Press.

Catholic University of America. (2018). *Crime prevention—"safety first, safety always."* Retrieved from http://publicsafety.cua.edu/prevention.cfm

Cohen, L. E., & Felson, M. (1979). "Social change and crime rate trends: A routine activity approach." *American Sociological Review, 44*(4), 588–608.

Cole, G. E., Smith, C. S., & DeJong, C. (2018). *Criminal justice in America* (9th ed.). Boston, MA: Cengage Learning.

Crank, J. P. (2003). *Imagining justice.* Cincinnati, OH: Anderson Publishing.

Davis, M. S. (2016). *The concise dictionary of crime and justice* (2nd ed.). Los Angeles, CA: Sage, p. 75.

Eisenstein, J., & Jacob. H. (1970). *Felony justice: An organizational analysis of criminal courts.* Boston, MA: Little, Brown.

Fuller, J. R. (2003). "Peacemaking criminology." In M. D. Schwartz & S. E. Hatty (Eds.), *Controversies in critical criminology* (pp. 85–95). Cincinnati, OH: Anderson Publishing.

Hawkins, I., & Scherr, K. (2017). Engaging the CSI effect: The influences of experience-taking, type of evidence, viewing frequency on juror decision-making. *Journal of Criminal Justice, 48,* 45–52.

Hayes-Smith, R. M., & Levitt, L. M. (2011). "Jury's still out: How television and crime show viewing influences jurors' evaluations of evidence." *Applied Psychology in Criminal Justice, 7(1),* 29–46.

Hunter, R. D., Barker, T., & de Guzman, M. C. (2018). *Police community relations and the administration of justice* (9th ed.). New York, NY: Pearson.

Lab, S. S. (2004). Crime prevention, politics, and the art of going nowhere fast. *Justice Quarterly, 21*(4), 681–692, 861.

Lambertus, S., & Yakimchuk, R. (2007). *Future of policing in Alberta: International trends and case studies* (A discussion paper). Alberta, Canada: Alberta Solicitor General and Public Security Office Research Unit.

Leventhal, G. S. (1980). "What should be done with equity theory? New approaches to the study of fairness in social relationships." In K. Gergen, M. Greenberg, & R. Willis (Eds.), *Social exchange* (pp. 27–55). New York, NY: Plenum.

Lynch, G. E. (2003). "Screening vs plea bargaining: Exactly what are we trading off?" *Stanford Law Review, 55*, 1399–1408.

Maeder, E. M., & Corbett, R. (2015). "Beyond frequency: Perceived realism and the CSI effect." *Canadian Journal of Criminology and Criminal Justice, 57*, 83–114.

Maguire, E. R., & Katz, C. M. (2002). "Community policing, loose coupling, and sensemaking in American police agencies." *Justice Quarterly, 19*(3), 503–536.

Maiese, M. (2003). "Types of justice." In G. Burgess & H. Burgess (Eds.), *Beyond intractability*. Boulder, CO: Conflict Information Consortium, University of Colorado. Retrieved from http://www.beyondintractability org/essay/ types-of-justice

Mentor, (2013). *Criminal justice*. Dubuque, IA: Kendall Hunt.

Meyer, P. N. (2018). Evoking jurors' sympathetic imagination is a key for lawyer storytellers." *ABA Journal, 104*(2), 10.

Miltner, C. C. (1931). "Legal versus moral justice." *Notre Dame Law Review, 6*(4), 451–457.

Neubauer, D. W., & Fradella, H. E. (2011). *America's courts and the criminal justice system* (10th ed.). Belmont, CA: Wadsworth Cengage Learning.

Packer, H. L. (1968). *The limits of criminal sanction*. Stanford, CA: Stanford University Press.

Pozzulo, J. D., Lemieux, J. M., Wilson, A., Crescini, C., & Girardi, A. (2009). "The influence of identification decision and DNA evidence on juror decision making." *Journal of Applied Social Psychology, 39*, 2069–2088.

Pozzulo, J. D., Dempsey, J., Maeder, E., & Allen, L. (2010). "The effects of victim gender, defendant gender, and defendant age on juror decision making." *Criminal Justice and Behavior, 37*, 47–63.

Reichel, P. L. (2018). *Comparative criminal justice systems: A topical approach* (7th ed.). New York, NY: Pearson.

Rush, G. E. (2004). *Dictionary of criminal justice*. New York, NY: McGraw-Hill.

Schweitzer, N. J., & Saks, M. J. (2007). "The CSI effect: Popular fiction about forensic science affects the public's expectations about real forensic science." *Jurimetrics, 47*, 357–364.

Stevens, D. J. (2008). "Forensic science, wrongful convictions, and American prosecutor discretion." *The Howard Journal of Criminal Justice, 47*, 31–51.

Taylor, C. J., & Auerhan, K. (2015). "Community justice and public safety: Assessing criminal justice policy through the lens of the social contract." *Criminology & Criminal Justice 15(3)*, 300–320.

Thibaut, J., & Walker, L. (1975). *Procedural justice: A psychological analysis.* Hillsdale, NJ: Erlbaum.

Thibaut, J., Walker, L., LaTour, S., & Houlden, P. (1974). "Procedural justice as fairness." *Stanford Law Review, 26,* 1271–1289.

Thibaut, J, Walker, L., & Lind, E. A. (1972). "Adversary presentation and bias in legal decision making." *Harvard Law Review, 86,* 386–401.

Travis, L. F., & Langworthy, R. H. (2008). *Policing in America: A balance of forces* (4th ed.). Cincinnati, OH: Prentice Hall.

Tyler, T. R. (2006). "Viewing CSI and the threshold of guilt: Managing truth and justice in reality and fiction." *The Yale Law Journal, 115,* 1050–1085.

Tyler, T.R. (2017). "Procedural justice and policing: A rush to judgment?" *Annual Review of Law and Social Science, 13,* 29–53.

Van Ness, D. W., & Strong, K, H. (2006). *Restoring justice: An introduction to restorative justice* (3rd ed.). Cincinnati, OH: Anderson Publishing.

Walker, S. L. (2011). *Sense and non-sense about crime, drugs, and communities* (7th ed.). Belmont, CA: Wadsworth Cengage.

Worrall, J. & Schmalleger, F. (2018). *Policing* (2nd ed.). New York, NY: Pearson.

Endnotes

[1] Stare decisis is a legal principle where earlier decisions made by the highest court should bind lower courts when interpreting similar disputes.

[2] Double jeopardy is a legal principle that bars the prosecution of an offender for the same offense twice within the same jurisdiction. Since the federal and state governments are two different jurisdictions, the processing of the same offense in these two levels is not in violation of the due process clause and double jeopardy.

Crime and the Law

LEARNING OBJECTIVES

After reading this chapter, the student should be able to

1 Identify the different types of law

2 Understand the categories of crime

3 Explain the elements of a crime

4 Describe the seven principles of criminal law

5 Discuss the various defenses used to challenge criminal intent

Introduction

Put simply, laws tell us what we can and cannot do. In the United States, we are all expected to follow the law. In fact, even those who hold the highest powers must make decisions within the limits imposed by law. Government officials are expected to both follow and enforce the law. In a democracy like ours, laws are fundamental in preventing government officials from seizing too much power or using it improperly. Further, the government can only seek to punish those who violate defined laws, and their guilt must be determined through procedures established by law.

In this chapter, we discuss the different types of law, including criminal and civil law. We will also provide an explanation of the categories of crime and the elements that must be present in order for a crime to have occurred. We will then provide an overview of the seven principles of criminal law. Finally, we will discuss the defenses used to challenge criminal intent in a court of law.

Types of Law

© Billion Photos/Shutterstock.com

Criminal Law

© izzet ugutmen/Shutterstock.com

Criminal law deals with behaviors that can be understood as an offense against the public, society, or the state, even if there is an individual victim; it is the part of law that is concerned with the punishment of those who commit crimes. In criminal cases, only the federal or state government (i.e., the prosecution) can bring about charges or initiate a case; most cases that go to trial are then decided by a jury. It is important to note here, however, that the majority of criminal cases do not go to trial, but end in a plea bargain instead. During a trial, the prosecution has the burden of proof in criminal cases, and must prove the defendant's guilt "beyond a reasonable doubt." This means that it is the prosecution's responsibility to prove to the jury that the defendant committed the crime. The defense does not have to prove that the defendant did not commit the crime, although this is a common way for the defense to dispute the prosecution's case and insert reasonable doubt into the mind of the jury.

One category of criminal law, **substantive criminal law**, defines the acts that the government can punish and indicates the punishments for those crimes. Legislatures define this type of law through statutes. A second category, **procedural criminal law**, defines the procedures that criminal justice officials must follow in all subunits of our criminal justice system, enforcement, adjudication, and corrections. Defined by courts through judicial rulings, procedural law specifies how the state must process cases. The US Supreme Court plays a large part in defining procedural criminal law.

Civil Law

Civil law regulates the relationships between or among individuals, typically involving property, contracts, or business disputes. It deals with behaviors that constitute injury to an individual or other private party, such as a corporation. It is civil law that is in effect when you hear of one person suing another in court. Different from criminal cases, civil cases are filed by a private party, known as the **plaintiff**. Cases are typically decided by a judge, although larger cases may be decided by a jury. Punishment almost always involves a monetary reward and never includes incarceration. In civil cases, the plaintiff must establish the defendant's liability by a "preponderance of evidence." This means that they must prove their case by 51 percent or greater, instead of "beyond a reasonable doubt," which is needed in criminal cases.

Administrative Law

Administrative law refers to the body of law governing the operation and procedures of federal and state government agencies that these agencies must follow when making determinations and rulings. An administrative agency's primary purpose is usually to protect the public at large and ensure the public's safety. These agencies create, implement, and enforce regulations. For example, the US Food and Drug Administration (FDA) "is responsible for protecting the public health by ensuring the safety, efficacy, and security of human and veterinary drugs, biological products, and medical devices; and by ensuring the safety of our nation's food supply, cosmetics, and products that emit radiation" (U.S. Food and Drug Administration, 2018).

Case Law

Case law is the law established through previous judicial decisions or former cases. These rulings then become **precedent**, and all courts in the same jurisdiction must adhere to them as law in any cases that are similar in nature. *Roe v. Wade* (1973) is a landmark Supreme Court case that set the precedent for abortion in the United States. At the time, Texas criminal law made aborting a fetus a felony, unless the pregnancy risked the woman's health. Jane Roe, unmarried and pregnant, filed a class action lawsuit against Dallas County District Attorney Henry Wade to challenge the constitutionality of this law. The Court determined that it is

© Rob Crandall/Shutterstock.com

the woman's constitutional right to privacy and her decision to have an abortion. The case also gave states the right to regulate abortions based on the trimester of the pregnancy, the protection of prenatal life, and the mother's health. *Roe v. Wade* (1973) is perhaps one of the most controversial Supreme Court cases in history and is still debated to this day.

Categories of Crime

Each state and the federal government define crime differently, but offenses are typically broken down into one of three categories:

1. **Felonies**: Serious crimes punishable by incarceration for a year or more in prison.
2. **Misdemeanors**: Less serious crimes typically punishable by incarceration for up to a year in county jail.
3. **Civil infractions**: Punishable only by fines and do not result in an arrest or criminal record.

It is important to note that crimes within these categories vary from state to state. Additionally, categories of crime are not always defined solely on the seriousness of the offense. For example, after the wave of mass incarceration and the overcrowding in many jails and prisons, some state legislatures have redefined certain nonviolent felonies as misdemeanors in an attempt to reduce the number of people being incarcerated.

Elements of a Crime

Criminal laws must be carefully drafted in order to define the specific actions and intentions that are considered deserving of punishment. Thus, an individual will have committed a crime if his or her actions fulfill every element of an offense. In most cases, the statute that establishes the crime will also establish the specific elements of the crime. In general, every crime involves three elements.

© GraphicsRF/Shutterstock.com

The Act

Also referred to as ***actus reus***, meaning "the guilty act," this element constitutes the wrongful deed that, in combination with the other elements, may result in an arrest, trial, and conviction of an individual. It is important to note that this can be an act either of commission or omission, meaning that the individual may have committed the act or may have failed to act when the law imposes a duty to do so. This element generally prohibits the punishment of someone for holding a particular status or condition. For example, it is not a crime to be *addicted to* drugs, while it can be a crime to *sell* drugs or *possess* drugs.

© Syda Productions/Shutterstock.com

The State of Mind (Intent)

This element regards the individual's mental state at the time of the act. Referred to as ***mens rea*** or criminal intent, this element involves the guilty or evil mind required for criminal liability. What is in question here is whether or not the act was committed or omitted *willfully*. Did the accused have the intent necessary to make the act a crime? Establishing criminal intent typically involves the role of motive (although this does not have to be proven and is not an element of crime in and of itself), inferences, and circumstantial evidence.

© Becris/Shutterstock.com

The Attendant Circumstances

The final element concerns the attendant circumstances, or other facts surrounding the case that, in conjunction with the act and the state of mind, make for the commission of a crime. In some cases, it must be proven that certain events occurred or certain facts are true (i.e., attendant circumstances) in order for a defendant to be found guilty of the crime. For example, suppose the law states that it is illegal to wave to others while standing in the driveway. The act here would be waving and the state of mind would be that the individual was waving to someone on purpose. However, these alone would not constitute a crime under the law. Instead, the attendant circumstances would have to be present as well—the individual would have to be willfully waving to someone while *standing in the driveway*. Thus, all three elements must be present in order for a crime to have taken place.

Principles of Criminal Law

Legal scholar Jerome Hall summarized seven principles of law that must be present to define acts as criminal, and the conditions required for successful prosecution. According to Hall (1947), the act must be *legally proscribed*. In other words, there must be a law that defines the act as a crime. Next, *actus reus* affirms that there must be a human act of either commission or omission. *Mens rea* must also be present. Therefore, the act must be accompanied by a guilty mind, or there must be criminal intent present. Relatedly, the act and the intent must be present at the same time (i.e., *concurrence*). The act or failure to act must also cause *harm* to something that is protected under the law. Additionally, there must be a *causal relationship* between the act and the harm suffered. Finally, there must be a provision in the law that warrants *punishment* of individuals found guilty of breaking a law.

Defenses Used in a Court of Law

Alibi

When suspected of or charged with a crime, most people quickly develop or provide an alibi. An **alibi** is an account of one's whereabouts at the time the alleged criminal act took place. An alibi can simply be a claim put forth by the individual, or it can include evidence to substantiate the individual's explanation. If verified, an alibi can demonstrate that the accused could not have committed the crime because he or she was somewhere else when the crime occurred.

There are various defenses that can be used in an attempt to avoid the conviction of defendants who do not deny the claim of having committed the criminal act, but argue that the criminal intent (*mens rea*) was not present. Because all three elements (the act, the state of mind, and the attendant circumstances) must be present to establish responsibility for the criminal act, demonstrating the absence of one of these elements—the state of mind, in this case—may result in an acquittal. When arguing that *mens rea* was not present, the defendant is admitting that he or she committed the harmful act, but that it was not intentional (an accident is the most obvious example). This does not mean, however, a guaranteed not guilty verdict, although in most cases it does relieve defendants of responsibility for acts that otherwise would have been labeled criminal had they been intentional. In addition to accidents, there are eight defenses based on the lack of criminal intent. These defenses are typically divided into two categories: justifications and excuses.

Justifications

There are two defenses based on the lack of criminal intent, which fall under the category of justifications. **Justifications** focus on the act itself and whether the circumstances surrounding it make the act socially acceptable. Put another way, the individual's actions are deemed socially acceptable under the circumstances, even though they caused a harm that is otherwise breaking the law. In these cases, members of the public view and accept the act as being essential to the person's self-preservation.

Self-Defense

The **self-defense** justification gives us the right to defend ourselves with reasonable force against a perceived threat. If a person feels that he or she is in immediate danger of being harmed by another person, he or she may ward off an attack in self-defense. Here, the level of force used by the individual defending oneself cannot exceed the perceived threat (Simons, 2008). One can only defend one's self using lethal force if he or she reasonably perceives that the threat is both imminent and potentially lethal. For example, a homeowner comes home to find a burglar inside his/her home, stealing his/her possessions. The  burglar is just as startled by the homeowner and begins to run out the door. Because there is no reasonable threat of immediate danger here, the homeowner could not decide to use deadly force in self-defense to take down the burglar. If, however, the burglar charges at the homeowner, the homeowner could use an appropriate amount of force to defend him/herself. Most states also recognize the right to defend others, to protect property, and to prevent the commission of a crime.

The law of self-defense rests on the concept of reasonableness. If a person reasonably believes there is a serious threat of harm, and uses reasonable force to meet that threat, the law justifies even deadly force. People have differing views on what is considered reasonable, though, so self-defense laws must attempt to further define the concept. Typically, a person is justified in using only the force necessary to respond to an imminent threat, and these same principles apply to cases involving defense of another. Although self-defense laws vary by state, they generally fall into the three categories below.

The Castle Doctrine

The common law principle of the castle doctrine provides that individuals have the right to use reasonable force, including deadly force, to protect themselves against an intruder in their home. This legal concept is derived from the philosophy that every person is the king or queen of his or her castle (i.e., home). As the king or queen, you have no duty to retreat when an outsider invades. Thus, if there is an intruder in your home, you have the right to defend your habitation. Most U.S. states have laws related to the castle doctrine that say there is no duty to retreat before using deadly force if you are in your home or yard (some states also include place of work and occupied vehicles).

Duty to Retreat

Some states include a stipulation regarding self-defense cases that hold that a person has a duty to retreat if he or she has a reasonable opportunity to do so. Here, an individual is not legally allowed to use deadly force if he or she can safely avoid the risk of death or serious bodily harm by retreating from the situation. It is important to understand, however, that even in duty to retreat states, there is no duty to retreat from an intruder in your home.

Stand Your Ground

In the substantial majority of states, there is no duty to retreat. This means that in these states, an individual is allowed to "stand his ground" when defending himself. There does not have to be an attempt to escape a situation before using force in these states. Many states have now also extended their stand your ground laws beyond the home to any place where a person might lawfully be found. It is also important to understand that even in states that have stand your ground laws, there are still certain restrictions regarding using force in self-defense. For example, some require that the individual be at the location lawfully, that the individual is not engaged in the commission of a crime, and that the individual was not the initial aggressor or did not provoke the victim with the specific purpose of getting the victim to attack or make a threat.

In 2005, Florida was the first state to pass a law that removed the duty to retreat before using force in self-defense. The tragic killing of Trayvon Martin in 2012 and the initial decision by police not to arrest George Zimmerman for that killing led to great public attention on Florida's "stand your ground" law. As one of the most far reaching stand your ground laws, Florida requires the prosecution to prove beyond a reasonable doubt that the defendant did not act in self-defense, which can be a heavy burden.

Necessity

Instead of using force to defend oneself, the justification defense of **necessity** is used when people commit crimes to save themselves or to prevent some greater harm, often in what is viewed as an emergency situation. In such situations, the harm caused must not be greater than the harm prevented. Additionally, the defendant will typically have to prove that there was a significant threat that presented imminent danger, that it was necessary to act immediately, that he or she did not contribute to or cause the threat, and that there was no practical alternative to the criminal act committed.

In cases of necessity, it is recognized that circumstances beyond one's control sometimes force people to engage in illegal behavior; breaking the law is necessary to prevent a harm worse than the one the law is aimed at preventing. For example, a 13-year-old girl is riding in the car with her mother who suddenly goes unconscious. To avoid going through a busy intersection, the girl grabs the steering wheel and swerves the car, crashing it into a parked vehicle on the side of the road. In this example, the girl crashed into the parked car in order to prevent the possible greater harm that could have come about by driving through the busy intersection.

Excuses

Whereas justifications focus on the act, **excuses** instead focus on the actor and whether he or she fulfilled the elements necessary to be held liable under criminal law. More specifically, did the individual possess the knowledge, state of mind, or intent required for a criminal conviction? The six excuse defenses can either reduce or eliminate criminal responsibility because they demonstrate a lack in the fulfillment of the elements of a crime.

Duress/Coercion

Sometimes also referred to as **coercion**, the **duress** defense can be used when people commit crimes because they have been coerced by others. A person must usually show that he or she tried to escape from the situation, if possible. For instance, if a suspect fleeing from a crime were to force an unsuspecting person at gunpoint to drive them away from the crime scene, the bystander essentially becomes a criminal by acting as the getaway driver. However, this person may not be liable for the criminal behavior because he or she was acting under duress, or was coerced by another.

Entrapment

Entrapment occurs when government agents induce a person to commit a crime that he or she would not have otherwise committed. When entrapment is used as a defense, judges must question, did the police go too far in making a crime occur that would not have otherwise? A key factor in question here is the predisposition of the defendant. The Supreme Court has declared that the prosecution must show beyond a reasonable doubt that the defendant was predisposed to commit the crime before approached by government agents. Importantly, entrapment does not include undercover traps or stings, and does not mean that law enforcement officers cannot provide ordinary opportunities for the commission of a crime.

Infancy/Immaturity

The excuse defense of **infancy** (also sometimes called **immaturity**) provides that *mens rea* is not present for children younger than 7 years. According to this defense, children do not have the mental capacity to understand right from wrong or the consequences of their actions, and therefore do not have the criminal intent necessary for conviction.

Mistake of Fact

You may have heard the phrase "ignorance is no excuse" before; and indeed it is not. But, a mistake regarding a crucial fact during the commission of a crime may be a defense in a criminal case. Mistake of fact can be used as a defense to show lack of intent when the accused person makes a mistake on some crucial fact in regards to the occurrence of the crime. Since mistake of fact is used to demonstrate that the defendant did not have the intent to commit the crime, if the prosecution cannot prove beyond a reasonable doubt that the defendant did in fact have the requisite intent, the defendant must be acquitted. For example, Armando left his bicycle outside the local corner store while he went inside to purchase a drink. When he came out, he hopped on his bike and rode home. The next thing he knew, the police showed up at his house and were arresting him for theft. As it turned out, Armando had gotten on someone else's bike when he came out of the grocery store. Because he believed he had gotten on his own bike and his intent was not to steal the bike, the court may find this mistake of fact negates the criminal intent necessary to convict Armando of a crime.

Intoxication

Here is another defense that may not be exactly how it sounds. The defense of **intoxication** does not include acts committed while intoxicated voluntarily. In other words, if a person makes an informed choice to consume a substance known to cause intoxication and then goes on to commit a crime, he or she cannot use intoxication as a defense, although it can sometimes be used as a mitigating factor to reduce the seriousness of the charge or the punishment. If the intoxication is involuntary, however, such as when someone has been tricked into consuming a substance without knowing that it may cause intoxication, then this defense may be used.

Insanity

The **insanity** defense may well be one of the most well-known defenses, but it is also one that has been the subject of much debate. The public tends to see the insanity defense as an excuse that people make up and skillfully use to get away with serious criminal acts. In reality, a very small number of criminal defendants use insanity as a defense, and less than 1 percent are found "not guilty by reason of insanity." Interestingly, four states (Idaho, Montana, Nevada, and Utah) no longer even allow this defense.

US courts have five tests of criminal responsibility involving insanity:

- M'Naghten Rule

  Developed in England in 1843, the M'Naghten Rule came about from a case where Daniel M'Naghten claimed he was delusional at the time he killed Edward Drummond, a man he believed to be Sir Robert Peel, the prime minister of Great Britain. The British court then developed the "right-from-wrong test," which asks whether "at the time of committing the act, the accused was laboring under such a defect of reason from disease of the mind, as not to know the nature and quality of the act he was doing, or if he did know it, he did not know what he was doing was wrong (*M'Naghten's Case*, 1843)." This test is currently used by more than twelve states in the United States.

- Irresistible Impulse Test

  The Irresistible Impulse Test supplements the M'Naghten Rule in four states because psychiatrists regularly argue that some people are compelled by their mental illness to commit criminal acts even though they understand them to be wrong. Therefore, this test excuses criminal defendants when a mental illness was controlling their behavior despite the fact they knew what they were doing was wrong.

- Durham Rule

  The Durham rule releases defendants of criminal responsibility if the criminal act was caused by the mental illness. This test was adopted by the Circuit Court of Appeals for the District of Columbia in 1954 after being originally developed in 1871 in New Hampshire.

- *Model Penal Code's* Substantive Capacity Test

  More than half the states and the federal government use the *Model Penal Code's* Substantial Capacity Test, which was developed in the early 1970s. This test came about after it was argued that the Durham rule did not provide a useful definition of "mental disease or defect." The *Model Penal Code's* Substantial Capacity Test broadens and modifies the M'Naghten and Irresistible Impulse Rules and does not require a defendant to not understand right and wrong. Instead, this test excuses criminal responsibility "if at the time of such conduct as a result of mental disease or defect he lacks substantial capacity either to appreciate the criminality (wrongfulness) of his conduct or to conform his conduct to the requirements of the law."

- The Comprehensive Crime Control Act of 1984

  In 1984, President Ronald Reagan signed into law the Comprehensive Crime Control Act, requiring defendants using the insanity defense in federal courts to prove by "clear and convincing evidence" that they did not understand the nature or wrongfulness of the crime due to severe mental disease or defect. The Act essentially brought back the standard of "knowing right from wrong" and disallowed the use of the Irresistible Impulse Test in federal courts. Moreover, instead of the prosecution having to prove their case, the burden now rests on the defendant, who has to prove his or her insanity.

Applicability of Insanity Tests

It is important to understand that for purposes of the law, insanity is a legal definition and not a psychiatric one. The idea of mental illness in psychiatry is often very different from the concept of insanity used as a defense in criminal cases. Differences between legal and psychiatric conceptualizations of insanity often lead to conflicting opinions and testimony regarding a defendant's sanity. Furthermore, it can be difficult to apply any of the tests of insanity, and the decision of how to proceed with someone who has been found not guilty by reason of insanity can be complex and difficult. Jurors are also often fearful of what may happen once a defendant is found to be legally insane (e.g., will they be released back into society?), potentially influencing decisions regarding whether the defendant was legally insane at the time of the crime.

BOX 2.1   CAREER HIGHLIGHT: FORENSIC PSYCHOLOGIST

Forensic psychologists apply psychological theory and practice to the police, courts, and correctional systems. The application of many legal concepts requires understanding various psychological principles, such as state of mind, memory, and perception. Forensic psychologists must possess advanced knowledge and skills reflecting the intersection of legal theories, procedures, and law with clinical issues, practice, and ethics. They most commonly are licensed psychologists who specialize in applying their psychological knowledge to legal matters, both in the criminal and civil arenas. Forensic psychologists work with defendants raising issues such as competency to stand trial, insanity, diminished capacity, sentencing considerations, juvenile waivers, and defendants found incompetent to stand trial or not guilty by reason of insanity and in need of treatment. They can also serve as expert witnesses to provide testimony regarding things like why the crime occurred and their belief about whether or not the defendant was likely to have committed the crime(s). Forensic psychologists can be found in academia, public service, and in the private sector. They assist in a wide variety of legal matters, including mental state examinations of criminal defendants, child custody/family law, violence risk assessment, civil law (personal injury cases), social science research, mediation/dispute resolution, and jury selection.

To become a forensic psychologist, you must obtain a bachelor's degree (e.g., major in Psychology, minor in Criminal Justice/Criminology or vice versa), as well as a master's degree and a doctorate (Ph.D. – research-oriented or Psy.D. – practitioner). There are some forensic psychology graduate programs, though many pursue a degree in Clinical Psychology and then pursue a postdoctoral specialization in forensics. State licensure is typically needed if evaluating people on behalf of the court or serving as an expert witness regarding competency is desired. Typically, there is a minimum number of postdoctoral training hours that are needed before applying for a license to practice independently. Professional certification with the American Board of Forensic Psychology (ABFP) is an option, but is not an absolute requirement for practice.

© YAKOBCHUK VIACHESLAV/ Shutterstock.com

Procedural Defenses

When the US Constitution was ratified in 1788 and 1789, it contained few references to criminal justice. This caused concern that the rights of the people were not specified in enough detail, leading to the addition of ten

amendments in 1791. These first ten amendments, collectively known as the Bill of Rights, provide specific rights, some of which have direct implications for criminal justice such as those concerning proper searches, trials, and punishments.

Some of the rights included in the Bill of Rights receive more attention than others. Indeed, most people can explain at least part of the First Amendment, and many people are aware of their right to bear arms, which is provided in the Second Amendment. Although these may be more well known, four amendments in particular play a role in criminal procedure and should be discussed here.

The Fourth Amendment forbids unreasonable searches and seizures. The Fifth Amendment provides basic due process rights such as rights against self-incrimination or double jeopardy. The Sixth Amendment gives the right to a speedy, fair, and public trial by a jury of our peers and the right to counsel. The Eighth Amendment bars excessive bail and cruel and unusual punishment.

The fundamental guarantees of the first ten amendments have been interpreted and clarified since their ratification on December 15, 1791. While the guarantee of due process is found in the Fifth Amendment, it also underlies the entire Bill of Rights. Many of the decisions made by the Supreme Court during the Warren Court era of the 1960s led to the due process standard as the basis of the US criminal justice system.

The exact words of the four amendments concerning procedural criminal law are below (The U.S. National Archives and Records Administration, 2017a, 2017b):

Amendment IV

The right of the people to be secure in their persons, houses, papers, and effects, against unreasonable searches and seizures, shall not be violated, and no Warrants shall issue, but upon probable cause, supported by Oath or affirmation, and particularly describing the place to be searched, and the persons or things to be seized.

Amendment V

No person shall be held to answer for a capital, or otherwise infamous crime, unless on a presentment or indictment of a Grand Jury, except in cases arising in the land or naval forces, or in the Militia, when in actual service in time of War or public danger; nor shall any person be subject for the same offence to be twice put in jeopardy of life or limb; nor shall be compelled in any criminal case to be a witness against himself, nor be deprived of life, liberty, or property, without due process of law; nor shall private property be taken for public use, without just compensation.

Amendment VI

In all criminal prosecutions, the accused shall enjoy the right to a speedy public trial, by an impartial jury of the State and district wherein the crime shall have been committed, which district shall have been previously ascertained by law, and to be informed of the nature and cause of the accusation; to be confronted with the witnesses against him; to have compulsory process for obtaining witnesses in his favor, and to have the Assistance of Counsel for his defence.

Amendment VIII

Excessive bail shall not be required, nor excessive fines imposed, nor cruel and unusual punishments inflicted.

Unfortunately, the Bill of Rights did not apply to many criminal cases throughout history because it was meant to protect individuals from the power of the federal government and most cases were handled by state or local officials. However, after the Civil War, three amendments were added to the US Constitution in an attempt to protect individuals from infringement by state and local government officials. The Thirteenth and Fifteenth Amendments had little impact on criminal justice, abolishing slavery and attempting to prohibit racial discrimination in voting, respectively. The Fourteenth Amendment, however, barred states from violating the right to due process of law, stating, "No State shall . . . deprive any person of life, liberty, or property, without due process of law; nor deny to any person within its jurisdiction, the equal protection of the laws." Still, with no specific definitions, the rights of "due process" and "equal protection" were left open to interpretation. It became the Supreme Court's responsibility to decide if and how these amendments applied to the criminal justice process. Owing to the decisions made by the Supreme Court, all US citizens now equally enjoy the same minimum protections against criminal justices processes, including illegal searches and seizures, improper police interrogations, and other violations of constitutional rights.

Comprehension Check

1. Discuss the different types of law, including criminal, civil, administrative, and case law.
2. Differentiate between the various categories of crime. How do the penalties differ?
3. What elements must be present in order to determine that a crime has occurred?
4. Describe the seven principles of law summarized by Jerome Hall.
5. What legal defenses can be used to excuse or justify a criminal act?

References

Hall, J. (1947). *General principles of criminal law* (2nd ed.). Indianapolis, IN: Bobbs-Merrill.

Roe v. Wade, 410 U.S. 113 (1973). Retrieved from LexisNexis database.

M'Naghten's Case, 8 ER 718 (1843).

Simons, K. W. (2008). "Self-defense: Reasonable belief or reasonable self-control?" *New Criminal Law Review, 11*, 51–90.

U.S. Food and Drug Administration. (2018). *What we do.* Retrieved from https://www.fda.gov/AboutFDA/WhatWeDo/default.htm

The U.S. National Archives and Records Administration. (2017a). *The bill of rights: A transcription.* National Archives, America's Founding Documents. Retrieved from https://www.archives.gov/founding-docs/bill-of-rights-transcript

The U.S. National Archives and Records Administration. (2017b). *The constitution: Amendments 11–27.* National Archives, America's Founding Documents. Retrieved from https://www.archives.gov/founding-docs/amendments-11-27

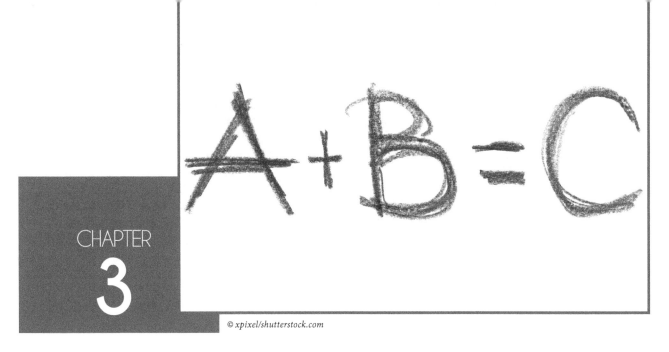

© xpixel/shutterstock.com

Criminology

LEARNING OBJECTIVES

After reading this chapter, the student should be able to

1 Identify some of the prominent criminological theories proposed to explain criminal behavior

2 Understand the relationship between theory and research

3 Recall the main ideas associated with the classical and positivist schools of criminology

Introduction

Wouldn't it be nice if we could pinpoint the cause of all criminal behavior? If we could say something as simple as A + B = crime, then we could likely prevent this unlawful behavior as well. Unfortunately (or maybe fortunately for those of us in this field!), this is not the case. Over the years, however, various explanations have been proposed in an attempt to better understand why some people engage in criminal behavior (and why others do not). Theory plays an important role in this effort to explain and understand crime.

The relationship between theory and research is an important one to understand. Not only are the two related, but they are also dependent upon one another. How so? Well, just about anyone can propose an explanation for something. A theory cannot gain credibility, however, unless it is testable. In other words, researchers often conduct studies to test these theories and their validity. Similarly, theories often serve as a foundation or rationale for what is being tested. Using the scientific method, criminologists develop hypotheses and collect and analyze data to determine which theories best explain criminal behavior. Then, if the findings support the tenets of the theory, the theory can establish a basis for new public policies aimed at preventing and controlling crime.

In this chapter, we discuss some of the causal explanations put forward to better understand criminal behavior. Focusing on the two major schools of criminological thought, we begin the chapter with a discussion on the classical school of criminology. It is within this school where the concept of rational thought began to influence our understanding of criminal behavior. We then move to positivism, where we review biological, psychological, and sociological causes of criminal behavior.

The Classical School

Prior to the eighteenth century, Europeans primarily explained criminal behavior as the work of supernatural forces. Criminals were believed to be "possessed" by the devil and defendants were left with few rights. Those accused of committing a crime were rarely given the chance to defend themselves and confessions were often obtained through torture. Penalties typically consisted of physical punishment or death.

Cesare Beccaria's (1764) *Essay on Crimes and Punishments* was the first attempt to explain criminal behavior in a different way. His ideas led to the development of **classical criminology**, where free will, rationality, and fear of punishment were the foundation of criminal behavior. Essentially, people are rational and concerned with minimizing their pain and maximizing their pleasure. Beccaria (1738–1794) argued that for punishment to be effective, it needed to be swift, certain, and severe. Accordingly, if these three principles were followed, potential criminals should be deterred from criminal behavior.

Beccaria's ideas had a profound impact on society, and criminal justice policies were soon modified with the expectation that crime would quickly decrease. There was, however, no way to determine whether crime rates were really dropping since there were no annual statistics to measure crime. In fact, the first annual national crime statistics were not published until more than sixty years later. Despite the changes, crime rates appeared to be on the rise and there was evidence of recidivism among punished offenders. In addition, the development of annual national crime statistics in France paralleled the development of a stable social and political organization in Europe. At this time, accurate official records were being maintained and could be counted and compared to analyze economic and social conditions and their consequences. Ultimately, classical theory began to lose its influence.

Neoclassical Criminology

Although Beccaria's ideas remained influential for over one hundred years, the popularity of the classical approach began to decline by the end of the 1800s. However, in the second half of the twentieth century, at a time when the United States became more conservative, classical ideas began to resurface and the principles of classical criminology saw a resurgence via rational choice theory.

Rooted in classical theory and owing to the perceived failure of rehabilitative technologies and the increase in maintenance of official records, attention returned in the 1970s and 1980s to an analysis of the criminal decision-making process. According to this contemporary approach to explaining criminal behavior, everyone has the ability to act on his or her own free will and make rational decisions. Offenders' rationality is thought to be structured by social and cultural forces, providing a more complex view of how offenders in particular situations calculate the costs and benefits of criminal behavior (Cornish & Clarke, 1986). Criminals, then, are rational actors who plan their crimes, are controlled by the fear of punishment, and should be punished for their wrongdoings.

Before making the decision to engage in criminal behavior, criminals weigh the benefits versus the costs of their actions, and only decide to commit a crime if the rewards are greater than the potential consequences. Offenders choose criminal behavior after considering both personal (e.g., money, thrill, entertainment, revenge) and situational (e.g., availability of targets, security) factors. In other words, criminals do not engage in random antisocial activities, but instead will carefully contemplate factors such as the risk of apprehension, the value of the crime commission, and the likelihood of success before making the decision on whether to proceed.

While the focus of neoclassical criminology rests on the idea that crime results from the rational decision-making of individuals after weighing the potential benefits of the crime against the costs of being caught and punished, it is also recognized that differences exist among individuals and the law must remember to take this into account. This renewed interest in classical ideas sparked many of the components of the crime control model (sentencing reform, mass incarceration, and criticisms of rehabilitation).

Deterrence

If people make rational decisions and do not fear the consequences of their behavior, then those who are motivated to do so will engage in criminal behavior. If this is the case, crime should be controlled by increasing the real or perceived threat of criminal punishment. Following Beccaria's ideas, making punishment swift, certain, and severe should reduce the amount of crime. This is reflected in modern deterrence theories, which focus on the impact of official punishments on crime.

General Deterrence

According to general deterrence theory, if people believe that the certainty of arrest, conviction, and punishment is high, they will refrain from criminal activity. Similarly, if they believe that the punishment will be severe enough to outweigh the potential benefits of committing the crime, they will forgo their criminal behavior. Finally, if people believe that they will be punished rather quickly for their crimes, they are likely to abstain from criminal behavior. General deterrence focuses on all people in society and seeks to prevent the commission of crime by all potential offenders.

Specific Deterrence

The theory of specific deterrence asserts that criminal sanctions should be so powerful that known criminals will never repeat their criminal acts. The idea behind this is that an association made between a planned action and memories of its consequence, which should be sufficiently severe, should prevent the action from reoccurring. For example, if an offender is convicted of theft and receives time in jail, specific deterrence says that because the offender will not want to go back to jail, he should decide not to steal again.

General Deterrence	Specific Deterrence
• Deterring people in the general population, including those who have not been punished before • Indirect experiences of punishment	• Punishing offenders for their crimes deters those specific offenders from future crime commission • Direct experiences with punishment

Positivism

In the second half of the nineteenth century, biological sciences and evolution were gaining popularity, and both countered the assumptions of classical theory. A new perspective of criminology began to take over, and criminologists began using the scientific method to explain crime and human behavior. Many began to hold the view that people behave in a predetermined manner. Criminal behavior, then, was believed to be the result of biological, psychological, or social forces beyond the control of the individual. These ideas shaped the foundation of what is known today as the positive school.

Although we saw a resurgence of classical ideas, the positivist school of thought dominated twentieth-century American criminology. Within the positivist school, there are three primary categories of theories: biological, psychological, and sociological. Although classical criminology and rational choice theory focus on the rationality and decision-making of the actor, positivistic theories hold that behavior is largely out of the actor's control.

Biological Theories

One branch of positivistic theories focuses on the biological conditions that control human behavior. These can be genetically predetermined or acquired through diet or the environment. As classical theories lost their credence, biological theories became the dominant explanation of crime in the late 1800s.

Influenced by Darwin (1859), and basing his theory on criminal anthropology and biological determinism, Cesare Lombroso argued that crime is the result of biological differences between criminals and "normal" individuals. He concluded that modern criminals shared physical characteristics with more primitive humans, and developed his concept of **atavism**, or the idea that criminals were biological throwbacks to an earlier evolutionary stage (Lombroso-Ferrero, 1979).

Although the individualistic theories of positivist criminology maintained popularity into the twentieth century, Lombroso's theories began to lose credit when several limitations were identified in his research. Years later, Charles Goring (1913) examined more closely some of Lombroso's ideas and concluded that there were no significant differences between criminals and noncriminals. Early biological theories were eventually characterized by a lack of knowledge regarding the human brain and methodological limitations. These theories were ultimately discarded after being recognized as unscientific, simplistic, and unicausal. Biological explanations began to reemerge, however, in the 1970s.

© Uncle Leo/Shutterstock.com

Modern biological theories explore variables such as diet, environmental pollution and toxins, and endocrine imbalance and their influence on criminality. For example, an improper diet can lead to an imbalance of the chemicals and minerals we need for normal brain functioning and growth. This imbalance has been associated with cognitive and learning issues and, in turn, antisocial behaviors. A potential relationship between hypoglycemia (low blood sugar) has also been discussed, with claims of a connection between this and impaired brain function and violent crime.

The Twinkie Defense

Myth: Junk food as a cause

Refined sugar in junk food → diminished capacity → inability to premeditate

Fact: Junk food as an indicator

Depression (evidenced by a diet consisting of junk food) → diminished capacity → inability to determine right and wrong

On November 27, 1978, Dan White, a former San Francisco city supervisor who had recently resigned from his position, entered San Francisco's city hall through a basement window and proceeded to shoot and kill the current city supervisor, Harvey Milk, and the mayor, George Moscone. It was during White's criminal trial for the murders that the term 'Twinkie defense' came about. Although it is now a widely recognized term, it is also quite the misconception.

The Twinkie defense is generally believed to have originated from White's defense attorney's ability to successfully argue that White's judgment was impaired due to his consumption of Twinkies and other junk foods. In fact, White's defense team never actually claimed that his consumption of junk food caused psychological or physiological changes that led him to act in a way that was inconsistent with his typical behavior. Instead, his defense was that he had been suffering from chronic, untreated depression that diminished his capacity to distinguish right from wrong. Thus, his defense team claimed, White was not capable of the premeditation that is required for the crime of first-degree murder. The defense called Dr. Martin Binder as an expert witness to testify that White went from being quite health-conscious to eating a diet consisting mostly of Twinkies and other junk foods, which was evidence of his depression.

White was ultimately convicted of the lesser charge of voluntary manslaughter, instead of first-degree murder, and was sentenced to seven years in prison. The jury determined White's actions were not premeditated, which was incomprehensible and unbelievable to most people, considering White's gun was already loaded with especially lethal ammunition, he had climbed through a basement window to avoid metal detectors, eluded Moscone's bodyguard, reloaded after killing Moscone, and walked across the building to find and shoot Milk. On the night of his conviction, violent riots broke out across the city.

The subtleties of his defense, however, were overlooked by much of the press and public. The claim of depression was largely ignored and the media essentially reported that White had claimed that the "Twinkies made him do it." The public essentially changed something they had heard into something they wanted to believe they had heard.

The Twinkie defense is now a term used to represent the attempt of offenders to avoid responsibility of their actions by claiming some external force beyond their control caused them to act that way. When a defendant argues diminished capacity, he or she is claiming that a mental condition, emotional distress, or another factor prevented him or her from fully understanding the nature of the crime committed. "Twinkie defense," a term coined by the media during coverage of Dan White's trial, has become shorthand for any defense in which the accused blames the consumption or use of some substance for his or her actions (e.g., cough medicine, MSG, caffeine). The purpose of this argument, like other defenses discussed in the previous chapter, is to negate the element of intent and thus result in an acquittal or a conviction of a lesser charge.

Is it crazy to believe there is a possible connection between the use or consumption of other substances and violent crimes?

Theories concerning endocrine imbalance have explored a relationship between male (testosterone) and female (estrogen) hormones, but have typically been inconclusive. The premenstrual syndrome (PMS) defense came about in the 1980s when the murder charges of two women were reduced to manslaughter under the premise that their mental capacity was reduced due to severe PMS.

Sociobiological theories suggest that biological and genetic conditions affect how social behaviors are learned and perceived. Although it is not suggested that a single trait predisposes individuals to criminality, some criminologists have concluded that personal traits must be what separate the deviant members of society from the nondeviant, and that possessing these traits may help explain why, when faced with the same life situation, one person commits crime whereas another obeys the law.

Psychological Theories

Another branch of positivism centers on the relationship between psychological factors (e.g., personality, learning, intelligence) and criminal behavior. Originally developed by Sigmund Freud, psychoanalytic (or psychodynamic) theory claims that crime is caused by unconscious forces and drives. Additionally, Freud believed that childhood experiences played a significant role in personality development. His followers took these ideas a step further by saying that the personality consists of three parts: the id, the ego, and the superego. The **id** controls drives that are primarily sexual in nature, whereas the **ego** links desires to behaviors. The **superego,** also known as the conscience, determines right from wrong. As such, criminal behavior is said to be the result of an over- or underdeveloped superego.

Personality is said to differentiate individuals by their established patterns of thoughts, emotions, and behaviors. Accordingly, one's personality exhibits the various ways that individuals respond to strains and challenges. In other words, one's behavior is a function of how his or her personality facilitates analysis of events and the choices made in reaction to such events (Senna & Siegel, 2002). Psychological research has found that, when investigating the relationship of personality and crime, even aggressive adolescents have been shown to have unstable personality structures. In one study, Steiner, Cauffman, and Duxbury (1999) found personality traits to be predictive of both past and future criminal behavior, even after controlling for age, length of incarceration, number of previous offenses, and the seriousness of offense.

There is growing suspicion that heredity is largely responsible for one's personality. It appears that siblings tend to share comparable personality traits, suggesting that genes play a greater role in personality development than do common experiences (the nature vs. nurture debate). Currently, researchers have begun to concentrate not on whether genes have an influence on personality, but to what extent and in what ways they play a role (Hergenhahn & Olson, 2007). It remains likely, however, that some personality traits are determined by genetics, whereas other traits are learned through experience.

Personality disorders have also been thought to play a role in the commission of crime. For example, antisocial personality disorder is defined in the *Diagnostic and Statistical Manual of Mental Disorders* (*DSM-5*) as a diagnosis given to those who habitually and pervasively disregard or violate the rights of others with no sign of remorse. Similarly, psychopaths are typically willing to deceive, lie to, and manipulate others to get what they want, while doing so without feeling any remorse or guilt. Research has shown that adults with personality disorder have a higher risk for participation in violent behavior. It has also been demonstrated that when controlling for age, location, gender, and race, personality is a predictor of criminal behavior, although it is important to recognize that the relationship between personality and criminal behavior remains quite complex.

General Theory of Crime/Low Self-Control

More than two hundred years after Cesare Beccaria argued there was a strong relationship between hedonism and criminality, Michael Gottfredson and Travis Hirschi (1990) similarly argued that criminality was the result of selfish desires and impulsivity, which they said derived from low self-control. Rejecting biological determinism, association and learning, and subcultures, Gottfredson and Hirschi claimed that criminality is the instinctual longing of receiving instant gratification, and that the benefits and outcomes of criminality need not be learned or observed, but are instead simply intuitive. They argued that self-control was a direct result of ineffective childrearing, specifically parents failing to recognize deviant behavior, punishing it in a timely manner, and punishing it in a proper fashion. Gottfredson and Hirschi also argued that the level of self-control is determined by age 8 and remains stable from that point on.

Sociological Theories

Social Structure Theories

As part of another frame of reference, criminologists began exploring the potential influence of macrolevel factors on behavior. In the decades after World War II, the shift to a postindustrial society brought about massive changes in the social and economic structure of America. Many jobs now required increased education levels and those with little education or specific job skills were no longer needed. Those who could afford to move from the central city were leaving and those with few options, scarce or no work, little or no income, and lack of opportunity were isolated in the inner cities.

In their classic book *Juvenile Delinquency in Urban Areas*, Clifford Shaw and Henry McKay (1942) identified three structural factors (socioeconomic status, ethnic heterogeneity, and residential mobility) that lead to disruption of community social organization, giving rise to variations in crime and delinquency. Emile Durkheim believed that **anomie**, or the breakdown of social norms, would be worse during times of economic prosperity than in times of depression because, he speculated, prosperity stimulates the insatiable appetites of humans at a time when they need regulation the most.

Robert Merton (1949) later took Durkheim's theory of anomie and acclimated it to American society. He argued that this insatiable appetite is not natural, but instead a creation of American society. Certain individuals do not have the same opportunities to achieve society's goals through legitimate means and instead turn to crime. He contended that there are two elements of social and cultural structure that are important to his **strain theory**: culturally defined goals and legitimate means for obtaining these goals. A successful equilibrium is preserved if a balance is maintained between the goals of the culture and the available modes of obtaining the goals. When appropriate means are not accessible (e.g., the lower class has less opportunity for legitimate means), an individual may experience negative emotions such as anger and frustration, which can then lead to deviant or criminal behavior. In other words, the differential access to approved opportunities for appropriate modes of adaptation can lead to strain and anomie, which may initiate deviant behavior. According to Merton, some societies (e.g., America) place an overemphasis on the goal of economic success, and stress the importance of goal achievement rather than focusing on ways of achieving this insatiable cultural goal. Through this malintegration in society, individuals are forced to choose a mode of adaptation. Merton explained five modes of individual adaptation that individuals appear to choose through a nonrandom response to the strain experienced from the failure to achieve the culturally defined goals. These alternative responses are conformity, innovation, ritualism, retreatism, and rebellion. As demonstrated in Table 3.1, each of these modes of adaptation differs in whether or not they accept the cultural goals and/or the means to achieve them. Conformity is the most common type of adaptation. Conformists accept both the societal goals and the means approved for obtaining the goals; they follow the rules of society and obey the law. Innovators hold the same goals of society, but do not necessarily have the legitimate means to achieve them. Therefore, these individuals use their own means to get ahead, which may include robbery, embezzlement, or other types of criminal behavior. Ritualists have stopped trying to achieve the goals, but still believe in following conventional means (e.g., someone who stays in a dead-end job). Retreatists have abandoned both the culturally defined goals and the means to obtain them. These individuals often retreat into a world of alcohol abuse and drug addiction and become unproductive members of society. Finally, rebels reject the goals and means, but create their own, bringing about revolutionary change and creating a new society.

TABLE 3.1. MERTON'S INDIVIDUAL ADAPTATIONS TO ANOMIE.

Adaptation	Cultural Goals	Institutional Means
Conformity	+	+
Innovation	+	−
Ritualism	−	+
Retreatism	−	−
Rebellion	+/−	+/−

Robert Agnew (1992) attempted to elaborate upon Merton's strain theory to create a **general strain theory**. While Merton maintained that strain was a result of the failure to achieve positively valued goals (i.e., the disjunction between aspirations and expectations), Agnew expanded this theory by adding that strain could also result from the removal of positively valued stimuli and the presentation of negative stimuli. According to Agnew, experiencing each type of strain will increase the probability that an individual will suffer from at least one of several negative emotions. Anger, the most crucial negative emotion in general strain theory, results from the individual placing blame on others for his or her own hardship. Delinquency, then, becomes one possible response to this anger and the individual may attempt to alleviate strain through deviant behaviors. Agnew argued that his general strain theory is potentially capable of explaining a broad range of delinquency, unlike Merton's strain theory. Additionally, Agnew asserted that the magnitude, recency, duration, and clustering of adverse events also influence the amount of strain one experiences.

Steven Messner and Richard Rosenfeld's (2001) institutional anomie theory is the most contemporary version of anomie/strain theory. The central premise of their theory is that serious crime is a result of the routine functioning of the American social system. In other words, "high crime rates are intrinsic to the basic cultural commitments and institutional arrangements of American society" (Messner & Rosenfeld, 2001, p. 5). Messner and Rosenfeld say that the American Dream, or the commitment to the goal of material success shared and pursued by all members of society, refers to the insatiable appetite for monetary gain and material success found in our culture. The values fundamental to the American Dream include achievement, individualism, universalism, and materialism.

© danielfela/Shutterstock.com

Drawing from Merton's conceptualization of American culture, Messner and Rosenfeld agree that the American culture is characterized by severe imbalance and that economic success is promoted to the exclusion of all other goals. Although the American Dream has encouraged economic expansion, technological innovations, modernization, and social mobility, it has also fostered the pressure to succeed at any cost, and thus generates deviant and criminal behavior.

Subcultural Theories

A subculture is a group whose norms, values, and behaviors are distinct enough to set members off from mainstream culture. The main idea behind subcultural theories, then, is that conformity to the rules, values, and norms of unconventional subcultural groups is interpreted by conventional society as deviant or criminal.

Marvin Wolfgang and Franco Ferracuti (1967) developed the **subculture of violence theory** where they contend that there is a subcultural ethos that suggests that in some types of social interaction, a violent and physically aggressive response is expected or required. Accordingly, such force or violence is generally viewed as a reflection of values that stand apart from the dominant, mainstream culture. The basic premises of this theory state that:

- Violence is not completely different from the dominant culture.
- Those who participate in a subculture of violence are not necessarily violent all the time.
- The violence ethos is most prominent among adolescent to middle-aged males.
- Attitudes favorable to violence are learned through a process of differential learning and association.

Social Process Theories

Learning theorists contend that criminal behavior can be learned and unlearned just like any other behavior. Accordingly, these theorists say that deviant and criminal behaviors are learned and modified through the same cognitive mechanisms as conforming behavior (Akers, 1998). Essentially, people are born good and learn to be bad.

In the early 1900s, the behaviorist revolution replaced the ideas of mental images and consciousness with observable stimuli and responses, yet maintained the basic idea that learning is achieved through association. As a forerunner of modern-day learning theorists, Gabriel Tarde rejected popular biological theories of crime causation and initiated an offensive against the idea of the born criminal. He believed that criminality was a "profession" learned through interaction with and imitation of others (Tarde, 1903).

Differential Association

Until now, the dominant explanation for crime was a multiple factor approach. Criminal behavior was believed to be determined by a variety of factors including age, race, social class, and inadequate socialization. Edwin Sutherland's dissatisfaction with the nonscientific multiple-factor approach led to his attempt at the development of both a thorough definition and a satisfactory causal explanation. Sutherland's theory of **differential association** was the first and most prominent formal statement of microlevel learning theory. In 1939, Sutherland stated that the specific causal process in the development of criminal behavior is the differential association with people who commit crime and those who do not (Cullen & Agnew, 2006).

In 1947, Edwin Sutherland rejected the notions of biological determinism and instead focused on crime as a learned behavior. He believed that while crime was learned, it was intermediately affected through association with others, and the extent of deviant behavior was directly linked to the time spent with delinquent peers. As noncriminal behavior is also learned through association, the magnitude of both criminal and noncriminal learned behavior is dependent on degree of association and with whom an individual is associating. Accordingly, it is the element of interaction that is so imperative to the determination of behavior learned (Cressey, 1952; Sutherland, 1947).

Sutherland developed nine principles, contending that criminal behavior is learned through social interactions:

1. Criminal behavior is learned.
2. Criminal behavior is learned in interaction with other persons in a process of communication.
3. The principal part of the learning of criminal behavior occurs within intimate personal groups.
4. When criminal behavior is learned, the learning includes: (a) techniques of committing the crime and (b) the specific direction of

motives, drives, rationalizations, and attitudes necessary to engage in criminal behavior.

5. The specific direction of the motives and drives are learned from definitions of the legal codes that are either favorable or unfavorable to law violation.

6. A person becomes delinquent because of an excess of definitions favorable to violation of law over definitions unfavorable to violation of law.

7. Differential associations may vary in frequency, duration, priority, and intensity.

8. The process of learning criminal behavior by association with criminal and anticriminal patterns involves all of the mechanisms involved in any other learning.

9. Although criminal behavior may be an expression of general needs and values, it is not explained by those general needs and values since non-criminal behavior is also an expression of the same needs and values.

Ultimately, a person will become delinquent when exposure to definitions—defined as motives, attitudes, and rationalizations—favorable to law breaking are greater than exposure to definitions favorable to the opposite (i.e., conventional behavior) (Akers, 1998; Cressey, 1960; Sutherland, 1979; Sutherland, Cressey, & Luckenbill, 1992).

The basic elements of Sutherland's theory come from George Herbert Mead's theory of **symbolic interactionism**, or the idea that the self is determined through social interactions and symbolic definitions (Blumer, 1969). As Mead argued that "meanings" determine behavior, Sutherland similarly alleged that the primary determining factor for criminality is the meaning they give to the social conditions they experience. In the end, whether or not a person engages in criminal behavior depends on how he or she defines the situation (Sutherland, 1979; Sutherland & Luckenbill, 1992).

Social Learning

Presented as a general theory of crime and deviance, Ronald Akers' (1998) **social learning theory (SLT)** retains concepts from symbolic interactionism, Sutherland's focus on primary group interaction (e.g., peer groups, the family), and the idea of learning through association. According to this view, the learning process and behavior are related to the imitation and modeling of others with whom the individual is associated, as well as the frequency, amount, and probability of perceived or experienced rewards and punishments.

Expanding on the ideas of differential association and focusing on the psychological notions theorized by Bandura (1963, 1965) and Skinner (1938, 1958), Akers views SLT to be a broader theory that incorporates some of the same elements of Sutherland's theory, along with differential reinforcement and other principles of behavioral acquisition, continuation, and cessation.

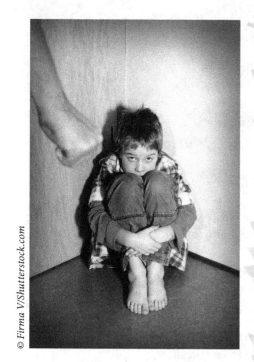

© Firma V/Shutterstock.com

The four primary concepts of SLT are differential association, definitions, differential reinforcement, and imitation.

Borrowed from Sutherland, **differential association** is the notion that people are exposed to various "role models" and assorted attitudes and values, and some will model criminal behavior and convey values that are consistent with such behavior. Akers (1998, p. 78) also uses **definitions** as a major concept of SLT and defines them as "normative attitudes or evaluative meanings attached to given behavior . . . that label the commission of an act as right or wrong, good or bad, desirable or undesirable, justified or unjustified." Akers adds the idea that behavior is a function of the frequency, amount, and probability of anticipated or actual rewards and punishments (i.e., **differential reinforcement**) and that the behavior of others and its consequences are observed and modeled (i.e., **imitation**).

SLT calls attention to the notion that behavior may be reinforced not only through rewards and punishments, but also through expectations that are learned by watching what happens to others. Since it is a general explanation of crime and deviance of all kinds, social learning is not simply a theory about how novel criminal behavior is learned or a theory regarding the positive causes of that behavior, but it embraces variables that operate to both motivate and control delinquent and criminal behavior, and to both promote and challenge conformity.

Neutralization

Building upon Sutherland's theory of differential association, Gresham Sykes and David Matza (1957) developed a theory of delinquency using techniques to rationalize or justify criminal behavior. They rejected the notion that delinquent subcultures maintain their own set of values independent from that of the dominant culture. Instead, Sykes and Matza believed that most delinquents hold conventional values and are only able to violate these social norms by developing a set of justifications to neutralize their behavior. The rationalizations make the delinquent behavior possible by allowing delinquents to avoid the guilt that might otherwise result from their behavior. In other words, the **techniques of neutralization** allow individuals to engage in deviant behavior while still protecting themselves from guilt, shame, or a negative self-image.

Society has certain expectations of how we are supposed to act. As part of the process of socialization, we internalize these norms. When the moral code is broken, then, we need a way to justify our actions so that we can see ourselves—and present ourselves to others—as moral members of society. Sykes and Matza's techniques of neutralization do just that—provide us with a rationale for norm violations. Although excuses are typically used to justify behavior after the fact, neutralizations, they contend, precede deviant behavior.

This theoretical model is based on four facts observed in society:

1. Delinquents express guilt over their illegal acts.
2. Delinquents frequently respect and admire honest, law-abiding individuals.
3. A line is drawn between those whom they can victimize and those they cannot.
4. Delinquents are not immune to the demands of conformity.

Sykes and Matza's (1957) neutralization theory includes five techniques that may be used by offenders to excuse unconventional behavior:

The Denial of Responsibility

In this first technique, the individual acknowledges the behavior, but claims that he or she had to do it or was forced to do it. This is not unlike the legal claims of diminished capacity. In this technique, the offender claims, "It was not my fault."

The Denial of Injury

In using this strategy, the individual acknowledges the behavior, but says that no one was harmed or the harm was not intended and it therefore should not be of concern. This is an attempt for the offender to negate the harm that was done to the victim. In this technique, the offender claims, "No one got hurt."

The Denial of the Victim

When using this technique, the offender agrees that deviant action was taken and somebody was hurt, but believes the action/injury was not wrong. The victim is said to have brought about or otherwise deserved the behavior. This is, once again, a way for the offender to excuse his or her behavior. In this technique, the offender claims, "They deserved it."

The Condemnation of the Condemners

The use of this technique is not necessarily to show that the behavior was wrong, but rather to deflect from the wrongfulness of the actions by shifting the focus to those who are doing the condemning. By using this technique, delinquents claim that those who condemn them engage in questionable behavior as well. This technique shifts the attention away from the offender and onto those who disapprove of the criminal actions. In this technique, the offender claims, "You are all hypocrites and have no right to judge me."

The Appeal to Higher Loyalties

Although it is acknowledged that some social norms were violated, the individual claims to have been adhering to other norms or loyalties, and these higher principles justify the behavior. In other words, loyalty to someone or something else may sometimes necessitate criminal behavior. In this technique, the offender claims, "I am loyal to a higher purpose." For example, the offender may say, "I was just helping a friend."

Offenders who justify or neutralize their criminal conduct are still able to view themselves as normal and conventional, but are able to offset any guilt or shame they feel about committing their crimes.

Although Sykes and Matza originally developed neutralization theory with regard to juvenile delinquency, techniques of neutralization may explain many types of deviant and criminal behavior, including violent crime (Agnew, 1994). Matza (1964) later discussed the idea that many delinquents go back and forth between conventional and criminal behavior, a concept he termed "drift." He maintained that people live their lives on a continuum, somewhere between complete freedom and complete restraint. Once an individual commits a crime, he or she feels guilt for the act and must balance his or her behavior by returning to law-abiding behavior.

Social Control Theories

Social Bond Theory

Travis Hirschi (1969) developed his **social control theory** as a theory on conformity rather than one on crime and delinquency, examining the variation in the degree to which individuals commit to the common values of society. The primary assumption of control theories is that crime and delinquency are a result of weakened or broken bonds to society. Hirschi used four elements to represent these bonds: attachment, commitment, involvement, and belief. First, a lack of **attachment** to others, or insensitivity to others' opinions, suggests that the individual is not bound by the norms of society and is thus free to deviate. Second, a **commitment** to obeying the rules of society simply for fear of consequence is viewed as one's common sense, the rational element in conformity. Third, lack of opportunity for participation in deviant behavior because of **involvement** in conventional activities eliminates both the time and prospect for involvement in delinquency. Fourth, **belief** in a common value system within the society elicits not the question of why people differ in their beliefs, but the question of why people violate the values or norms of which they believe. Instead of searching for an answer to the question of why some people violate the law, however, social control theory is grounded in answering the question of why some people conform to the law.

Labeling Theory

In the mid-twentieth century, labeling theorists began to focus on how and why society applies the label of "criminal" to certain people and behaviors to explore the effects the label has on the future behavior of the labeled individual. Stemming from symbolic interactionism, labeling theory is less concerned with the causes of crime and more interested in the societal reactions to and the stigma associated with crime. Howard Becker is associated with labeling theory and the idea that there is nothing inherently deviant about certain acts, and that those who face labels must adapt to the consequences that come with the labeling.

Social Development Theories

Developmental, or life-course, criminology integrates sociological, psychological, and economic elements into more complex developmental views of crime causation. Individual factors are said to interact with social factors to determine the onset, length, and end of criminal careers. Some of these theories predict continuity across the life course, others predict continuity from some offenders and change for others, and still others predict continuity and change for the same offenders (Gleuck & Gleuck, 1950; Moffitt, 1993; Sampson & Laub, 1995, 2003).

Terrie Moffitt (1993) presented a dual taxonomy to explain two categories of individuals and their involvement in antisocial behavior over time. The first category, life-course-persistent offenders, is said to begin antisocial behavior in early childhood and continue involvement in crime over every stage of the life course. Their antisocial behavior has its origins in neurodevelopmental processes. In contrast, adolescence-limited offenders engage in antisocial and deviant behavior only for a short period during adolescence. Their antisocial behavior originates in social processes and tends to desist in young adulthood.

Social Conflict Theories

Although pluralist conflict theories focus on power differences and divisions, radical or Marxist theories maintain that there is one power base and critical theories consist of transcending dominant social control ideas. Karl Marx focused on the economic conditions perpetrated by capitalists. He argued that unequal distribution of power and wealth produce crime. Essentially, crime develops as a result of social conflict.

Feminist Criminology

Three primary types of feminist theories dominate the literature. Liberal feminism highlights problems arising from gender discrimination and stereotypical views concerning the traditional roles of women in society and the equality of opportunities (Adler, 1975; Bottcher, 2001; Messerschmidt, 1993; Miller & Mullins, 2006). Radical feminism views the origins of patriarchy and subordination of women in male aggression and the control of female sexuality (Brownmiller, 1975; Griffin, 1971). Social feminism views gender discrimination as a function of capitalist society, which fosters both social class divisions and patriarchy (Messerschmidt, 1993).

Integrated Theories

Integrated theories merge several perspectives and/or different disciplines in an attempt to better understand crime causation. Integrated theories combine concepts from two or more existing theories to form a more inclusive theory of crime causation. Proponents of theoretical integration view it as an alternative method of theory development and testing that addresses some of the limitations found in more traditional strategies. They also argue that integration offers greater explanatory power and include more types of criminal behavior than single theories.

Indeed, crime exists on different levels of analysis, manifests itself in numerous ways throughout the life course, has been linked to forces both internal and external to the individual, and is implicated in a myriad of social, cultural, and political contexts. While criminologists attempt to determine the ultimate cause of criminal behavior, it is likely that we will continue to see new ideas emerge, old perspectives reappear, and integration of existing theories in the years soon to follow.

BOX 3.1 CAREER HIGHLIGHT: CRIMINOLOGIST

Criminologists analyze data to understand crime, its causes, how crimes are committed, and what information law enforcement might need to help aid in solving crime. They conduct research to determine what causes individuals to commit crimes and the effects those activities have on the perpetrators, victims, and society. The field is interdisciplinary, combining criminal justice, sociology, psychology, and other disciplines to develop an understanding of human behavior and to use that knowledge to analyze, predict, and prevent conditions leading to criminal acts.

A career as a criminologist is mostly research driven. It requires an advanced degree in some combination of criminology, criminal justice, sociology, or psychology. Criminologists need organizational, interpersonal communication, and strong writing skills, as well as knowledge in probability and statistics. They may interview criminals or work with law enforcement, community leaders, and politicians to develop policies to help reduce crime and ensure fair and humane treatment within the criminal justice system. Criminologists work for local, state, and federal governments, on policy advisory boards, or for legislative committees. Most often, criminologists are employed through colleges and universities, teaching and conducting research.

Comprehension Check

1. What are some of the principal theories put forward to explain criminal behavior?
2. How are theory and research related?
3. What are some of the main ideas associated with the classical school of criminology?

4. Discuss how positivism differs from the classical school.

5. What are some theories that fall under biological explanations? Psychological explanations? Sociological explanations?

References

Adler, F. (1975). *Sisters in crime: The rise of the new female criminal.* New York, NY: McGraw-Hill.

Agnew, R. (1992). "Foundations for a general strain theory of crime and delinquency." *Criminology, 30*(1), 47–87.

Agnew, R. (1994). "The techniques of neutralization and violence." *Criminology, 32*(4), 555–580.

Akers, R. (1998). *Social learning and social structure: A general theory of crime and deviance.* Boston, MA: Northeastern University Press.

Bandura, A. (1963). *Social learning and personality development.* Englewood Cliffs, NJ: Prentice Hall.

Bandura, A. (1965). "Influence of models' reinforcement contingencies on the acquisition of imitative responses." *Journal of Personality and Social Psychology, 1*(6), 589–595.

Beccaria, C. (1764). *On crimes and punishments.* Indianapolis, IN: Hackett Publishing Company.

Blumer, H. (1969). *Symbolic interactionism: Perspective and method.* Englewood Cliffs, NJ: Prentice Hall.

Bottcher, J. (2001). "Social practices of gender: How gender relates to delinquency in the everyday lives of high-risk youths." *Criminology, 39*(4), 893–932.

Brownmiller, S. (1975). *Against our will: Men, women, and rape.* New York, NY: Simon and Schuster.

Cornish, D. B., & Clarke, R. V. (1986). *The reasoning criminal: Rational choice perspectives on offending.* New York, NY: Springer-Verlag.

Cressey, D. R. (1952). "Application and verification of the differential association theory." *The Journal of Criminal Law, Criminology, and Police Science, 43*(1), 43–52.

Cressey, D. R. (1960). "The theory of differential association: An introduction." *Social Problems, 8*(1), 2–6.

Cullen, F. T., & Agnew, R. (2006). *Criminological theory: Past to present.* Los Angeles, CA: Roxbury Publishing Company.

Darwin, C. (1859). *On the origin of species by means of natural selection.* London, UK: J. Murray.

Gleuck, S., & Gleuck, E. (1950). *Unraveling Juvenile delinquency.* New York, NY: Commonwealth Fund.

Goring, C. (1913). *The English convict: A statistical study.* London, UK: H.M.S.

Gottfredson, M. R., & Hirschi, T. (1990). *A general theory of crime.* Stanford, CA: Stanford University Press.

Griffin, S. (1971). *Rape: The all-American crime.* New York, NY: Random House.

Hergenhahn, B. R., & Olson, M. H. (2007). *An introduction to theories of personality* (7th ed.). Upper Saddle River, NJ: Pearson Publishing.

Hirschi, T. (1969). *Causes of delinquency*. Berkeley, CA: University of California Press.

Lombroso-Ferrero, G. (1979). "Criminal man." In J. E. Jacoby (Ed.), *Classics of criminology* (pp. 75–88). Prospect Heights, NY: Waveland Press, Inc.

Matza, D. (1964). *Delinquency and drift*. New York, NY: Wiley.

Merton, R. K. (1949). *Social theory and social structure*. New York, NY: The Free Press of Glencoe.

Messerschmidt, J. W. (1993). *Masculinities and crime: Critique and reconceptualization of theory*. Lanham, MD: Rowman & Littlefield Publishers, Inc.

Messner, S. F., & Rosenfeld, R. (2001). *Crime and the American dream*. Belmont, CA: Wadsworth/Thomson Learning.

Miller, J., & Mullins, C. W. (2006). "Taking stock: The status of feminist theories in criminology." In F. Cullen, J. P. Wright, & K. Blevins (Eds.), *The status of criminological theory* (pp. 217–249). New York, NY: Routledge.

Moffitt, T. E. (1993). "Adolescence-limited and life-course-persistent antisocial behavior: A developmental taxonomy." *Psychological Review, 100*(4), 674–701.

Sampson, R. J., & Laub, J. H. (1995). *Crime in the making: Pathways and turning points through life*. Cambridge, MA: Harvard University Press.

Sampson, R. J., & Laub, J. H. (2003). "Life-course desisters? Trajectories of crime among delinquent boys followed to age 70." *Criminology, 41*(3), 555–592.

Senna, J. J., & Siegel, L. J. (2002). *Introduction to criminal justice*. Belmont, CA: Wadsworth.

Shaw, C. R., & McKay, H. D. (1942). *Juvenile delinquency in urban areas*. Chicago, IL: The University of Chicago Press.

Skinner, B. F. (1938). *The behavior of organisms*. New York, NY: Appleton-Century-Crofts.

Skinner, B. F. (1958). *Science and human behavior*. Oxford, UK: Macmillan.

Steiner, H., Cauffman, E., & Duxbury, E. (1999). Personality traits in juvenile delinquents: The relation to criminal behavior and recidivism. *Journal of the American Academy of Child & Adolescent Psychiatry, 38*, 256–262.

Sutherland, E. H. (1947). *Differential association: Principles of criminology*. Lanham, MD: AltaMira Press.

Sutherland, E. H. (1979). "Differential association." In J. E. Jacoby (Ed.), *Classics of criminology* (pp. 168–170). Prospect Heights: Waveland Press, Inc.

Sutherland, E. H., Cressey, D. R., & Luckenbill, D. F. (1992). *Principles of criminology* (11th ed.). Lanham, MD: General Hall.

Sykes, G. M., & Matza, D. (1957). "Techniques of neutralization: A theory of delinquency." *American Sociological Review, 22*, 664–670.

Tarde, G. (1903). *The laws of imitation*. New York, NY: Henry Holt and Company.

Wolfgang, M. E., & Ferracuti, F. (1967). *The subculture of violence: Toward an integrated theory in criminology*. New York, NY: Tavistock Publications.

© samuelwong/Shutterstock.com

Victimology

LEARNING OBJECTIVES

After reading this chapter, the student should be able to

1 Understand the basic concepts related to victimization

2 Consider the consequences/effects of victimization and the impact of crime

3 Discuss the victim's interactions with the criminal justice system

4 Better understand the costs of crime and compensation for crime victims

Introduction

The plight of victims has not always been a matter of great significance. In fact, crime victims were paid little attention until the 1950s when the field of victimology emerged. This subfield of criminology examines the role of the victim in precipitating a criminal event, as well as the impact of crime on victims and the community. Victimology essentially focuses on who is victimized, the effects of crime, and victims' interactions and experiences with the criminal justice system. Fortunately, in recent years, we have seen an increased interest in crime victims and their involvement in the criminal justice process.

This chapter examines the changing role of crime victims throughout history, including the relationship between victims and crime, and the victim's role in, and interaction with, the criminal justice system.

We also introduce the various methods of gathering data on crime victims, the costs of crime, and how victims are compensated.

Who Is Victimized?

Criminal victimization is a far too common experience. Indeed, many of you have likely been victims of crime and experienced physical, financial, or emotional harm as a result of the commission of a crime, or know someone who has. Victimization knows no boundaries—not age, gender, sexual orientation, disability status, race or ethnic identification, or any other category.

When it comes to victim selection, although it might sometimes appear to be random, not everyone shares an equal chance of victimization. Research has shown that demographic factors (e.g., age, gender, race, income) place some individuals at a greater risk for victimization. One explanation for this is that these demographic factors affect people's lifestyles. In other words, their everyday activities, such as work, home life, and recreation, are influenced by these demographic factors. In turn, these routine activities affect their exposure to dangerous places and people.

The Routine Activities Approach

Lawrence Cohen and Marcus Felson (1979) proposed a routine activities approach, arguing that potential offenders respond to opportunities to commit crime that are systematically related to the routine activities by which people live their lives. They believed that the dramatic increase in reported crime rates in the United States since 1960 could be linked to changes in the structure of American society (e.g., the dispersion of activities away from the household, the addition of women to the labor force, changes in the sales of consumer goods). Because of these changes, target suitability is believed to have increased as guardian presence decreased, explaining the increased crime rates.

Based on two general principles, the routine activities approach first argues that in order for crime to occur, motivated offenders must converge with suitable targets in the absence of capable guardians (see Figure 4.1). Capable guardians can include things like walking with a buddy instead of walking alone or arming a home alarm system. Second, this approach argues that the probability of these factors converging in time and space is influenced by our "routine activities," or things such as our work, leisure, recreation, family, and other activities in which we participate.

The routine activities approach typically takes the supply of motivated offenders for granted. In other words, it assumes that there will always be people who are willing to commit a crime if provided with the right opportunity. Thus, the theory instead focuses on the opportunity for crime on the premise that even when there is a motivated offender, no crime can occur

FIGURE 4.1 ELEMENTS OF THE ROUTINE ACTIVITIES APPROACH.

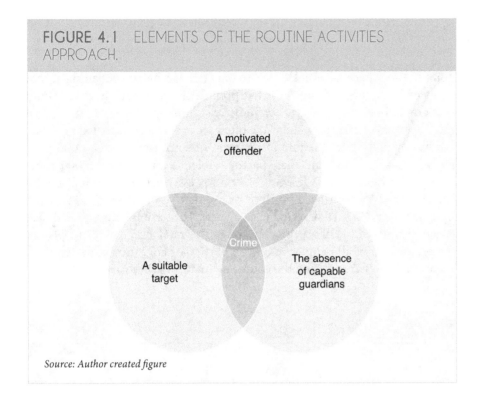

Source: Author created figure

if no opportunity is available (i.e., an attractive target and the absence of capable guardians).

Repeat Victimization

Although anyone can become a victim of crime, having been a victim once might make someone more likely to be a victim again. In fact, victimization is the single best predictor of victimization. This does not mean that every victim will become a victim a second time, but it does mean that victims may be more vulnerable due to circumstances or lifestyle. Thus, we should look at what victims can do to help minimize future vulnerability in the same way we look at what factors may contribute to crime in the first place.

Measuring Victimization

Incidence versus Prevalence

We can use different ways to measure crime, but the difference between incidence and prevalence is important to understanding what is actually being reported. **Incidence** is the number of new instances of a condition or an event that occur during a given period of time in a specified population. Therefore, incidence gives a snapshot of how many crimes occur during a particular period of time (often a year). Incidence only includes the new cases that occur during that period of time. For example, US residents age 12 and older experienced 5.7 million violent victimizations in 2016 (Morgan & Kena, 2017).

Prevalence, on the other hand, provides the number of existing cases of a condition or an event at a single point in time (not necessarily new cases, but the total number of cases). The important words here are "at a single point in time" because prevalence can only tell us what is happening at that point or has happened up until that point. It is important to understand that prevalence is a cumulative or additive summary of the total amount of existing cases of a phenomenon. We often see prevalence reported as a rate. For example, in 2016, the rate of stranger violence was 8.2 per 1,000 people, whereas the rate of intimate partner violence was 2.2 per 1,000 people (Morgan & Kena, 2017). The term **period prevalence** (e.g., annual prevalence) is used to describe conditions or events that have occurred at some time during a designated period (e.g., a year). The term **lifetime prevalence** is a useful way to express the concept of the total number of people (or the proportion of all people) who get a particular condition/experience an event, such as crime, during the course of an average lifetime.

Measurement Tools

The Uniform Crime Report

Although you will learn more about measuring crime in Chapter 5, it is important to understand the tools that help us to not only measure criminal behavior, but also to know more about victimization. The Uniform Crime Report (UCR) is one measurement tool we use to better understand the amount of crime that occurs. As a brief overview, the UCR is a system of reporting criminal statistics that is compiled by the Federal Bureau of Investigation (FBI). More than 17,000 law enforcement agencies voluntarily provide data on reported crimes. Because the information comes directly from various law enforcement agencies, only those crimes that are reported to the police are included in the annual report published by the FBI. Unfortunately, the UCR does not include any information on crime victims.

The National Incident-Based Reporting System

A newer system of reporting is the FBI's National Incident-Based Reporting System (NIBRS). This measurement tool collects data from local, state, and federal automated records systems on every incident and arrest within forty-six crime categories. The NIBRS includes information on the incident, victim (including the relationship between the victim and offender), property, offender, and the person arrested for the crime. This tool, however, is also only able to include crimes that are known/have been reported to the police.

The EZANIBRS (Easy Access to NIBRS Victims) allows access to state-level data on violence victims based on the information obtained from NIBRS. EZANIBRS allows users to explore various characteristics of victims of violence, including demographics (age, sex, race), injury, and victim–offender relationship (National Center for Juvenile Justice, 2015).

The National Crime Victimization Survey

The National Crime Victimization Survey (NCVS), designed to complement the UCR, includes a national representative sample of interviews regarding victimization. Conducted on an annual basis, this survey collects detailed information regarding the crimes of rape and sexual assault, robbery, assault, domestic violence, household burglary, personal household theft, and motor vehicle theft, but does not include the crimes of homicide, commercial crime, kidnapping, or what we refer to as victimless crimes. The NCVS does allow us to collect information regarding the victim's age, sex, race, ethnicity, marital status, income, and educational level, as well as data on the offender. Moreover, we are able to collect information on the victim's experience with the criminal justice system, any protective measures used, and possible substance abuse by offenders. As you can see, the NCVS offers us quite a bit more information on crime victims than some of the other measurement tools. This is due in large part to the fact that the NCVS data come directly from surveys of crime victims themselves, providing them with the opportunity to describe victimization events, even if they were not reported to the police.

The Role of Victims

The role the victim plays in the victimization can vary. In some cases, victims truly are in the wrong place at the wrong time. In other cases, however, some responsibility falls to the victim for contributing to the victimization in some way. The extent to which a victim is responsible for his or her own victimization is called **victim precipitation**. This takes into consideration that criminal victimization involves at least two parties—the perpetrator and the victim—and that both are acting and, in many cases, reacting before, during, and after the crime occurred.

© Straight 8 Photography/Shutterstock.com

At one end of the spectrum, a victim may unintentionally make it easier for an offender to commit a crime. For example, a man accidentally leaves his vehicle unlocked, making it easier for an offender to enter the vehicle and steal the laptop that was left inside. This is referred to as **victim facilitation**. At the other end of the spectrum, **victim provocation** occurs when someone does something to incite another person to commit an illegal act. This suggests that a crime would not have occurred without the victim's behavior and that the offender is in no way responsible for the crime. For example, a man intends to burglarize a house, but upon entering the residence realizes that someone is home. The homeowner, fearing for his life, shoots and kills the intruder. Even though the original offender is ultimately a victim, he would not have been shot and killed had he not entered the residence without permission. While these behaviors do lead us to consider aspects of the crime that we may not have initially thought about, it is important to understand that these behaviors do not excuse criminal acts, nor do they mean that it was the victim's fault that the crime occurred.

The Impact of Crime

© Doidam 10/Shutterstock.com

Victimization can also be understood by looking at its costs. Costs can be seen in how a person reacts to becoming a victim, as well as the financial and physical damages or injuries caused by the person who committed the crime. When a person becomes a victim of a crime, he or she will experience varying degrees of physical, financial, and psychological trauma and loss. Typically, victims of nonviolent crime experience lower levels of trauma than their violent crime counterparts, but that is not always the case. Indeed, victimization is a very personal phenomenon, and people respond and react differently.

The cost of victimization has three general dimensions: physical injuries, financial losses, and emotional stress. These primary costs will vary by victim, depending on the individual victim and the severity of the crime. Physical injuries consist of bruises, cuts, or broken bones, but the stress of the crime might also cause issues such as sleeplessness, fatigue, and appetite changes. Financial costs are the monetary losses sustained as a result of becoming a victim. Victims are often faced with having to replace stolen or damaged property; loss of productivity, income, and/or wages (e.g., missing work for court or medical appointments, unable to work because of injury); and extensive medical bills. Emotional costs are more difficult to quantify because they include how becoming a victim has forever changed their emotional state and their life in general, but are no less significant to crime victims.

When an individual experiences victimization, there are a variety of supports and interventions put into place to help the victim repair the damage and move beyond the incident. However, if a victim does not receive this help and support, he or she may experience secondary costs. The victim may even feel as though he or she is being victimized for a second time because valuable resources and support were not provided to them.

Fear of Crime

Fear of crime, or the sense of danger and anxiety at the prospect of being victimized, does not always correlate with the realities of victimization. Research shows, for example, that women tend to be more fearful than men of becoming victims of crime, yet men actually have higher rates of victimization for all crimes except rape and sexual assault. Similarly, most studies indicate that despite the fact that the elderly have the lowest risk of victimization, they actually fear criminal victimization the most. However, it should be noted that fear of victimization may lead the elderly to curtail their activities so that they do not leave the home or go out, thereby limiting their activities and, in turn, lowering their risk of victimization.

Despite the fact that we have seen crime rates declining since the 1980s, nearly every year when asked whether there is "more crime in the United States than there was a year ago," the majority has answered "yes." This erroneous image of increasing crime rates may very well result from the fact that most people obtain their information about crime from the news media, which by focusing on violent criminal activity, may give the impression that the crime situation is continually becoming worse, when research shows the reality to be much different. Similarly, with increasing and advancing technology, our exposure to the news media has changed as well. With real-time notifications via social media and instant access to live news stories from various outlets, the fact that we hear more about events as they occur is likely to lead to an increase in fear and the belief that more crime is occurring.

Victims' Interactions and Experiences With the Criminal Justice System

While victims are left to contend with a variety of physical, psychological, and economic losses, they are often forgotten after the crime has occurred, as our criminal justice system tends to focus on the apprehension and prosecution of the offender. In fact, victims often feel left out of the process and that our criminal justice system is not sensitive to their needs. From seemingly hostile questioning by law enforcement during the immediate investigation following the crime, to missing work due to repeated judicial proceedings, and many times never even hearing the outcome of the case, victims frequently feel as though they have been victimized twice—once by the offender and a second time by our criminal justice system.

© Macrovector/Shutterstock.com

Victim surveys have revealed that more than half of violent crime victimizations go unreported to the police. When asked why they did not report their victimizations, victims offer a variety of reasons. In most cases, victims report that the offender was unsuccessful in the crime (i.e., nothing was lost, there were no injuries). Others claim that the police cannot or will not do anything or that the courts will not punish the offender sufficiently. Many victims also report that they did not notify the police because of past experiences with the criminal justice system, to minimize losses or avoid double victimization, or there was a lack of confidence in the criminal justice system.

Over the last thirty years, crime victims have begun to receive greater attention and sensitivity from the criminal justice system. This is in part because victims many times are the only eyewitnesses to the crime, so their help and cooperation are needed. Still, this help may come at further cost to the victim (e.g., financial and emotional costs), making many of them unwilling to provide such assistance.

The victims movement initially focused on serious violent crime, so the question remains: What about victims of other types of crime, like property crime, fraud, or white-collar crime? Researchers are calling for more information about these other types of crime and asking what can be done to help all victims.

In recent years, new laws have been put into place that help increase the rights and benefits of victims. The core rights for victims of crime are included below (Office of Justice Programs, n.d.).

- The right to be treated with fairness, dignity, sensitivity, and respect
- The right to attend and be present at criminal justice proceedings
- The right to be heard in the criminal justice process, including the right to confer with the prosecutor and submit a victim impact statement at sentencing, parole, and other similar proceedings
- The right to be informed of proceedings and events in the criminal justice process, including the release or escape of the offender, legal rights and remedies, and available benefits and services, and access to records, referrals, and other information
- The right to protection from intimidation and harassment
- The right to restitution from the offender
- The right to privacy
- The right to apply for crime victim compensation
- The right to restitution from the offender
- The right to the expeditious return of personal property seized as evidence whenever possible
- The right to a speedy trial and other proceedings free from unreasonable delay
- The right to enforcement of these rights and access to other available remedies.

In addition to the core rights for victims, most states have adopted amendments to their state constitution, securing even more rights for crime victims. While there is currently no amendment to the US Constitution providing rights to victims of crime, the Crime Victims' Rights Act (CVRA), part of the Justice for All Act of 2004, gives crime victims' rights in federal criminal justice proceedings, ways for victims to enforce those rights, and provides victims and prosecutors standing to assert victims' rights.

BOX 4.1 CAREER HIGHLIGHT: VICTIMS ADVOCATE

A victims advocate is a trained professional that works with victims of crime or abuse. They are often employed by non-profit organizations, state or federal legal offices, and shelters and community centers. Victims advocates help victims cope with the stress and trauma following victimization by offering support and guidance to victims through the entire process. They provide assistance to individuals who need help dealing with the aftermath of a traumatic experience. Some common responsibilities of victims advocates include:

- Offer emotional support
- Help create safety plan/find safe place to go
- Inform victims of their rights and what to expect from the legal process
- Assist in completing and submitting applications for victims compensation
- Accompany victims to court hearings and other legal proceedings
- Contact victims to inform of offender release or escape

Victims advocates should be prepared to be on call for clients experiencing personal emergencies or for new clients who have been recently victimized. They are required to maintain confidentiality to protect victims. Victims advocates work within almost every part of the criminal justice system:

- Police: As liaisons to investigators
- Courts: Help victims navigate through the legal process
- Corrections: Help determine issues regarding restitution and sentencing

To become a victims advocate, a bachelor's degree (psychology, criminal justice, social work, or education) is usually required, with a master's degree preferred. Coursework, along with intense practical training in social work, is required.

Victims advocates should possess empathy, patience, compassion, a desire to help others, strong listening skills, knowledge of the criminal justice system and legal processes, and should be familiar with resources available for victims of crime. The ability to speak a second language is often a desirable attribute. Many employers prefer previous experience working with victims, which can be obtained through volunteer work, internships, or a previous position in law enforcement or social work. Advocacy organizations are often looking for licensed social workers or licensed therapists.

Cost Remedies

While crime victims may seek recourse through the criminal justice system to punish the offender, victims can also receive financial remedy for the harm they have suffered. As you read earlier about the various costs associated with victimization, to help remedy some of these costs, offenders may be ordered to pay restitution to the victim or victims can seek financial compensation from the state.

Offender restitution involves payment of money or services to the victim by the offender for the damages he or she inflicted. Restitution can take a variety of forms, including the most common type, financial, in which the offender makes payments directly to the crime victim. Restitution can also take the form of service, either performed for the actual victim or as some beneficial service to the community.

One "catch" to restitution is that the offender must be caught and convicted of the crime and then sentenced to pay restitution. Additionally, in many cases, the offender has no resources to make any payments. In these cases, financial payments may not be possible, but the offender could perform a service either to the individual victim or to the community as a form of payment. Similarly, juvenile offenders are often incapable of obtaining or holding a job, making it difficult to acquire the funds needed to pay.

Another form of financial remedy for crime victims, **victim compensation**, differs from restitution in that instead of the offender paying the victim, the state reimburses the victim for the losses suffered from the victimization. The first compensation program began in California in 1965, but all fifty states and the District of Columbia now have crime victim compensation programs. Many of these programs cover costs associated with things such as medical and dental care, mental health counseling, lost wages, moving expenses, crime scene cleanup, and in homicide cases, funeral costs and loss of support. Other services offered to support victims include temporary housing, advocacy, crisis intervention, emergency transportation to court, and criminal justice support.

There are, however, requirements that must be met to apply for victim compensation, and certain factors that can make a victim ineligible to receive compensation. In general, requirements often include reporting the crime to police (sometimes this includes within a certain period of time like seventy-two hours from the discovery of the crime), filing claims by certain deadlines, and requiring the victim cooperate in any subsequent investigation or court proceedings. In contrast to restitution, the offender does not have to be apprehended or convicted to receive compensation from the state.

Most states limit compensation to those who have suffered injury as a result of a crime, as well as survivors of homicide victims. Victims must not have contributed to the crime in any way. Although cases associated with drunk driving used to be excluded, all states now consider it to be a violent crime where victims are eligible for compensation. All states also now include domestic violence as a compensable crime.

In the state of Georgia, to qualify for victim compensation, the crime must have occurred in Georgia in the last three years and must have been reported to the authorities. One of the following must describe the victim's experience related to a violent crime:

- Physical injury or witness to a crime
- Hurt trying to help a victim
- Parent or guardian of someone who was killed or injured
- Dependent on someone for financial support who was killed
- Not the victim, but have been paying bills related to the crime
- A child was the victim and the offender was relied on for financial support
- Victim of family violence who relied on the offender for financial support
- Suffered serious mental or emotional trauma as a result of being threatened or being present during a crime

Additionally, it must not have been only a property crime or identity theft victimization and the victim must have one or more of the following expenses as a result of the crime that was not reimbursed by insurance or another source:

- Medical, dental, or counseling expenses (including copays or deductibles)
- Loss of income or support
- Funeral expenses
- Crime scene sanitization expenses

Source: Georgia Crime Victims Compensation Program, Criminal Justice Coordinating Council (Crime Victims Compensation Program, 2018).

Restorative Justice

Restorative justice involves a system of "righting wrongs" that aims to solve problems and help all parties move forward, rather than just punishing offenders or simply preventing them from recidivating. Although typical punish-ment focuses solely on the offender, restorative justice brings together the offender, the victim, and the community in an attempt to repair the harm done by the offender and address the needs of all parties impacted by the crime.

© Photographee.eu/Shutter stock.com

This type of justice can take different forms, but often involves dispute resolution or mediation. The idea here is to bring the involved parties together in an attempt to figure out a mutually agreeable solution. In doing so, these programs typically involve a third-party mediator to ensure the interaction remains civil and focused. This generally occurs in a nonconfrontational setting, where the interested parties, including the victim and offender, friends and family, criminal justice system personnel, and members of the community, come together.

As a group, they attempt to understand what led to the commission of the crime, discuss the feelings and concerns of all parties, agree upon an acceptable solution, and decide how to implement the solution. It is important to understand that most mediation programs require participation to be voluntary and the process is rather informal compared to resolution of a case via the criminal justice system.

Comprehension Check

1. What are some of the important concepts to understand related to victimology?
2. How does crime impact the victim? What are some of the costs associated with victimization?
3. Describe the victim's interactions with the criminal justice system.
4. What type of compensation is available to crime victims?

References

Cohen, L. E., & Felson, M. (1979). "Social change and crime rate trends: A routine activity approach." *American Sociological Review, 44* (4), 588–608.

Crime Victims Compensation Program. (2018). *Criminal justice coordinating council.* Retrieved from http://crimevictimscomp.ga.gov/for-victims/

Morgan, R. E., & Kena, G. (2017). *Criminal victimization, 2016.* Bureau of Justice Statistics. Retrieved from https://www.bjs.gov/index.cfm?ty=pbdetail&iid=6686

National Center for Juvenile Justice. (2015). *EZANIBRS. Office of Juvenile Justice and Delinquency Prevention (OJJDP), Office of Justice Programs, U.S. Department of Justice.* Retrieved from https://www.ojjdp.gov/ojstatbb/ ezanibrsdv/

Office of Justice Programs. (n.d.). *About victims' rights.* Office of Justice Programs, Office for Victims of Crime. Retrieved from https://www.victimlaw.org/ victimlaw/pages/victimsRight.jsp

© Zoomphoto Stock/Shutterstock.com

CHAPTER 5

Crime Measurement Tools and Other Criminal Justice Databases

LEARNING OBJECTIVES

After reading this chapter, the student is expected to

1   Identify the different methods of measuring crimes in the United States

2   Evaluate the strengths and weaknesses of the different methods of measuring crime

3   Describe the different types of criminal justice databases

4   Identify the different international crime and criminal justice databases

5   Explain the uses of these databases in research and practice

Introduction

Information is key to understanding crime and the criminal justice system. Not only are data important for research, but they are central to informed decision-making and developing intervention programs. Criminal justice and criminology are data-driven professions. Criminal justice practitioners collect all kinds of data for their plans and programs and criminologists analyze these data to advance knowledge in the field.

A student of criminal justice needs to be able to locate appropriate data for their projects and papers. The multiplicity of data and crime statistics can be overwhelming at this time and age. But not all data are equal. In research, the criteria for evaluating the data are its validity and reliability. Validity refers to the ability of the measure to capture the essence of the phenomenon being measured. Reliability is the ability to produce a result that will be similar upon repeated measurements (Bachman & Schutt, 2015). The ideal situation is that the data should be both valid and reliable for usable information to emerge.

This chapter expands on previous textbooks by not only discussing the crime databases, but also other major criminal justice databases and statistical sources including courts, corrections, terrorism, and drugs. In addition, this chapter includes measurements of crime and criminal justice that are not only about the United States, but also about international databases. In a globalized world, it becomes more important to examine how the US compares to the other countries in the world both in its crime rates and its comparison in terms of the institutions and functions of various justice systems. Hence, students who are interested in doing comparative studies are exposed to these sources. This approach will prepare the student to evaluate statistics and information that they will be confronted with in the future. Likewise, the student will accumulate information about sources that will assist them in their quests for deeper understanding about the phenomena of crime and criminal justice.

US Official Crime Measures

Measuring crime in society is a very important undertaking.[1] From these data, crime reports, priorities, policies, and interventions are formulated by criminal justice agencies. For ordinary citizens, crime statistics are necessary for choosing residences, workplaces, and schools for themselves and their family. Businesses also make decisions about their enterprises based on the crime situation of an area. Indeed, some scholars have contended that crime statistics affect the economy (Chalfin, 2015). In a summary of estimates made about the cost of crime, Chalfin (2015) examined and generated estimates of the cost of crime based on studies done over twenty-five years adjusted for valuation. His estimates show that the cost of crime constitutes approximately 2 percent of gross domestic product (GDP). He states that this GDP value is almost double the amount of revenue generated by the education sector and half the amount of revenue produced by the US entertainment industry.

Measurements of crime require certain criteria for it to become a basis for action. First, the data must be valid. Research scientists consider the quality of the validity of the measure to be the ability to actually capture the meaning of the concept being measured. This issue will be further illustrated in the criticisms of the different measures below. The other desirable quality of the data is its reliability. Reliability is the ability of the measure to accurately estimate the magnitude of the phenomenon. For example, overcounting and undercounting a phenomenon or event is a form of reliability issue. In social science research, there are several factors that might undermine the accuracy of collecting information. Discussions on some of these reliability issues in measuring crime will be highlighted in the succeeding sections.

The other concepts important for beginning students to know about crime measurements is generalizability. One way to achieve this is through a process of standardizing the data. In this context, one should ask whether or not data can be used to compare crime and criminal justice data across multiple jurisdictions. Standardizing the measure usually through the number of population controls for the effects that the actual number of population in the jurisdiction have on crime. A higher level of crime is expected in areas with a greater number of people. The key is to frame the data so that the numbers become comparable among different population sizes. In this regard, the concepts of crime incidences, crime concentration, and crime prevalence are the three most important concepts. Rogerson (2004) differentiates these three different terms as follows:

- **Crime prevalence** refers to the proportion of people (or targets, e.g., households, properties, or cars) in an area who/that are victimized.
- **Crime concentration** refers to the number of victimizations per victim (or victimized place).
- **Crime incidence** is a product of crime prevalence and crime concentration. It refers to the number of crimes that have occurred in a given area. Incidence is usually expressed as a rate per head of population. Therefore, it is synonymous to the term crime rate. A crime rate is calculated by dividing the number of reported crimes by the total population; the result is multiplied by 100,000. For example, in 2010 there were 58,100 robberies in California and the population was 38,826,898. This equals a robbery crime rate of 149.6 per 100,000 general population.

The Uniform Crime Report

The Uniform Crime Report (UCR) is a Federal Bureau of Investigation (FBI) compilation of all crimes reported or that have come to the attention of the police. This UCR is collated from the local police agencies' records and are submitted on a voluntary basis to the FBI (Barnett-Ryan, 2007). For organizational purposes, criminal offenses are divided into two major groups: Part I offenses and Part II offenses. In Part I, the UCR indices reported incidents of **index crimes**,[2] which are broken into two categories: violent crimes and property crimes. Aggravated assault, forcible rape, murder/willful homicide, and robbery are classified as violent crimes. Arson, burglary, larceny-theft, and motor vehicle theft are classified as property crimes. More recently, human trafficking (trafficking for commercial sex acts and trafficking for involuntary servitude) is now included in Part I offenses (FBI, 2013). Human trafficking is a recent addition and seems ill-fitted to either of the two categories. Robbery is placed under violent crimes because of the attendant circumstance of the use of force. Table 5.1 summarizes these categories below.

TABLE 5.1 PART I INDEX CRIMES.

Violent Crimes	Property Crimes
Willful homicide	Burglary
Forcible rape	Larceny-theft (commercial and household)
Aggravated assault	Motor vehicle theft
Robbery	Arson
Source: Author created table.	

These crimes are reported via the document named Return A—Monthly Return of Offenses Known to the Police. These crimes are deemed the most serious ones and are the ones reported to the police instead of being reported to other agencies (e.g., Internal Revenue Service [IRS], Immigration and Customs Enforcement [ICE]) who do not contribute to the UCR. Part I crimes are the ones that the public and government pay more attention to as they tend to create greater alarm and damage among residents.

In Part II, the following crimes are tracked: simple assault, curfew offenses and loitering, embezzlement, forgery and counterfeiting, disorderly conduct, driving under the influence, drug offenses, fraud, gambling, liquor offenses, offenses against the family, prostitution, public drunkenness, runaways, sex offenses, stolen property, vandalism, vagrancy, and weapons offenses. These are also known as less serious offenses.

Criticism of the UCR

The UCR has been known to suffer from several shortcomings. Primarily, it has been criticized for its validity and reliability. These errors in measurement are considered to be more benign. The more severe criticism about the data is the manipulation of the numbers at the department level (Eterno & Silverman, 2012). The crime numbers have certain professional repercussions that sometimes the recording and reporting of crimes are carefully scrutinized.

Validity

A criticism of the UCR is that it cannot accurately measure crime because of the recorder bias that might happen (Block & Block, 1984). There are crimes reported to the police that are either upgraded or downgraded during the filing of the investigation report (Lynch & Jarvis, 2008; Maltz, 2007). Ansari and He (2017) noted that this problem occurs due to the hotel counting method and the hierarchy rule. In the hotel counting method, if a number of dwelling units under a single manager are burglarized and the offenses are more likely to be reported to the police by the manager rather than the individual tenants, the burglary must be scored as one offense (FBI, 2013).

According to the classifying and scoring rule of hierarchy, law enforcement agencies are required to identify and report the most serious crime in a multiple-offense situation in which several offenses have been committed at the same time and place (FBI, 2013).

Also, since these crimes are recorded prior to adjudication, the final recorded report might not reflect the real crime situation. For example, false accusations (e.g., someone claiming victimization when there was none), are included in that report. The other threat to the validity of the report is the fact that crimes are classified based on the individual judgment of a police officer. One officer might label the offense differently than another officer. Thus, the reported crimes are not true events, but the individually constructed crime event in the officer's own understanding. The biggest problem with its validity is the measure's ability to represent the conceptual meaning of crime. Is this really a measure of crime in society or is it measuring the reporting habits of citizens? Some scholars have inferred that the UCR is only a measure of police efficiency or effectiveness in detecting crimes (Berg & Lauritzen, 2016; Biderman, 1967; Biderman & Reiss, 1967; Langan & Farrington, 1998; O'Brien, 1999).

Reliability

Several factors might undermine the reliability of the crime measured under the UCR. The first is the social desirability effect or the stigma associated with reporting crimes. For example, sex crimes are consistently underreported to the police (Ansari & He, 2017). These errors might be random, which can be easily corrected through statistical manipulation. The greater threat to its reliability is the measurement error known as systematic measurement errors (Bachman & Schutt, 2015). Systematic measurement errors are produced due to the bias in the instrument or the collector of the data. This is more serious because the errors could be deliberate. For example, there is evidence to show that police crime data are sometimes manipulated due to the impact on work performance and the political repercussions of high crime rates (Eterno & Silverman, 2012; Strom & Smith, 2017).

The Dark Figure of Crime

Because not all crimes are detected by the police or reported to the police, the actual figures arrived at through the UCR have been touted as an undercounting of crime (Block & Block, 1984). On top of the nonreporting, not all crimes are manifested in the database because there are only about thirty crimes reported through the UCR's Summary Reporting System (SRS). As a result, some observers use the analogy of the iceberg for the crime statistics in the United States. The crime figures that are compiled represent just the tip of the iceberg. This phenomenon results in the so-called dark figure of crime. Biderman and Reiss (1967, p. 2) defined the **dark figure of crime** as "occurrences that by some criteria are called crime yet that are not registered in the statistics of whatever agency was the source of the data being used."

The Crime Picture from the UCR

The FBI (2017) recently has published the crime rates for the year 2016. These data are found on their website and reported in a series entitled, *Crime in the United States*. The report depicts the crime situation as follows. Among violent crimes, aggravated assault tends to be the majority of crimes committed, with 64.3 percent of crime committed. Robbery is the next most committed violent crime (26.6 percent). With respect to property crimes, larceny-theft is the most committed property crime (71.2 percent), followed by motor vehicle theft, with 9.7 percent of crimes committed. Compared to 2015, violent crime rose by 4.1 percent, whereas property decreased by 1.3 percent (See Figure 5.1). The preliminary report of the FBI (2017, 2018) indicates that crime overall for the first six months of 2017 showed a decline in all categories.

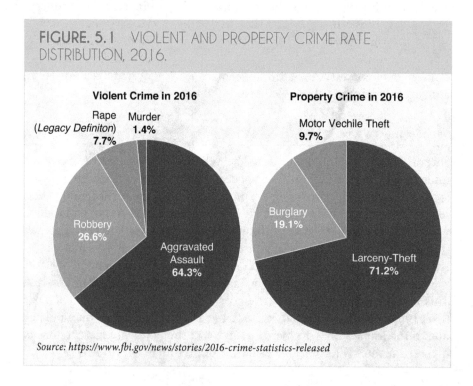

FIGURE. 5.1 VIOLENT AND PROPERTY CRIME RATE DISTRIBUTION, 2016.

Source: https://www.fbi.gov/news/stories/2016-crime-statistics-released

The National Crime Victimization Survey

The National Crime Victimization Survey (NCVS) provides a picture of crime from the eyes of the victims (Block & Block, 1984). The survey consists of a multistage cluster survey of households inquiring about their victimization in the last six months. The US Census Bureau collects NCVS and the surveys are compiled by the Bureau of Justice Statistics (BJS) of the National Institute of Justice (NIJ). These surveys are conducted in person or by phone. Samples for the survey are households with a resident member of that household who is 12 years old or above as qualified respondents. Surveys from these samples are conducted every six months and are kept in the respondent pool for a period of three years. This panel sampling design was utilized in order to avoid "telescoping" (Neter & Waksberg, 1964). **Telescoping** is the bringing of the incidents into the current period of observation that were outside of the time frame. In order to avoid such over counting, the NCVS used bounding. **Bounding** is the framing of the question so that a previously reported event will not be reported again (BJS, 2017).

Unlike the UCR, the NCVS only gathers information on six crimes, namely, rape, robbery, assault, household burglary, larceny, and motor vehicle theft. The NCVS was primarily created to discover unreported crime (Block & Block, 1984). Arson and homicide are excluded from the survey. A unique feature of the NCVS is that it collects both reported and unreported crimes and reasons why the crime was or was not reported (FBI, 2014). It also asks about crime-specific information such as hate, the emotional toll of the crime, and if the victim is pregnant.

The survey process does not ask respondents which type of crime they experienced, but rather collects the detailed elements of each incident and uses an algorithm to categorize each victimization into a standardized taxonomy. This approach is taken because legal definitions vary by jurisdiction and use of the algorithm allows for a uniform classification of events at the national level (BJS, 2014).

Each year, data are obtained from a nationally representative sample of about 135,000 households, composed of nearly 225,000 persons, on the frequency, characteristics, and consequences of criminal victimization in the United States. Survey respondents provide information about themselves (e.g., age, sex, race and Hispanic origin, marital status, education level, and income) and whether they or any of their household members experienced a victimization. For each victimization incident, the NCVS collects information about the offender (e.g., age, race and Hispanic origin, sex, and victim–offender relationship), characteristics of the crime (e.g., time and place of occurrence, use of weapons, nature of injury, and economic consequences), whether the crime was reported to police, reasons the crime was or was not reported, and victim experiences with the criminal justice system (BJS, 2018).

Recent innovations to the survey include questionnaires in Spanish and there are several supplemental surveys such as the School Incident Report, Identity Theft Report, Crime Incident Report, and the Supplemental Victimization Survey (SVS). The SVS collects information about stalking experiences of the members of the household. The Crime Incident Report is a supplemental report that gathers specifics surrounding the crime such as the time, day, and other circumstances.

The Crime Picture from the NCVS

The BJS (2018) has indicated that crime victimization has declined over the years from 2012 to 2015. Violent crimes have generally declined. However, there was no significant decline in violent victimization observed between 2014 and 2015 although the rate is still lower for 2015 with the exception of intimate partner violence (IPV) which registered a higher rate. Table 5.2 presents that latest violent crime victimization data from the NCVS (BJS 2016 revised March 2018).

TABLE 5.2 VIOLENT VICTIMIZATION BY TYPE OF VIOLENT CRIME, 2014 AND 2015.

Type of Violent Crime	Number		Rate per 1,000 Persons age 12 or Older	
	2014*	2015	2014*	2015
Violent Crime[a]	5,359,570	5,006,620	20.1	18.6
Rape/sexual assault[b]	284,350	431,840 ‡	1.1	1.6 ‡
Robbery	664,210	578,580	2.5	2.1
Assault	4,411,010	3,996,200	16.5	14.8
Aggravated assault	1,092,090	816,760 ‡	4.1	3.0 ‡
Simple assault	3,318,920	3,179,440	12.4	11.8
Domestic violence[c]	1,109,880	1,094,660	4.2	4.1
Intimate partner violence[d]	634,610	806,050	2.4	3.0
Stranger violence	2,166,130	1,821,310	8.1	6.8
Violent crime involving injury	1,375,950	1,303,290	5.2	4.8
Serious Violent Crime[e]	2,040,650	1,827,170	7.7	6.8
Serious domestic violence[c]	400,030	460,450	1.5	1.7
Serious intimate partner violence[d]	265,890	333,210	1.0	1.2
Serious stranger violence	930,690	690,550	3.5	2.6
Serious violent crime involving weapons	1,306,900	977,840	4.9	3.6 ‡
Serious violent crime involving injury	692,470	658,040	2.6	2.4

Note: Detail may not sum to total due to rounding. Total population age 12 or older was 266,665,160 in 2014 and 269,526,470 in 2015.

*Comparison year.

†Significant difference from comparison year at 95 percent confidence level.

‡Significant difference from comparison year at 90 percent confidence level.

[a]Excludes homicide because the NCVS is based on interviews with victims and therefore cannot measure murder.

[b]BJS has initiated projects examining collection methods for self-report data on rape and sexual assault. See *NCVS measurement of rape and sexual assault* in *Methodology* for more information.

[c]Includes victimization committed by intimate partners and family members.

[d]Includes victimization committed by current or former spouses, boyfriends, or girlfriends.

[e]In the NCVS, serious violent crime includes rape or sexual assault, robbery, and aggravated assault.

Source: Bureau of Justice Statistics, National Crime Victimization Survey (NCVS), 2014 and 2015; BJS (2016)

Similar patterns emerge for property crime offenses—there was a decline between the years 2014 and 2015, but these differences are not significant (see Table 5.3). Comparing the violent crime victimization and property crime victimization, the report suggests that there are more violent crime victimizations than property crime victimizations every year from 2013 to 2015 (see Figure. 5.2).

Type of Property Crime	Number		Rate per 1,000 Households	
	2014*	2015	2014*	2015
Total	15,288,470	14,611,040 ‡	118.1	110.7 †
Burglary	2,993,480	2,904,570	23.1	22.0
Motor vehicle theft	534,370	564,160	4.1	4.3
Theft	11,760,620	11,142,310 †	90.8	84.4 †

Note: Detail may not sum to total due to rounding. Total number of households was 129,492,740 in 2014 and 131,962,260 in 2015.
*Comparison year.
†Significant difference from comparison year at 95 percent confidence level.
‡Significant difference from comparison year at 90 percent confidence level.

Source: BJS, 2016.

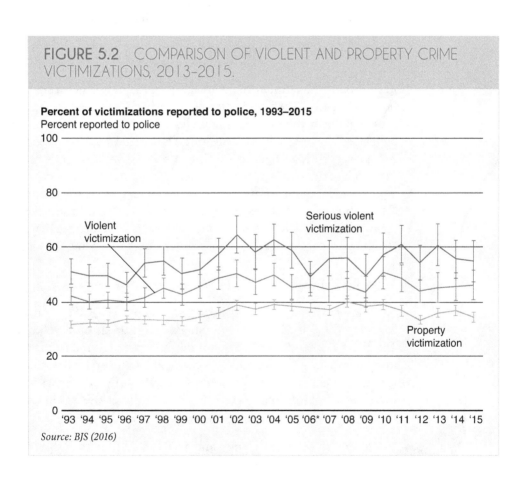

Percent of victimizations reported to police, 1993–2015
Percent reported to police

Source: BJS (2016)

Several criticisms can be levied against the NCVS regarding its reliability and validity. First, the social desirability effect is a serious threat to the data's reliability. Social desirability is the tendency to portray one's self in a positive light. Another threat to reliability is the respondent's ability to recall or know about victimization. In this error, respondents might forget or are not aware about the victimization in their households. This is known as memory decay. Although this has been claimed as being remedied by the latest protocol, it is still suspected to occur (Langton, Planty, & Lynch, 2017). There is also a halo effect of the survey where respondents might not want to divulge some traumatic incidents in their household. Included in this error is the effect of self-blame that might have occurred in their victimization and therefore the victim will try to discount that experience as victimization (Block & Block, 1984). The opposite might also be true that respondents might try to answer the question based on the expectations of the interviewer (i.e., the Hawthorne effect).

Another problem includes misplacing the respondents' victimizations within the time cutoff or forgetting about some events at the time of the interview. The interval of six months is very susceptible to this error. The NCVS technical description recognizes the potential for this occurrence and concedes that doing the survey in three-month intervals will reduce this problem. However, costs could become more prohibitive and the six-month interval is likely the best compromise solution (Block & Block, 1984). Finally, respondent competency can contribute to the potential for error. A respondent 12-year-old might not be too familiar in formulating a best judgment on the categorization of the event. They might also not have been informed about the victimization of the members of their household. This undercounting phenomenon by the NCVS is particularly true for certain crimes such as rape (Biderman & Lynch, 1991; Eigenberg, 1990; Koss, 1992). As various crime reports indicate, both in the UCR and the NCVS, rape remains the lowest crime reported among violent crimes if murder is not included. Despite the redefinition and clarification of rape crimes during interviews, rape is still consistently undercounted (Ross, 1996). Therefore, it is not farfetched to deduce that the associated threats to the reliability of the measure are influencing this outcome.

The National Incident-Based Reporting System

The National Incident-Based Reporting System (NIBRS) is another database that the FBI collects from police organizations on a voluntary basis. The NIBRS expands on the eight index crimes measured in the UCR summary reporting program and collects incident and arrest information from law enforcement agencies for twenty-four categories of offenses in Group A, as well as arrest information only for ten additional offenses in Group B (see Figure 5.3 for these groups of offenses).

In addition to counts of crimes and arrests, NIBRS was designed to collect detailed information on the attributes of each crime incident known to law enforcement, including:

- the date, time, and location of the incident
- a detailed list of all offenses that occurred in the incident, not just the most serious offense
- demographic information on each victim and offender involved in the incident
- the relationships between each of the victims and the offenders
- other details of the incident, including victim injury, type of weapon involved, alcohol or drug involvement, property loss, and drugs seized
- clearance information, including both arrest and clearances by exceptional means
- date of arrest and arrestee demographics

FIGURE 5.3 GROUP A AND GROUP B OFFENSES UNDER NIBRS.

Group "A" Offenses

NIBRS OFFENSES	HIBRS CODES	NIBRS OFFENSES	HIBRS CODES
Arson	200	Human Trafficking	
		-Commercial Sex Acts	64A
Assault offenses		-Involuntary Servitude	64B
-Aggravated Assault	13A		
-Simple Assault	13B	Kidnapping/Abduction	100
-Intimidation	13C		
		Larceny/Theft Offenses	
Bribery	510	-Pocket Picking	23A
		-Purse Snatching	23B
Burglary/B&E	220	- Shoplifting	23C
		-Theft from Building	23D
Counterfeiting/Forgery	250	-Theft from Coin-Operated	23E
		Machine or Device	
Destruction/Damage/Vandalism		-Theft from Motor Vehicle	23F
of Property	290	-Theft of Motor Vehicle Parts	
		or Accessories	23G
Drug/Narcotic Offenses		-All Other Larceny	23H
-Drug/Narcotic Violations	35A		
-Drug/Narcotic Equip. Violations	35B	Motor Vehicle Theft	240
Embezzlement	270	Pornography/Obscene	370
		Material	
Extortion/Blackmail	210		
		Prostitution Offenses	
Fraud Offenses		-Prostitution	40A
-False Pretenses/Swindle/	26A	-Assisting or Promoting	40B
Confidence Games		Prostitution	
-Credit Card/Automatic Teller	26B	-Purchasing Prostitution	40C
Machine Fraud			
-Impersonation	26C	Robbery	120
-Welfare Fraud	26D		
-Wire Fraud	26E	Sex Offenses (Forcible)	
		-Forcible Rape	11A
Gambling Offenses		-Forcible Sodomy	11B
-Betting/Wagering	39A	-Sexual Assault with An Object	11C
-Operating/Promoting/ Assisting	39B	-Forcible Fondling	11D
Gambling			
-Gambling Equip. Violations	39C	Sex Offenses (Non-Forcible)	
-Sports Tampering	39D	-Incest	36A
		-Statutory Rape	36B
Homicide Offenses			
-Murder/Non-Negligent	09A	Stolen Property Offenses	280
Manslaughter			
-Negligent Manslaughter	09B	Weapon Law Violations	520
-Justifiable Homicide	09C		

Source: BJS (2018b).

Group "B" Offenses

Group B's MUST have an arrest to be NIBRS Reportable

NIBRS OFFENSES	HIBRS CODES	NIBRS OFFENSES	HIBRS CODES
Bad Checks	90A	Family Offenses, Non-Violent	90F
Curfew/Loitering/Vagrancy Violations	90B	Liquor Law Violations	90G
Disorderly Conduct	90C	Peeping Tom	90H
Driving Under the Influence	90D	Trespassing	90J
Drunkenness	90E	All Other Offenses	90Z

Source: Association of State Uniform Crime Reporting Programs (ASUCRP). Accessed on June 6, 2014.

Similarities between the UCR and NIBRS

The general concepts, such as jurisdictional rules, of collecting and reporting data are the same as in NIBRS. However, NIBRS goes into much greater detail than the UCR. NIBRS includes twenty-four Group A crime categories, whereas the UCR only has nine crime categories classified as Part I.

In NIBRS, the definition of rape has been expanded to include male victims. The UCR, until recently, defined rape as "the carnal knowledge of a female forcibly and against her will," but has since expanded the definition. Formerly in the UCR, sex attacks against males were to be classified only as either assaults or "other sex offenses," depending on the nature of the crime and the extent of the injury.

When multiple crimes are committed by a single person or group of persons during the same basic period of time and same basic location, the UCR uses a "hierarchy rule" to determine which offenses will be reported for that incident. Only the most serious offense is reported. For example, if a criminal burglarizes a residence and assaults the inhabitant, only the assault is reported, as it takes precedence over the burglary on the "hierarchy rule." NIBRS reports all offenses involved in a particular incident.

The UCR has only two crime categories: crimes against persons (e.g., murder, rape, assault, robbery) and crimes against property (e.g., car theft, burglary, larceny, arson). NIBRS adds a third category titled "crimes against society" for activities such as drug or narcotic offenses and other activities prohibited by society's rules. Finally, agencies submit UCR data in written documents that must then be entered by hand into a computer system for statistical analysis. NIBRS data are submitted electronically in the form of ASCII text files. These files are then processed without the need for a person to input the data (except at the originating agency's initial filing of the report into their computer system).

Criticisms against NIBRS

Although many proclaim the usefulness of NIBRS in understanding the attendant circumstances surrounding the crimes as well as the expansion of the reporting involving some crimes, shortcomings are still noted with this database. Jarvis (2015) summarized these shortcomings as:

1. The NIBRS does not overcome the weaknesses of the UCR (e.g., administrative recording mistakes and data manipulations such as victim's losses)
2. The determination of recording the motives for the crime might become arbitrary and misleading
3. There is some hesitancy for recording some circumstances (e.g., drug use) because the lack of real evidence might impede the prosecution of the offense
4. The circumstances of how the weapons or paraphernalia of the crime are not captured. Although the type of weapon is provided, it does not provide for how this weapon was used and the circumstances of how it was used

Although there are criticisms to the database, it is a significant improvement from the terse reporting system of the UCR and the NCVS. Jarvis (2015) reminds the consumers of this database that these information are primarily collected for law enforcement purposes and not for academic purposes. In other words, conceptual accuracy and measurement reliabilities should be diligently examined when conducting research using this database. These data are normally used for tactical purposes rather than research purposes (Lauritzen & Cork, 2017).

Criminal Justice Databases

When it comes to criminal justice databases, the US Department of Justice's NIJ, together with the BJS, has a wide array of databases and statistics concerning the operations of the criminal justice system. Their databases include data about crime, gun violence, school shooting, terrorism, drugs, corrections, police, probation, and parole among others. Some of these databases are collected directly by the bureau, whereas others are collated from various federal and state sources. The sections below present some of these databases.

Policing Databases

Police statistics are collected on different levels. The most popular are summarized in this section. The databases are collated by the US Department of Justice through the FBI and BJS. These databases are periodically collected following certain intervals. Hence, they can be considered as panel data, but are collective in the universe of samples available.

Law Enforcement Management and Administrative Statistics

Conducted periodically since 1987, Law Enforcement Management and Administrative Statistics (LEMAS) collects data from more than 3,000 general purpose state and local law enforcement agencies, including all those that employ one hundred or more sworn officers and a nationally representative sample of smaller agencies. Data obtained include agency responsibilities, operating expenditures, job functions of sworn and civilian employees, officer salaries and special pay, demographic characteristics of officers, weapons and armor policies, education and training requirements, computers and information systems, vehicles, special units, and community policing activities (Bureau of Justice Statistics, 2018a).

This database has been used in various research studies to determine the organizational correlates of police practices and capabilities among local law enforcement. Except the questions on personnel information, the questionnaires are sometimes revised to measure significant police operations such as the implementation of community policing or capabilities of local police agencies to perform homeland security and intelligence functions. Lately, these data include reports about police departments' implementation of community policing (Wilson, 1999). The latest survey included questions about their implementation of homeland security policing or antiterrorism policing (Kim & de Guzman, 2012).

Beginning in 1937, the FBI's UCR program collected and published statistics on law enforcement officers killed in the line of duty in its annual publication, *Crime in the United States*. Statistics regarding assaults on officers were added in 1960. In June 1971, executives from the law enforcement conference, "Prevention of Police Killings," called for an increase in the FBI's involvement in preventing and investigating officers' deaths. In response to this directive, the UCR Program expanded its collection of data to include more details about the incidents in which law enforcement officers were killed and assaulted. Recently, in February 2016, the criteria for participation in the national Law Enforcement Officers Killed and Assaulted (LEOKA) program included military and civilian police and law enforcement officers of the Department of Defense (DoD) who are killed or assaulted while performing law enforcement functions and/or duties and who are not in a military combat or deployed-for-mission status. These subjects include DoD police and law enforcement officers who perform policing and criminal investigative functions while stationed (not deployed) on overseas bases, just as if they were based in the United States. The collection of these data have begun and the FBI could begin publishing these data soon.

Court Databases

Court behaviors are mostly studied using case decisions. Some of the case variables that are mostly studied are the conviction rates, punitiveness, and the factors involved in these decisions, such as race, gender, class, and immigrant status. Court behaviors can also be studied by attending court hearings or interviewing judges and prosecutors. However, these kinds of methods are sometimes time consuming and subjects might not be willing to serve as research participants. In addition, recording devices are not generally allowed in the courts. This restriction will not allow a researcher to be able to observe demeanors of court actors. Thus, databases and information about courts are a more efficient way of conducting academic research.

Federal Judicial Center Integrated Database

The federal government provides information about cases in its jurisdiction through its Integrated Database (IDB). The Federal Judicial Center (FJC) provides an Internet site for public access to its IDB. The IDB contains data on civil case and criminal defendant filings and terminations in the district courts, along with bankruptcy court and appellate court case information. The FJC receives regular updates of the case-related data that are routinely reported by the courts. The FJC then postprocesses the data, consistent with the policies of the Judicial Conference of the United States governing access to these data, into a unified longitudinal database, the IDB.

Up to 1992, the reporting period, or statistical year, went from July to June (e.g., statistical year 1990 covered the period July 1, 1989 to June 30, 1990). In 1992, the statistical reporting period was changed to conform to the federal government's standard fiscal year, October to September (e.g., fiscal year 1993 covered the period October 1, 1992 to September 30, 1993). All of the previous data files in the IDB conform to the old statistical year (SY70–SY91). The 1992 files cover a fifteen-month time span (July 1, 1991 to September 30, 1992) to accommodate this conversion period. The 1993 file and all subsequent files conform to the new fiscal year (October 1 to September 30) (Federal Judicial Center, 2018).

Public Access to Court Electronic Record (PACER)

Public Access to Court Electronic Record (PACER) allows anyone with an account to search and locate appellate, district, and bankruptcy court case and docket information using PACER Case Locator (http://www.uscourts.gov/court-records/find-case-pacer). Only cases after 1999 are available electronically. Paper cases are available in the court where the case was filed or at the Federal Court Centers. For historical decisions, the cases are available through the National Archives and Records Administration (NARA).

State Court Database

On the state level, The National Center for State Courts (NCSC) is a site that may assist on information about the personnel and workloads of state courts. This center creates a database called the Court Statistics Project (CSP). CSP—a joint project of the NCSC and the Conference of State Court Administrators (COSCA)—publishes caseload data from the courts of the fifty states, the District of Columbia, and Puerto Rico. These data are provided by the offices of the state court administrator in those jurisdictions. The data reported conform to the definitions and case counting rules in the *State Court Guide to Statistical Reporting*. States publish their own data that may be more extensive, although not directly comparable to other states for a variety of reasons, including differences in court structure, case definitions and counting practices, court rules, statutes, or terminology (National Center for State Courts, 2018).

Corrections Databases

Corrections databases abound, but are sometimes not accessible to the public. Just as the UCR and NIBRS are collected for tactical purposes, most corrections databases are also collected relative to the need of the agencies. The following databases and reports are mostly available to researchers.

Sex Offender Registry

The sex offender registry is a database of individuals convicted of sex offenses. This registry was precipitated by Megan's Law in order to protect children from being sexually assaulted and molested. Today, the National Sex Offender Public Registry (NSOPR) maintains a clearinghouse on information about sex offenders in the registry. First established in 2005 as NSOPR, the National Sex Offender Public Website (NSOPW) was renamed by the Adam Walsh Child Protection and Safety Act of 2006 in honor of

22-year-old college student Dru Sjodin of Grand Forks, North Dakota, a young woman who was kidnapped and murdered by a sex offender who was registered in Minnesota.

NSOPW is the only US government website that links public state, territorial, and tribal sex offender registries from one national search site. Parents, employers, and other concerned residents can utilize the website's search tool to identify location information on sex offenders residing, working, and attending school not only in their own neighborhoods, but also in other nearby states and communities. In addition, the website provides visitors with information about sexual abuse and how to protect themselves and loved ones from potential victimization.

NSOPW's advanced search tool provides information about sex offenders through a number of search options:

- Search by name nationally or with an individual jurisdiction
- Search by address (if provided by jurisdiction)
- Search by zip code
- Search by county (if provided by jurisdiction)
- Search by city/town (if provided by jurisdiction)

NSOPW presents the most up-to-date information as provided by each jurisdiction. Information is hosted by each jurisdiction, not by NSOPW or the federal government. The search criteria available for searches are limited to what each individual jurisdiction may provide.

National Prisoner Statistics

The National Prisoner Statistics Program produces annual national- and state-level data on the number of prisoners in state and federal prison facilities. Aggregate data are collected on race and sex of prison inmates, inmates held in private facilities and local jails, system capacity, noncitizens, and persons age 17 or younger. Findings are released in the Prisoners series and the Corrections Statistical Analysis Tool (CSAT)—Prisoners. Data are from the fifty states departments of corrections, the Federal Bureau of Prisons, and until 2001, from the District of Columbia (after 2001, felons sentenced under the District of Columbia criminal code were housed in federal facilities).

Probation Statistics

The BJS maintains the Annual Probation Survey, an annual data series designed to provide national-, federal-, and jurisdiction-level data from administrative records on adults supervised in the community on probation. Data include the total number of probationers supervised, by jurisdiction, on January 1 and December 31 of each year and the number of adults who entered and exited probation supervision during the year. Additional data include demographic characteristics, such as sex, race and Hispanic or Latino origin, and offense of probationers under supervision at the end of each year.

The BJS maintains the Annual Probation and Parole Survey, an annual data series designed to provide national-, federal-, and jurisdiction-level data from administrative records on adults supervised in the community on parole. Data include the total number of parolees supervised, by jurisdiction, on January 1 and December 31 of each year and the number of adults who entered and exited parole supervision during the year. Additional data include demographic characteristics, such as sex, race and Hispanic or Latino origin, and offense of parolee under supervision at the end of each year.

Terrorism Databases

The Global Terrorism Database (GTD) is the most extensive repository of terrorism activities and information including attacks, weapons used, and the locations of the attacks, among other information. The National Consortium for the Study of Terrorism and Responses to Terrorism maintains the database housed at the University of Maryland College Park.

The GTD is an open-source database including information on terrorist events around the world from 1970 to 2016 (with additional annual updates planned for the future). Unlike many other event databases, the GTD includes systematic data on domestic as well as transnational and international terrorist incidents that have occurred during this time period and now includes more than 170,000 cases. For each GTD incident, information is available on the date and location of the incident, the weapons used and nature of the target, the number of casualties, and—when identifiable—the group or individual responsible.

Statistical information contained in the GTD is based on reports from a variety of open media sources. Information is not added to the GTD unless and until the center has determined the sources are credible. Users are advised not to infer any additional actions or results beyond what is presented in a GTD entry and specifically, users should not infer an individual associated with a particular incident was tried and convicted of terrorism or any other criminal offense. If new documentation about an event becomes available, an entry may be modified, as necessary and appropriate (University of Maryland, 2018).

Drugs Statistics

The National Institute on Drug Abuse (NIDA) is the biggest repository of databases, reports, and studies about drugs and substance abuses. Likewise, the Substance Abuse and Mental Health Services Administration (SAMHSA) also maintains several databases particularly involving treatment of substance abuses. In particular, SAMHSA's national surveys on drug use and mental health is the most often used database for research and planning.

When it comes to criminal justice, the Drug Enforcement Administration (DEA) provides several databases regarding the arrests of drug dealers and operations against drugs. The drug courts also provide several information and statistics about their accomplishments and clients. From these publications, treatment intervention practices are derived. The BJS also maintains several databases regarding the drug-addicted population, particularly with those within the correctional supervision of the federal government and states.

As regards international databases, the United Nations (UN) Office on Drugs and Crime publishes a yearly report of its surveys regarding the trends of drug abuse and the criminal justice agencies activities regarding its efforts against drugs and substances abuses. It provides extensive information about sources and transit of drugs across the globe.

Other Data and Statistics

The NIJ, through its National Criminal Justice Reference Service (www.ncjrs.gov), has a vast repository of data and reports about criminal justice. The reports consist of information about policing, courts, drugs, corrections, juvenile justice, victimology, and others. The institute provides some of these data in raw form. The data are sometimes reported in summarized form through the BJS.

There are other data sources maintained by private institutions, but they are available only through subscription or fees. The more popular ones are the Inter-university Consortium for Political and Social Research (ICPSR). The General Social Survey is another resource that are used in some criminological research. The National Youth Survey (NYS) is another popular database for those interested in examining criminal justice issues as reported by the youth and their parents.

International Criminal Justice Statistics

International Classification of Crimes for Statistical Purposes

The UN developed an international crime reporting system to be able to compare countries on their crime situation. One of the challenges to international data gathering is that the legal definitions of crimes across countries have considerable nuances and variations. In order to overcome such challenges, the approach used by the International Classification of Crimes for Statistical Purposes (ICCS) is to consider the "criminal" acts in national and international laws as the universe of acts that are subject to classification within the ICCS (Bisogno, Dawson-Faber, & Jandl, 2015). However, the specific classification of such acts, that is, their allocation to analytical categories, is based on behavioral descriptions rather than legal specifications derived from criminal laws. "Crimes as defined in criminal law are typically associated with actions or behavioral and contextual attributes that are universally considered to be an offence (e.g., wounding or injuring, or taking property without consent). This event-based approach avoids issues created by legal complexities, resulting in a simplified and globally applicable classification" (UNODC, 2015, p. 8).

Despite such standardized classifications, Reichel (2018) issues caution regarding the comparison of states using this database. He argues that crime-specific comparison is still problematic as the legal definitions are still the operative mind-set in the original collection of these data. Instead, he suggests that comparison should be based on the disaggregated data. For example, he suggests that since homicide crimes are particularly universal, countries can be compared using this crime. Another approach that Reichel (2018) suggests in the use of these local data is to compare crime trends among countries along specific crime criteria. For examples, rape crime trends among different countries could be compared. However, a student should use caution in comparing these trends as countries' definitions of crimes can sometimes change over time.

The Impunity Index

Another database that collates information about the justice systems of other countries is the Impunity Index. The UN defines impunity as "the impossibility, de jure or de facto, of bringing the perpetrators of violations to account—whether in criminal, civil, administrative or disciplinary proceedings—since they are not subject to any inquiry that might lead to their being accused, arrested, tried and, if found guilty, sentenced to appropriate penalties, and to making reparations to their victims (United Nations Commission on Human Rights, 2015)." In short, people get away with violations because the state apparatus lacks the structure in terms of its security system and justice system to protect human rights.

Impunity is a multidimensional phenomenon that goes beyond the analysis of crimes that could be punished, such as homicide. Instead, it seeks to find an explanation as to why people would not be punished for their crimes. To measure this phenomenon, the Impunity Index is estimated using three major dimensions: security, justice, and human rights. The security dimension refers to the ability of the justice system to provide protection to its inhabitants. The justice dimension refers to the ability of the criminal justice system to adjudicate cases that occur. The human rights component involves the respect of the rights that is accorded to offenders. Thus, the structural as well as the functional capabilities of the justice system are analyzed. Figure 5.4 illustrates how the index is created using several indicators. As can be seen from the figure, the index is created by getting different ratios for structural dimensions (e.g., police to citizen ratio, the availability of facilities in jails and prisons, the ratio of judges to its inhabitants), functional dimensions (e.g., number of persons under preventive detention or the length of time that a person awaits trial), and the observance of human rights (protection of the dignity of individuals) by the government from criminalization all the way up to corrections are also estimated. Information from this database are collected from different countries on their justice system as reported to the UN.

FIGURE 5.4 THE INDICATORS AND COMPUTATIONS OF THE IMPUNITY INDEX.

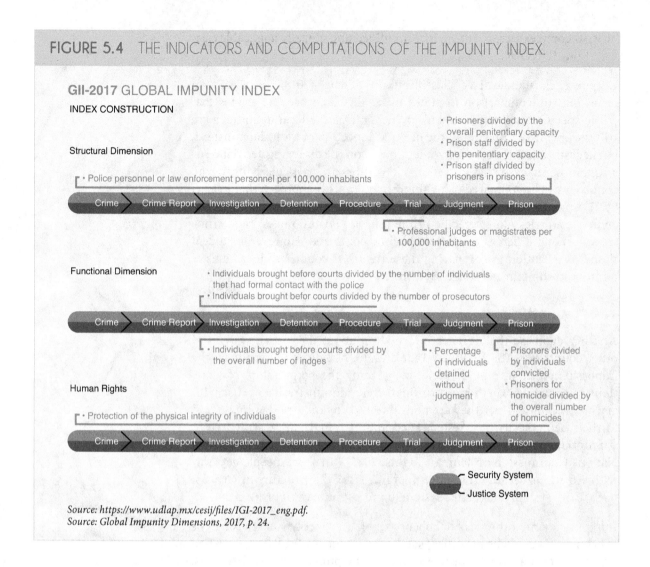

GII-2017 GLOBAL IMPUNITY INDEX

INDEX CONSTRUCTION

Structural Dimension

- Prisoners divided by the overall penitentiary capacity
- Prison staff divided by the penitentiary capacity
- Prison staff divided by prisoners in prisons

- Police personnel or law enforcement personnel per 100,000 inhabitants

Crime > Crime Report > Investigation > Detention > Procedure > Trial > Judgment > Prison

- Professional judges or magistrates per 100,000 inhabitants

Functional Dimension

- Individuals brought before courts divided by the number of individuals thet had formal contact with the police
- Individuals brought befor courts divided by the number of prosecutors

Crime > Crime Report > Investigation > Detention > Procedure > Trial > Judgment > Prison

- Individuals brought before courts divided by the overall number of indges

- Percentage of individuals detained without judgment

- Prisoners divided by individuals convicted
- Prisoners for homicide divided by the overall number of homicides

Human Rights

- Protection of the physical integrity of individuals

Crime > Crime Report > Investigation > Detention > Procedure > Trial > Judgment > Prison

Security System
Justice System

Source: https://www.udlap.mx/cesij/files/IGI-2017_eng.pdf.
Source: Global Impunity Dimensions, 2017, p. 24.

Uses of These Data in Research and Practice

Uses of Data among Practitioners

Evidenced-based intervention is now a buzzword in policing. Sherman (1998) describes this approach as basing practices on evidence about what works best. The key to documenting the ingredients for this success is to gather data. At the very least, practitioners should learn how to gather this information by using sound research methodologies. Most government agencies have now received assistance in their efforts to gather data and understand the information that these data are telling them. In criminal justice, the BJS, the National Institute of Drug Abuse, and SAMHSA provides guidance and assistance of this matter.

Practitioners should also remember that they are the front lines for the gathering of these information. Therefore, they should exercise diligence and care in the reporting of these data. In effect, the practitioners are the producers and consumers of these data. Several notable practices have emerged due to data and an evidenced-based approach. The other chapters in this book have cited several innovative practices whose data have been generated by practitioners and have become the evidence that other agencies needed to adopt the innovation in their own jurisdictions.

Uses of Data among Academics

The production of new knowledge is the business of the academe. Hard and soft technologies are produced due to the work of the academe. Hard technology refers to the actual hardware and tools that are being used by the agencies. Soft technology refers to the less tangible materials such as the intervention practices or computer software that they utilize in their work. For instance, the use of geographic information systems (GIS) has now become part of the technology of the police, probation, and parole. This technology has been used in geography and public health, but has now found its way into crime analysis. Several theories have also been developed out of these data. For instance, the Broken Windows Theory (Wilson & Kelling, 1982) was conceptualized and is now used in policing practices.

The world of practice can gain a lot of insights from these theories and data. There were times when there was a great divide between theory and practice, especially in criminal justice. However, lessons from the field demonstrate that criminal justice practices are greatly enhanced with the assistance of academics in understanding what works. Likewise, the data gathered by the academics become more relevant, valid, and robust when they are collected in collaboration with practitioners in the field. Several of these interventions that have been produced are research that have the greatest impact and the most relevance to the world of the practitioners.

Challenges in Data Collection

The criminal justice system will be facing several challenges in the future in data collection. The method of data collection is changing. Internet surveys are becoming more of a trend in information gathering, but it is also becoming more challenging to entice voluntary participation. Virtual data collection is also becoming a challenge for the future. Information shared through the Internet is slowly being regulated and "sleuthing" in the Internet by criminal justice agents is becoming more legally constricted. For example, law enforcement agencies can only collect metadata (e.g., communication patterns), but not the content of those communications. These information are being protected by the Fourth Amendment against unnecessary intrusions by the criminal justice system. The ability to collect these information is critical in some crimes such as drug, terrorism, and other transnational crimes. The fact that crimes can now be committed through the Internet will have an impact on the data collection of crimes (Lauritzen & Cork, 1997). These mobile communication devices are being used for drug trafficking even from within the prisons (see, e.g., the Philippines' experience with drug lords inside prison directing trafficking activities through cellphones) (Wikipedia, 2017). Crime events and victimization are conducted in cyberspace, but they are also being shared through social media. The possibility for generating crime data through social media should be something that needs to be explored for its potential to measure the extent of crime in society.

Comprehension Check

1. Describe the major means of measuring crime in the United States.
2. What are the weaknesses and strengths of the different ways of measuring crime in the United States?
3. What are the major databases that has been used to study policing in the United States?
4. Identify the various court databases and the information they contain?
5. What are several databases to study international crime and criminal justice system?

References

Ansari, S., & He, N. (2017). "Explaining the UCR-NCVS convergence: A time series analysis." *Asian Criminology, 12,* 39–62.

Bachman, R. D., & Schutt, R. K. (2015). *The practice of research in criminology and criminal justice* (6th ed.). New York, NY: Sage.

Barnett-Ryan, C. (2007). "Introduction to the uniform crime reporting program." In J. P. Lynch & L. A. Addington (Eds.), *Understanding crime statistics: Revisiting the divergence of NCVS and UCR* (pp. 225–250). New York, NY: Cambridge University Press.

Berg, M. T., & Lauritzen, J. L. (2016). "Telling a similar story twice? NCVS/ UCR convergence in serious violent crime rates in rural, suburban, and urban places (1973–2010)." *Journal of Quantitative Criminology, 32,* 91–87.

Biderman, A. D. (1967). "Surveys of population samples for estimating crime incidence." *The Annals of the American Academy of Political and Social Science, 374*(1), 16–33.

Biderman, A. D., & Lynch, J. P. (1991). *Understanding rape incidence statistics.* Secaucas, NJ: Springer-Verlag.

Biderman, A. D., & Reiss, A. J. (1967). "On exploring the "dark figure" of crime." *The Annals of the American Academy of Political and Social Science, 374*(1), 1–15.

Bisogno, E., Dawson-Faber, J., & Jandl, M. (2015). "The international classification of crime for statistical purposes: A new instrument to improve comparative criminological research." *European Journal of Criminology, 12*(15), 535–550.

Block, C. R., & Block, R. L. (1984). "Crime definition, crime measurement, and victim surveys." *Journal of Social Issues, 40*(1), 137–160.

Bureau of Justice Statistics. (2014). *Criminal victimization, 2014.* US Department of Justice, Office of Justice Programs.

Bureau of Justice Statistics. (2016). *Criminal victimization, 2015* (revised March 2018). Retrieved from https://www.bjs.gov/content/pub/pdf/cv15.pdf

Bureau of Justice Statistics. (2017). *The national crime victimization survey, 2016: Technical documentation.* Washington, DC: National Institute of Justice.

Bureau of Justice Statistics. (2018a). *Data collection: Law Enforcement Management and Administrative Statistics (LEMAS).* Retrieved from https://www.bjs.gov/ index.cfm?ty=dcdetail&iid=248

Bureau of Justice Statistics. (2018b). Retrieved from https://www.bjs.gov/ content/pub/pdf/offensea_offenseb.pdf

Chalfin, A. (2015). *Economic costs of crime. Encyclopedia of crime and punishment.* Hoboken, NJ: John Wiley & Sons.

Eigenberg, H. M. (1990). "The national crime survey and rape: The case of missing questions." *Justice Quarterly, 7,* 655–672.

Eterno, J. A., & Silverman, E. B. (2012). *The crime numbers game: Management by manipulation.* Boca Raton, FL: CRC Press/Taylor and Francis.

Federal Bureau of Investigation. (2013). *Summary Reporting System (SRS) user manual.* Washington, DC: U.S. Department of Justice.

Federal Bureau of Investigation. (2014). *Crime in the United States.* Washington, DC: U.S. Department of Justice.

Federal Bureau of Investigation. (2017). *2016 crime statistics released.* Retrieved from https://ucr.fbi.gov/crime-in-the-u.s/2017/preliminary-report/home on May 30, 2018

Federal Bureau of Investigation. (2018). *Preliminary semiannual uniform crime report, January-June, 2017.* Retrieved from https://www.fjc.gov/research/idb on May 30, 2018

Federal Judicial Center. (2018). *Integrated Database (IDB).* Retrieved from https://www.fjc.gov/research/idb

Ibid.

Jarvis. J. P. (2015). "Examining National Incident-Based Reporting System (NIBRS): Perspectives from a quarter century analysis efforts." *Justice Research & Policy, 16*(2), 195–210.

Kim, M., & de Guzman, M. C. (2012). "Police paradigm shift after 9/11 terrorist attacks: The empirical evidence from the united states municipal police departments." *Criminal Justice Studies: A Critical Journal of Crime, Law and Society, 25*(4), 323–342.

Koss, M. P. (1992). "The underdetection of rape." *Journal of Social Issues, 48*, 63–75.

Langan, P. A., & Farrington, D. P. (1998). *Crime and justice in the United States and in England and Wales, 1981–96* (NCJ No. 169284). Washington, DC: Government Printing Office.

Langton, L., Planty, M., & Lynch, J. P. (2017). "Second major redesign of the National Crime Victimization Survey (NCVS)." *Criminology & Public Policy, 16*, 1049–1074.

Lauritzen, J. L., & Cork, D. L. (2017). "Expanding our understanding of crime: The national academies report on the future of crime statistics and measurement." *Criminology & Public Policy, 16*, 1075–1098.

Lynch, J. P., & Jarvis, J. P. (2008). "Missing data and imputation in the uniform crime reports and the effects on national estimates." *Journal of Contemporary Criminal Justice, 24*(1), 69–85.

Maltz, M. D. (2007). *"Uniform crime reports of the federal bureau of investigation 1960-2004."* Criminal Justice Research Center, Columbus, OH: The Ohio State University.

National Center for State Courts. (2018). *Court Statistics Project (CSP).* Retrieved from http://www.courtstatistics.org/

Neter, J., & Waksberg, J. (1964). "A study of response errors in expenditures data from household interviews." *Journal of the American Statistical Association, 59*, 17–55.

O'Brien, R. M. (1999). "Measuring the convergence/divergence of "serious crime" arrest rates for males and females: 1960-1995." *Journal of Quantitative Criminology, 15*(1), 97–114.

Reichel, P. L. (2018). *Comparative criminal justice systems: A topical approach.* New York, NY: Pearson.

Rogerson, M. (2004). *Crime incidence, prevalence, and concentrations among NDCs: Research report no. 45.* Sheffield, UK: The Neighborhood Renewal Unit/Sheffield Hallam University.

Ross, M. (1996). "Measurement of rape victimization in rape surveys." *Criminal Justice and Behavior, 23*(1), 55–69.

Sherman, L. W. (1998). *Ideas in policing: Evidence-based policing.* Washington, DC: Police Foundation.

Strom, K. J., & Smith, E. L. (2017). "The future of crime data: The case for the National Incident-Based Reporting System (NIBRS) as a primary data source for policy evaluation and crime analysis." *Criminology & Public Policy, 16*, 1027–1048.

United Nations Commission on Human Rights. (2015). *Global impunity index, 2017.* Puebla, Mexico: University of the Americas Puebla.

University of Maryland. (2018). *Overview of the GTD.* Retrieved from https://www.start.umd.edu/gtd/about/

UNODC (2015). International Classification of Crime for Statistical Purposes (Version 1.0), Vienna, Austria: United nations Office on Drugs and Crime

Wikipedia. (2017). *New bilibid prison drug trafficking scandal.* Retrieved from https://en.wikipedia.org/wiki/New_BilibidPrison_drug_traffick ing_scandal, posted on October 2017

Wilson, J. (1999). *Community policing in America.* New York, NY: Taylor and Francis.

Wilson, J. Q., & Kelling, G. L. (1982). "Broken windows: Police and neighborhood safety." *Atlantic Monthly, 249,* 29–38.

Endnotes

[1] These databases can be explored by visiting the FBI website such as these sites https://www.ucrdatatool.gov/twomeasures.cfm or https://ucr.fbi.gov/nibrs-overview/ The student can explore the various information from the local level all the way to the national level.

[2] Index crimes are the eight crimes the FBI combines to produce its annual crime index. These offenses include willful homicide, forcible rape, robbery, burglary, aggravated assault, larceny over $50, motor vehicle theft, and arson. (https://definitions.uslegal.com/i/index-crimes/)

Editorial credit: Victor Moussa/Shutterstock.com

SECTION 2
THE CRIMINAL JUSTICE AGENCIES

Chapter 6
The US Police System

Chapter 7
The Police Process

Chapter 8
The Judicial System

© gerasimov_foto_174/Shutterstock.com

The US Police System

LEARNING OBJECTIVES

After reading this chapter, the student should be able to

1 Trace the development of modern policing in the United States

2 Outline the organization of policing in the United States

3 Identify the emerging models of policing in the United States

4 Explain the core essence of policing

5 Explain the requirements and process of becoming a law enforcement officer

Introduction

This chapter explains the police as a system in a democratic society. We examine the concepts and philosophical foundations of the police system in the United States. Klockars (1985) argues that for a useful discussion of the police, it is important to remove the biases that everyone has about the police. Instead, he argues that a more useful conceptualization about the police would be something that is objective, comprehensive, and mutually exclusive.

This chapter provides insights on the factors that shape the origin, development, organization, and central features of the police in the United States. The past defines and explains the state of the present. In this regard, a historical overview about the police is central to understanding the current state of the police. This chapter illustrates the central feature of policing in the United States as well as the existence of multiple policing agencies that are administratively decentralized and uncoordinated in most of their operations (Bayley, 1985, 1992). Some scholars would call these a fragmented system (Cole, Smith, & DeJong, 2018; Cordner, 2010) while others call this system loosely-coupled (Katz & Webb, 2006; Maguire & Katz, 2002). In Chapter 1, we discussed this characteristic of criminal justice. To reiterate, loosely-coupled organizations are those that have independent jurisdictions and that are operationally and administratively autonomous, but work in conjunction with other agencies to achieve common objectives (Carter, Phillips, & Gayadeen, 2014). These features of US policing are primarily due to the country's federated nature. The federal government as well as the fifty states and other US territories enforce laws in these jurisdictions. Likewise, each of the police levels and units provide policing services that address the needs of their specific constituents and mandates (Langworthy & Travis, 2008). According to Johnson and Vaughn (2016), the loosely coupled nature of these agencies are actually beneficial, as departments can tailor their responses to unique needs of the policing environment while at the same time pursuing the overall goal of addressing crime and administering justice (Hunter, Barker, & de Guzman, 2018). The overall nature and characteristics of these various police organizations in the United States are explored in this chapter. In addition, the chapter points out the primary organizational characteristics of these different policing agencies.

This chapter also discusses the evolution of US police. It offers theoretical explanations as well as empirical evidence of these developments. Police services provisions in the United States continue to evolve due to multiple factors. Technology and social movements have been argued to be instrumental in this aspect of policing evolution (de Guzman, Das, & Das, 2012; de Guzman & Kumar, 2011). Subsumed in this discussion is an analysis of trends that may shape the future of policing. The section argues that provisions of public safety are no longer a monopoly of government. Instead, the notion of public safety and the means to achieve this desired state is a shared responsibility of the police and the community. It will be highlighted that the models that emerge would consist not only of the traditional bureaucratic model, but a more hybrid type where provisions of safety, that is policing, could not only be a shared or collaborative enterprise, but also a form of self-help (Bayley & Shearing, 2001; Klockars, 1985).

Core Essence of Policing

Policing is a unique profession. Klockars (1985) attributes the unique nature of policing to being a state-sanctioned organization whose job is to distribute nonnegotiable coercive force in society in an exigent manner (Bittner, 1970; Klockars, 1985). Langworthy and Travis (2008) formally define **police** as "institutions or individuals given the general right to use coercive force by the state within the state's domestic territory." This definition underscores some of the basic tenets of policing in society, namely, that:

1. The police have the power to decide what kind of force should be applied. They have the discretion to decide whether a mere verbal command or lethal force is necessary (Sykes & Brent, 1980). This application of force is something that the police do sometimes in a split-second decision in certain circumstances (Fyfe, 1981).

2. The police have the decision to apply the force option to the appropriate situation and specific citizens. In their interaction with citizens, the police decide who among the members of the population would require police intervention and who would not require police use of force (Black, 1973).

3. This force is coercive and something that citizens could not resist at the exigent time (Bittner, 1980). Thus, the resistance to the use of force is often itself a criminal offense (i.e., resisting arrest).

This core essence of policing is controversial in all societies. Bittner (1980) calls the police anomalies in democratic societies. He argues that settling disputes through force runs counter to the democratic ideals of settling disputes through peaceful means. Even in communist Russia, the police have been argued as unnecessary in a communist regime (Lenin, 1917). Lenin (1917) claimed that the police are only temporary institutions during the infancy of communism. These contentions about the nonnecessity of the police are negated by current facts about the police. Today, we have witnessed an increasing number and uses of police forces instead of their diminutions.

The use of force in policing has several implications on its organization and functions. First, the "business" of policing could not be privatized. Police personnel should be state agents because force is such a delicate nature, and its applications have damaging and long-lasting consequences. The state has to train personnel (police officers) who can be accountable for the unnecessary use of force. Second, managers of police should be state agents and seasoned sworn personnel. This means that civilians might not be qualified to lead. The legal and social implications of the use of force are very sensitive that only those that have acquired sufficient training and experience with its use and deployment should be responsible in making those decisions. Third, the use of force must be restricted. Law should be the sole basis for the use of force. This means that distribution of force in society should be nondiscriminatory.

With the emergence of community policing, some argue that the core essence of policing is order maintenance (Wilson & Kelling, 1982) or service (Landau, 1996). Some have even argued for the use of so-called "soft policing" in combination with the traditional hard-core use of force enforcement (Innes, 2005). However, the dominance of these other competing functions have been recently clouded with the development of homeland security policing (HSP) in the United States (Kim & de Guzman, 2012). Likewise, the recent controversial events involving the police use of force have again brought front and center the core essence of policing as the use of force and, therefore, highlight the necessity of controlling those that decide on its applications.

Theories and Historical Evolutions of the Police

Police in the United States have gone several evolutions. The evolution of the police in the United States could be traced to its colonial, cultural, technological, and social movements (de Guzman et al., 2012; Travis & Langworthy, 2008; Worrall & Schmalleger, 2018).

Early on, the history of the US police shows the vestiges of its colonial pasts. As a colony of England, the police system in the United States displays several traces of the English police models. For example, the sheriff's office has its roots in the English community of one hundred families known as the shire, which was headed by a **shire reeve**. The shire reeve performs various governmental services including the provisions of public safety. Thus, counties are normally policed through the sheriff's office.

In most societies, policing began as a self-help model (Klockars, 1985). This means that anyone or any group in the society can define the safety that they need and the individual or group can use personal means for providing that safety (Bayley & Shearing, 2001). Eventually, as communities became more organized, the performance of such function slowly became organized with the use of volunteers such as the **night watches** or **thief takers**. This semiorganized form of policing is necessary as crime has also become more organized with bands of robbers and as the disorders or crimes would become more pronounced (Lundman, 1980).

In 1829, Sir Robert Peel institutionalized the creation of the police built on several principles, as seen in Figure 6.1. The first formal police established in London was justified by expanding the purposes of the police from crime control to crime prevention. These purposes were accomplished by introducing the concept of a 24/7 patrol. It also included the use of a distinctive uniform that would make them easily identifiable. Peel's proposal for a modern police was also justified using the concepts of professionalism. He presented an organization where officers will be trained and selected from the "best of the best." Finally, he allayed the fears of the citizens about the potential for abuse of these new groups of law enforcers by arguing that they will not be armed and will have limited jurisdiction. In this effort, he also introduced the concepts of accountability and control. On top of these tenets, he retained the importance of the community in the preservation of law and order as well as the observance of the rule of law in performance of police functions. All these tenets are embodied in what is now known as the nine principles of policing.

Several observations should be made with these principles. First, policing in London was based on community needs and consent. In its modern concept, the first principle is known as the principle of policing by consent. Second, policing highlights the principles of training and accountability mechanisms to control the use of force. Third, policing emphasizes the concept of crime prevention through police presence in certain geographic boundaries. They were only allowed to operate within the city of London. This principle of bounded territoriality is now being assailed as a barrier to law enforcement effectiveness in the emerging trend of the transnational and international

FIGURE 6.1 THE NINE PRINCIPLES OF POLICING

Peel's Principles of Policing

1. The basic mission for which police exist is to prevent crime and disorder as an alternative to the repression of crime and disorder by military force and severity of legal punishment.

2. The ability of the police to perform their duties is dependent upon public approval of police existence, actions, behavior and the ability of the police to secure and maintain public respect.

3. The police must secure the willing cooperation of the public in voluntary observance of the law to be able to secure and maintain public respect.

4. The degree of cooperation of the public that can be secured diminishes, proportionately, the necessity for the use of physical force and compulsion in achieving police objectives.

5. The police seek and preserve public favor, not by catering to public opinion, but by constantly demonstrating absolutely impartial service to the law, in complete independence of policy, and without regard to the justice or injustice of the substance of individual laws; by ready offering of individual service and friendship to all members of the society without regard to their race or social standing; by ready exercise of courtesy and friendly good humor; and by ready offering of individual sacrifice in protecting and preserving life.

6. The police should use physical force to the extent necessary to secure observance of the law or to restore order only when the exercise of persuasion, advice and warning is found to be insufficient to achieve police objectives; and police should use only the minimum degree of physical force which is necessary on any particular occasion for achieving a police objective.

7. The police at all times should maintain a relationship with the public that gives reality to the historic tradition that the police are the public and that the public are the police; the police are the only members of the public who are paid to give full-time attention to duties which are incumbent on every citizen in the interest of the community welfare.

8. The police should always direct their actions toward their functions and never appear to usurp the powers of the judiciary by avenging individuals or the state, or authoritatively judging guilt or punishing the guilty.

9. The test of police efficiency is the absence of crime and disorder, not the visible evidence of police action in dealing with them.

(Adapted from: https://www.durham.police.uk/About-Us/Documents/Peels_Principles_Of_Law_Enforcement.pdf.)

characteristic of some crimes (Sheptycki, 1999). Fourth and perhaps the most important feature of the London police was the nonuse of firearms and their provision of a unique control known now as the police badge. Thus, the London police were fondly called the "coppers" due to the issuance of a copper badge, which is now a popular moniker for police officers being called "cops." The other name given to these police officers was "bobbies" in reference to Robert Peel's nickname. Being the creator of this modern police force, Peel became the first administrator of the very first police organization.

The Police Traditions in the United States

Caldero and Crank (2004) suggest that the type of policing that will emerge is a product of the environmental and social factors that exist at the time. The effects of these conditions are reflected in the now universally considered policing traditions in the United States. Except for the tradition in the Northeast, traces of the other police traditions are hardly in existence. The society is now witnessing the seeming uniformity among police departments with very little noticeable influence from the other traditions (Travis & Langworthy, 2008).

Policing in the Northeast

Since territories in the Northeast were under British rule, the models of policing from the United Kingdom were transported over to these US colonies. Thus, the early forms of policing in the Northeast are characterized by limited jurisdiction, local in orientation, and more bureaucratic in organization. These characteristics are based on the Peelian model of policing that was established in London. Police have to be more available at the locality and became more accountable and professional at least to the polity. They embody the purposes and ideals of their original creation. Thus, there are expectations that police officers should be prevention focused and have strict accountability. However, as we shall see in the later section, the US police have undergone several reformations before its current state.

Policing in the South

The economic need for workers in the South has precipitated certain laws and social institutions to reflect such need (Chambliss, 1964). Policing was used as means to perpetrate the interest of the elite (de Guzman & Kumar, 2011; Lenin, 1917; Lundman, 1980). As a result, policing was instituted primarily to control workers in the plantations of the South (Chambliss, 1964). Most textbooks called the early police organizations that emerged in the South as the **slave patrols**. Due to their organizational origin, the police tend to enforce laws that are mostly unfavorable to the working class (i.e., slaves). As the police have to run after plantation workers, they need to have wider scope of jurisdictions to be able to perform their functions. Thus, the county level policing was more dominant in the early history of policing in the South. This form of policing was contrary to the principle of limited jurisdiction that was a used to justify the creation of the London police. Instead, the police should be allowed to exercise greater scope of authority particularly in the rural areas where a runaway worker might tend to hide. As one can see, the emergence of this form of policing bears witness to the influence of social, economic, and political conditions that existed during this time.

Policing in the West

The West was an open territory in the early histories of policing. In a lot of discourses of Dinesh D'Souza on YouTube, he claims that the early history of the earth was governed by the principle of conquest where territories and properties are acquired by force and protected by force. Thus, the popular media used to depict the old West as the "Wild, Wild, West" where justice can be achieved at the end of the barrel of a gun. Due to this nature of the West being an open territory, the provision of safety was dependent on the individual's perception of safety. It is in this context that the self-help form of policing (Klockars, 1985; Travis & Langworthy, 2008) became the dominant form of policing in the West. If there was ever an organized policing in the West, it can be called a feudal or clannish form of policing where families band together to protect themselves. It was also due to these circumstances that justice was something that was personally undertaken by the aggrieved individual. Hence, the nature of policing that emerged in the West was that of vigilantism.

Over time, because of the United States' liberation from colonial powers and the establishment of the Union as well as the incorporation of other territories into the Union, the police have evolved as exhibiting a seemingly singular or homogeneous character. Thus, the concept of modern police in the United States is viewed as a homogeneous group of state-sanctioned personnel who use similar technologies and govern by approximately similar laws. As a result, the policing traditions' characteristics are no longer as imminent in today's police organizations, except for the bureaucratic tradition that emerged in the Northeast.

The Evolution of Modern Police in the United States

de Guzman et al. (2012) argued in their introduction to their book, *Evolution of Policing*, that policing has evolved as a product of societal and technological evolutions. Lundman (1980) has also presented a theory of the evolution of modern police, but it only goes as far as explaining the emergence of the formal type of police. In an international research study, applying Lundman's theory involving India, de Guzman and Kumar (2011) found that the forces responsible for the emergence of formal police could be used to explain other characteristics of modern police. Several historical accounts, however, have also cited technological developments, politics, ideological developments, and public safety challenges, and have influenced the evolution of policing in the United States.

Lundman's Theory on the Evolutions of the Police

Several scholars have suggested that early policing is a form of self-help (Klockars, 1985; Travis & Langworthy, 2008). This means that public safety needs are primarily defined by individuals and they, in turn, devise means of being able to achieve that level of safety that someone needed (Bayley & Shearing, 2001). The question becomes, "How did we get from policing being a personal, non-paid, voluntary endeavor to become a formally organized and paid profession?" Lundman (1980) developed a theoretical model to explain the emergence of professional policing. This theoretical model is depicted in Figure 6.2. This model was later expanded and modified by de

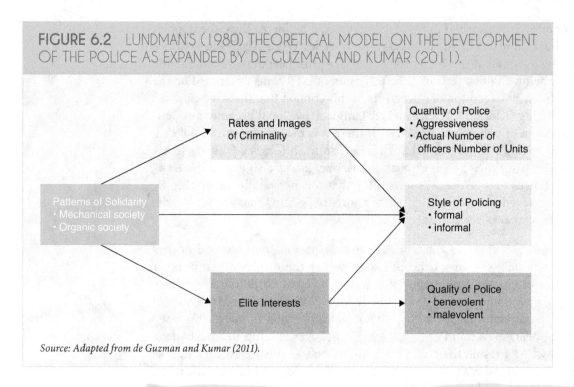

Source: Adapted from de Guzman and Kumar (2011).

Guzman and Kumar (2011) and showed that such factors could also explain the quantity and quality of the police in society. Although the de Guzman and Kumar study was situated in India, the extended theoretical model could be applied to the development of policing in the United States.

In this theoretical model, Lundman (1980) argues that the reason why society has adopted formal policing is primarily due to the evolutions of the patterns of solidarity, rates, and images of criminality, and the preservation of elite interest. The first two correlates are due to societal infrastructure, whereas the third correlate explains the influence of class conflict in the formation of the police. Primarily, however, patterns of solidarity evolving from mechanistic to organic society were predominantly responsible for images of disorders and class stratification in society. Lundman (1980) argues that when a society is simple or mechanistic where there is hardly no division of labor, it does not call for the need of a formal organized policing. Instead, individuals and communities provide for their own safety. As societies become more complex or organic, division of labor becomes more pronounced and urbanization and its accompanying effects of immigration and emigration as well as increased social alienation produce an image of chaos that heightened people's fears for their safety (Wilson & Kelling, 1982). As people become more preoccupied with their engagement with urban life and economy (i.e., means of production), they have to rely on some other people to provide for their safety. As a consequence, the citizens have to rely on another group to provide safety—a formal policing organization. Finally, when society becomes more complex, social stratification and elitism emerge. These elites need an instrument to maintain their dominance. Hence, they rely on the instrument that can monopolize the use of force toward the underclass (Chambliss, 1964)—the police. Thus, even though Lenin (1917) believed that the police are not necessary in a communist system, he argued for the temporary maintenance of the police to protect the working class' dominance. Unfortunately, Lenin's dream of the police withering away did not happen. Instead, the police have become permanent fixtures in communist regimes.

de Guzman and Kumar (2011) applied Lundman's theory in the Indian context and found the need to extend the explanatory powers of the identified factors. In their research, the authors found that rates and images of criminality are primarily responsible for the quantity of police in society which they operationalized in terms of actual number of officers and increased aggressiveness of police actions. In addition, de Guzman and Kumar (2011) found that the nature of the elite predominantly influence the quality of the police. They found that benevolent elites would produce a more humane police, whereas a more malevolent elite group would induce the police to be more abusive. This phenomenon supports the contention of Caldero and Crank (2004) that the police cannot rise above the society that it serves.

The Eras of Modern Police in the United States

Most police historians (e.g., Kelling & Moore, 1991; Wilson & Kelling, 1982) delineate the eras of modern policing into three: political era, reform era, and community era. Aside from these eras, this text presents an argument that a new era has emerged following the 9/11 attacks in the United States. Empirical evidence as well as practical considerations show that the terrorist attacks in the United States as well as the intensified activities of international terrorists has precipitated the emergence of a new era—the HSP era.

The Eras of Policing

Most textbooks cite Kelling and Moore (1991) for the major eras of policing in the United States. However, the 9/11 terror attacks in the United States in 2001 was remote from the minds of scholars when these eras were created. Definitely, the attack has shifted the paradigm of policing in this country. Thus, a fourth era of HSP is being presented in this text as the future paradigm of public safety services provision in the United States (Kim & de Guzman, 2012). Thus, we now have four eras in policing evolution in the United States.

The Political Era (1830–1920)

Policing is characterized by domination of political bosses during this regime. It is a time when police officers were selected based on their political affiliation. In this atmosphere where appointment is not based on merit, police officers were expendable and had no security of tenure. Thus, the political era has the following features:

- Police appointment—There was political patronage where entry and promotion into policing are based on the arbitrary wishes of the political lords.
- Tenure—The officers have no security of tenure.
- Training—The appointed police have no formal training.
- Duties—Police performed a broad range of functions but they cater more to serve the political bosses. The police are primarily service oriented but delivery of such service comes with a twist (i.e., political affiliates receive the best service but nonaffiliates are not given good services).

The Reform Era (1920–1970)

The progressive movement during this era resulted in the propagation of professional ideals and the emergence of the bureaucratic principle. The police were swept into this wave of change that engulfed the United States. The first feature of the political era that was dismantled was the clout of political bosses over the police. In place of patronage system, a merit-based selection was implemented through the use of civil service system. The civil service also provided a security of tenure for police officers. This period was also the era of major scientific revolutions in transportation, communication, and other technological advances. It was during this time that the fingerprint system was invented. The police embraced these technologies and incorporated them in the performance of their functions. The era also produced two major principles that emerged within the police force. The first was the embrace of militarism in policing. Militarism was intended to remedy the perceived lack of discipline among officers. The second principle is the adherence to professionalism. Professional standards were intended to insulate the police from political influences and address the practice of discriminatory policing where nonpolitical affiliates were not given fair provision of police services. This adherence to professionalism has been associated with the narrow focus on their roles as law enforcers rather than service providers.

Despite these reforms, the police were still unfavorably viewed in society. For one, they failed to meet the expectations of the public to reduce crime and disorders despite their training and use of modern technology. The urban riots and the drugs menace in the 1960s and the 1970s highlighted the seeming inability of the police to maintain law and order. As far as some scholars were concerned, bureaucratization and militarism produced the twin effects of the police as becoming aloof and unresponsive to the needs of the community. More importantly, it has been noted by Wilson and Kelling (1982) that technology created a chasm in the police–community relationships as they became less mutually engaged in a more personal and positive way. Furthermore, technology has increased the public expectations about the effectiveness of the police, but society at this time had experienced continued spikes in criminality.

The academic community, led by Goldstein (1979, 1987), argued that police ineffectiveness was due to the isolation of the police from the community that they serve. It was also at this time that the leading proponents of community policing shifted the focus of law enforcement effectiveness away from crime and identified fear of crime and quality of life as the more important barometers for measuring police effectiveness (Skolnick & Bayley, 1986). By the year 2000, community policing had become the dominant policing paradigm in the United States (Wilson, 2006).

Despite continuing adherence to community policing, several problems still plague the police (Williams & Murphy, 1990). In the last decade, police–community relations have not really improved that much (Hunter et al., 2018). Social movements such as Black Lives Matter lament the fact that police abuses bring to question the achievements of the community policing era. Much like the era before it, the community policing era seems hard pressed in fostering a healthy and collaborative relationship with the police. Skogan and Hartnett (1997) found that comprehensive community policing programs, such as the Chicago Alternative Policing System (CAPS), have failed to see significant involvement of communities with police activities and programs. So much so that they concluded that better off communities benefitted more with community-oriented policing (COP), but disadvantaged communities were worse off. Despite some of these less glowing outcomes of COP, it had become the dominant philosophy until the early 2000s. Plus, some reanalysis of the CAPS data suggests that communities that have been covered by CAPS had greater satisfaction with the police than non-CAPS communities (Lombardo, Olson, & Staton, 2010).

The Homeland Security Era (2001–present)

HSP is a recent phenomenon. Immediately after the 9/11 attacks, several scholars have noted the potential paradigm shift that may occur in policing. One scholar in particular noted that the tenets of community policing that operated in building trusts and cooperation among communities are really incongruent with the tenets of antiterrorism policing that thrived on surveillance and suspicion in order to thwart terrorist attacks (de Guzman, 2002). This dramatic and traumatic terrorism event in US history did not only impact federal law enforcement activities, but also local law enforcements' way of policing (Maguire & King, 2011). The central focus of the homeland security era became the promotion of national security. The event has also intensified the antiterrorism tactics of the local police in response to the demands of the time.

At the height of the community policing era, Wilson (2006) conducted a nationwide examination of the implementation of COP in the United States. He found the extensive implementation of community policing among an overwhelming number of local police departments in the United States. After the 9/11 attacks, there have been thoughts about the viability of community policing to counterterrorism (de Guzman, 2002). Likewise, the federal government have reorganized its counterterrorism law enforcement efforts and vigorously enjoined local policing to collaborate in this counterterrorism efforts. Suspecting the effects of these developments to policing, Kim and de Guzman (2012) revisited Wilson's (2006) study with the purpose of finding empirical evidence for the shift of community policing to HSP. In their review of the literature, Kim and de Guzman (2012) stated that there are numerous clues after 9/11 that showed police departments have shifted their focus to homeland security. The authors noticed that several police departments had significantly reduced their adherence to several components of community policing implementations evidencing a shift toward homeland security.

At the moment, community policing and HSP are competing paradigms in policing. There are efforts to maintain the two philosophies. Several scholars have argued that community policing and HSP are compatible. Police departments still proclaim themselves as community policing. However, others contend that community policing is incompatible with HSP. The recent evidence shows too that police departments have deescalated their community policing efforts and titled their efforts toward HSP.

Policing Systems in the United States

The United States has a federal form of government. As such, the various political divisions in the country have different ways of providing for public safety. The federal government implements its own system of public safety services provisions. Each of the fifty states also establishes its own state police system. Counties have the county police or the sheriff's offices that take care of the unincorporated areas in the state. Finally, The United States has police agencies that are organized at the municipal, city, and village levels, which are commonly called local police agencies. On top of these police systems located at the government levels, there are different forms of police agencies that are maintained, such as special purpose police that may include the likes of transit police, university police, or park police. These are special purpose police due to the limited exercise of their jurisdictions. On top of these law enforcement offices, there are several security agencies that provide security for fees. These personnel are either contracted by private or public organizations or are appointed by the organizations. However, private police do not only have limited jurisdiction, but also limited intervention powers. In fact, most of them are not authorized to use firearms. In this sense, private police are not real police forces since they lack the necessary element of using nonnegotiable coercive force.

The Federal Police System

The federal police have gradually evolved and are continuing to evolve to respond to the need of the times. Several developments that happened over the last two decades are the reorganization of the law enforcement agencies due to the creation of the Department of Homeland Security (DHS) (Hunter et al., 2018). The mandates of other agencies have also been expanded. For example, the Federal Bureau of Investigation (FBI) has become more concerned about antiterrorism. As a result of the terrorist attacks, several task forces have been formed, such as the Joint Anti-Terrorism Task Force (JTTF), that aim to provide a collaborative law enforcement effort among local, county, state, and federal agencies. Intelligence and Fusion Centers were also created as a nucleus for understanding threats of terrorism and provide actionable intelligence for the law enforcement communities.

The emergences of cybercrimes and transnational crimes have also altered the federal law enforcement landscape. A lot of investigative and law enforcement agencies at the federal level have created units that are involved in the detection and intervention of these crimes. Thus, we now see the proliferation of policing units to address specific crimes such as antimoney laundering, organized crime, terrorism, human trafficking, smuggling, and others. Several federal law enforcement agencies have agents deployed across the world in order to gather intelligence against some of these types of crimes.

These movements and developments lend credence to the thesis of Travis and Langworthy (2008) that federal law enforcement agencies are products of security needs that emerge at a particular time and locale. For example, they cited the expansion of the Secret Service. The Secret Service was given the extended mandate of providing protection to the President instead of being confined to its original mandate of investigating counterfeit activities. With respect to the Central Intelligence Agency (CIA), its original mandate was to gather human intelligence in response to the attacks in Pearl Harbor. In 1947, it was created through the National Security Act. The CIA has now become involved in some covert operations particularly against terrorism and cybercrimes.

The administration of the federal police agencies is fragmented. The law enforcement units are primarily dispersed through the different line departments in the Executive Department. For example, the duty to protect the border of the United States is given to the Border Patrol and the Coast Guard, which are both under the DHS. The provision of security for federal courts, serving of federal warrants, and protection of federal witnesses are with the US Marshal's Office that is under the Department of Justice (DOJ). In addition, the FBI is also under the DOJ. Below are descriptions of some of the more prominent federal law enforcement agencies.

Federal Police Agencies

By including all units that have arrest and firearm authority, there are approximately one hundred different federal police agencies. The largest agencies are formally located within the Justice and the Treasury Departments. Since the creation of the DHS, several agencies have been moved.

Department of Treasury Agencies

Established in 1789, the Treasury's enforcement function is investigation of counterfeit and collection of revenues. Originally, the four primary law enforcement agencies were the Bureau of Alcohol, Tobacco, and Firearms; the US Customs Service; the Internal Revenue Service (IRS); and the US Secret Service. After the 9/11 attacks and the creation of Homeland Security, the US Secret Service and the US Customs Service are now located within the DHS. Likewise, the Bureau of Alcohol, Tobacco, and Firearms (ATF) is now located within the DOJ. The IRS was the only major enforcement agency that was retained in the Treasury and according to the 2008 census (Reaves, 2012), its criminal investigation division employs 2,636 federal law enforcement officers.

BOX 6.1 LAW ENFORCEMENT AGENCIES IN THE US FEDERAL GOVERNMENT BY BRANCH OF GOVERNMENT AND DEPARTMENTS.

Executive Branch

Department of Agriculture (USDA)

- Office of Inspector General **(USDAOIG)**
- US Forest Service **(USFS)**
  - ‣ US Forest Service Law Enforcement and Investigations (USFSLEI)

Department of Commerce (DOC)

- National Institute of Standards and Technology **(NIST)**
  - ‣ National Institute of Standards and Technology Police (NIST Police)
- National Oceanic and Atmospheric Administration **(NOAA)**
  - ‣ National Oceanic and Atmospheric Administration Fisheries Office for Law Enforcement (OLE)
- Department of Commerce Office of Inspector General **(DOCOIG)**

Department of Education

- Office of the Inspector General **(EDOIG)**

Department of Energy (DOE)

- Office of Inspector General **(DOEOIG)**
- Office of Health, Safety and Security **(DOEHSS)**

Department of Health and Human Services

- US Food and Drug Administration **(HHSFDA)**
  - ❯ Office of Criminal Investigations (OCI)
- National Institutes of Health **(NIH)**
  - ❯ National Institutes of Health Police (NIH Police)
- Office of Inspector General **(HHSOIG)**

Department of Homeland Security (DHS)

- National Protection and Programs Directorate
  - ❯ Federal Protective Service (FPS)
- US Coast Guard **(USCG)**
  - ❯ Coast Guard Investigative Service (CGIS)
- US Customs and Border Protection **(CBP)**
  - ❯ Office of Air and Marine (OAM)
  - ❯ Office of Border Patrol (OBP)
  - ❯ Office of Field Operations (OFO)
- US Immigration and Customs Enforcement **(ICE)**
  - ❯ Enforcement Removal Operations (ERO)
  - ❯ Homeland Security Investigations (HSI)
  - ❯ Office of Intelligence
  - ❯ Office of Professional Responsibility (OPR)
- US Citizenship and Immigration Services **(USCIS)**
- US Secret Service **(USSS)**
- Transportation Security Administration **(TSA)**
  - ❯ Office of Law Enforcement/Federal Air Marshal Service (OLE/FAMS)
- Department of Homeland Security Office of Inspector General **(DHSOIG)**

Department of Housing and Urban Development

- Office of Inspector General **(HUD/OIG)**
- Protective Service Division **(HUDPSD)**

US Department of the Interior (USDI)

- Bureau of Indian Affairs **(BIA)**
  - ❯ Bureau of Indian Affairs Police (BIA Police)

- Bureau of Land Management **(BLM)**
  - Bureau of Land Management Office of Law Enforcement (BLM Rangers and Special Agents)
- Bureau of Reclamation **(BOR)**
  - Bureau of Reclamation Office of Law Enforcement (BOR Rangers)
  - Hoover Dam Police aka Bureau of Reclamation Police
- National Park Service **(NPS)**
  - Division of Law Enforcement, Security and Emergency Services (US Park Rangers-Law Enforcement)
  - US Park Police
- Office of Inspector General **(DOIOIG)**
- US Fish and Wildlife Service **(USFWS)**
  - Office of Law Enforcement
  - Division of Refuge Law Enforcement

Department of Justice (USDOJ)

- Bureau of Alcohol, Tobacco, Firearms, and Explosives **(ATF)**
- US Drug Enforcement Administration **(DEA) (since 1973)**
- Federal Bureau of Investigation **(FBI)**
  - Federal Bureau of Investigation Police (FBI Police)
- Federal Bureau of Prisons **(BOP)**
- Office of Inspector General **(DOJOIG)**
- US Marshals Service **(USMS)**

Department of Labor

- Office of Inspector General **(DOLOIG)**

Department of State (DoS)

- Bureau of Diplomatic Security **(DS)**
  - US Diplomatic Security Service (DSS)
- Office of the Inspector General of the Department of State

Department of Transportation

- Office of Inspector General **(DOTOIG)**

Department of the Treasury

- Bureau of Engraving and Printing (**BEP**)
  - › Bureau of Engraving and Printing Police (BEP Police)
- Internal Revenue Service Criminal Investigation Division (**IRS-CI**)
- Office of Inspector General (**TREASOIG**)
- Treasury Inspector General for Tax Administration (**TIGTA**)
- US Mint Police (**USMP**)
- Special Inspector General for the Troubled Asset Relief Program (**SIGTARP**)

Department of Veterans Affairs

- Office of Inspector General (**VAOIG**)
- Veterans Affairs Police

Legislative Branch

- US Capitol Police (**USCP**)
- US Government Printing Office Police
- Office of Inspector General, US Government Printing Office

Judicial Branch

- Marshal of the US Supreme Court
  - › US Supreme Court Police
- Administrative Office of the US Courts, Office of Probation and Pretrial Services (**AOUSC**)

Other federal law enforcement agencies

- Central Intelligence Agency Security Protective Service (**CIASPS**)
- US Environmental Protection Agency
  - › Criminal Investigation Division (EPACID)
  - › Office of Inspector General (EPAOIG)
- National Aeronautics and Space Administration
  - › Office of Inspector General (NASAOIG)
  - › NASA Protective Services
- Nuclear Regulatory Commission, Office of Inspector General (**NRCOIG**)
- Office of Personnel Management, Office of Inspector General (**OPMOIG**)

- Railroad Retirement Board, Office of Inspector General **(RRBOIG)**
- Small Business Administration, Office of Inspector General **(SBAOIG)**
- Federal Deposit Insurance Corporation, Office of Inspector General **(FDICOIG)**
- General Services Administration, Office of Inspector General **(GSAOIG)**
- Social Security Administration Office of Inspector General **(SSAOIG)**
- US Postal Service **(USPS)**
  - USPS Office of Inspector General (USPSOIG)
  - US Postal Inspection Service (USPIS)
  - US Postal Police
- Smithsonian Institution
  - Office of Protection Services (SI)
  - National Zoological Park Police (NZPP)
  - Office of the Inspector General (OIG)
- Amtrak
  - Amtrak Office of Inspector General
  - Amtrak Police
- Federal Reserve Bank: Federal Reserve Police
- Tennessee Valley Authority Office of Inspector General **(TVAOIG)**
- US Agency for International Development, Office of Inspector General **(AIDOIG)**

Note: This list was edited from the original source list to reflect only law enforcement agencies. Defense and Military Police were also excluded from the list. Inspector General's Offices are included.

Source: World Heritage Encyclopedia (2018).

DOJ AGENCIES

The Department of Justice, created in 1870, is responsible for enforcing federal crime statutes. The largest DOJ agency is the Bureau of Prisons. Other DOJ units having law enforcement authority are the Antitrust Division, the Civil Rights Division, and the Office of Inspector General. The four primary law enforcement agencies within the department are the ATF; DEA; USMS; and FBI.

Bureau of Alcohol, Tobacco, Firearms, and Explosives

Aside from enforcing federal criminal laws, the ATF regulates the firearms and explosives industries. The ATF is engaged in the investigation and reduction of crime involving firearms and explosives, acts of arson, and illegal trafficking of alcohol and tobacco products. Pursuant to the Homeland Security Act, the Bureau of ATF was transferred to the DOJ in 2003. The law enforcement functions of ATF under the Department of the Treasury were transferred to the DOJ. The tax and trade functions of the former ATF remained in the Treasury Department with a new Alcohol and Tobacco Tax and Trade Bureau. The agency's name was changed to ATF to reflect its new mission in the DOJ.

The ATF mainly works collaboratively with local law enforcement to identify, arrest, and prosecute the most violent criminals in designated cities. Likewise, the ATF investigates fire and explosives incidents throughout the United States. The ATF is also instrumental in counterterrorism measures by investigating alcohol and tobacco trafficking and diversion, thereby reducing the source of funding to criminal and terrorist organizations, and stemming the loss of revenue to affected states and the federal government.

Drug Enforcement Administration

The DEA was created in 1973. It is currently one of the larger federal law enforcement agencies, with 4,308 full-time law enforcement officers (World Heritage Encyclopedia, 2018). The mission of the DEA is to enforce the controlled substances laws and regulations of the United States and bring to the criminal and civil justice systems of the United States, or any other competent jurisdiction, those organizations and principal members of organizations involved in the growing, manufacture, or distribution of controlled substances appearing in or destined for illicit traffic in the United States; and to recommend and support nonenforcement programs aimed at reducing the availability of illicit controlled substances on the domestic and international markets (Drug Enforcement Administration, 2018).

In carrying out its mission as the agency responsible for enforcing the controlled substances laws and regulations of the United States, the DEA's primary responsibilities include

> Investigation and preparation for the prosecution of major violators of controlled substance laws operating at interstate and international levels.
>
> Investigation and preparation for prosecution of criminals and drug gangs who perpetrate violence in our communities and terrorize citizens through fear and intimidation.
>
> Management of a national drug intelligence program in cooperation with federal, state, local, and foreign officials to collect, analyze, and disseminate strategic and operational drug intelligence information.
>
> Seizure and forfeiture of assets derived from, traceable to, or intended to be used for illicit drug trafficking.
>
> Enforcement of the provisions of the Controlled Substances Act as they pertain to the manufacture, distribution, and dispensing of legally produced controlled substances.

Coordination and cooperation with federal, state, and local law enforcement officials on mutual drug enforcement efforts and enhancement of such efforts through exploitation of potential interstate and international investigations beyond local or limited federal jurisdictions and resources.

Coordination and cooperation with federal, state, and local agencies, and with foreign governments, in programs designed to reduce the availability of illicit abuse-type drugs on the US market through nonenforcement methods such as crop eradication, crop substitution, and training of foreign officials.

Responsibility, under the policy guidance of the Secretary of State and US Ambassadors, for all programs associated with drug law enforcement counterparts in foreign countries.

Liaison with the United Nations, Interpol, and other organizations on matters relating to international drug control programs.

U.S. Marshal Service (USMS)

Created by Congress in 1789, the USMS is the oldest federal law enforcement agency. Its full-time law enforcement officers stand at 3,314 (Drug Enforcement Administration, 2018). While the ninety-four Marshals are appointed by the President and approved by Congress, in 1969, the agency's regulations, training, and duties were standardized to ensure uniformity and professionalism among its offices. The Marshals Service is one of the more diverse law enforcement agencies, with a variety of duties that once included conducting the US Census. Today, the US Marshals Service is responsible for apprehending fugitives, protecting federal judges and courts, managing and selling seized assets, transporting prisoners, managing prisoners, protecting witnesses, and serving court documents. As claimed on its website, the US Marshals have no specialties, as they serve general law enforcement and administrative functions (U.S. Marshalls Service, 2018).

Federal Bureau of Investigation (FBI)

The FBI is the primary investigative agency of the federal government and arguably the most famous of the federal law enforcement agencies. The primary responsibility of the FBI is to investigate violations of federal criminal law and to assist local and state agencies in investigations. These include crimes such as kidnapping, bank robbery, art and cultural property crime, jewelry and gem theft, white-collar crime, and organized crime. The FBI is also responsible for investigating corporate fraud, health-care fraud, mortgage fraud, identity theft, insurance fraud, telemarketing fraud, Internet fraud, and money laundering.

In addition to the above crimes, the FBI is engaged in counterterrorism activities, counterintelligence activities, and cybercrime investigations (including stopping those behind serious computer intrusions and the spread of malicious code as well as identifying and thwarting online sexual predators who use the Internet to meet and exploit children and produce, share, or possess child pornography). The FBI also counteracts operations that target US intellectual property and endanger national security and competitiveness.

The FBI's other duties include investigating public corruption at all levels of government; investigating all allegations regarding violations of applicable federal civil rights laws (its Civil Rights program consists of the following subprograms: Hate Crimes, Color of Law/Police Misconduct, Involuntary Servitude/Slavery, and Freedom of Access to Clinic Entrances); and suppressing violent street gangs, motorcycle gangs, and prison gangs. In addition, the FBI has federal law enforcement responsibility on more than two hundred of the nation's 267 Indian reservations.

Department of Homeland Security (DHS)

The DHS was created on November 25, 2002. A response to the terrorist attacks in 2001 in the US mainland, the department was created to better coordinate intelligence and law enforcement efforts to protect the United States from terrorism. The organizational chart for DHS is displayed in Figure 6.1. The largest agencies transferred into the DHS were the US Secret Service and the US Customs Service (from the Treasury Department), the Immigration and Naturalization Service (INS) and US Border Patrol (from DOJ), the Federal Emergency Management Agency (formerly independent), and the Transportation Security Administration (TSA) and the US Coast Guard (from the Department of Transportation). Close to half (45.5 percent) of all federal law enforcement officers come from the DHS (Reaves, 2012).

Customs and Border Protection

US Customs and Border Protection (CBP) is the unified border agency within the DHS. According to the 2008 Census of Federal Law Enforcement (Reaves, 2012), the agency employs the most number of federal employees with 36,863 full-time law enforcement officers. This number is over 33 percent more than its former number of employees in 2004. The largest concentration of these officers could be found in the US-Mexico border of the United States (Reaves, 2012). CBP combined the inspectional workforces and broad border authorities of US Customs, US Immigration, Animal and Plant Health Inspection Service, and the entire US Border Patrol. CBP's mission is to safeguard America's borders thereby protecting the public from dangerous people and materials, while enhancing the nation's global economic competitiveness by enabling legitimate trade and travel (Customs and Border Patrol, 2018).

Immigration and Customs Enforcement

Created in March 2003, the Immigration and Customs Enforcement (ICE) is the largest investigative branch of the DHS with more than 12,000 federal law enforcement officers (Reaves, 2012). The agency was created after 9/11 by combining the law enforcement arms of the former INS and the former US Customs Service to more effectively enforce immigration and customs laws and to protect the United States against terrorist attacks. ICE does this by targeting illegal immigrants: the people, money, and materials that support terrorism and other criminal activities. The ICE website now reports that it has more than 20,000 employees. The agency has an annual budget of approximately $6 billion, primarily devoted to three operational directorates—Homeland Security Investigations (HSI), Enforcement and Removal Operations (ERO), and Office of the Principal Legal Advisor (OPLA) (Immigration and Customs Enforcement, 2018).

Transportation Security Administration

TSA was created in response to the terrorist attacks of September 11, 2001, as part of the Aviation and Transportation Security Act that was signed into law by President George W. Bush on November 19, 2001. TSA was originally in the Department of Transportation, but was moved to the DHS in March 2003.

TSA's mission is to protect the nation's transportation systems by ensuring the freedom of movement for people and commerce. In February 2002, TSA assumed responsibility for security at the nation's airports and by the end of the year had deployed a federal workforce to meet congressional deadlines for screening all passengers and baggage (Department of Homeland Security, 2018).

The US Coast Guard

The US Coast Guard is a military, multimission, maritime service and may be considered one of the nation's five armed services. Its mission is to protect the public, the environment, and US economic interests—in the nation's ports and waterways, along the coast, on international waters, or in any maritime region as required to support national security. Its numerous cutters, aircraft, and boats carry out these functions. In wartime, the Coast Guard operates under the aegis of the US Navy.

The Coast Guard is given several homeland security missions that include prevention of terrorism and enhancement of security, security and management of the borders (especially in the maritime jurisdiction of the United States), enforcement and administration of immigration laws, and strengthening of the national preparedness and resilience. The US Coast Guard normally conduct its activities involving its six operational programs, namely, (1) maritime law enforcement, (2) maritime response, (3) maritime

FIGURE 6.3 DEPARTMENT OF HOMELAND SECURITY (DHS) ORGANIZATIONAL CHART.

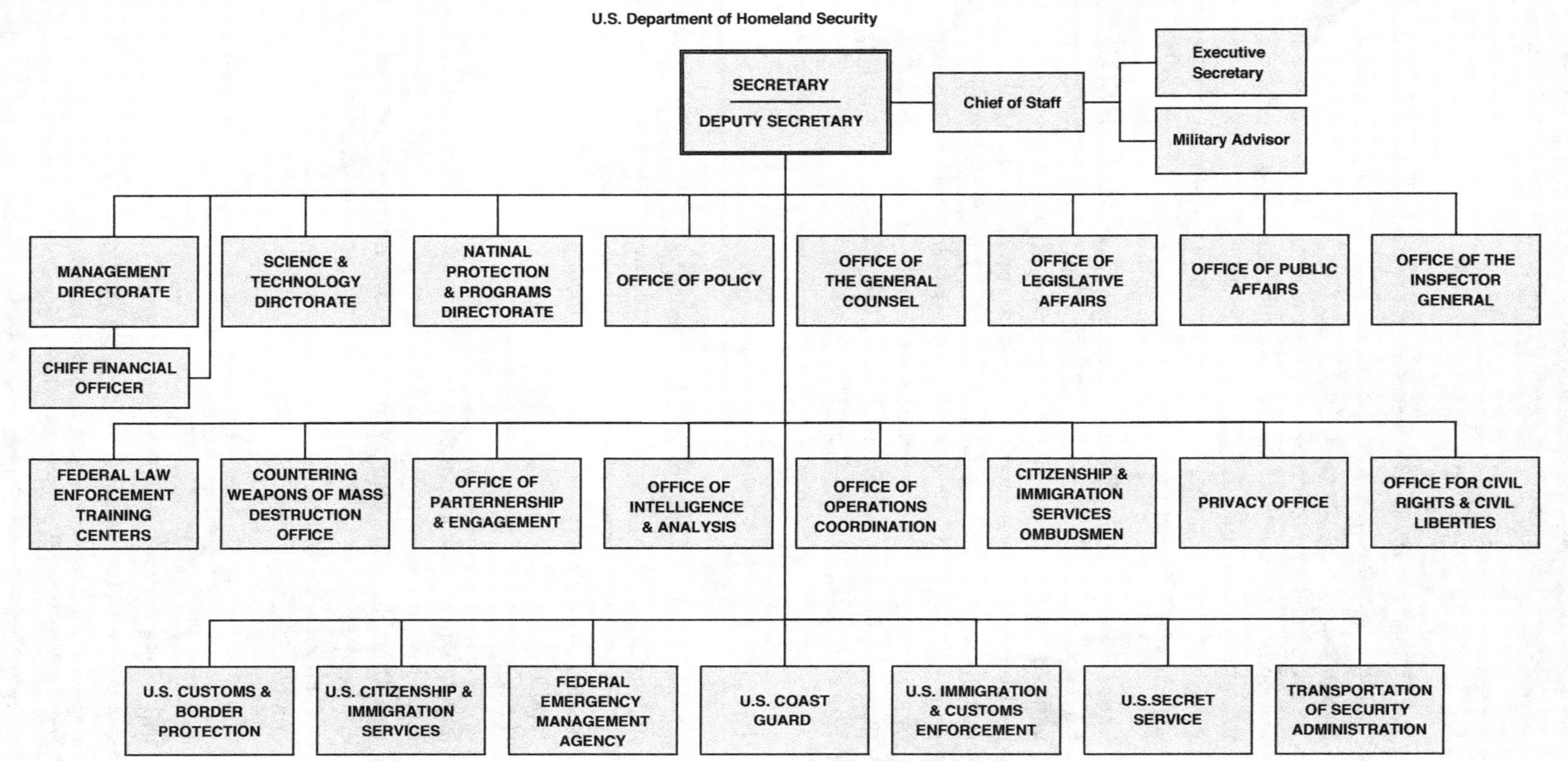

https://www.dhs.gov/sites/default/files/publications/17_1219_DHS_Organizational_Chart.pdf, retrieved on January 15, 2018.

prevention, (4) maritime transportation system management, (5) maritime security operations, and (6) defense operations (U.S. Coast Guard, 2018).

US Secret Service

The US Secret Service Division originally had the mandate to investigate counterfeit currency. Its mandate was later broadened to investigate any person defrauding the government. Due to the alarming assassinations of US Presidents, the Secret Service assumed full-time responsibility for protection of the President, which was again expanded to provide protections to former Presidents, the President's family, candidates for President, the President elect, and the Vice President. The division also protects foreign dignitaries and other protectees.

The passing of the PATRIOT Act in 2001 (Public Law 107-56) increased the Secret Service's role in investigating fraud and related activity in connection with computer-related offenses. Likewise, they are involved in enforcing environmental laws as well as the protection of US financial infrastructures that are vulnerable to attacks, particularly to protect American financial payment systems while combating transnational financial crimes directed by terrorists or other criminals. In March 2003, the Secret Service was transferred from the Department of the Treasury to the Department of Homeland Security (DHS; 2018) (Figure 6.3).

State Police Agencies

The latest LEMAS (Reaves, 2015) survey report that all fifty states have some form of state police. Previously, Hawaii was claimed to be the only state that has no state police. However, Hawaii's Department of Public Safety was labeled as a primary state law enforcement agency. Hence, it is now being reported that there are now fifty primary state law enforcement agencies (Reaves, 2015).

The state police system enforces laws of the state. They provide law enforcement functions including the protection of the governor and state facilities. The state police also perform support functions to the state's local law enforcement agencies especially those that are too small to handle training of their local officers or academy or those that may be inadequate to handle complex criminal investigations.

Organizational Models

The state agencies have typically two types of organizational structure. One is a centralized state law enforcement system where the police and investigative functions are under one central administrative agency. The other structure is a decentralized model where the police patrol and/or enforcement bureau is separate from the investigation bureau. An example of such model is the state of Georgia, which has the Georgia Bureau of Investigation (GBI) and the State Police. New York State is a good example of a centralized state police structure (Worrall & Schmalleger, 2015).

State police functions are normally organized into three major divisions: highway patrols, highway inspections, and investigations. Aside from enforcing traffic and safety rules in the highways, the patrol units also perform general police functions such as responding to incidents. Highway inspection patrols are those that conduct inspections of trucks, movers, and hazardous materials in the highways. The state also maintains an investigation unit that not only investigates state crimes, but also provides investigative assistance to local police departments within the state. Since most local police agencies within the state may not have enough personnel or resources to respond to and investigate crimes, the state agencies lend assistance to police agencies and centralize the use of highly sophisticated investigative tools such as forensic investigation equipment at the state level.

The County Police System

Sheriffs and **deputy sheriffs** enforce the law on the county level. Sheriffs are usually elected to their posts and perform duties similar to those of a local police chief. Deputy sheriffs often have law enforcement duties similar to those of officers in police departments. Police and deputies who provide security in city and county courts are sometimes called bailiffs (IACP, 2018). In 2008, there were 3,063 sheriff's offices with 182,879 full-time sworn and 11,334 part-time sworn personnel (Reaves, 2011). It must be noted that about half of those employed at the sheriff's offices are civilians (Reaves, 2011). This means that sheriff's offices are viable paths for civilian employment. Local police departments have lesser numbers of civilians in their employment.

The careers in the sheriff's offices are unique as the sheriffs are elected for a fixed term in their offices. The deputies are selected in a competitive selection process. However, the job assignments vary from being assigned to law enforcement operations, jail operations, or court operations. There are also several states (e.g., Alaska, Connecticut, Hawaii, and Rhode Island) that do not have a sheriff's office. Sheriffs' responsibilities in these states are performed by state agencies (Reaves, 2011).

The Local Police System

Local police agencies refer to the city and municipal police offices. Included in this category are the university or college police and other special purpose police.

The Local Police Profiles

Local police departments employ the largest number of sworn personnel comprising about 60 percent of the total number of those that operate at the state and local level. In 2013, there were 12,326 local police agencies with a total of 477,317 full-time sworn officers and more than 26,000 part-time sworn officers (Reaves, 2015). In 2016, there are now about 652,936 law enforcement officers and more than 280,000 civilian employees in more than 13,000 agencies (FBI, 2017). About half (48 percent) of local police agencies employ fewer than ten, but the majority (54 percent) are employed in jurisdictions that have at least 100,000 residents. It has been observed that a typical local police department employs less than twenty-five employees. The estimated ratio of police to citizens overall is one officer for every four hundred residents, but the ratio on the municipal and township level is about 1:500 (Reaves, 2015). The New York City Police Department employs the highest number of local police officers with Chicago, Los Angeles, Philadelphia, and Houston making up the rest of the five biggest departments in the United States (Reaves, 2015).

Figure 6.4 illustrates the profile of the local US police departments. Through this information we can describe a typical police officer in the United States as a white, middle class, male with some college education. It should be noted that there have been increases in the minority officers compared to previous surveys. The 2013 survey reports that 27 percent of local police officers were members of racial or ethnic minority groups, with Latinos registering a 16 percent increase in 2013 compared to the 2007 data. Females to male ratio stands at 1 for every 8 (Reaves, 2015).

FIGURE 6.4 PROFILE OF LOCAL POLICE OFFICERS IN THE UNITED STATES.

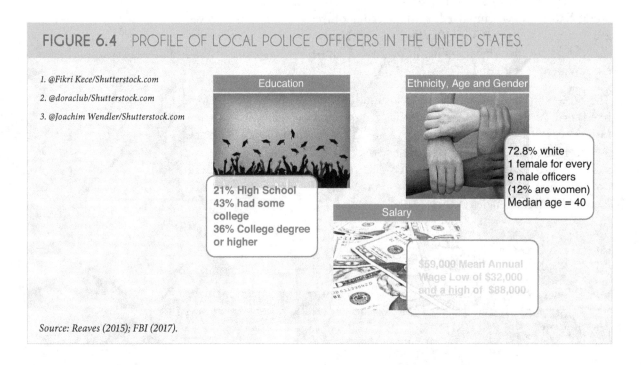

1. @Fikri Kece/Shutterstock.com
2. @doraclub/Shutterstock.com
3. @Joachim Wendler/Shutterstock.com

Education

21% High School
43% had some college
36% College degree or higher

Ethnicity, Age and Gender

72.8% white
1 female for every 8 male officers
(12% are women)
Median age = 40

Salary

$59,000 Mean Annual Wage Low of $32,000 and a high of $88,000

Source: Reaves (2015); FBI (2017).

Special Police Units

Special police units are law enforcement entities that have special jurisdictions. Reaves (2011) noted that there are five categories of the special jurisdiction police.

1. Public building/facilities. These police units are involved in policing universities and colleges, public housing, state buildings, hospitals, and other state-owned facilities.

2. Natural resources. These police units are more involved in enforcement of regulatory laws involving fishing, parks and recreation areas, and the protection of the natural resources.

3. Transportation system/facilities. These units enforce laws involving public transport including airports, railroads, bridges/tunnels, harbors/ports, and commercial vehicles.

4. Criminal investigations. These are special units that are assigned to investigate specific crimes such as fraud, fire, tax, or other crimes.

5. Special enforcement. Included in this category are those that enforce vice laws (e.g., racing, alcohol, narcotics) and agricultural laws.

The difference of these police units with some of the private police is the source of their funding or authority from which they are created. For example, private universities might also have their own complement of security personnel, but they are not funded from public funds nor created by a political entity. Hence, private police are more limited in their powers and performance of their law enforcement functions. These private police are also governed by different standards and legal expectations (Bayley & Shearing, 2001).

BOX 6.2 REQUIREMENTS AND DISQUALIFIERS TO BECOME A POLICE OFFICER.

Each state has a Commission on Peace Officer Standards and Training (POST) or similar entity that establishes minimum selection standards for law enforcement officers. Individual agencies must meet or exceed these minimum standards. While requirements may vary from state to state and agency to agency, typical basic requirements include the following:

- *Citizenship Requirement.* Agencies require applicants to be US citizens, or in some cases, permanent resident aliens who have applied for citizenship. Some agencies require officers to reside within their jurisdictions while others do not.

- *Minimum/Maximum Age Requirement.* While most agencies require you to be 21 by academy graduation date, some take cadets as young as 18. The maximum age can vary widely. Do not assume that just because you are over 30, your chances of becoming a police officer are over. Some agencies have no maximum age.

- *Education Requirement.* Most agencies expect officers to have a high school diploma or General Educational Development (GED) at a minimum. Some agencies require a bachelor's degree or a minimum number of college credit hours. Others offer additional pay based on educational attainment. Regardless, education beyond high school will only help you in your law enforcement career. Having a four-year degree or an advanced degree is an asset in your career progression, particularly when seeking a promotion or specialized assignment. While criminal justice studies are the traditional route for those aspiring to a career in law enforcement, many other fields provide you with a good foundation. Sociology, psychology, and social work are a few other fields that are particularly well suited for police work.

- *Valid Driver's License.* Since most officers start out on patrol, a valid driver's license is a requirement for any law enforcement position. Your driving history will also be reviewed during the background check.

- *Minimum Fitness Requirement.* The type and rigor of these requirements vary by agency. With enough training and preparation, you can meet the challenge.

Disqualifiers

While specific disqualifiers vary from department to department, any of the items listed below may disqualify you from police service. Agencies use their discretion when reviewing past infractions. Some come with a sliding time limit that may adjust based on the severity of the crime. For example, marijuana use once in college ten years ago might not be disqualifying, but marijuana use ten days ago probably would. *Please keep in mind that departments have different requirements. If you are found to be unsuitable for one department, there may be other departments that find you suitable.* Following are some typical disqualifiers:

- Felony conviction (adult or juvenile)

- A misdemeanor conviction involving domestic abuse or a sexual component

- Illegal drug use

- Poor driving record (including reckless driving conviction)

- Driving while intoxicated (DWI)/driving under the influence (DUI) conviction

- Poor credit history or other financial problems

Source: IACP (2018). What does it take? The basic requirements. http://www.discoverpolicing.org/what_does_take/?fa=requirements. Retrieved on January 18, 2018.

BOX 6.3 THE HIRING PROCESS.

Unlike most jobs, becoming a law enforcement officer involves far more than completing an application and interview. Agencies run their applicants through a comprehensive series of tests and exams, each designed to narrow the field of applicants to advance only those who are most qualified.

As with the basic requirements, each state has a Commission on POST or similar entity that establishes minimum selection standards for law enforcement officers. Recognizing that each state and each agency may differ, below is a summary of the steps you are likely to see in the hiring process.

Basic Application/Prescreening Questionnaire

The initial application and prescreening questionnaire convey an applicant's interest and eligibility. Based on a review of this material, candidates are invited back to take the written exam.

Written Exam/Entrance Test

The written exam is typically a standardized test used to assess general aptitude and does not require or assume any knowledge specific to law enforcement. Written exams typically test an applicant's

- reading comprehension
- problem-solving/judgment skills
- memory
- writing skills

Some agencies or state POSTs offer study guides to assist applicants preparing for the exam. Alternatively, there are private sector publications available online and at local bookstores that are designed to help with test preparation.

Video Exam

During video exams, applicants watch a scenario and provide a verbal response that is rated and scored. Some agencies use video simulations to assess an applicant's interpersonal skills and judgment.

Physical Fitness/Ability Test

Law enforcement has physical demands, and employers are keen to ensure their recruits are fit to serve. Applicants can expect to take some sort of physical ability test during the hiring process. Agencies typically use a fitness test, a job simulation test, or a combination of both. A fitness test measures a candidate's overall level of fitness through structured activities that assess strength, endurance, and cardiovascular health. Job simulation tests are designed to be job samples, measuring your ability to perform certain job-specific tasks such as running stairs, dragging a weight, or climbing a wall. While each agency sets its own minimum requirements, with enough training and determination anyone can achieve success.

Background Investigation

A thorough background check will be conducted to ensure that you do not have any personal or professional issues that would preclude you from police service. Background investigators will review your employment history, character references, academic records, residency history, criminal history, and credit history. A background investigation typically includes a fingerprint check and interviews with those who know you, including previous employers, school or military personnel, neighbors, and family members.

Drug Testing

Drug tests are routinely administered to check for the presence of illegal substances. Each agency establishes the type of test.

Psychological Testing

Just as agencies want to ensure you are physically fit for the job, they also want to ensure that you are psychologically stable and mentally fit to handle the job. This evaluation is typically made through written psychological exams and may be supplemented with an interview by a psychologist. Psychological testing serves two functions: to evaluate your character and emotional makeup and to ensure you are well suited to the job from a psychological standpoint.

Polygraph

Many department use a polygraph, commonly known as lie detector, to verify information submitted throughout the application process.

Oral Board

The oral board is a chance for members of the hiring authority to meet and talk with you face to face. Oral interviews serve as a chance to discuss your qualifications and gauge your fit with the agency. During the oral interview, you may be evaluated on your:

- General appearance and demeanor
- Communication skills
- Understanding of and interest in policing as a career
- Response to questions and scenarios

Medical Exam

Generally, only those applicants who have been given a conditional offer of employment will be subject to the medical exam. This physical exam will evaluate if you are medically fit to meet the physical requirements of the job. Specifically, you should be able to perform the "essential job functions" as listed by the employer. For example, to drive a vehicle, your vision will be assessed and you should have a low risk of sudden incapacitation, such as seizure or heart attack.

A typical medical exam may include the following elements:

- Height
- Weight
- Vision
- Hearing
- Chest x-ray
- Blood test
- Urine test
- Blood pressure

- Electrocardiogram

- Screening tests for illegal drugs

Most law enforcement agencies have vision and hearing criteria, as well as criteria based on specific diseases or conditions. The specific requirements vary by agency and what is acceptable by one department may not be by another.

Source: IACP (2018). What does it take? The hiring process. http://www.discoverpolicing.org/what_does_take/?fa=hiring_process. Retrieved on January 18, 2018.

Becoming a State and Local Law Enforcement Police Officer

The International Association of Chiefs of Police (IACP), through its law enforcement job information board, publishes some generic qualifications, disqualifiers, and hiring process for local law enforcement. As outlined in Boxes 6.2 and 6.3, the selection of a police officer is a rigorous process. On top of these requirements, a recruit must also undergo academy training for about four weeks to six months (Reaves, 2016). After graduation from the academy, the recruit must undergo another orientation phase known as field training under a Field Training Officer (FTO). The median time for field training has been noted as 180 hours or eight weeks (Reaves, 2016). Thus, a new police officer has to be mentally, physically, and psychologically prepared for the job.

The Emerging Models of Policing

After the international terrorist attacks on the United States on 9/11, policing was thoroughly examined and overhauled. Several changes were implemented as a result of these developments. One of the major changes was the creation of the DHS where a major realignment of the law enforcement and intelligence units of the federal government were realigned. The other major change is the shift in focus of the local police units to include counterterrorism in its policing efforts (Kim & de Guzman, 2012). However, even without the 9/11 attacks, several factors are precipitating the emergence of different models of policing. Sheptycki (1999) has pointed out that the fragmented type of policing is no longer viable in the transnational and global nature of some crimes. He also argued that there was an increasing marketization of insecurity that not only precipitated the commodification of safety services (examples are the home and personal security measures), but also in certain circumstances the commodification of public policing. This led Bayley and Shearing (2001) to write that policing is undergoing major restructuring. They argue that the new structures are primarily a product of the phenomenon that definitions of safety and its provision are no longer a monopoly of government.

In the latest edition of their book, Hunter et al. (2018, p. 75) outlined these developments as argued by Bayley and Shearing (2001):

> *In supporting their thesis, they first differentiated the two major actors in making society safe—auspices and providers.* **Auspices** *are those entities that define the safety needs of the community.* **Providers** *are those that actually do policing. They argued that early on the formation of policing as a formal organization, auspices and providers are one and the same, that is, government defines the safety needs of society and organize the means to provide such desired state of safety. In the modern age, particularly with the emergence of community policing, these domains have been become distinct. The government slowly allowed non-government entities to define their safety needs with government supplying the providers (i.e., public police). Eventually, not only are non-government entities allowed to define their own safety need but they were allowed to form their own providers (i.e., private police).*

Furthermore, the analysis of Hunter et al (2018, p. 76). brought to light four coexisting models of police services delivery in society:

1. Traditional—This model is where government defines safety needs of the community and utilizes the public police for achieving that state of safety.
2. Augmentation—This model is where government defines its safety needs but allow private providers to be engaged in that duty.
3. Commodification—This model makes public policing available to private entities who feel the need for a different level of safety. Normally this model includes an additional fee such as when a business provides compensation to public police to secure an event or the police department provides more manpower on top of its regularly deployed officers.
4. Responsibilization—This model allows private entities to define their own safety needs and allows them to hire or seek the help of private providers to attain such safety.

Comprehension Check

1. What is the essence of policing?
2. Explain the foundational roots of policing in England and U.S. societies.

3. Describe the different eras of policing in the United States and identify the characteristics of each era.

4. Outline the policing system in the United States.

5. Provide a summary of the general qualifications for becoming a local law enforcement officer in the United States.

6. What are the various emerging models of police services provision in the United States?

References

Bayley, D. H. (1985). *Patterns of policing: A comparative international analysis.* New Brunswick, NJ: Rutgers University Press.

Bayley, D. H. (1992). "Comparative organization of the police in English-speaking countries." In M. Tonry & N. Morris (Eds.), *Crime and justice: A review of research* (Vol. 21, pp. 509–545). Chicago, IL: University of Chicago Press.

Bayley, D. H., & Shearing, C. D. (2001). *The new structure of policing: Description, conceptualization, and research agenda.* Washington, DC: Office of Justice Programs, National Institute of Justice.

Bittner, E. (1970). *The functions of police in modern society.* Rockville, MD: National Institute of Mental Health.

Bittner, E. (1980). *Police behavior: A sociological perspective* (R. J. Lundman, Ed.). New York, NY: Oxford University Press.

Black, D. J. (1973). "The mobilization of law." *Journal of Legal Studies, 2*(1), 125–149.

Caldero, M., & Crank, J. P. (2004). *Police ethics: Corruption of a noble cause* (4th ed.). Cincinnati, OH: Anderson Publishing.

Carter, J. G., Phillips, S. W., & Gayadeen, S. M. (2014). Implementing intelligence-led policing: An application of loose-coupling theory." *Journal of Criminal Justice, 42*, 433–442.

Chambliss, W. (1964). "A sociological analysis of the law of vagrancy." *Social Problems, 12*, 67–77.

Cole, G. E., Smith, C. S., & DeJong, C. (2018). *Criminal justice in America* (9th ed.). Boston, MA: Cengage Learning.

Cordner, G. W. (2010). "The architecture of U.S. policing. Variations among 50 states." *Police Practice and Research: An International Journal, 12*(2), 107–119.

Customs and Border Patrol. (2018). Retrieved from https://www.cbp.gov/about

de Guzman, M. C. (2002). "The changing roles and strategies of the police in time of terror." In J. Victor & J. Naughton (Eds.), *Criminal justice annual editions 03/04* (pp. 84–94). New York, NY: McGraw-Hill.

de Guzman, M. C., & Kumar, S. K. (2011). "Extending Lundman's theory on policing: The evidence from the literature focusing on India." *Policing: An International Journal of Police Strategies & Management, 34*(3), 403–418. https://doi.org/10.1108/13639511111157483

de Guzman, M. C., Das, D. K., & Das, A. M. (2012). *The evolution of policing: Worldwide innovations and insights.* Boca Raton, FL: CRC Press/Taylor and Francis.

Department of Homeland Security. (2018a). Retrieved from https://www.tsa.gov/about/tsa-mission

Department of Homeland Security. (2018b). Retrieved from https://www.secret-service.gov/

Drug Enforcement Administration. (2018). Retrieved from https://www.dea.gov/about/mission.shtml

FBI. (2017). *Crime in the U.S., 2016: Police employee data.* Retrieved from https://ucr.fbi.gov/crime-in-the-u.s/2016/crime-in-the-u.s.-2016/topicpages/police-employees

Fyfe, J. (1981). "Observations on police deadly force." *Crime and Delinquency, 27*(3), 376–390.

Goldstein, H. (1979). "Improving policing: A problem-oriented approach." *Crime and Delinquency, 25*(2), 236–258.

Goldstein, H. (1987). "Toward community-oriented policing: Potential, basic requirements, and threshold questions." *Crime and Delinquency, 33*(1), 6–30.

Hunter, R. D., Barker, T., & de Guzman, M. C. (2018). *Police and the community in the administration of justice* (9th ed.). New York, NY: Pearson.

IACP. (2018). Retrieved from http://www.discoverpolicing.org/whats_like/?fa=types_careers

Immigration and Customs Enforcement. (2018). Retrieved from https://www.ice.gov/about

Innes, M. (2005). "Why 'soft' policing is hard: On the curious development of reassurance policing, how it became neighborhood policing, and what this signifies about the politics of police reform." *Journal of Community and Applied Social Psychology, 15*, 156–169.

Johnson, A. D., & Vaughn, M. S. (2016). "Decoupling police organizational structure." *Administrative Theory and Praxis, 38*(3), 157–167.

Katz, C., & Webb, V. (2006). *Policing gangs in America.* Cambridge, UK: Cambridge University Press.

Kelling, G., & Moore, M. (1991). "From political to reform to community: The evolving strategy of the police." In J. R. Greene & S. D. Mastrofski (Eds.), *Community policing: Rhetoric or reality.* New York, NY: Praeger Publishers.

Kim, M., & de Guzman, M. C. (2012). "Police paradigm shift after the 9/11: An empirical evidence from the united states municipal police departments." *Criminal Justice Studies: A Critical Journal of Crime, Law and Society, 25*(4), 323–342.

Klockars, C. B. (1985). *The idea of police.* Beverly Hills, CA: Sage.

Landau, T. (1996). "Policing and security in four remote aboriginal communities: A challenge to coercive models of police work." *Canadian Journal of Criminology, 38*(1), 1–32.

Langworthy, R. H., & Travis, L. F. III. (2008a). *Policing in America: A balance of forces* (2nd ed., p. 8). Upper Saddle River, NJ: Prentice Hall.

Langworthy, R. H., & Travis, L. F. III. (2008b). *Policing in America: A balance of forces* (4th ed.). Upper Saddle River, NJ: Prentice Hall.

Lenin, V. I. (1917). *State and revolution.* London, UK: Penguin Books.

Lombardo, R. M., Olson, D., & Staton, M. (2010). "The Chicago alternative policing strategy: A reassessment of the CAPS program." *Policing: An International of Police Science and Management, 33*, (4), 586–606.

Lundman, R. J. (1980). *Police and policing: An introduction.* New York, NY: Holt, Rinehart, & Winston.

Maguire, E. R., & Katz, C. M. (2002). "Community policing, loose coupling, and sensemaking in American police agencies. *Justice Quarterly, 19*(3), 503–536.

Maguire, E. R., & King, W. R. (2011). "Federal-local coordination in homeland security." In B. Forst, J. R. Greene, & J. P. Lynch (Eds.), *Criminologists on terrorism and homeland security.* New York, NY: Cambridge University Press.

Reaves, B. A. (2011). *Census of state and local law enforcement agencies, 2008.* Washington, DC: U.S. Department of Justice, Office of Justice Programs, Bureau of Justice Statistics.

Reaves, B. A. (2012). *Federal law enforcement officers, 2008.* Washington, DC: U.S. Department of Justice, Office of Justice Programs, Bureau of Justice Statistics.

Reaves, B. A. (2015). *Local police departments, 2013.* Washington, DC: U.S. Department of Justice, Office of Justice Programs, Bureau of Justice Statistics.

Reaves, B. A. (2016). *State and local law enforcement training academies, 2013.* Washington, DC: U.S. Department of Justice, Office of Justice Programs, Bureau of Justice Statistics.

Sheptycki, J. (1999). "Policing, postmodernism and transnationalization." In R. Smandych (Ed.), *Governable places: Readings on governmentality and crime control* (pp. 215–238). Brookfield, VT: Ashgate.

Skogan, W., & Hartnett, S. (1997). *Community policing: Chicago style.* New York, NY: Oxford University Press.

Skolnick, J. H., & Bayley, D. H. (1986). *The new blue line: Police innovation in six American Cities.* New York, NY: Free Press.

Sykes, R. E., & Brent, E. E. (1980). "The regulation of interaction by the police: A systems view of taking charge." *Criminology, 18*(2), 182–197.

U.S. Coast Guard. (2018). Retrieved from https://www.overview.uscg.mil/Missions/

U.S. Marshalls Service. (2018). Retrieved from https://www.usmarshals.gov/history/general_practitioners.htm

Williams, H., & Murphy, P. V. (1990). *The evolving strategy of the police: A minority view.* Washington, DC: U.S. Department of Justice.

Wilson, J. M. (2006). *Community policing in America.* New York, NY: Routledge/Taylor and Francis.

Wilson, J. Q., & Kelling, G. L. (1982). "Broken windows: Police and neighborhood safety." *Atlantic Monthly, 249*, 29–38.

World Heritage Encyclopedia. (2018). *List of US federal law enforcement agencies.* Retrieved from http://self.gutenberg.org/articles/eng/List_of_United_States_federal_law_enforcement_agencies

Worrall, J. L., & Schmalleger, F. (2015). *Policing* (2nd ed.). New York, NY: Pearson.

Worrall, J. L., & Schmalleger, F. (2018). *Policing* (3rd ed.). New York, NY: Pearson.

© Bumble Dee / Shutterstock.com

The Police Process

LEARNING OBJECTIVES

After reading this chapter, the student should be able to

1 Identify the formal functions that police perform in a democratic society

2 Describe the different operational units of the police

3 Analyze the impact of different police strategies on crime

4 Critique the problems that the police face in the United States

5 Evaluate the various mechanisms to control the police

Introduction

Most textbooks identify the police as the gateway to the criminal justice system (Cole, Smith, & DeJong, 2018). The police are primarily responsible for initiating the individual into the criminal justice system either as a victim or a perpetrator of a crime. The police are also the immediate face of the criminal justice system, as they are directly involved in the everyday lives of citizens (Travis & Langworthy, 2008). Likewise, the police's decisions and interventions have significant impact on citizens' lives. Thus, it is important to understand their operations, behaviors, programs, and practices.

The police are considered a multipurpose agency whose duty is not only to confront crime and criminals in a legally consistent manner, but also to provide other social services (Wilson, 1968). While most

141

scholars consider the police as law enforcers, others consider them by some other names, and therefore, expect them to behave accordingly. For example, Muir (1977) calls them street corner politicians, whereas Landau (1996) would like to consider them as social workers. If you adhere to Muir's view, then you would expect the police to be very legalistic in their approach of enforcing the law. If you adhere to Landau's view, then you expect the police to place paramount humanitarian considerations secondary to law. The perceptions about the police and their roles run a whole gamut of spectrum, from being law enforcers to social workers and even avoiders (Muir, 1977).

In this chapter, readers will learn about the functions of the police in a democratic society. Readers will understand police practices and the technology police employ in law enforcement. Likewise, it is imperative to understand the empirical evidence on the effectiveness of these practices as well as the shortcomings by the police in the performance of their functions. Readers will also study police culture, as they are influential factors in the performance of police functions. Additionally, we will examine the problems that police officers face in the performance of their functions. Finally, we discuss the different mechanisms of control that influence police practice in the United States.

The Functions of the Police in a Democratic Society

The police in the United States operate in the backdrop and in accordance with democratic principles (Bayley, 2001; Manning, 2010; Skolnick, 1993). Surveying the literature on the concept of democratic policing, Cao, Huang, and Sun (2016) describe democratic policing as the "police practice where political neutrality holds in domestic conflicts and a civilian supremacy prevails." This definition demands that the police are nondiscriminatory and that they are subject to the consent of the governed. Thus, other scholars have opined that under the principle of democratic policing, police officers should be accountable under the law and the people's duly elected representative (Cao & Dai, 2006). Likewise, the police are expected to serve the needs of the individual citizens (Bailey, 2001), and provide immediate relief to their exigent needs (Klockars, 1985; Manning, 2010).

Shilston's (2015) discourse on the components of democratic policing have echoed the same conceptualizations mentioned above. He argued that the components of a democratic policing ideal are most closely associated with the core building blocks of democracy itself, namely, accountability, transparency, participation, and responsiveness. These components are the principal reasons for the continuing calls for reforms in policing even in the most advanced democracy in the world such as the United States.

Three Main Functions of the Police in the United States

The police perform three main functions: (1) law enforcement, (2) order maintenance, and (3) service. Travis and Langworthy (2008) argue that police departments have to exercise all of these functions in a balanced way.

This means that the police should try to minimally satisfy these functions in order to be a viable organization. Although the police have to maintain good political relationships (Fogelson, 1977), the performance of these three main functions tends to influence the relationships and the satisfaction of different audiences with the police (Travis & Langworthy, 2008).

Law Enforcement

Law enforcement as a police function involves crime control and crime prevention. As discussed in Chapter 6, the creation of the police was premised on an added feature of crime prevention. This crime prevention function is founded on the belief that police presence has a deterrent effect on crime. Thus, the modern police have pursued this strategy by deploying police officers geographically and making them available perpetually, twenty-four hours a day. Lately, departments have employed several tactics to increase police presence such as situating marked but unmanned vehicles in strategic locations as well as allowing police officers to take their patrol vehicles home. Departments have also added "eyes and ears" on the watch out for criminal activities through operations such as community night watches, citizen's patrols, street cameras, and drones.

Crime control has always been the main concern of policing. Crime control refers to the ability of the police to respond to infringements of law and to stop the crime from continuing or spreading as well as to solve the crime through arrests. In pursuit of this goal, the police employed rapid response as well as efficient crime reporting. Lately, the police have employed closed-circuit television (CCTV) in order to instantly know if crime is happening and to respond immediately. Research on police response to crime shows that for the crime to be solved through suspect apprehension, the police should be at the scene of the crime in less than two minutes (Cole et al., 2018). Otherwise, the possibility of apprehending the suspect goes down abruptly. This research again justifies the strategic omnipresence of the police particularly in the field through patrol. Recently, crime control focus was not only about controlling the situation and the suspect, but also in minimizing victims and injuries. Thus, most police departments have Emergency Medical/Management Services (EMS) units or collaborations with health services providers. Police departments have also improved on their hostage, active shooter, or protest protocols in order to effectively minimize harm during emergency crime or crisis situations.

Order Maintenance

Order maintenance has also been associated with the crime prevention function of the police. Wilson and Kelling (1982) argued in **broken windows theory** that addressing disorders in society is the best crime prevention measure. It has also been argued by Eck and Spelman (1987) that disorders could be the ultimate cause for crime and, therefore, should be addressed immediately. Thus, police departments started addressing disorders, most particularly in the community policing era (Goldstein, 1990; Skolnick & Bayley, 1986). As defined in most textbooks, order maintenance situations as a police function are those that disturb the peace. Therefore, to maintain peace in society, disorders must be addressed (Wilson, 1968; Wilson & Kelling, 1982a). Disorders have been categorized into physical and social disorders. **Physical disorders** refer to those deteriorated environmental conditions in society (e.g., graffiti, abandoned houses, or trash). **Social disorders** are those behaviors that convey a sense of chaos and disturbance of the peace (Reisig & Parks, 2000; 2004). Examples of social disorders might include kids hanging out in the streets, loud parties, skateboarding in unauthorized places, or unruly behaviors on the street. The reasons for the police in addressing these activities are not merely to maintain the peace, but to improve perceptions of qualities of life and to reduce fears in society. In addition, these disorderly behaviors or artifacts invite conflict that may lead to some aggressive behaviors. For example, neighbors fight due to trash, or individuals argue because of unruly or disruptive behaviors. Thus, if indeed disorders lead to crime, then it is imperative for the police to embrace them as their primary function.

Service

Service is those activities that promote citizens' welfare in society. It might be peripheral to police activities, but they are performed because of the expectations from the public for the police as an all-purpose agency. These activities include welfare checks, home checks during vacation time, and others. In fact, service is the catch-all phrase for all the other activities that police do.

Policing Styles

Travis and Langworthy (2008) suggest that the degree of emphasis of these roles will project the character of the police. However, they cautioned police departments that all of these functions must be performed and minimally satisfied in order to make the organization viable. Any of the functions not sufficiently addressed will potentially result in the withdrawal of support from any of the major constituents of the police. This withdrawal of support might eventually lead to crisis in the organization and ultimately death or disbanding of the organization (King, 2014). Despite such prescription by Travis and Langworthy (2008), they did not provide how these department personalities are formed. It was James Q. Wilson (1968) that provided empirical evidence of how these identities and behaviors are formed. He suggested that these behaviors are observable only with police street activities involving traffic enforcement. His classic work produced what is now known as the varieties of police behavior. He argued that the frequency of interventions by the police and the formality they exhibit during these situations produced three different policing styles.

The Legalistic Style

The legalistic style is characterized by a high frequency of intervention and high formality. In this situation, the police will seldom ignore violations of the law and if they do intervene, it is expected that they will abide by the legal requirement for that situation. This situation is characterized by high probability of formal sanctions such as a citation or arrest.

The Watchman Style

This is a style that addresses disturbances of peace. The police department is characterized by low frequency of intervention, but formality is expected once an intervention occurs. This means that police can ignore some minor violations of the law, but they have to make it worth their while when they intervene because it has reached a level of intolerance where something has to be done.

The Service Style

This style is a customer-oriented approach. The primary motivation is the desire to find an alternative other than the law that redounds to the welfare of the individual. Although the department is compelled to act in most situations, they will not necessarily use enforcement actions. Arrest can also be resorted to, in case it is beneficial to the individual, such as in cases of mercy arrests (e.g., arresting a homeless person so he or she will have shelter for the night).

The Do Nothing Style

This is a style where the department as a whole does not want to intervene, and even if they do, they will not do anything that would require them to do more work. This is not originally included in the work of Wilson, and it has not been empirically tested. Perhaps the reason for not finding this type of department is that a do nothing agency will suffer death as it is not performing any of its mandated functions (Figure 7.1).

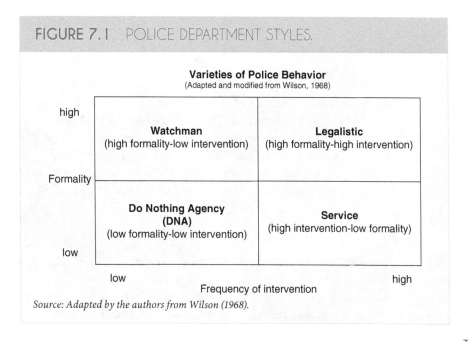

FIGURE 7.1 POLICE DEPARTMENT STYLES.

Varieties of Police Behavior
(Adapted and modified from Wilson, 1968)

Source: Adapted by the authors from Wilson (1968).

Police as Organizations

The police organization has been described as bureaucratic (Worrall & Schmalleger, 2018), hierarchical (Angell, 1971), and paramilitary (Caldero & Crank, 2011; Kraska, 2001, 2007; Kraska & Cubellis, 1997). As a bureaucracy, the police adhere to the principles that were laid out in the management literature. These principles include division of labor, merit promotion, specialization, among others. Thus, it has become the central feature in most police departments that each unit has specialized activities and observes the separation of these functional differentiations strictly. In addition, police departments observe merit not only for promotion, but initial entry to the police department (Discoverpolicing.org, (2020)).

The next characteristic of the police being hierarchical is embodied in several major principles. These principles include limited span of control, unity of command, and chain of command. It has been established that supervision becomes more effective if there is a rational number of employees being supervised (i.e., limited span of control). Unity and chain of command are established as means of having clear lines of authority and accountability. As policing is involved in the management and distribution of nonnegotiable coercive use of force (Klockars, 1985), it is imperative that police are appropriately guided and that clear lines of accountability are established. The communication is mostly top-down where only those that are in the chain receive such commands.

Finally, the police are paramilitary in nature where their mobilizations, operations, and traditions mimic the military from the use of the uniforms, movements, and ceremonies. This paramilitary character has been noted by researchers (Kraska, 2001, 2007) as important in achieving functional efficiency by the police. Paramilitarism has also been noted as important for morale and sense-making of the job that police officers do (Caldero & Crank, 2011; Kraska & Cubellis, 1997; Kraska & Kappeler, 1997).

Major Police Divisions

Every police organization seems to be functionally arranged under three major divisions: operational, administrative, and auxiliary services. However, these divisions are generally nonexistent in small departments. Thus, the operational units may perform administrative functions every now and then. Likewise, auxiliary services are sometimes contracted out. As the department becomes bigger, however, these divisions become more necessary.

The Operations Division

The operations division of a police department consists of those units that directly deliver safety services to the public. These are the ones who perform the essential function of the police organization in terms of crime fighting, service, or order maintenance. The operations units are normally reserved for sworn personnel. This division normally consists of two major units—patrol and investigation. Among bigger departments, they might have specialized units such as Special Weapons and Tactics (SWAT), Special Victims Unit (SVU), or community policing units.

The Administrative Division

The administrative division provides personnel services necessary for the organization to exist and operate. Examples of the units in this division are the training unit, planning office, human resources office, payroll services, among others. Employees in these units are combinations of sworn and nonsworn personnel. As a practice, however, personnel in the leadership positions of this division are mostly uniformed sworn personnel. The primary reason that heads of such units are mostly sworn personnel is due to the sensitive or confidential nature of some information that might come to their offices such as the intelligence officers and assets being paid for by the department. The personnel information of officers are also normally handled as confidential documents.

The Auxiliary Services Division

The auxiliary services division is sometimes referred to as support services. Units in this division provide services that maintain the building or equipment of the police departments. Examples of the services that are auxiliary in nature are the motor pool, inspections, engineering, chaplain, health, or sometimes house counsels.

They are not directly involved in any operations of the police department, nor are they providing administrative support for the personnel. Some believe that these functions should not be separated from the administrative functions, as their designations may not be apparent in small departments.

Major Police Operational Units

Patrol

Patrol has been called the backbone of policing. The majority of officers are assigned as patrols. Patrols are normally divided into three eight-hour shifts per day. In smaller departments, two twelve-hour shifts are being implemented. They are deployed geographically over their area of jurisdictions. Over the years, patrol has taken various forms such as foot patrol, motorized patrol, bike patrol, or mounted patrols. If they have the resources, police departments use all of these forms of patrol.

Several experiments have been conducted with patrol deployments. Some departments have random patrols where officers decide how they would go about patrolling their beats. Other departments employ directed patrol where officers are instructed where to patrol, or officers might be required to constantly communicate their locations during their shifts. Patrols have also been either proactive or reactive. Reactive patrols are mobilized only when a call for service comes through the department. Proactive patrols or preventive patrols are those that are situated in locations that can optimally deter crime or potentially apprehend a suspect when a crime occurs.

Types of Patrol

Patrol has taken various forms. Patrol was first conceived by Robert Peel to be done on foot. Over the years, due to technological developments and strides in management science, the police have experimented on and instituted various means of patrol–**foot, motorized, mounted**, and **technology**.

Foot Patrol

Foot patrol requires the police to circle their area of responsibility on foot. Adams (1971) suggested that foot patrol is the most effective type of patrol. Trojanowicz (1983) did not find foot patrol as effective against crime prevention. However, foot patrol has facilitated the development of better police community relations as it lessened the fear of crime in the neighborhood. In a more recent experiment of foot patrol in Philadelphia, researchers found foot patrol as significantly reducing violent crimes (Ratcliffe, Taniguchi, Groff, & Wood, 2011).

Motorized Patrol

This form of patrol takes different forms. The most popular of motorized patrol is the use of an automobile. Some jurisdictions, however, use other forms such as motor bikes, boats, or airplanes and helicopters. The use of these vehicles is based on the geographic territory of the police department as well as the mode of criminal activities. Jurisdictions that have bodies of water where criminal activities can happen, employ boats to patrol their areas. In big cities where heavy traffic situations occur, air patrols may be necessary.

Mounted Patrol

This form of patrol takes on different forms. Police officers might use a bicycle or an animal such as a horse to patrol. A bicycle patrol is more effective in getting into tight spaces or parks where cars may not be able to traverse. A horse patrol does not only serve the purpose of being able to access tight spaces, but also provides an additional advantage of being able to see over large crowds. Thus, horse patrol is most often used for rallies and other crowd control situations.

Technological Patrol

This type uses technology in order to have a watchful eye over the department's area of responsibility. This type takes the form of the use of drones, cameras or CCTVs, or radars. Technology is often used in places where physical access or presence may not always be available.

Forms of Patrol

The scientific management of patrol has been the preoccupation of the police. Patrol was used to have a quick response to an incident as well as to prevent crime. Several of these patrols have been experimented on over the years.

Reactive Patrol versus Proactive Patrol

Reactive patrol refers to situations where police officers wait for calls or incidents and then respond to the incident or call. **Proactive patrol** is a situation where the police on their own initiative patrol neighborhoods that they believe might potentially need their intervention prior to the occurrence of an incident.

One of the classic studies in the field is the Kansas City Preventive Patrol experiment (Kelling, Pate, Dickman, & Brown, 1974). In this study, the researchers tried to determine whether increasing patrol in the area even without an incident (proactive patrol) would experience less crime compared to those that only get police service when a call is made (reactive patrol). The experiment has shown that neither patrol areas had significant differences in property crime rates.

Random Patrol versus Directed Patrol

Random patrol demands that officers will have discretion on where to situate themselves during their shift. **Directed patrol** consists of a predetermined concentration of patrol efforts, or the officers are directed where to go during their patrol. The main difference between the two is the amount of discretion that an officer has during the shift. Directed patrol is sometimes conceptualized into aggressive patrols, hot spots, or saturation patrol. In aggressive patrol, officers are expected to make frequent stops of suspicious vehicles and people to uncover potential crimes. Saturation patrol is directed toward a specific area of the community to target individuals or groups that are most likely to be involved in crime. In both of these patrol tactics, field interrogation is the norm. A field interrogation is a temporary detention of a person in order to question a person about a suspicious circumstance.

Investigation

Investigations are those that are undertaken to ascertain the facts of a case as well as to identify and apprehend the suspect. Investigation normally includes two phases—(1) preliminary and (2) follow-up investigations. **Preliminary investigations** are normally conducted at the scene of the crime. It establishes potential suspects, victims, and witnesses to the crime. It also gathers facts and evidence at the scene of the crime. Normally, investigators or detectives are seldom involved in the preliminary investigations, but do more follow-up investigations. Preliminary investigations are first conducted by a responding officer whose primary duty is to apprehend suspects if present, assist victims, and gather and preserve evidence, including the initial interviews of witnesses, and the questioning of suspects if available. When the crime scene has been secured, the responding officer might call the investigation units, especially the crime scene investigators, to conduct the crime scene investigations. After these processes, the follow-up investigation kicks in.

Follow-up investigations involve two major tasks—the first is suspect identification and the other is suspect apprehension. For suspect identification, the police may use the Automated Fingerprint Identification System (AFIS), where latent prints found at the scene of the crime are entered into and compared with the sets stored in the database.

When suspects are not apprehended at the scene of the crime, investigators have to interview witnesses and gather evidence to identify the suspect. In this phase, several investigation practices are employed. One approach is the use of criminalistics. **Criminalistics** is the application of scientific techniques in the collection and analysis of physical evidence. This approach might include the lifting of fingerprints, ballistics examinations, DNA analysis, and crime analysis. The police use the Integrated Ballistics Identification System (IBIS) to identify the gun used and its registered owner.

Another investigation approach is **questioning or interrogation**. Here, the police bring in witnesses who can provide a description or draw a cartographic sketch of the suspect. They can also bring in potential suspects to conduct interrogations or potentially extract confessions. Suspect identification might also involve the surveillance of the potential suspect. Surveillances are normally done through a court-issued warrant. After the identity of the suspect has been established, the investigators need to locate the suspect and apply for a warrant of arrest to apprehend the suspect. **Psychological profiling** is another technique used by investigators to uncover series of crimes. Crimes that are normally subjected to this investigative tools are those involving serial offenders such as murderers, sex offenders, or arsonists.

Traffic

Traffic enforcement and accident investigation have become routine tasks for police officers. Thus, in most departments, a traffic unit is an essential component of policing. Traffic as a police operation involves three tasks:

- Enforcing laws pertaining to motor vehicles and their operation.
- The relief of congestion and the reduction of accidents.
- Enforcement of safety standards on the road.

Although traffic violations are essentially a shared function with regular patrols, traffic accident investigations are more scientific and specialized that police departments designate a trained and certified traffic investigator. If no trained traffic investigator exists, some departments enter into collaborations with other departments to seek the assistance from the state police in investigating traffic accidents.

Special Police Units

Several departments create specialized police units. One of the units that has gained prominence over the years is SWAT (Figure 7.2). According to Kraska and Kappeler (1997), SWAT teams have mushroomed in the US police departments. SWAT's engagements in critical incidents have likewise gradually increased. Aside from the SWAT, other specialized units have recently emerged in the major operations of the department. Thus, there are specialized patrol units such as hot-spots patrol officers, community policing officers, gang units, scene of the crime operatives, and so on. The investigation operations also have specialized units such as the special victims, serial crimes, vice squads, and counterterrorism. Among large departments, specialized units are more prominent, whereas smaller departments create ad-hoc specialized units from time to time.

FIGURE 7.2 FEMALE POLICE OFFICER SPECIAL WEAPONS AND TACTICS (SWAT) DURING POLICE OPERATIONS.

© getmilitaryphotos/Shutterstock.com

Modern Police Approaches

The police have become more scientific in their approach. In the current era, evidenced-based policing is vigorously being promoted. **Evidence-based policing** was first introduced by Lawrence W. Sherman (1998), where he advocated that police practices should be guided by research. Likewise, he expounded on the idea that research should focus on how their findings and evaluations could be integrated into policies and practices. Hence, researches and practitioners have witnessed the emergence of various police programs and interventions that are based on theory and research. Alongside this new approach, traditional police practices that are perceived as not having significant impact are slowly being replaced.

Community-Oriented Policing

Community-oriented policing or COP has been touted as the dominant and overarching philosophy for the modern police. The turbulent times of the 1960s and the perceived strained community relationships during that time ushered in this new approach in policing (Kelling & Moore, 1988; Williams & Murphy, 1990; Wilson & Kelling, 1982b).

Police officers have been considered as pariahs from the community they served in the 1960s–1970s. Furthermore, the segmentation within police departments among its different personnel have made the police become inefficient. Sherman, Milton, and Kelly (1973) advocated for team policing as a solution to these organizational deficits. **Team policing** has meant to deploy police officers in the communities to be accessible to the public. On top of local deployment, the team consisted of patrol officers, detectives, and other personnel necessary. The idea was to have collaboration among different units in the department and to be more efficiently accessible to the public. This was considered as a failed experiment and, as a result, it fizzled.

A new idea sprung up afterward that involved problem-solving. This new idea was dubbed as problem-oriented policing or POP (Goldstein, 1990). As POP was gaining traction, this new idea was overwhelmed by the much broader concept of COP. Hence, POP became a mere strategy for the COP philosophy.

The Meaning of COP

Several scholars have defined COP differently. Despite such differences, it is always emphasized that there is a proactive reliance on the community (Friedmann, 1996; Travis & Langworthy, 2008) where members are empowered to define their safety needs and sometimes allowed to take responsibility for providing and maintaining safety levels (Bayley & Shearing, 2001; de Guzman & Kim, 2017).

Perhaps the most popular definition of community policing is the one offered by Trojanowicz and Bucqueroux (1994). They defined community policing as . . .

> a philosophy of full service, personalized police where the same officer patrols and works in the same area on a permanent basis, from a decentralized place, working in proactive partnership with citizens to identify and solve problems.

COP Principles

Based on the previous definition, community era reformers have come up with several principles that encompass COP.

1. Consent: The actions and operations need to have the authorization from community members. This authorization comes from expressed documents such as the professional code, the statement of mission and purpose of the police, and the legal mandate that has been promulgated. Sometimes, this consent is tacit such as when the community initiates grievance actions, complaints, or dialogs and petitions.

2. Participation: The community must have extensive citizen support to the police. This participation may come from their willingness of performing their civic duties and reporting crimes or actively engaging in becoming witnesses during investigations.

3. The police must be all-purpose: Shilston (2015) laments the vagueness of this principle. However, over the years, the principle has come to mean that police should maintain a balance of the performance of all expected police functions and minimally satisfy these three main police functions of law enforcement, service, and order maintenance (Travis & Langworthy, 2008). This means that the police cannot compartmentalize themselves into just one function and use only one technology for solving community issues.

4. Accessible: Police departments must be available to the public. This principle has been embodied now in such practices as decentralization and responsive organizational structure. Access to police services should be equally available to all and police services should be equitably dispersed (i.e., those that need more police services should be given greater access to the police).

5. Citizen satisfaction: Skolnick (1993) has identified efficiency as one of the working personalities of the police. However, efficiency can sometimes sacrifice effectiveness and responsiveness. The unbalanced attainment of these objectives might lead to citizen satisfaction. Tyler (1990) adds the component of procedural justice as a necessary aspect of increasing police legitimacy and citizen satisfaction.

The Elements of COP

Gary Cordner's (1999) work on the essential elements of policing has been the most used reference for this topic (Box 7.1). The most important of these elements is the idea that community policing is a philosophy. As a philosophy, it is the guide for organizing and reforming the organization. He believes that the entire organization should value citizen input and provide personalized service using varieties of intervention presumably to provide solutions to the problem. The strategic and tactical dimensions of the element are envisioned to accomplish the goals of community policing. Thus, these dimensions prescribe several operational and behavioral components. The most important element is a face-to-face interaction that happens not only during crisis, but more importantly in normal times. The use of bike patrol is one of the innovations that was perceived to have increased this face-to-face interaction with the public (Figure 7.3). This strategy is supposed to enhance positive interactions, partnerships, and problem-solving in the community. More importantly, the strategic dimension seems to suggest changes in two paradigms with policing. One is crime prevention focus. This means that police should be more proactive in identifying potential crime precipitating conditions. The other is geographic focus. This means that police officers have more permanency in their beat assignments and stop juggling patrol around. This strategy is important in increasing face time, knowing the members of the community and their problems, and increasing more trust and cooperation from the public. Finally, Cordner believes that the entire organization should undergo some indoctrination and change management skills in order to reduce resistance from the personnel. It might also require the reorientation of the organizational structure in order to achieve more inter- and intraunit cooperation and communications. As noted by some scholars, communication is central to the development of police-community relations (Hunter, Barker, & de Guzman, 2018).

BOX 7.1 THE ELEMENTS OF COMMUNITY-ORIENTED POLICING.

Essential Elements of COP

1. The Philosophical Dimension
   citizen input
   broadened police function
   personalized service
2. The Strategic Dimension
   reoriented operations (face-to-face)
   geographic focus
   prevention emphasis
3. The Tactical Dimension
   positive interactions
   partnerships
   problem-solving
4. The Organizational Dimension
   reoriented structure (functions, hierarchy, communications)
   indoctrinated personnel
   change management

Source: Cordner (1999).

FIGURE 7.3 POLICE OFFICERS PATROL THE STREETS ON BICYCLE.

© James Greenshields/Shutterstock.com

Challenges and Issues with COP

Although COP has become the dominant police paradigm in the United States (Schmalleger & Worrall, 2018; Shilston, 2015; Wilson, 2006), scholars have noted several problems that still plague COP (Grinc, 1994; Kerley & Benson, 2000; Reisig & Parks, 2000, 2004; Schmalleger & Worrall, 2018; Walker, 1977; Williams & Murphy, 1990). Their critique hinges on the difficulty of measuring the effectiveness of COP due to the range, complexity, and development of community policing. Travis and Langworthy (2008) note that community policing is implemented in a variety of ways and for a variety of targets. These variations lead to the second critique, which is that citizen satisfaction with police performance can be difficult to conceptualize and quantify. The third critique lies in the elusive conceptualization of community. According to Schmalleger and Worrall (2018), communities are mostly based on interests and less on the geographic concept. Again, the satisfaction measures are not resident specific, but may include transient groups. Finally, authors noted that it is not a concept totally embraced among police managers. The police seem less willing to let go of their nontraditional image of police work. They remain legalistic and law enforcement oriented rather than order maintenance and service oriented. Thus, when 9/11 happened, the de-escalation of COP happened in most police departments (Kim & de Guzman, 2012).

Problem-Oriented Policing

The POP policing strategy has been proposed prior to the full-blown development of community-oriented policing. Indeed, the Community Oriented Policing Services (COPS) office has touted the strategy as integral to community policing. Problem-solving advocates for more permanent solutions to problems by addressing the ultimate cause of crime incidents (Eck & Spelman, 1987; Goldstein, 1990; Skolnick & Bayley, 1986). The POP approach assumes that several criminal or disorder incidents are precipitated by the same cause. Thus, the ideal strategy is for the police to address the ultimate cause of the problem (Eck & Spelman, 1987).

The POP Process

The Eck and Spelman (1987) model of problem-solving has been adopted as the process for doing POP. The SARA approach has also been promoted by the COPS as the model to follow for problem-solving. SARA, an acronym, is explained below:

S—Scanning. Refers to the gathering of data to identify if a problem exists and to describe the nature of the problem.

A—Analysis. Refers to the identification of persons involved and to document the scope of the problem. This stage of the process also investigates the geographic and temporal factors associated with the incidents. The ultimate outcome is the identification of the ultimate cause of the problem.

R—Response. It is at this stage where the police come up with possible solutions to the problem. At the inception of the practice, the police should provide the remedy or response. Recently, it has been advocated that community and other resource groups should be included in the implementation of the remedy.

A—Assessment. The police department should examine the impact of the intervention. Primarily, the symptoms of the problem (i.e., crime or disorder) should have been significantly reduced.

If no significant impact is seen, Eck and Spelman (1987) suggested that the police try to examine where the process might have gone wrong, or where some adjustments might be needed. It could be that the assessment was not thoroughly or appropriately done. The police can also examine if an alternative intervention should have been implemented instead. It was even suggested to go back to the initial stages of the process and determine whether more data need to be collected or the analyses were not adequate.

Broken Windows and Zero-Tolerance Policing

The broken windows approach (a.k.a. zero tolerance policing) is a crime prevention model propounded by Wilson and Kelling (1982). The basic premise of broken windows theory is that disorders in society would breed an environment where no one cares. In his earlier work, Wilson (1968) called this area where no one cares the zone of indifference. It is in this zone, according to Wilson, that criminals are more emboldened to commit crime because the communities are permissive, or they are afraid to get involved.

Police have operationalized broken windows as a metaphor for disorders in society. It is different from problem-solving policing as any form of disorder in broken windows should be addressed. It is also more proactive in its stance as the police will seek to use their initiative in addressing disorders in society.

The New York City Police Department (NYPD) has pushed this disorder policing model into zero-tolerance policing. Under the zero-tolerance model, police will vigorously enforce laws that involve disturbing the peace. However, the NYPD has only used arrests and banishment as tools for maintaining order. Due to this overreliance on a singular police tactic, zero tolerance is not widely regarded as a community policing approach.

Intelligence-Led Policing (ILP)

The International Association of Chiefs of Police (2005) has suggested that intelligence is not merely information gathering, but it should include the analysis of the collected data. Based on this description, we can define **intelligence** as information that has been analyzed and evaluated that provides a basis for action. Adopting this definition, it means that information can only be considered intelligence when it has been evaluated as coming from credible sources. The process of evaluation includes the determination of the authenticity or veracity of the information. This process is called the authentication of the information. After the information has been authenticated, the totality of information must be analyzed to determine whether the information could provide a potential target, when the attack will happen, where the attack potentially will happen, and how the attack would be executed.

Ratcliffe (2005) has come up with a rational model for intelligence-led policing (ILP). He said that the information from the criminal environment must be gathered and interpreted. The department must also come up with interventions and tactics on the bases of the information analyzed. The intelligence can then be used to influence decision-makers about the utility, practicality, and feasibility of the intervention. Such information can be used by decision-makers to develop policies that can impact the criminal environments. This model is known as the 3i (interpret, influence, impact) model of ILP (see Figure 7.4).

The International Association of Chiefs of Police (2005) identifies several key elements of ILP such as:

1. Making collection of intelligence and analysis of information as collaborative enterprise. The model should enjoin a comprehensive number of stakeholders and information.
2. Applying the principles and processes of community policing and POP. For example, it should use the SARA model in the analysis of events.

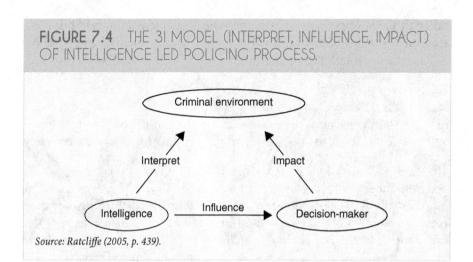

FIGURE 7.4 THE 3I MODEL (INTERPRET, INFLUENCE, IMPACT) OF INTELLIGENCE LED POLICING PROCESS.

Source: Ratcliffe (2005, p. 439).

3. Incorporating intelligence into the planning process.
4. Sharing and dissemination of information to key personnel and stakeholders.
5. Employing competent data analysis and sophisticated quality of data analysis technology.

Several police practices have already applied some of these principles. For example, CompStat demands the grassroots and extensive gathering and analysis of information using computing technology to assist in the interpretation of the data (McDonald, 2002). Another example was the onset of POP where the SARA model was clearly the center of the processing of the information. In other words, ILP enhances the current practices adding another component (i.e., processing and sharing of intelligence information), which for a long time has been strictly shared on a "need to know" basis. Under ILP, the process of dissemination is one of the key steps in the process (see Figure 7.5). Thus, it has become a norm for law enforcement units to access some of the intelligence databases.

Due to this new paradigm, we have experienced uses of intelligence surveillance information being merged with community surveys to verify the information and to design appropriate responses. To demonstrate the enhanced techniques, analyses of information have now incorporated the use of geographic information systems (GIS), network analyses, event analyses, and other scientific data processing approaches. The police have also utilized closed circuit television (CCTV), computing and mobile technology surveillance, and drones to gather more information. Thus, intelligence gathering has now combined both human and technological sources.

Tactical Intelligence versus Strategic Intelligence

The International Association of Chiefs of Police (2005, p. 3) has identified two key distinctions between tactical intelligence and strategic intelligence. The document states, "**Tactical intelligence** contributes directly to

FIGURE 7.5 THE INTELLIGENCE PROCESS.

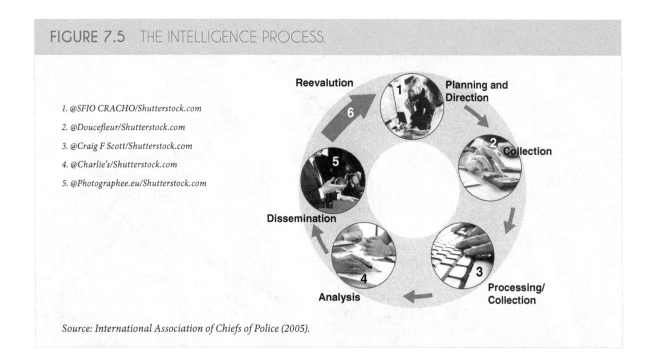

1. @SFIO CRACHO/Shutterstock.com

2. @Doucefleur/Shutterstock.com

3. @Craig F Scott/Shutterstock.com

4. @Charlie's/Shutterstock.com

5. @Photographee.eu/Shutterstock.com

Source: International Association of Chiefs of Police (2005).

the success of specific investigations. **Strategic intelligence** deals with 'big-picture' issues, such as planning and manpower allocation. Tactical intelligence directs immediate action, whereas strategic intelligence evolves over time and explores long-term, large-scope solutions."

The same document clarified the distinction between evidential intelligence and operational intelligence. It states that **evidential intelligence** refers to those information in which "certain pieces of evidence indicate where other evidence may be found. Evidential intelligence can help prove a criminal violation or provide leads for investigators to follow up. **Operational intelligence** is sometimes used to refer to intelligence that supports long-term investigations into multiple, similar targets. Operational intelligence is concerned primarily with identifying, targeting, detecting, and intervening in criminal activity (International Association of Chiefs of Police, 2005, p. 13)."

Levels of Intelligence

The National Institute of Justice (2005) has also categorized police departments into different intelligence capability levels. Their categorization is based on the extensiveness of the intelligence operations and network of the organization. The following is a description of these levels (International Association of Chiefs of Police, 2005, pp. 12–13).

Level 1 intelligence is the highest level ILP scenario wherein agencies produce tactical and strategic intelligence products that benefit their own department as well as other law enforcement agencies. The law enforcement agency at this level employs an intelligence manager, intelligence officers, and professional intelligence analysts. Examples of level 1 intelligence agencies include the High Intensity Drug Trafficking Area (HIDTA) Intelligence

Support Centers, the Financial Crimes Enforcement Network, and some state agencies that provide intelligence products, by request, to local law enforcement, such as the California Department of Justice, the Florida Department of Law Enforcement, the Arizona Department of Public Safety, and the Illinois State Police. Probably fewer than three hundred agencies in the United States operate at level 1. These agencies may have hundreds or even thousands of sworn personnel.

Level 2 intelligence includes police agencies that produce tactical and strategic intelligence for internal consumption. In other words, these agencies generally use intelligence to support investigations rather than to direct operations. Such agencies ILP may have a computerized database that is accessible to other departments, but they typically do not assign personnel to provide significant intelligence products to other agencies. These departments may have intelligence units and intelligence officers, analysts, and an intelligence manager. Some examples of level 2 intelligence agencies are state police agencies, large city police departments, and some investigating commissions. Agencies at this level may have hundreds to thousands of sworn personnel. Probably fewer than five hundred agencies in the United States operate at this level.

Level 3 intelligence is the most common level of intelligence function in the United States. It includes law enforcement agencies with anywhere from dozens to hundreds of sworn employees. These agencies may be capable of developing intelligence products internally, but they are more likely to rely on products developed by partner agencies, such as Regional Information Sharing Systems (RISS) centers, HIDTAs, federal intelligence centers, and state agencies. Some level 3 agencies may hire private intelligence analysts for complex cases. These types of departments do not normally employ analysts or intelligence managers, but they may have named one or more sworn individuals as their "intelligence officers" and may have sent them to intelligence and/or analytic training. Thousands of agencies nationwide are in this category.

Level 4 intelligence is the category that comprises most agencies in the United States. These agencies, often with a few dozen employees or less, do not employ intelligence personnel. If they assign someone to intelligence operations, that person generally has officer, gang officer, or counterterrorism officer status. Most are involved in a limited information-sharing network made up of county or regional databases. Some departments have received intelligence awareness training and may be able to interpret analytic products.

Focused Deterrence

Focused deterrence is one of the recent innovations in police intervention that incorporates ILP and COP. Briefly, **focused deterrence** strategies seek to change offender behavior by understanding underlying crime-producing dynamics and conditions that sustain recurring crime problems and by implementing a blended strategy of law enforcement, community mobilization, and social service actions (Kennedy, 1997, 2008). Direct communications of increased enforcement risks and the availability of social service assistance to target groups and individuals are the defining characteristics of focused deterrence programs. Brunson (2015) describes focused deterrence as being consistent with the POP framework and "rely on data driven intelligence gathering to identify carefully and target repeat, high-risk offenders for increased interagency law enforcement attention and individualized social service programming."

The Process of Focused Deterrence

Two major works have comprehensively described the process of focused deterrence—The High Point, North Carolina drug offender intervention and the Cincinnati Initiative for Reduction of Violence (CIRV). The processes of both programs contain elements of intelligence gathering, targeting serious and verified offenders, providing information to the victims and their families about the risk of full enforcement against the targeted offender, and consultation and solicitation of community support for the reformation of the offender. Due to its rehabilitative and nonaggressive law enforcement stances, this model has been referred to as "soft policing" or "reassurance policing."

In a focused deterrence intervention model in (North Carolina, Frabutt, Hefner, Di Luca, Shelton, & Harvey, 2010) report three key processes that are followed in succession.

1. **Information gathering and target identification.** Using community surveys, crime suspect data, and surveillance, the police department identified their targets.

2. **Notification.** The suspect, the suspects' family members, and community members were informed about the result of the information gathering and analysis that were done. This effort was done to achieve two ends: (1) to convince the offender that he or she would not be able to escape enforcement and (2) to muster support for the intervention that the police will do regardless of whether or not to arrest or divert the individual to a life of noncrime. Thus, family members and community are included in the process to convince the offender to accept the intervention.

3. **Resource delivery.** This stage occurs when the offender needed assistance in terms of looking for alternative livelihood, counseling, skills development, or education.

These processes are followed in various ways in different jurisdictions. However, the essential elements remain the same. In the CIRV (Engel, Tillyer, & Corsaro, 2013), the organization of the program intervention is more elaborate in Cincinnati as formal boards and councils were established. However, the intervention maintained the essential components of collaboration, information gathering, and resource allocations.

CompStat

CompStat is the use of computers to analyze crime statistics and to provide guidance on police concentration of efforts (MacDonald, 2002). CompStat emphasizes information-sharing, responsibility, and accountability, and improving effectiveness. It includes four generally recognized core components:

1. Timely and accurate information or intelligence
2. Rapid deployment of resources
3. Effective tactics
4. Relentless follow-up

The Bureau of Justice Assistance suggests that the legacy of CompStat can be seen in the significant changes that were made in three areas of the organization:

1. Information-sharing—CompStat helps to facilitate the flow of information between divisions and from the top-down. This enabled leaders to have a more holistic view of the entire organization.
2. Decision-making—CompStat helps in moving away from a hierarchical bureaucracy allowed for "taking the handcuffs off cops." Commanders were provided with greater authority.
3. Organizational culture—The agency became more creative, flexible, and better equipped to manage risk.

Challenges to Policing

Despite the growing sophistication of the police in performing their tasks, they still face major challenges in their policing environment. These challenges are brought about by the changing landscapes in US society and the police are caught in the middle of all of these changes.

Policing a Multicultural Society

The United States has undergone a paradigmatic change in its assimilation process (Caldero & Crank, 2011). In the past, there is a melting pot theory that was being implemented in the assimilation process. This assimilation process means that immigrants who come to the United States are expected to fully assimilate in society from language, customs, and way of life. Thus, it is mandatory that everyone looks, acts, and talks in basically uniform fashion. The new form of assimilation is designated by Caldero and Crank (2011) as the **distinctiveness theory**. In a nutshell, it is no longer a requirement that immigrants divest themselves of their culture, but that they could maintain those indigenous cultures in the assimilation process. Moreover, there is an expectation that the population and the government agencies need to adjust, tolerate, and accommodate them. Thus, police departments have instituted reforms in these endeavors. Some departments have begun issuing forms in different languages. Departments have also tried to recruit police officers that can communicate or liaison with the dominant immigrant group in their communities.

This new form of assimilation presents several challenges for the police. For one, the police might not be properly trained to engage and communicate with some of these new cultures (Caldero & Crank, 2004). Thus, street encounters can become more tenuous and have the potential for misunderstandings (Hunter et al., 2018). It is also incumbent for government agencies, including the police, to accommodate the needs of their constituents. The challenge is not the willingness of the police to accommodate this new assimilation paradigm, but the lack of resources to be effective in this new environment.

Policing and Terrorism

Police strategies against terror are anchored in a more collaborative and in-depth intelligence gathering. Since the outcome desired in the policing of terrorism is the prevention of an attack, a sophisticated gathering of intelligence and swift analysis of the information should be done so that the intelligence can be disseminated and acted upon (National Institute of Justice, 2005). Immediately after the 9/11 attacks, several scholars have begun questioning the appropriateness of community-oriented policing paradigm (Brown, 2007; Deflem, 2004; de Guzman, 2002; Friedmann & Cannon, 2007). Even the police activities and planning have changed after the 9/11 attacks (Lee, 2010). Kim and de Guzman (2012) have investigated the practice of community policing among local police agencies to test the hypothesis that police departments have shifted their priorities to homeland security policing (HSP). Compared to the earlier findings of Wilson (2006) that community policing is widely and vigorously practiced by police departments, Kim and de Guzman (2012) noted that a significant number of police departments have scaled down their community policing efforts. In fact, most resources coming from the federal government have been noted to have been diverted to counterterrorism measures.

COP versus HSP: Are they compatible?

This question was debated primarily by several quarters. Brown (2007) and Deflem (2004) believe that COP and HSP are compatible. Contrary to the ideas of compatibility of COP with HSP, de Guzman (2002) believes that COP is incompatible with HSP. His arguments are anchored in a fundamental principle of COP that tends to clash with HSP—trust. COP operates on the assumption that community members are mostly law abiding and well intentioned. This element of trust is not central to HSP, which operates on suspicion.

Some empirical studies have found that community can be effective against terrorism (Dunn et al., 2015). A group of scholars have investigated the use of COP and its influence of the satisfaction of a Muslim community with the strategy. The respondents did not produce a negative impact on their satisfaction with the program, but there was pronounced suspicion among pockets of the community members that were studied (Dunn et al., 2015). Thus, more studies are necessary to investigate this matter.

Police, Mass Media, and the Digital Media

Technological evolutions in society have major impact on police operations and strategies (de Guzman, Das, & Das, 2012). One of the most influential factors on innovations in policing is the influences of the mass media and the use of digital media, especially social media.

Mass Media's Impact on the Police

The relationship of the police with the mass media can sometimes become tenuous. Marsh (2014) has identified two types of mass media—the fictional media and the factional media. The fictional media is referred to as those that portray the police in fiction dramas or shows. It might also include print media that are included in such outlets as fiction novels and cartoons. Factional media are those that tend to portray the police as they perform their jobs in the real world. Hence, reality shows on TV such as COPS or 48 Hours are examples of these broadcast media. However, there are also factional information about the police, such as the news (print, digital, and broadcast) or interviews of police officers.

Marsh's (2014) findings are interesting. Several scholars have noted the so-called CSI effect of the mass media on citizen expectations about the police. The public have been conditioned to think that the most important part of police work is the use of forensic sciences. On the other hand, there is the other side known as the CNN or Fox effect. This latter effect means that portrayal of police activities only highlighted their worst behaviors. Alternatively, the TV show COPS portrays the police as extremely polite and highly professional workers that project the image of service-oriented police officers. According to Marsh (2014), these factional media present distorted images of the police. On one extreme, these factional shows portray the police as kind and service oriented. On the other extreme, the police are being portrayed in these shows as abusing their powers. He concluded by saying that fictional media portray the police in a more realistic and balanced way. Thus, it becomes amusing that fictional media does not really shape our rational expectations about the police. Instead, the factional media that should greatly shape our perceptions through the more realistic portrayal of police activities distort or slant our views about them.

Social Media Use by the Police

Social media refers to those self-run digital platforms such as Facebook, Twitter, YouTube, among others. These media have become an important tool for the police to reach the public. The advantage of these media is that the police have more control over their contents, they reach a wide audience, and sometimes, instantaneously. In 2010, the International Association of Chiefs of Police encouraged police departments to take advantage of social media in their operations (Jones & de Guzman, 2011). As a result, the police have tremendously increased their digital and social media presence (Jones, & de Guzman, 2011; Jones, de Guzman, & Kumar, 2011). However, the use of social media is sometimes relegated to mere information instead of a platform for collaborative endeavors (Jones et al., 2011). Today, a lot of police departments are using social media to communicate with citizens (de Guzman & Hunter, 2015). Worrall and Schmalleger (2018) have categorized COP strategies into crime control and prevention, informing citizens and engaging with citizens. The studies done on social media use by police indicate that police are primarily using these media for informational purposes (de Guzman & Hunter, 2015; Jones & de Guzman, 2011).

The Police Subculture, Ethics, and the Use of Force

The police have been considered to display a unique occupational subculture. Some scholars attribute the development of this culture to natural selection. This means that certain individuals who are imbued with distinct characteristics are naturally attracted to become police officers (Cole et al., 2018). Others believe that the police subculture is a product of socialization of those that enter the profession (Niederhoffer, 1969; Van Maanen, 1973). There is a belief that there are merits to both contentions. Perhaps, individuals who possess those characteristics are drawn to policing and these characteristics are reinforced by the profession.

A classic work by Van Maanen (1973) suggests that socialization is a more viable explanation for police culture. He argues that anybody who enters the police force is drawn into the profession by altruistic ideals of helping people. In fact, Caldero and Crank (2011) argue that these ideals are the source of noble cause corruption by the police. Eventually, police officers are socialized into the working personality and develop cynicism toward their job and the community they serve. Neiderhoffer (1969) predicted that such cynicism will primarily be responsible for two dysfunctional behaviors. One is that the disillusionment will lead to a police officer deciding to leave the service. The other form of adaptation is worse. He says that the officer might stay in the force, but he or she would participate in a delinquent subculture. Neiderhoffer (1969) suggests that the negative effects of cynicism can be alleviated by going back to the academy or by recommitting to the ideals of the profession.

Sheriff Clark Cottom is featured in this chapter as a career profile (see Box 7.2). He is an example of someone who was drawn to the profession at a very early age, but avoided the negative consequences of socialization in the job. Thus, his story is a case study for Van Maanen's (1973) thesis about the attraction and socialization of the police. All throughout his career, he maintained the ideals of the profession and he constantly recommitted himself to the ideals of the job. As a result, he avoided being cynical about his job. He remained optimistic that he could make a difference in people's lives, and he self-actualized his role as a helping professional in his job. Consequently, he did not leave his job and instead he sought positions that enabled him to make a difference in people's lives. Because he remained committed to the ideals

BOX 7.2 CAREER IN PROFILE

Sheriff Clark Cottom is the County Sheriff for Sullivan County in the state of Indiana. His passion for police service was inspired by a fireman at a very early age. Even before reaching his teen years, he was already committed to becoming a cop. He reached the pinnacle of his success becoming the top law enforcement officer in Sullivan County by being elected as Sheriff. His ascent to the top was a bit circuitous and it started at a young age. He started as a volunteer for the fire department. Eventually, he became a volunteer police officer. The career path he took is something he is proud of and would suggest as a path that aspiring police officers should take. He believes that starting as a volunteer inspired him to achieve more and his reminiscence of his past kept him motivated to achieve more.

Sheriff Cottom has a deep commitment to his job. Early on, he had already resigned himself to foregoing with holidays being a police officer. His reward comes in the joy of helping people and keeping society sage. He kept his ideals and his passion for helping people in whatever way. One of his most difficult jobs is informing families about their loved ones being involved in fatalities. He makes sure that he is the first to deliver the news to the family, even before the news announces the events. He takes it as his obligation to the families that he serves to be there in their hour of grief and be able to assist them in their trying times.

Photo courtesy of Jason P. Bobbitt

Sheriff Clark Cottom

Sullivan County, Indiana

He understands and embraces the utility of technology in his job. He considers mobile devices to be both useful for crime solution, but at the same time might compromise other people's safety. He has relied on information embedded in mobile technology and computers to solve some of the most challenging crimes he has investigated. At the same time, he acknowledges the dangers that new technology can present to safety, such as the technology being the cause of accidents, victimization, or perpetration of crimes.

He epitomizes the idealist, being someone who never fails to do his best in his job and holds faith in the ability of a person to do reform. One of his noted programs involves an appreciation day for inmates in his county. He takes delight when offenders are touched by the acts of kindness that he and his police officers extend to them. These beliefs and activities have provided him with passion to do his job. By doing these activities, Sheriff Cottom avoided the path that Van Maanen[162] says leads to cynicism and eventually becoming disillusioned with the job. By maintaining his idealist attitude and his constant recommitment to the profession, he was able to persist in the force and reach the pinnacle of success.

of his job, he avoided the pitfalls of being part of a delinquent subculture in policing. His strategy exemplifies the method by which a police officer avoids the negative consequences of cynicism.

Discretion in Policing

Muir (1977) describes the police as street-corner politicians. As part of their job, they find themselves constantly making decisions. Policing is a unique profession because the lowest workers (i.e., patrol officers) are given the widest latitude of discretion. Likewise, the use of their discretion can have grave consequences. The danger of reposing this discretion to the lowest level of employees is the potential for committing mistake in judgments. This judgment is also being granted to someone who may not have had significant and long experience in the job that may influence those choices of actions. Indeed, it has been found that more seasoned officers use better judgment and produce better results compared to their younger and less experienced counterparts.

Despite these risks, the granting of street-level discretion to police officers is necessary for both their safety and the sound administration of justice. Every situation is different and the police officer must be given all the available arsenal to resolve the situation, including the use of force. Also, it is impossible to micromanage the police on the streets (Hunter et al., 2018).

On the contrary, discretion in the hands of malevolent officers could be dangerous to society. Officers work alone and they have the capacity to cover their actions from the eyes of the public (Skolnick, 1993). Thus, it is necessary to control the officer's use of discretion. Several measures have been implemented in order to advance this objective. One is to fashion discretion by limiting its use in specific situations. For example, some departments have issued mandatory arrest policies for domestic violence and driving under the influence situations. Others use technology to control the use of discretion and enable the review of the use of their discretion. One of the most recent technologies for this effort is the use of body-worn cameras (BWCs).

The Use of Force and Misconduct

The use of force is a controversial aspect of policing. Force has been conceptualized as including verbal and physical dimensions. However, none is more controversial than the use of physical force by the police. Although the use of force raises the greatest concern, it has been noted that the use of physical force in policing is rare. It has even been noted that in rare instances when force was used, the police have been found to have used their power in a justifiable and necessary way.

The use of force by the police is categorized into three types:

1. Legal and necessary use of force. This is a situation where the police are authorized to use force because it requires the enforcement of the law or the maintenance of order. It also demands that the force used is reasonable to control the situation.
2. Legal but excessive use of force. This is a middle ground situation. There is a legally justifiable reason for the police to intervene such as a law is being broken or a disturbance of order is happening that may lead to crime. However, the force used goes beyond after the threat has been neutralized or that it is an overwhelming force to control the situation.

3. Illegal and unnecessary use of force. This is where the police have no legal justification to intervene and they use force. In this situation, it is not necessary if the force is calibrated. The premise is that force is used when there is no reason to do so.

Police Misconduct

Police misconduct is a catch-all phrase that includes violating the code of conduct of the profession all the way to the act of committing a crime. Police misconduct would open the department or the police officer for civil liability or an initiation of a criminal proceeding against a police officer. Ordinarily, police have absolute immunity when damages are incurred in the legitimate performance of their duty. However, courts have taken the doctrine of qualified immunity where the police need to show that the damages incurred are without malice or negligence to be excused from liabilities. Among the variety of misconduct that police are engaged in, corruption is the focal concern in society. Corruption has been classified by the Wickersham Commission as committed by grass eaters or meat eaters. Grass eaters are those that commit corruption as an incidental matter. They do not actively seek financial gains through the use of their office, but they do not reject bribes or any other perks that are offered to them voluntarily. Meat eaters are those who use their authority and seek opportunities to use their power and influence in order to elicit financial favors from their victims.

Use of Force as a Conditioned Response

One of the most influential findings about the working personality of the police is suspiciousness and being authoritarian. This tendency by the police has been explained by Smith and Alpert (2007) as a conditioned response that is a product of social conditions. Likewise, the working personality has been explained by Skolnick (1993) as a product of policing being perceived as dangerous and the importance of taking control. In these regards, Skolnick (1993) states that the working personality of the police is defined by **danger and authority**. The perception that police work is dangerous leads the police to be suspicious. The police locker rooms are replete of this warning that no one should be trusted and to search thoroughly. Muir (1977) argued that the cost of not being suspicious might be an officer's life. Thus, suspiciousness serves as a survival tool for the police and becomes part of their psyche.

Maintaining control is another aspect of police personality. As such, the police take tremendous efforts that their authority is not questioned. An undermining of their authority during an encounter is a disturbing situation for the police. Sykes and Brent (1980) noted that the entry and exit of the police to a situation are controlled in such a way that their authority is intact all throughout the process of police intervention. Thus, they noted that the police encounter is actually a "taking control" situation.

Police are constantly challenged about their lack of legitimacy in society (Tyler, 1990) that it becomes imperative for them to constantly assert this authority. When their authority is questioned, they sometimes resort to the use of force in order to gain compliance. The use of force is a calibrated response to an affront to their authority (Sykes & Brent, 1980).

Control of the Police

The police are heavily controlled institutions in society. This concern for control has been prominently voiced, even in the inception of professional policing in London (Travis & Langworthy, 2008). The source of control of the police comes from all directions and forms. Figure 7.6 categorized these controls based on the adjudication process involved and the locus of such control. There are controls that are internal and external to the department. The processes for such control also vary where some are adversarial and others are nonadversarial. Figure 7.6 illustrates these different forms of control (de Guzman, 2001). Two forms of control seem to be very influential in controlling police behavior. The first is the judicial control and the other is the administrative control.

Judicial Control

The courts have been very influential in their control of the police. Judicial control comes mostly in the form of judicial decisions, particularly on questions of constitutionality of police conduct. Certainly, there is a long line of jurisprudence that have made a major impact on the police. The most popular is the guidelines laid out in *Miranda v. Arizona* (1966), which is known as the Miranda rule. Under the Miranda rule, it is required for the police to inform the offender of their constitutional rights at the moment of arrest or during custodial investigation. The other influential judicial ruling is known as the exclusionary rule. Under the exclusionary rule, any evidence that is obtained in violation of the person's constitutional rights is not admissible as evidence in a court proceeding (1914). As a result of these rulings, the police have been more careful in their apprehension, interrogation, and investigation of suspects. Similarly, stops have been regulated by the courts in the leading case of *Terry v. Ohio* (1968) where police are only allowed to detain a person within a reasonable time and apply only a pat-down search. The courts have also laid down the levels of proof for different police intervention decisions. Thus, probable cause is needed for arrest situations and reasonable suspicion is required for a temporary stop (Figure 7.6).

The Administrative Control

Two of the most influential informal controls on the police are the use of policies, rules, or the use of an investigatory unit known as the internal affairs unit. It has been noted by Wilson (1968) that the chief is the most

FIGURE 7.6 TYPOLOGY OF POLICE CONTROL MODELS.

	External	Internal
Non-adversarial	Legislatures Executives Police commissions Ombudsperson Media/Watchdogs	Rule and Regulations Professionalization Supervision Compstat
Adversarial	Courts Civilian review boards	Internal Affairs Inspectorate Trial Boards

Process (vertical axis)

Location of Control (horizontal axis)

Source: de Guzman (2001, p.73).

influential person when it comes to controlling police behavior. The wishes of the chief are normally expressed through the policies, procedures, internal memoranda, and rules and regulations within the department.

Internal affairs is one of the most dreaded investigatory agencies in the police department. Compared to other disciplinary agencies, the internal affairs are more proactive and have been found to find police officers accountable and give out more punitive sanctions compared to other agencies such as civilian review boards or ombudspersons (de Guzman, 2001).

These two forms of control do not negate the impact of other controls. More recently, professional organizations such as the International Association of Chiefs of Police through the requirements of accreditation have instituted reforms and controlled departments across the country. The federal government's enforcement of civil and political rights has precipitated the use of consent decrees. Consent decrees are court-ordered documents to force departments to comply with certain organizational and personnel standards. These decrees have also controlled police departments.

Mechanisms of control are constantly evolving. Despite the multiplicity of controls, communities are still uneasy about police exercise of their powers. The current protests and mass movements against police brutality are solid proof of this unease. These concerns about police abuse of power were echoed at the inception of the creation of formal police in London and still reverberate up to now.

Comprehension Check

1. Differentiate the 3 main functions of the police.
2. Explain the different styles of policing.

3. Describe the essential units of a police department and the specific functions of each major units.

4. What are current innovations being used by the police in the performance of their functions?

5. Explain the major challenges that police officers face in the performance of their functions.

References

Adams, T. F. (1971). *Police patrol*. Englewood Cliffs, NJ: Prentice-Hall Inc.

Angell, J. (1971). Toward an alternative to the classic police organizational arrangement. *Criminology, 9*, 185–207.

Bayley, D. H. (2001) *Democratizing the police abroad: What to do and how to do it.* Washington, DC: U.S. Department of Justice.

Bayley, D., & Shearing, C. (2001). *The new structure of policing: Description, concpetualization, and research agenda.* Washington, DC: National Institute of Justice, Office of Justice Programs.

Brown, B. (2007). "Community policing in post-September 11 America: A comment on the concept of community-oriented counterterrorism." *Police Practice & Research, 8*, 239–251.

Brunson, R. K. (2015). "Focused deterrence and improved police-community relations: Unpacking the proverbial "black box"." *Criminology & Public Policy, 14*(3), 507–514.

Caldero, M. A., & Crank, J. P. (2004). *Police ethics: Corruption of a noble cause* (2nd ed.). Cincinnati, OH: Anderson.

Caldero, M. A., & Crank, J. P. (2011). *Police ethics: A corruption of a noble cause.* New York, NY: Taylor & Francis.

Cao, L., & Dai, M. (2006). "Confidence in the police: Where does Taiwan rank in the world?" *Asian Journal of Criminology, 1*(1), 71–84.

Cao, L., Huang, L., & Sun, I. S. (2016). "From authoritarian policing to democratic policing: A case study of Taiwan." *Policing and Society, 26*(6), 642–658.

Cole, G. F., Smith, C. F., & DeJong, C. (2018). *Criminal justice in America* (9th ed.). Boston, MA: Cengage Learning.

Cordner, G. W. (1999). "The elements of community policing." In G. W. Cordner & L. K. Gaines (Eds.), *Policing perspectices: An anthology* (pp. 137–149). Beverly Hills, CA: Roxbury Publishing.

de Guzman, M. C. (2001). *Integrity, legitimacy, efficiency, and impact: Do all these matter in the civilian review of the police?* Unpublished dissertation, University of Cincinnati, Cincinnati, OH.

de Guzman, M. C. (2002). "The changing roles and strategies of the police in time of terror." *ACJS Today, 22*(3), 8–13.

de Guzman, M. C., Das, A. M., & Das, D. K. (2012). *The evolution of policing: Worldwide Innovations and insights.* Boca Raton, FL: CRC Press/Taylor and Francis.

de Guzman, M. C., & Hunter, R. D. (2015). *Social media and police: Technology uses and challenges*. In Research Presentation during the Annual Conference of the Criminal Justice Association of Georgia, Morrow, GA.

de Guzman, M. C., & Kim, M. (2017). "Community hierarchy of needs and policing models: Toward a new theory of police organizational behavior." *Police Practice & Research: An International Journal, 18*(4), 339–365.

Discoverpolicing.org (2020). Skills and Abilities. Retrieved from https://www.discoverpolicing.org/about-policing/skills-and-abilities/ on June 1, 2020.

Dunn, K. M., Atie, R., Kennedy, M., Ali, J. A., O'Reilly, J., & Rogerson, L. (2015). "Can you use community policing for counter terrorism? Evidence from NSW, Australia." *Police Practice & Research: An International Journal, 17*(3), 196–211.

Eck, J., & Spelman, W. (1987). "Who you gonna call? The police as problem busters." *Crime and Delinquency, 33*, 31–52.

Engel, R. S., Tillyer, M. S., & Corsaro, N. (2013). "Reducing gang violence using focused deterrence: Evaluating the Cincinnati Initiative to Reduce Violence (CIRV)." *Justice Quarterly, 30*, 403–439.

Fogelson, R. M. (1977). *Big-city police*. Cambridge, MA: Harvard University Press.

Frabutt, J. M., Hefner, M. K., Di Luca, K. L., Shelton, T. L., & Harvey, L. K. (2010). "A street-drug elimination initiative: The law enforcement perspective." *Policing: An International Journal of Police Strategies & Management, 33*(3), 452–472.

Friedmann, R. R. (1996). "Community policing: Some conceptual and practical considerations." *Home Affairs Review, 34*(6), 114–123.

Friedmann, R. R., & Cannon, W. J. (2007). "Homeland security and community policing: Competing or complementing public safety policies." *Journal of Homeland Security and Emergency Management, 4*(4), 1–22.

Goldstein, H. (1990). *Problem-oriented policing*. New York, NY: McGraw-Hill.

Grinc, R. (1994). "Angels in marble: Problems in stimulating community involvement in community policing." *Crime and Delinquency, 40*, 437–68.

Hunter, R. D., Barker, T., & de Guzman, M. C. (2018). *Police community relations and the administration of justice* (9th ed.). New York, NY: Pearson.

International Association of Chiefs of Police (2005). *Intelligence led policing: The new intelligence architecture*. Washington, DC: Bureau of Justice Assistance.

Jones, M. A., & de Guzman, M. C. (2011). "E-policing: The value of police websites for citizen empowered participation." In E. Downey, C. D. Ekstrom, & M. A. Jones (Eds.), *E-government website development: Future trends and strategic models* (pp. 211–227). Hershey, PA: Information Reference Service, IGI Global.

Jones, M. A., de Guzman, M. C., & Kumar, K. S. (2011). "Using web 2.0 as a community policing strategy: An examination of United States municipal police departments." In E. Downey & M. A. Jones (Eds.), *Public service, and web 02.0 technologies: Future trends in social media*. Hershey, PA: Information Reference Service, IGI Global.

Kelling, G. L., & Moore, M. H. (1988)."The evolving strategy of policing." *Perspectives on Policing, 4*, 1–16.

Kelling, G. L., Pate, A., Dickman, D., & Brown, C. (1974). *The Kansas City preventive patrol experiment*. Washington, DC: Police Foundation.

Kennedy, D. (1997). "Pulling levers: Chronic offenders, high crime settings, and a theory of prevention." *Valparaiso University Law Review, 31*(2), 449–484.

Kennedy, D. (2008). *Deterrence and crime prevention*. New York, NY: Routledge.

Kerley, K. R., & Benson, M. L. (2000). "Does community-oriented policing help build stronger communities?" *Police Quarterly, 3*(1), 46–69.

Kim, M., & de Guzman, M. C. (2012). "Police paradigm shift after the 9/11 terrorist attacks: The empirical evidence from the United States municipal police departments." *Criminal Justice Studies: A Critical Journal of Crime, Law and Society, 25*(4), 323–342.

King, W. R. (2014). "Organizational failure and disbanding of local police agencies." *Crime and Delinquency, 60*(5), 667–692.

Klockars, C. B. (1985). *The idea of police* (2nd ed.). Beverly Hills, CA: Sage.

Kraska, P. B. (2001). *Militarizing the American criminal justice system: The changing roles of the armed forces and the police*. Boston, MA: Northeastern University Press.

Kraska, P. B. (2007). "Militarization and policing: Its relevance to 21st century police." *Policing, 1*(4), 501–513.

Kraska, P. B., & Cubellis, L. J. (1997). "Militarizing mayberry and beyond: Making sense of American paramilitary policing." *Justice Quarterly, 14*(4), 607–629.

Kraska, P. B., & Kappeler, V. E. (1997). "Militarizing American police: The rise and normalization of paramilitary units." *Social Problems, 44*(1), 1–18.

Landau, T. (1996). "Policing and security in four remote aboriginal communities: A challenge to coercive models of policing." *Canadian Journal of Criminology, January, 38*, 1–32.

Lee, J. V. (2010). "Policing after 9/11: Community policing in an age of homeland security." *Police Quarterly, 13*, 347–366.

Manning, P. K. (2010). *Democratic policing in a changing world*. Boulder, CO: Paradigm.

Marsh, I. (2014). "Representations of the police in the British media: Hard cops and soft cops." In M. C. de Guzman, D. K. Das, & A. M. Das (Eds.), *The evolution of policing: Worldwide Innovations and Insights*, (pp. 33–347). Boca Raton, FL: CRC Press/Taylor and Francis.

McDonald, P. (2002). *Managing police operations: Implementing the New York crime control model CompStat*. Belmont, CA: Wadsworth/Thompson Learning.

Miranda v. Arizona, 386 U.S. Supreme Court (1966).

Muir, L. K. (1977). *Police: Street corner politicians*. Chicago, IL: Chicago University Press.

National Institute of Justice. (2005). *Intelligence-led policing: The new intelligence architecture*. Washington, DC: Bureau of Justice Assistance.

Niederhoffer, A. G. (1969). *Behind the shield: The police in urban society*. Garden City, NY: Anchor Books.

Ratcliffe, J. H., Taniguchi, T., Groff, E. R., & Wood, J. D. (2011). "The Philadelphia foot patrol experiment: A randomized controlled trial of foot patrol effectiveness in violent crime hotspots." *Criminology, 49*(3), 795–831.

Rattclife, J. (2005). "The effectiveness of police intelligence management: A New Zealand study.' *Police Practice and Research: An International Journal, 6*(5), 435–451.

Reisig, M. D., & Parks, R. B. (2000). "Experience, quality of life, and neighbourhood context." *Justice Quarterly, 17,* 607–629.

Reisig, M. D., & Parks, R. B. (2004). "Can community policing help the truly disadvantaged?" *Crime & Delinquency, 50*(2), 139–167.

Schmalleger, F., & Worrall, J. L. (2018). *Policing* (3rd ed.). New York, NY: Pearson.

Sherman, L. W. (1998). *Evidenced-based policing.* Washington, DC: Police Foundation.

Shilston, T. (2015). "Democratic policing, community policing, and the fallacy of conflation in international development missions." *International Journal of Police Science & Management, 17*(4), 207–215.

Skolnick, J. H. (1993). *Justice without trial* (3rd ed.). Upper Saddle River, NJ: Prentice Hall.

Skolnick, J. H., & Bayley, D. H. (1986). *The new blue line: Innovation in six American cities.* New York, NY: The Free Press.

Smith, M. R., & Alpert, G. (2007). "Explaining police bias: A theory of social conditioning and illusory correlation." *Criminal Justice and Behavior, 34*(10), 1262–1283.

Sykes, R., & Brent, E. (1980). "The regulation of interaction by the police." *Criminology, 18*(2), 182–197.

Terry v. Ohio 392 U.S. 1 (1968).

Travis, L. F., & Langworthy, R. H. (2008). *Police in America: A balance of forces.* Upper Saddle River, NJ: Pearson.

Trojanowicz, R. C. (1983). "An evaluation of neighborhood foot patrol program." *Journal of Police Science and Administration, 11,* 110–119.

Trojanowicz, R. C., & Bucqueroux, B. (1994). *Community policing: How to get started.* Cincinnati, OH: Anderson.

Tyler, T. (1990). *Why people obey the law.* New Haven, CT: Yale University Press.

Van Maanen, J. (1973). "Observations on the making of policemen." *Human Organizations, 32,* 407–418.

Walker, S. L. (1977). *A critical history of police reform: The emergence of police professionalism.* Lexington, MA: Lexington Books.

Weeks v. U.S., 232 U.S. 383 U.S. Supreme Court (1914).

Williams, H., & Murphy, P. V. (1990). "The evolving strategy of the police: A minority view." In V. Kappeler (Ed.), *The police and society: Touchstone readings.* Prospect Heights, IL: Waveland Press.

Wilson, J. Q. (1968). *Varieties of police behavior: The management of law and order in eight communities.* Cambridge, MA: Harvard University Press.

Wilson, J. Q. (2006). *Community policing in America.* New York, NY: Taylor & Francis.

Wilson, J. Q., & Kelling, G. L. (1982a). "Broken windows." *Atlantic Monthly, 211,* 29–38.

Wilson, J. Q., & Kelling, G. L. (1982b). "Broken windows: The police and neighborhood safety." *Atlantic Monthly, 249*(3), 29–38.

Worrall, J. L., & Schmalleger, F. (2018). *Policing* (3nd ed.). New York, NY: Pearson.

© blurAZ/Shutterstock.com

The Judicial System

LEARNING OBJECTIVES

After reading this chapter, the student should be able to

1 Describe the dual structure of the US court system

2 Explain the adversarial process

3 Discuss the courtroom workgroup and its various functions

4 Understand problem-solving courts

Introduction

The express purpose of our judicial system is to uphold due process and the legal rights of the accused individual. The judiciary is the branch of government that interprets the law. Courts resolve disputes by applying the law to the facts specific to each case, independently and impartially. It is the responsibility of the judiciary to resolve conflicts between individuals, the government and the governed, individuals and corporations, and organizations (both public and private). Everyone involved in the court process must be treated equally and fairly. The processing of cases and the application of the law should be predictable and consistent as facts are applied to individual cases.

© Alexander Kirch/Shutterstock.com

In this chapter, we discuss the dual structure of the US judicial system, including both the federal and state court systems. Then, we describe the adversarial process. We also identify the primary actors involved in the courtroom work group and examine their functions. Finally, we explore problem-solving courts and their role in our criminal justice system.

Structure of the US Court System

While many other countries have a single national court system, the United States has a dual court system. This means that we have separate federal and state court systems that are organized into separate hierarchies and handle legal matters throughout the country.

In both the state and federal systems, cases are initially filed and tried in courts of original jurisdiction. The jurisdiction of these courts can be based off of geographic location or subject matter. Then, each system has intermediate appellate courts, where appeals from the trial courts are heard. An appeal is a claim that the lower court made some mistake of law. Typically, the losing party is entitled to one appeal as a matter of right. At the highest level, each court system has a supreme court. Supreme courts hear appeals from the appellate courts. These appeals are usually discretionary in nature, meaning that the court can choose whether or not to hear the appeal.

Federal Courts

The US federal court system was created in Article III of the US Constitution. Additionally, Article III establishes the jurisdiction of federal courts, or the types of cases they may hear. In the US, there are 94 federal judicial districts

© Nagel Photography/Shutterstock.com

organized into 13 regional circuits, each of which has a court of appeals, and one Supreme Court (United States Department of Justice, 2018). A court may hear and decide only those cases that fall under the court's jurisdiction, which is established by statute or constitution. The jurisdiction of the federal court system is much more limited than that of state courts, and is restricted to only those cases that are expressly listed in Article III as being within their "judicial power." Once a case begins in a particular system (state or federal), it almost always stays in that system throughout the entire case, including on appeal. One exception to this is if a case in state court contains a significant issue of federal law, it may be appealed to the US Supreme Court after being heard by the state supreme court. Interestingly, the concept of double jeopardy, where a defendant may not be tried twice for the same charge, does not apply between federal and state government. In other words, if an individual is acquitted of a crime in the state system, it is possible that the federal government could file charges against the defendant for the same crime if the act is also illegal under federal law.

Article III of the Constitution provides for a Supreme Court and gives Congress the authority to establish other, lower courts. The first Congress established the Supreme Court of the United States, and a system of trial courts and appellate courts. As such, the federal court system has three main levels: district courts, circuit courts of appeal, and the Supreme Court of the United States. District courts are the general trial courts of the federal court system. They handle both criminal and civil trials. Circuit courts are the first level of appeal. Once a case has been decided by the federal district court, the case can be appealed to a federal court of appeal, or circuit court. These appeals are heard by a panel of three circuit court judges. Both parties file "briefs," which argue why the trial court's decision should be "affirmed" (upheld) or "reversed." Then, the lawyers for both sides make oral arguments before the court and answer questions asked by the judges.

The Supreme Court of the United States is the highest level of appeal in the federal system and the highest court overall in the American judicial system. Appeals to the US Supreme Court are discretionary, meaning the Court has complete freedom of choice in deciding whether to hear a particular case, with the exception of capital cases. Once the petitioner, or the person bringing the appeal, files a petition for a writ of certiorari, it takes a vote from at least four out of the nine justices to grant the petition and hear the case. If the writ is not granted, the lower court's opinion stands. The Supreme Court meets in Washington, DC, and conducts its annual term from October to late June. Out of the more than 7,000 cases it is asked to review each year, the Supreme Court agrees to hear only about one hundred cases annually (The Supreme Court of the United States).

© Brandon Bourdages/Shutterstock.com

All federal judges—and, in the case of the Supreme Court, "justices"—are appointed by the President of the United States and are confirmed by a majority vote of the Senate. They serve a life term, although they can retire or resign earlier, and can only be removed for serious offenses through the impeachment process.

Most recently, we saw the retirement of Supreme Court Justice Anthony Kennedy in July 2018. Justice Kennedy was a critical swing vote in several cases, as he held liberal views on issues such as gay rights, abortion, and the death penalty, but also helped conservatives block gun control measures and reduce voting rights. When a justice retires, resigns, or dies, it then becomes the responsibility of the President of the United States to nominate a replacement and the Senate to confirm the President's appointment. In this case, a conservative justice could jeopardize some landmark Supreme Court precedents on a variety of social issues where Justice Kennedy tended to side with his liberal colleagues.

In fact, this is precisely what we have seen with the filling of this recent vacancy. President Donald Trump nominated, and—in a controversial decision—the Senate voted to confirm, conservative Brett Kavanaugh by a vote of 50–48. Justice Kavanaugh took the oath of office the same day, October 6, 2018.

State Courts

© DW labs Incorporated/Shutterstock.com

Both Article VII and the Tenth Amendment to the US Constitution provide that state courts have the right to hear and decide legal matters that are not expressly under federal jurisdiction. The US Constitution also gives each state independent power to decide both the structure and procedure of the state court system. Most states have a three-tiered system that includes trial courts, intermediate appellate courts, and the court of last resort (the state supreme court). The lowest level of court in the state judicial system is the trial court, where cases and lawsuits typically originate. Most state courts are courts of general jurisdiction, meaning that they can hear most types of cases. Trial courts of general jurisdiction will usually handle both criminal and civil cases. Some trial courts, however, are courts of special or limited jurisdiction, which handle certain types of cases, such as traffic, juvenile, or family.

The appeals process also varies by state, but in the typical three-tiered system, the intermediate appellate court will usually review verdicts handed down by juries or the opinions of judges in the trial courts. These cases are heard on a limited basis and must meet certain criteria in order to be considered.

The state's highest court—the "court of last resort"—is the state's supreme court. Indeed, some states only have one level of appeals, and so in these states, appeals of trial court decisions go straight to the supreme court. The only available appeal after a decision is made by the state supreme court is to the US Supreme Court. However, as you learned earlier, the US Supreme Court only agrees to hear a very small percentage of cases.

While federal judges are appointed to their positions, most state trial court judges are elected into their positions by the general public. State appellate justices are usually appointed by the state's governor or legislatures, but are also in some cases elected by voters. State courts usually employ a large number of support staff. In addition to private assistants, law clerks, court reporters, and bailiffs, the clerk of the court performs a variety of important duties including posting legal notices, subpoenaing witnesses, summonsing and preparing juries, and maintaining court records.

Setting and Following Precedent

All courts must follow precedent set by courts above them. Put more simply, when issuing a decision on a similar issue, the court must follow any rulings made by courts of a higher level. All courts, both in the federal system and the state system, must follow any precedent set by the US Supreme Court. State courts are required to follow precedent set by the US Supreme Court and the Federal Courts of Appeal for issues regarding federal law, but not issues of state law. Therefore, each state supreme court is left to interpret the laws of its state as it sees fit, provided it does not violate the US Constitution. All lower courts in the state must follow the state supreme court precedent on issues regarding state law, as must federal courts in the state.

The Adversarial Process

In the United States, all state and federal courts follow an **adversarial process,** wherein lawyers for opposing sides represent their clients' best interests. Most other countries use an **inquisitorial process,** where the judge takes an active role in examining evidence and investigating the facts of the case. In an adversarial process, both sides—the prosecution and the defense—formulate arguments and offer their cases to an impartial judge (and possible jury) by presenting evidence and challenging the arguments

Courtroom
Lorem ipsum dolor sit amet,
sed illud percipit interesset .

© Macrovector/Shutterstock.com

and evidence of the opposing side in an attempt to uncover the truth. You will learn more about the trial process in Chapter 9.

The Courtroom Work Group

The various actors that make up the **courtroom work group** fulfill many functions, and their roles are interdependent. Although each individual has specialized functions to perform, incentives and shared goals influence the manner in which the individual members fulfill their duties. Such incentives and shared goals serve as motivation to maintain a cooperative courtroom work group, despite the adversarial process followed in our trial courts (Worden, 1995). The three primary players included in the courtroom work group are the judge, the prosecutor, and the defense attorney, all of whom must work together to move cases through the court system. Interaction and cooperation must take place between the various actors of the courtroom work group so that they can process the large number of cases, prevent delays, and ensure that they do not infringe upon the rights of the defendant in the process.

© *VP Photo Studio/Shutterstock.com*

Prosecutors represent the government (both state and federal) in bringing criminal charges against a person accused of committing a crime. Prosecuting attorneys have the ability to use discretion in making various decisions throughout the criminal justice process, including whether to pursue criminal charges, which charges to pursue, and what sentence to recommend once a defendant has been convicted. In other words, prosecutors possess significant authority to make important decisions throughout various stages of the criminal justice process (Spohn, Beichner, & Davis-Frenzel, 2001). There is typically not a higher authority that can overrule the decisions of a prosecutor, like deciding to file multiple charges against a defendant or declining to prosecute a suspect (*nolle prosequi*).

BOX 8.1 CAREER HIGHLIGHT: PROSECUTOR.

Prosecutors represent local, state, or federal governments in criminal court cases. In addition to trying cases in court, they conduct interviews of witnesses and victims, take evidence and dispositions, analyze and synthesize information, evaluate police reports, perform legal research, argue motions before a judge, and put together a strong case with a firm evidentiary foundation. Prosecuting attorneys work in different organizations, including the United States Attorney's Office, the Department of Justice, offices of local district attorneys and state attorneys general, and enforcement components of regulatory agencies. Large cities may have special units that hire prosecutors to focus on specific crimes.

Prosecutors have the power to initiate criminal investigations, help guide the sentencing of offenders, and are the only attorneys that can participate in grand jury proceedings. They must be sensitive to the needs of the community they represent, consider independently the facts of each situation before even deciding to pursue a case. Prosecutors must understand and remember the burden to make their case. The presentation of solid evidence and testimony are paramount, and prosecutors must balance extensive preparation with the flexibility to address any surprises. They must be able to adequately explain evidence to the jury. Prosecutors must have keen attention to detail, a passion for justice, and the ability to communicate effectively with a variety of individuals—witnesses, victims, defendants, and law enforcement officials.

To become a prosecuting attorney, you must obtain a bachelor's degree and complete law school at an institution accredited by the American Bar Association (ABA), obtaining a Juris Doctor (J.D.) degree. Afterwards, you must pass the bar exam for the state in which you plan to practice. Most positions require at least a year of postgraduate legal experience and satisfactory completion of a background investigation and drug test. Trial experience of any kind will help immensely with acquiring the skills necessary to be a successful prosecutor. This can be achieved through a judicial clerkship, participation in a law school clinical program, working for a government agency, or being an associate at a law firm. In fact, many prosecutorial positions require at least a few years of legal practice before even being considered.

The Defense

Defense attorneys represent accused and convicted offenders by advising defendants and protecting their constitutional rights at each stage of the criminal justice process (Flowers, 2010). Defense attorneys can be present and advise their clients during questioning by police; represent defendants during arraignments, hearings, and trials; and serve as advocates during the appeal process. While private practice defense attorneys may earn significant incomes, often defending wealthy defendants in highly publicized cases, more private defense attorneys instead accept court appointments where they handle cases involving indigent defendants for relatively low fees (Farole & Langton, 2010).

© sirtravelalot/Shutterstock.com

The Sixth Amendment guarantees the right to legal counsel at all stages of a criminal proceeding, but what happens to those who are too poor to afford their own lawyers? In the case of indigent defendants, the Supreme Court has interpreted the Sixth Amendment as requiring that the government provide such individuals with attorneys (*Argersinger v. Hamlin*, 1972; *Gideon v. Wainwright*, 1963; *Powell v. Alabama*, 1932). **Public defenders** are government-salaried attorneys who represent criminal defendants who do not have the funds to pay for an attorney. As the number of indigent defendants provided with counsel has significantly increased over the past three decades, public defenders often have excessively heavy caseloads and thus cannot always devote the amount of time needed (or wanted) to each case. This presents a challenge and a question of equity within our criminal justice system.

The Judge

© Andrey_Popov/Shutterstock.com

Judges preside over court proceedings and serve as impartial arbitrators in the courtroom. They enjoy several benefits of office, but can also face various challenges as well. In addition to life terms for federal positions, judges are in a position that typically holds considerable respect and prestige. However, judges must know and apply a wide range of law, always staying up to date on the most current precedent and law (McKee, 2007).

Judges also play multiple roles as part of their duties. Acting as **administrator** (Levy, 2011; Smith & Feldman, 2001), it is the judge's responsibility to manage the courthouse. The judge has control over the court and the docket, and must also supervise court staff. Judges also play the role of **adjudicator** (Geyh, 2012) in that they act as the neutral party in overseeing opposing parties in our adversarial system. Additionally, judges must also be **negotiators** (Carodine, 2010) by encouraging cooperation and collaboration between various parties in the courtroom. These negotiation skills may be necessary for things like plea bargains or to ensure that courtroom procedures run as smoothly as possible so that the many cases can move through quickly.

Problem-Solving Courts: A Different Kind of "Court"

The emergence of problem-solving courts began in the 1990s, as these specialized courts were created for certain types of cases (e.g., domestic violence, drug treatment (Drugs Courts Program Office, 1998), mental health (Rossman et al., 2012)), particular groups of people (e.g., female offenders), specific issues (e.g., drug addiction), or in certain locations (e.g., neighborhoods). Today, there are more than 3,000 problem-solving courts in the United States (Hughes & Reichert, 2017). These specialized courts do away with the traditional concept of determining guilt, and instead target the factors that lead to criminal behavior by assuming guilt and placing a greater focus on rehabilitation. Problem-solving courts usually incorporate treatment and/or counselling into the plan of action as alternatives to incarceration, and typically provide better supervision of offenders to ensure they are complying with the treatment plan. Referred to as "clients," defendants are monitored by judges for extended periods of time, to include months or even years. In fact, although called problem-solving "courts," they tend to actually be more like diversionary programs with their social work and treatment focus. In problem-solving courts, offenders are able to get help for the underlying problem that may have contributed to their criminal behavior, while avoiding jail time.

Comprehension Check

1. What does it mean to say that the U.S. has a dual court system?
2. What is the adversarial process? How does it differ from what we see in other countries?
3. Who makes up the courtroom work group? What do they do?
4. What are problem-solving courts?

References

Argersinger v. Hamlin, 407 U.S. 25, 92 S.Ct. 2006, 32 L.Ed. 2d 530 (1972).

Carodine, M. (2010). "Keeping it real: Reform of the 'untried conviction' impeachment rule." *Maryland Law Review, 69*, 501–586.

Drugs Courts Program Office. (1998). *Looking at a decade of drug courts*. Washington, DC: U.S. Department of Justice.

Farole, D. J., & Langton, L. (2010). *"County-based and local public defender offices, 2007."* (Bureau of Justice Statistics Special Report, NCJ 231175). Retrieved from http://bjs.ojp.usdoj.gov/index.cfm?ty=pbdetail&iid=2211

Flowers, R. (2010). "The role of the defense attorney: Not just an advocate." *Ohio State Journal of Criminal Law, 7,* 647–652.

Geyh, C. (2012). "Can the rule of law survive judicial politics?" *Cornell Law Review, 97,* 191–253.

Gideon v. Wainwright, 372 U.S. 335, 83 S.Ct. 792, 9 L.Ed. 2d 799 (1963).

Hughes, E., & Reichert, J. (2017). *An overview of problem-solving courts and implications for practice.* Illinois Criminal Justice Information Authority (ICJIA). Retrieved from http://www.icjia.state.il.us/articles/an-overview-of-problem-solving-courts-and-implications-for-practice

Levy, M. (2011). "The mechanics of federal appeals: Uniformity and case management in circuit courts." *Duke Law Journal, 61,* 315–391.

McKee, T. A. (2007). "Judges as umpires." *Hofstra Law Review, 35,* 1709–1724.

Powell v. Alabama, 287 U.S. 45, 53 S.Ct. 55, 77 L.Ed. 158 (1932).

Rossman, S. B., Willison, J. B., Mallik-Kane, D., Kim, K., Debus-Sherrill, S., & Downey, P. M. (2012). *"Criminal justice interventions for offenders with mental illness: Eevaluation of mental health courts in Bronx and Brooklyn, New York."* Retrieved from https://www.ncjrs.gov/pdffiles1/nij/grants/238264.pdf

Smith, C. E., & Feldman, H. (2001). "Burdens of the bench: State supreme courts' non-judicial tasks." *Judicature, 84,* 304–309.

Spohn, C., Beichner, D., & Davis-Frenzel, E. (2001). "Prosecutorial justifications for sexual assault case rejection: Guarding the 'gateway to justice.'" *Social Problems, 48,* 206–235.

The Supreme Court of the United States. *"About the court."* Retrieved from http://www.supremecourt.gov

United States Department of Justice. (2018). *"Introduction to the federal court system."* Offices of the United States Attorneys. Retrieved from http://www.justice.gov/usao/justice-101/federal-courts.

Worden, A. P. (1995). "The judge's role in plea bargaining: An analysis of judges' agreement with prosecutors' sentencing recommendations." *Justice Quarterly, 12,* 257–278.

The Adjudication Process

LEARNING OBJECTIVES

After reading this chapter, the student should be able to

1 Describe the pretrial process

2 Understand the bail system and identify alternatives to bail

3 Explain preventive detention

4 Discuss plea bargaining

5 Understand the criminal trial process

6 Explain the appeals process after conviction

Introduction

The process of the criminal justice system begins from the moment a crime has been committed and reported to the police. The police begin their investigation and, once a suspect is identified and arrested, that individual begins the journey into the criminal justice system.

In this chapter, we discuss the pretrial process, including what happens after the arrest of a suspect, up to the criminal trial or plea bargain. We also explain the bail system, which involves pretrial release, as well as some alternatives to bail and preventive detention. We then explain the prevalence of plea bargains. Finally, we discuss the criminal trial process and end the chapter with a discussion on appeals.

Courtroom Process

The Pretrial Process

As you have learned, Americans have the right to due process. From this stems the basis for the pretrial process, which allows members of the criminal justice system to review the available evidence and determine whether that evidence supports a suspect moving to the next stage of the criminal justice process. A warrantless arrest may take place, or if an investigation reveals probable cause, the police can obtain an arrest warrant and take the suspect into custody. After the **arrest**, the accused goes through the **booking** process at the police station. This includes photographing the individual's mug shots, taking their fingerprints, and typically placing the individual in a cell in the jail.

If a warrantless arrest took place, the accused will usually be taken to court within forty-eight hours for the **initial appearance** to hear the charges being pursued, be informed of his or her rights, and receive the opportunity for bail. It is at this initial appearance that the judge will also review the evidence that has been obtained against the suspect to determine if there is probable cause that the suspect committed the crime and is therefore eligible to be prosecuted. If the police had first obtained a warrant for the accused's arrest, evidence was previously presented to a judge to determine probable cause to arrest the suspect.

© MR. Yanukit/Shutterstock.com

The **arraignment** is often the first formal meeting between the prosecution and the defense attorney. During this court appearance, the charges are read to the defendant and the defendant will enter in a plea of guilty or not guilty. At this point, there likely has not been a discussion between the prosecution and defense regarding any form of plea deal, so most defendants plead not guilty at the arraignment, even if they will go on to plead guilty at a later time.

At this stage of the process, prosecutors begin to assess the evidence to determine the strength of their case. If the prosecutor believes there is not enough evidence against the defendant, he or she may decide to drop the charges. The prosecutor may also drop charges for other reasons, including if the crime was minor, if the defendant is a first-time offender, or if the prosecutor thinks that the few days spent in jail were punishment enough for the defendant.

During these pretrial proceedings, the defense is also using this time to evaluate the strength of the prosecution's case. The defense may file **motions**, or applications to the court requesting that a certain action be taken. For instance, the defense may file a motion to exclude certain evidence in the case on the basis that it was improperly obtained by law enforcement.

The pretrial process often takes place in an "assembly line fashion," meaning that initial appearances, bail hearings, and arraignments typically occur at a rapid pace in an attempt to move many cases through the system as quickly as possible. This is often what we see in misdemeanor cases as well. Although this haste could affect the decisions of prosecutors and judges, the criminal justice system would simply become too backed up with cases to function efficiently if cases were not pushed through quickly. Courts in the United States ultimately do not have the funds, resources, or staff to provide detailed attention to each case.

The Bail System

Bail: Pretrial Release

There seems to be a conflict between American values and the US criminal justice system. In America, we are supposed to be "innocent until proven guilty." However, those who are accused of committing crimes are arrested and taken to jail, where they lose their freedom (sometimes for quite a while awaiting trial). It can be a bit disheartening to think that innocent people are sometimes wrongfully accused, leading them to be held in and subjected to poor living conditions while awaiting processing of their cases.

It is inevitable, however, for there to be clashes between our American values of freedom and liberty and the need to keep potentially dangerous criminals or individuals who may try to escape prosecution away from the rest of society. Nevertheless, not every person arrested for a crime needs to be detained while awaiting trial or processing of his or her case (a practice referred to as **pretrial detention**). Thus, most defendants are provided the opportunity to "post bail" as a way to obtain pretrial release on the condition that they will appear in court as required.

Bail involves the posting of a bond or a sum of money, which is specified by a judge and paid by the defendant or someone acting on his or her behalf, as a way of promising to return to court on an assigned date. If the defendant does not appear in court as scheduled, he or she forfeits the bail money. As part of their right to due process, accused criminals are generally entitled to a bail hearing, but there is no constitutional right to bail or pretrial release. Furthermore, while the Eighth Amendment to the US Constitution forbids excessive bail and states typically have bail guidelines to prevent discrimination in setting bail, there is no guarantee that defendants have a realistic chance of being released before trial. In other words, bail is more of a privilege than a right.

Bail bonds are usually cash deposits, but can also include property or other valuables. Sometimes, if the defendant cannot pay the full amount of the bail, the defendant can seek a privately secured bail through the services of a professional **bail bondsman**. The bondsman will charge a percentage of the required

bond as a fee, requiring the defendant to pay this amount up front. The bondsman will then put up the full bail amount. If the defendant flees or does not show up to court as required (thus forfeiting the bail bond), many states give bail bondsmen the power to track down and bring back the defendant. In fact, some jurisdictions provide bondsmen with the power to pursue, arrest, and forcibly extradite their charges from foreign jurisdiction without consideration of the due process rights or statutory limitations required by law enforcement officers (*Taylor v. Taintor*, 1873).

In the typical money bail system, the amount is set by the judge who makes the decision based on the seriousness of the crime and the defendant's criminal record. The judge typically can use his or her discretion when setting bail, sometimes having to stay within guidelines set by the state. Because bail is typically determined within twenty-four to forty-eight hours after an arrest, however, there is often not enough time for the judge to conduct a thorough assessment of the factors involved in each specific case. This can lead to judges having predetermined amounts for certain crimes and sometimes setting high bail amounts because the police or prosecutor want a specific individual kept off the streets.

Discrimination within the Bail System

Unfortunately, even for those granted bail, it does not always mean that they will be released to await trial free from the confinement of jail. For many, bail is set at an amount that they simply cannot afford. Unable to pay, these individuals—presumed innocent because they have not yet pleaded or been proven guilty—must await trial in jail. Accordingly, critics of the bail system argue that it operates to facilitate discrimination, particularly against the poor.

Here are a few questions to consider:

- Should a violent, dangerous offender be allowed out on bail simply because he or she is wealthy, whereas a nonviolent suspect must remain incarcerated because he or she is too poor to afford bail?
- Should people be denied a chance at freedom because they are poor?
- If you have a limited amount of money, do you use it to pay bail or do you use it to hire an attorney?

Reforming the System

Because so many cannot afford bail and are forced to await trial in jail, and because of the discrimination that many argue is a result of the current bail system, critics have begun calling for reform of the cash bail system.

In 2017, US Senators Kamala Harris (Democrat-California) and Rand Paul (Republican-Kentucky) introduced the Pretrial Integrity and Safety Act. This legislation is an attempt to reform the money bail system by providing grants to states. These grants would be used to make changes to the criminal justice system, including replacing the payment of money as a condition of pretrial release in criminal cases (Pretrial Integrity and Safety Act of 2017).

Kentucky and New Jersey are two examples of states that use alternatives to the money bail system, such as personalized risk assessments, which examine indicators of whether a defendant is a flight risk or threat to the public. Alaska has also recently switched to a new system in place of bail. Judges now use a point-based system to grade each defendant on the likelihood of showing up to court and the risk of committing a new crime if released while awaiting trial. A decision is then made, based on these two scores, as to whether the defendant will be released and under what, if any, restrictions. All defendants released under this new system are monitored by a new branch of the Alaska Department of Corrections (Brooks, 2018).

Bail Guidelines

As a way of protecting against discrimination within the bail system, many states have set bail guidelines. These guidelines provide standards for judges to follow when setting bail and provide appropriate bail amounts. The guidelines typically take into account the crime committed, including the seriousness of the offense, and the defendant's criminal history.

Alternatives to Bail

As part of the reform to the bail system that we have seen taking place in recent years, there are also several other mechanisms used for pretrial release to reduce the number of defendants detained while awaiting trial, eliminating the possible damage to employment, family, housing, and general stability that results from pretrial detention.

Citation

© sirtravelalot/Shutterstock.com

A **citation** is a summons or a written order to appear in court at a specific time to answer to a criminal charge. We often hear a citation referred to as a "ticket," something that is usually issued for minor crimes such as traffic offenses. State laws guide the circumstances under which a citation can be issued. By issuing a citation, law enforcement officers are able to avoid taking the individual into custody and going through the booking process and arraignment and bail hearings. Defendants are still required to appear in court on the specified date, or can sometimes pay a fine instead. Citations can help reduce jail populations and provide local cost savings. Lower risk individuals are diverted from detention, reserving limited space and resources for those who are more dangerous.

Release on Recognizance

Release on recognizance (ROR) is a form of pretrial release where the judge releases the defendant on the basis that he or she is believed to be reliable and has ties to the community. The idea behind this approach is that the defendant's roots in the community (e.g., family, job, status) will guarantee that the defendant will not flee and will show up to court. ROR does not involve a cash bond and requires only that the defendant agree in writing to return for court hearings.

Percentage Cash Bail

Sometimes, judges are not willing to simply release defendants on their own recognizance. Some states will instead allow a defendant to pay a percentage of the set bail amount (usually 10 percent). If the defendant shows up to court as promised, the percentage is returned (typically minus about 1 percent, which is used to cover administrative fees). If the defendant does not show up to court, he or she must pay the full bail amount. This alternative method allows for more defendants to gain pretrial release while still paying a cash sum as a promise to appear in court, but without having to use bail bondsmen.

Preventive Detention

Critics of the bail system argue that letting defendants out on bail while awaiting trial provides them with the opportunity to commit new crimes during this time. In an attempt to prevent this, legislatures have passed laws allowing for detention of defendants without bail. Prior to 1970, however, judges could not preventively detain defendants to maintain safety in the community. The District of Columbia Court Reform and Criminal Procedure Act of 1970 was the first statute that allowed judges to consider the dangerousness of the offender and the risk of fleeing in making a decision to deny pretrial release (Pretrial Justice Center for Courts, n.d.). The Bail Reform Act of 1984 permits preventive detention in federal criminal cases, but requires certain procedural safeguards. Under this act, if a prosecutor recommends a defendant be detained while awaiting trial, a federal judge will hold a hearing to assess multiple factors, including flight risk, if the defendant poses a threat to anyone in the community, and the seriousness of the offense and possible penalty. If the judge determines that any of these factors make it impossible to release the defendant on bail without endangering the community, the decision can be made to hold the defendant in jail until the conclusion of the case.

Although some argue that preventive detention violates due process rights, the Supreme Court upheld the provisions of the Bail Reform Act of 1984 in *United States v. Salerno* (1987). In this case, the justices asserted that preventive detention is a legitimate use of governmental power to prevent people from committing further crimes while out on bail. Research has shown that the type of crime and seriousness of the charge, criminal history, and drug use strongly influence the likelihood that a defendant will commit another crime while released on bail.

Plea Bargains

Contrary to popular belief, most cases do not actually go to trial. Instead, the vast majority of cases end via plea bargain. A **plea bargain** involves a guilty plea arrived at through negotiations between the prosecutor, the defense, and the judge. In exchange for an agreed upon punishment, the defendant enters a plea of guilty.

Plea bargains allow for the quick resolution of cases, saving time and resources while still protecting the community. There are advantages to plea bargains for all parties involved. Prosecutors gain an easy conviction, even in cases where evidence may have been lacking or a weak case might have presented a challenge at trial. Plea bargains also save time and valuable resources by disposing of cases without having to prepare for and go through a criminal trial. Defense attorneys also save time and resources by not having to prepare for a trial. They can earn their fee quickly and move on to the next case. Plea bargains also help control the extensive caseloads of public defenders. Defendants benefit from negotiated guilty pleas by having their cases disposed of quickly, not having to wait for the case to move through each step of the criminal justice process. Defendants also have the benefit of knowing what their punishment will be before agreeing to plead guilty. Moreover, defendants typically receive a lesser punishment than they would have had they gone to trial and been convicted. Judges also benefit from plea bargains by avoiding lengthy criminal trials and having to make the decision of the appropriate sentence for the defendant.

The public, however, has a tendency to see plea bargaining as a way for offenders to "get off easy" or not receive the punishment appropriate for the crime committed. Critics of plea bargaining argue that defendants give up some of their constitutional rights when agreeing to a plea deal (e.g., right to trial by jury). Another criticism of plea bargaining is that it breeds disrespect and even contempt for the law by making the criminal justice process appear as a sham. An additional concern is that innocent people may agree to plead guilty to a crime they did not commit. While it may be difficult to understand how or why someone would plead guilty when in fact innocent, people with little education or low social status may not have the understanding or confidence to say no to an attorney who advises them to do so. People may also determine that it is in their best interest to plead guilty and take a lesser sentence than to risk being convicted at trial and being sentenced to the maximum penalty.

Trials

Cases that are not dismissed or disposed of through plea bargains will go to trial. As discussed earlier, even though it is our constitutional right to a trial by jury, most cases do not make it to this point in the criminal justice system. Preparing for and going to trial takes extensive amounts of time and resources. Attorneys must prepare by gathering evidence, responding to motions by the opposing side, strategizing, and presenting the case in court.

Of the cases that go to trial, some are **jury trials** and the others are **bench trials**, or trials conducted by a judge as the finder of fact and ruler on matters of law and procedure. In a bench trial, there is no jury involved. The defendant makes the decision as to the type of trial he or she wishes to have.

Bench trials are often speedier than jury trials because attorneys do not have to go through the process of jury selection or take the time necessary to instruct the jury. Bench trials can be useful in particularly complex cases involving issues or technical aspects that a jury might not understand. A disadvantage of a bench trial is that there is only one fact finder, so the opportunity to convince at least one person to agree with a given side does not exist as it does in a jury trial.

© Aleutie/Shutterstock.com

Jury trials are composed of members of the community who act as the finders of fact. Each side presents evidence to the jury and argues their side of the case. The jury ultimately makes a decision of guilt based on the persuasiveness of each side's evidence. The judge manages questions or issues pertaining to law and procedure. One benefit of a jury trial is that juries do not have to defend their decisions, whereas a judge may be an elected official and may have to take reelection into consideration or may face review by the governor, which may influence decisions. A drawback of jury trials is that they are time consuming, sometimes lasting weeks or even months. Additionally, juries may sometimes not understand the law or make decisions based solely on the law, but instead may render verdicts based on emotions.

The Trial Process

The trial process typically follows eight general steps. Although most cases never go to trial, understanding the steps of the process remains important. The eight steps of the trial process include the following:

1. Jury selection
2. Opening statements
3. The prosecution's case
4. The defense's case
5. Rebuttal
6. Closing arguments
7. Instructions to the jury
8. The verdict

© Macrovector/Shutterstock.com

JURY TRIAL

Jury Selection

The first step, jury selection, is an important step in the trial process. Both the prosecution and the defense seek to find potential jurors that can be impartial, deciding the case based on the evidence presented in the courtroom.

© Jillian Cain Photography/Shutterstock.com

Accordingly, they also seek to determine potential jurors that may be more likely to make decisions based on personal values, beliefs, and experiences. They also strive to identify those who may favor their side, and attempt to exclude those who appear sympathetic to the opposing side.

Jurors are ultimately selected from a jury pool, of which citizens' names are typically drawn from a list of registered voters. Once called for jury duty, potential jurors begin with the courtroom process of **voir dire**. During this process, attorneys for both sides and the judge question the prospective jurors to screen out those individuals who may be biased in some way or otherwise incapable of making a fair decision. Questions may be about the individual's background, victimization experiences, and knowledge of the current case. If either side feels that an individual may not be able to make a fair decision based on the responses given, the attorney can **challenge for cause**. The judge will rule on the challenge, and if the judge agrees, the juror will be excused from the case. Attorneys can usually challenge for cause an unlimited number of potential jurors.

Attorneys have a bit more power over the composition of the jury through the use of **peremptory challenges**. Using peremptory challenges, the prosecution and defense can exclude certain members of the jury pool from being included in the jury without providing any specific reason. Attorneys typically use these to exclude those individuals they think will be sympathetic to the other side or unsympathetic to their own arguments. Unlike challenges for cause, attorneys are usually limited to a certain number of peremptory challenges in each case.

Some attorneys believe that trials are won or lost in the jury selection process. If successful in seating a favorable jury, they may have an audience that is receptive and supportive of the arguments and evidence presented in court.

Opening Statements

Once the jury has been selected, the trial can begin. The prosecution and the defense will each present opening statements to the jury, summarizing the position they intend to take during the trial. No evidence is presented at this point, and the jury is not to use the opening statements as a way of anything being proven or disproven about the case.

The Prosecution's Case

Next, the prosecution begins their presentation of evidence. Remember, the prosecution carries the burden in criminal cases and must prove to the jury, beyond a reasonable doubt, that the defendant is the individual who committed the crime. Therefore, the prosecution will use this time to present their case in a way as to try to remove any reasonable doubt from the jury's minds. After all of the prosecution's evidence is presented, including physical evidence, witness testimony, expert testimony, and circumstantial evidence, the prosecution will rest their case.

The Defense's Case

After the prosecution rests, the defense will present their case. The defense is not required to answer to the case presented by the prosecution, as it is the prosecution's responsibility to prove their case beyond a reasonable doubt. Instead, the defense typically takes one of three approaches: (1) present evidence to rebut the prosecution's evidence (insert reasonable doubt), (2) offer an alibi, or (3) present an affirmative defense (refer to the defenses discussed in Chapter 2).

BOX 9.1 CAREER HIGHLIGHT: DEFENSE ATTORNEY.

The defense attorney represents those accused of committing crimes. Defense attorneys interview clients, research cases and the law, file motions with the court, review evidence, form defenses, and negotiate deals with prosecutors. A defense attorney should have strong analytical, language, communication, and interpersonal skills, as they often work with a variety of people from diverse backgrounds and cultures.

To become a defense attorney, you must obtain a four-year college degree, three years of law school to obtain a Juris Doctor (J.D.) degree, and pass the state bar exam. Law schools accredited by The American Bar Association (ABA) require taking the Law School Admissions Test (LSAT). Law school applicants are considered through undergraduate GPA, quality of undergraduate institution, work experience, letters of recommendation, personal statement, and LSAT score. Subsequent to law school, you must pass the state bar exam and be licensed by the state where you plan to practice law. Most states require the six-hour Multistate Bar Examination.

Rebuttal

When the defense rests their case, the prosecution is then given the opportunity to present witnesses whose testimony may discredit or counteract any testimony or evidence that was presented by the defense. If the prosecution presents rebuttal witnesses, the defense has the opportunity to question them and to present new witnesses in rebuttal.

Closing Arguments

Once the prosecution and defense have completed their presentations of the evidence, each side will make closing arguments to the jury. During closing arguments, the attorneys review and summarize the evidence and provide interpretations to support their side. The prosecutor may try to show the jury how the evidence supports the claim that the defendant is guilty of the crime, while the defense may attempt to demonstrate that the prosecution did not prove their case beyond a reasonable doubt. Attorneys from both sides often also use this time to remind jurors the importance of remaining impartial and deciding the case based on the evidence presented and not emotions.

© Anna Violet/Shutterstock.com

After the closing arguments, the judge instructs the jury on the law and how the jury should use the law to guide their decision in the verdict. The judge may discuss important concepts such as reasonable doubt, rights of the defendant, law that applies to the case, or other legal requirements.

The Verdict

After the prosecution and defense have presented their cases and the jury has been instructed by the judge, the jury will be excused from the courtroom and will retire to a private room. The jury will elect a foreperson to lead the discussions and then deliberations begin. The jurors are now able, for the first time, to discuss the case with each other, including the evidence and facts presented.

If the jury is unable to come to a decision, the trial may end in a hung jury. When this occurs, the prosecutor must then decide whether to try the case again before another jury. Conversely, if a verdict is reached, the jury will notify the judge and then everyone will reconvene in the courtroom for the reading of the verdict.

Appeals

Once a verdict has been reached and, if convicted, a sentence is imposed, many believe the case to be over. However, the defendant typically has the right to appeal the verdict to a higher court. An **appeal** cannot be made solely on disagreement with the verdict, however, and must be based on questions of procedure. When filing an appeal, the defendant must have a claim that one or more errors of law or procedure were made at some point in the criminal justice process (e.g., investigation, arrest, trial). Thus, an appellate court will assess whether the trial followed proper procedures. If the appellate court determines that significant errors were present, the conviction is set aside. It is then up to the prosecutor to decide whether to pursue the case and retry the defendant.

Throughout the pretrial process and pretrial release, courts must balance protecting the rights of the accused with the safety of the citizens in the community. A significant issue related to pretrial release is how to ensure that all defendants, no matter their race, sex, or income level, are afforded these same protections. Although most cases never actually go to trial, the criminal trial remains the hallmark of American criminal justice. Based on an adversarial process, where the prosecution is pitted against the defense, the criminal trial developed from the democratic principles of Western society.

Comprehension Check

1. What are the steps in the pretrial process?
2. How does the bail system work in the U.S.? What are some alternatives to bail?
3. What is preventive detention?
4. What is plea bargaining? Why are a majority of cases disposed of through plea bargaining rather than by going to trial?
5. Explain the various steps in the criminal trial process.
6. What does the appeals process entail?

References

Brooks, J. (2018). *Goodbye bail: Alaska switches to new system of criminal justice.* Juneau Empire.com. Retrieved from http://juneauempire.com/state/news/2017-12-20/goodbye-bail-alaska-switches-new-system-criminal-justice

Pretrial Justice Center for Courts. (n.d.). *Preventive detention.* National Center for State Courts. Retrieved from http://www.ncsc.org/Microsites/PJCC/Home/Topics/Preventive-Detention.aspx

S.1593—Pretrial Integrity and Safety Act of 2017. 115th Congress (2017–2018).

Taylor v. Taintor, 83 U.S. 66 (1873).

United States v. Salerno, 481 U.S. 739 (1987).

10

The Corrections System

LEARNING OBJECTIVES

After reading the chapter, the student should be able to

1 Explain the roles and functions of corrections in the criminal justice system

2 Define the meaning of the corrections system and its goals

3 Differentiate the various agencies involved in the corrections systems

4 Describe the management and administration of correctional systems in the United States

5 Articulate the visions for the future of corrections

Introduction

Correctional institutions bear the brunt of the criminal justice decisions. Of all the criminal justice agencies, the corrections system agents are mere implementers of the decisions made by other actors in the criminal justice system. Thus, correctional institutions are the most passive among the actors in the criminal justice system. To illustrate, the legislature has the ability to define criminal conduct and punishments that would have an impact on the inmate or offender population. Toward this end, the legislatures may criminalize behaviors that would unduly burden correctional resources and yet correctional workers are powerless to oppose these decisions. On the other hand, legislatures might decide to decriminalize an act and the correctional institutions have to release those people under their custody or supervision in compliance with the new law due to the retroactive application of *ex-post facto*[1] laws when they favor the offender. Likewise, correctional agencies do not have effective control over police, judges, or jury decisions regarding who would be confined over to correctional facilities or units. In effect, correctional institutions have little control over the quality and quantity of their clients. Furthermore, correctional workers are very much restricted in their management of people under their supervision due to the dictates of resources, human rights (Sen, 1996), civil and political rights, and the constitutional rights of individuals under their supervision (Cole, Smith, & DeJong, 2018). Although there are some coping mechanisms that correctional systems can do to alleviate the adverse decisions made by other actors (see criminal justice thermodynamics in Chapter 1), the correctional agencies have limited discretion on their clients and the manner of handling them.

Despite this seeming lack of controls over the workload of correctional institutions, correctional systems occupy a critical position in the justice system and have certain powers that they could exercise. First, they exercise discretion in the manner of supervision and control of those under their care. Under the *hands-off policy (HOP) of the courts*, institutions are free from the influence of courts in the administration of those that are under their supervision. In other words, the courts have limited power to supervise prison administration or interfere with ordinary prison rules and regulations *(Davis v Finney, 1995)*. Second, the corrections system also has discretions on parole and other forms of releases such as furloughs or work releases. Third, they have the ability to coerce compliance from inmates through the use of good time credits and threat of discipline. Through these discretionary powers, the correctional institutions somewhat alleviate their predicaments about their lack of control over the type of clients that they receive and the level of supervision they can exercise.

Aside from these autonomies in the performance of the correctional workers' administrative functions, they perform significant roles in protecting society and the rehabilitation goals for the offenders. Corrections, therefore, have the dual roles of **law enforcement and social worker**. Because they control the offender's behavior either in the facilities or in the community, correctional officers have to take on the role of being law enforcers that apprehend inmates' rule infractions and impose the appropriate sanctions. Correctional workers also make sure that inmates will not escape from the facilities or are returned in their facilities when inmates flee from institutions or do not report to the supervising state agents when the inmate is in parole or probation.

Correctional officers also perform social work functions for both the inmate and the victim. The agents of corrections seek to rehabilitate the offenders either through the delivery of treatment or imposition of discipline or, sometimes, the balancing of both discipline and treatment. Likewise, corrections provide services to victims. The current movement for restorative justice endeavors to restore the victim from losses and fears due to crime. This dual role makes corrections deal with a lot of paradoxes in their job. They have to be compassionate but firm. They have to be restrictive and yet need to show sincere efforts toward the betterment and well-being of both the offenders and the victims.

This chapter throws light on the realities about the correctional systems in the United States. This chapter outlines the management and administration of the different agencies within the correctional system of the United States. It outlines the goals and the associated means of punishment employed in the correctional system. It begins with the most severe and stringent punishment all the way to the least stringent and least severe forms of punishment. The basis for this classification is the impact of the punishment on one's freedoms. Toward the end, this chapter tries to provide some future trends for corrections in the United States.

Meaning of Corrections in the U.S. Context

Corrections is an umbrella term describing a variety of functions typically carried out by government agencies, and involving the punishment, treatment, and supervision of persons who have been convicted of crimes (Stohr, Walsh, & Hemmens, 2013). These functions commonly include detention, parole, and probation. A *corrections system*, also known as a *penal system*, refers to a network of agencies that administer a jurisdiction's institutional and community-based programs. It becomes a system as these various correctional agencies are typically under the control and supervision of the executive branch of governments.

Goals of Punishment

Generally, punishments are handed to a person who has committed criminal offenses. Offenders are punished to promote understanding of the law, to alleviate behavioral norms, and to maintain the public's trust in criminal justice. Thus, punishments are justified through utilitarian reasons. It is this utilitarian principle that distinguishes some of the analogous acts by the state from acts committed by individuals. For example, the killing of a person by the state through the death penalty is used for retributive or deterrent purposes. The killing engaged in by private individuals are presumably devoid of these utilitarian considerations. Instead, the act simply satisfies the basic instinct of human beings for revenge. Thus, a distinction has to be made between expressive acts and instrumental acts. **Expressive acts** are those that are ends in themselves. For example, inflicting pain on someone for no articulated reason is pursued as an end in itself, such as acts of sadism or spite. **Instrumental acts** are those that are pursued due to another or ultimate ends, for example, inflicting pain on someone to teach that person a lesson. An individual's acts can be punished simply because it is an illegal act. In this situation, the ends are irrelevant. This lack of a higher purpose makes punishment of a person an expressive act. Instrumental acts are always pursued for an ultimate purpose. The government's action must always be couched in an instrumental fashion to be considered justified. It is in this utilitarian ideal that punishment gets to be seen as a legitimate action of the state.

Goals of Punishment

The goals of punishment are generally categorized into five dimensions:

Retribution or Restitution. This form of punishment has two main rationales. The first rationale is called *retribution*, where the punishment is imposed to satisfy society's or an individual's need for revenge (Davis, 2016, p. 231). The second rationale is for *restitution*, where society needs to maintain equity by compensating for the loss that someone or society has suffered for the crime. In both rationales, compensation for material and emotional damages are primary considerations. Hence, this form of punishment is also known as "*just deserts*" where an individual who commits a crime deserves the punishment regardless of its harshness (Orth, 2003, p. 174). The outcome under this goal is what is known as *distributive justice*—one where an equilibrium is sought to restore the previous order of things that was disturbed by crime (Hunter, Barker, & de Guzman, 2018).

Underlying this just deserts principle are two standard expectations:

a. Proportionality—The reward or punishment should be in proportion to what one deserves. Therefore, a proper calibration of punishments and fines becomes the goal. The lack of proportionality will redound to the undue benefit of either the victim or the offender. Any perception of lack of proportionality would give rise to an injustice under this principle.

b. Nondiscriminatory—It should be meted out impartially (nondiscriminatory). In most circles, this philosophy is couched in the saying, "If you do the crime, you must do the time." The expectation is that the application of the law should not be clouded by extrajudicial factors particularly involving race, class, and gender.

It should be stressed that the utilitarian purpose of retribution or restitution is merely to restore the equilibrium. This form of punishment does not necessarily include the purposes of educating the offender or improving the welfare of the victim. If these two latter outcomes happen, they occur simply just by accident rather than by design.

Deterrence. Deterrence aims to educate the offender and the masses. In popular media, deterrence is often colloquially called "scared straight." It is a form of punishment that does not seek an equilibrium but rather a supremacy of the punishment in order to scare the individual from transgressing the laws. Thus, the punishment is not about symmetry but asymmetry. This means that punishments are not meted out to fit the offense or the offender. Instead, punishment should be meted out to prevent crime and, thereby, protect society. The major justification for the punishment of deterrence is to convey a legal threat to prospective offenders that criminals suffer when they commit a crime. "Deterrence is thought by many to dissuade would-be offenders from engaging in criminal behavior" (Davis, 2016, p. 87).

This form of punishment operates under the **pleasure principle**. This principle invokes the assumption that individuals will avoid unpleasant outcomes in favor of pleasurable ones. In addition, this goal of punishment assumes that humans are rational and will seek the most utilitarian outcomes that will benefit them. For deterrence to work, the punishment must be perceived to be painful or a negative expected value outcome (Newman, 1983). Newman (1983) argues that a punishment that is not painful would not be a deterrent for future misbehavior.

Forms of Deterrence

General deterrence. Punishments are meted out to convey to the general population the consequences of crime and that crime does not pay and is not pleasurable. It tends to make an example of an individual offender to the general population in regards to the outcome of their offenses.

Specific deterrence. Punishments are meted out to those that are at risk or current offenders so that they will not engage in the act or repeat the offense. The punishment seeks to impart to the offender lessons about their offenses.

Two problems have been associated with deterrence as a philosophy of punishment. The first one is intrinsic in the punishment itself. There is really no perfect formula for calibrating the deterrent effect of a specific punishment. This problem is known as the *severity* problem. How severe should punishment be set that it has the capacity to dissuade people from committing the offense? This brings about two related issues: finding the right dose and avoiding overdose. Both extremes are criminogenic. In a study by Cochran, Chamlin, and Seth (1994) about the effectiveness of the death penalty, they found that state executions of offenders have a deterrent effect. However, they noted that there is a tipping point where more executions not only did not have a deterrent effect, but have emboldened individuals to increase the gravity of their offending. This phenomenon was called the *brutalization effect* of punishment (Cochran et al., 1994). The other issue with the severity of punishment is the nonimposition of the actual punishment. It has been noted that incarcerated offenders serve only half of their actual sentences due to good time credits and other discretionary releases. Thus, punishments seem only severe in law but not really in practice. This practice of the lessened sentences produces a learning experience about the lack of severity in the actual imposition of punishment undermining the severity of the law.

The second problem with deterrence is associated with the application of the punishment. The twin objectives are for the punishment to be **swift and**

certain. The application of swift and certain justice has been a major issue in criminal justice. The processes in each stage are full of uncertainties. Starting from the detection of the crime by the police and the prosecution of the crime, the offender can potentially get away from the punishment. The trial process also undermines the certainty of punishment as the conviction and punishments are not guaranteed to be commensurate enough to deter an offender. Thus, the certainty of punishment is severely compromised.

The other problem with the application of deterrence is the lack of swiftness in the imposition of the punishment. It is often lamented that the wheels of justice turns ever so slowly. Even if the person has been convicted, the application of the punishment is sometimes suspended due to appeals and motions for reconsiderations. For example, the deterrent effects of the death penalty become less pronounced when death convicts are only executed after several years.

Incapacitation. Incapacitation refers to the imposition of restrictions on the capacity of an individual to re-offend. This form of punishment works on the principle of restraint. In the United States, the major form of restraint is through incarceration where the offender cannot re-offend because they are physically restrained. Likewise, death is another form of physical incapacitation. In fact, it is the ultimate form of incapacitation. Other countries incapacitate individuals through corporal punishments that particularly refer to the instrument of the crime such as the castration of their genitals for rape, cutting of their extremities for crimes such as theft or robbery, or the banishment of the offender to a remote island. In the United States, incapacitation through denial of the instruments of the crime is done through prohibitions such as nonuse of computers for hackers. Incapacitation of the offender could also be done virtually through the use of such means as electronic monitoring or the use of offender registry and prohibition in the practice of their professions where the offender and the victim might be in close proximity. Examples are money launderers not being allowed to work in financial institutions or sex offenders not allowed to tutor school kids.

Forms of Incapacitation

Just like deterrence, incapacitation could be either general incapacitation, selective incapacitation, permanent incapacitation, or more recently, civil incapacitation. **General incapacitation** happens when there is a systematic pattern of applying a specific form of incapacitation method without regard to other factors. For example, a mandatory incarceration for convicted drug offenders is a form of general incapacitation. At times, a specific individual offender is targeted such as a repeat sex offender is a form of **selective incapacitation**. The punishment is applied to that specific offender. The **three-strikes rule** of using the maximum penalty of 20 years for a conviction of a third felony offense regardless of the degree or seriousness is another specific incapacitation targeting repeat felony offenders. The policy in this case is make the punishment harsher for particular offenses or offenders.

Permanent incapacitation is normally imposed by means of corporal punishment such as decapitation, mutilation, or similar forms. **Civil incapacitation** happens as an effect of collateral punishments such as when an offender is placed on restraining orders, electronic monitoring, registry lists, or exercise of profession and limited movement.

Rehabilitation. Rehabilitation follows a different mantra in its application of punishment, that is, *let the punishment fit the offender for the betterment of that person.* The assumption is that character and personality deficiencies are the root causes of the offender's problems. Thus, addressing those problems will benefit not only the individual, but society as a whole. In this philosophy, the criminal justice system must have a whole host of intervention techniques that would address these criminogenic needs. In some circles, they call this the *medical model.* This model implies that an individual is afflicted with disorders that are criminogenic. Those criminogenic needs must be addressed for an individual to be rehabilitated.

This philosophy of punishment was severely criticized in the 1980s with Martinson's (1974) seminal article that boldly proclaimed *"nothing works"* in rehabilitation. These pronouncements were met with reforms that instituted more severe forms of punishments that led back to the retributive, deterrence, or incapacitation models of penal sanctions.

Restoration. This philosophy acknowledges the harm that crime inflicts on both the victim and society (Braithwaite, 1989). At the same time, this philosophy provides a pragmatic view that an offender will eventually rejoin society and will need to have the social support in order for that person to be reformed and become reintegrated back to society as a law abiding member. The philosophy still supports the imposition of appropriate punishments including retribution in order to restore society and individuals to a state prior to the harm that was inflicted. Thus, it is also a victim-centric philosophy. At the same time, it aims to prevent crime by providing rehabilitation to an individual offender including mandating his or her incapacitation through institutional confinement or being under state supervision while being reintroduced to society. Perhaps, the novel aspect of this philosophy is the acknowledgment that there should be reconciliation between the offender and the victims (i.e., individuals and society). These reconciliation efforts are normally conducted through a mediation process either prior to commitment or during the period of inmate's confinement.

Modes of Punishment

Corporal Punishments

The earliest forms of punishment were corporal punishments. Corporal punishments are those that inflict physical forms of punishment including the death penalty. Newman (1983) suggested that corporal punishments are really the most appropriate ones because they are just (i.e., only the offender gets punished and gets what he or she deserves) and painful (i.e., it serves as a deterrent).

The earliest pronouncements of corporal punishments are found in the code of Hammurabi (Cole et al., 2018). In the imposition of corporal punishments, the person could be flogged, exposed to the elements, mutilated, and killed. However, corporal punishments in the United States are no longer applied except perhaps in the form of the death penalty. The United States has also outlawed some forms of the imposition of the death penalty because of the Supreme Court's interpretation of the Eighth Amendment of the Constitution that several forms of executions are cruel and unusual. The Courts have also limited the prerogative of the state in putting to death certain populations such the youth (*Roper v Simmons*, 2005), those with mental disorders [*Ford v. Wainwright*, 1986; *Atkins v. Virginia* (122 S.Ct. 2242, 2002)]. More recently, certain petitions have been filed to exempt the elderly from the death penalty (Zimmerman, 2018).

Institutional Corrections

Writing for the Prison Policy Initiative, Sawyer and Wagner (2019) reported that the U.S. criminal justice system holds an estimated 2.3 million people in various facilities. These institutionalized individuals are distributed as follows—1,719 state prisons, 109 federal prisons, 1,772 juvenile correctional facilities, 3,163 local jails, and 80 Indian Country jails as well as in military prisons, immigration detention facilities, civil commitment centers, state psychiatric hospitals, and prisons in the U.S. territories. These numbers show how the criminal justice system relies on institutionalization as a form of punishment. As prisons and jails hold most of these individuals, a broader discussion of these two forms of institutionalization will be undertaken.

Prisons

Prisons are the institutions where individuals who have been convicted of felonies are confined. Individuals who are also convicted of crimes involving capital punishments are held in custody while awaiting their executions. The federal government and the 50 states operate prisons. Bronson and Carson (2019) reported that about 1.4 million are confined in federal and state prisons in 2017. They noted that this is a decline of 1.2% compared to 2016, which is a part of the declining trend in prison population in the United States. Black males remain overrepresented in the prison population by almost six times that of White males. While nearly half of federal prisoners are due to drugs convictions, the majority of those held in state prisons are for violent offenses. California and Texas have the most number of prisoners with each having more than 100,000 in custody for 2017 (Figure 10.1).

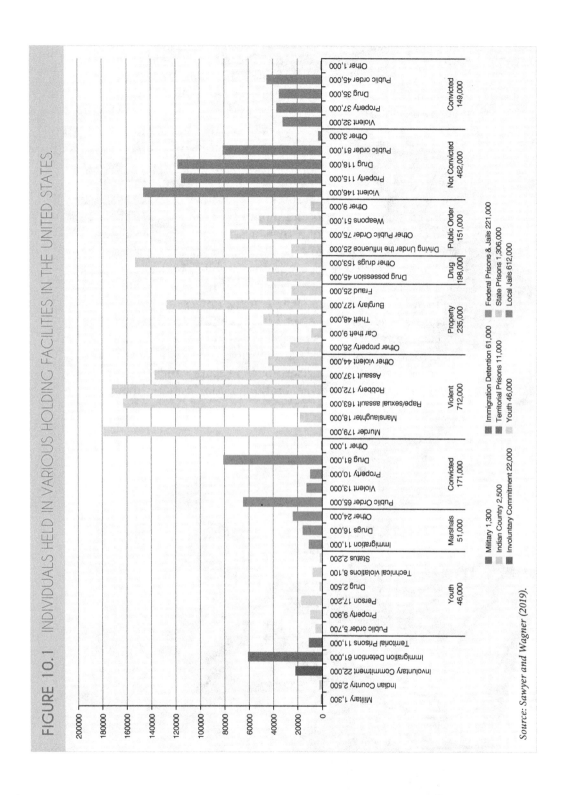

FIGURE 10.1 INDIVIDUALS HELD IN VARIOUS HOLDING FACILITIES IN THE UNITED STATES.

Source: Sawyer and Wagner (2019).

Prison Classification Systems. Prisons are normally classified in terms of their security levels and facilities that cater to gender variations. Security levels are determined by the intensity and restrictions of inmates in custody. Prisons are classified into minimum, medium, maximum, and supermax or admax. **Minimum security prisons** are normally structured resembling community settings where inmates might be free to roam around and the facility is not secured by fortified walls. **Medium security prisons** are a notch higher in terms of security. There are clear signs of confinement such as walls and prison cells. However, there is more freedom for inmates to roam around areas of the facilities. **Maximum facility** has all the trappings of confinement such as high walls and more presence of guards and monitoring capabilities. The architectural of most prisons resembles that of a panopticon (see Figure 10.2) and there are observation towers situated in strategic places. The inmates are more regulated in terms of their mobility and access to instruments or tools. Normally, they are prohibited to possess materials that could be turned into a weapon such as pens, knives, and metal objects. More serious offenders are confined in maximum security facilities. Inmates in maximum security prisons are also normally segregated along racial or gang affiliations as intragroup riots occur when they are not segregated. The practice in prison to avoid gang violence is the isolation of gang members from the general population and put them in restrictive housing (Pyrooz, 2018).

FIGURE 10.2 PANOPTICON PRISON DESIGN IN THE NETHERLANDS.

© Uwe Aranas/Shutterstock.com

Supermax or admax (maximum administration) are the confinement institutions for dangerous and hardened offenders. There is no set definition of a supermax prison; however, the U.S. Department of Justice (DOJ) and the National Institute of Corrections agree that "these units have basically the same function: to provide long-term, segregated housing for inmates classified as the highest security risks in a state's prison system" (Collins, 2004). Once confined in these facilities, inmates tend to stay in such detention units for a long time (Kurki & Morris, 2001). Offenders in these facilities are normally in solitary confinement. They are mostly restrained by handcuffs or leg restraints when they are out of their cells. They are also more closely watched when they are in a congregate activity. Inmates are locked down most of the time and receive only an hour of recreation and have limited contact and interaction of staff and visitors. They also have lower staff to inmate ratio in order to facilitate management, not including the need for more staff due to closer supervision and the need for a lower inmate to guard ratio (Hurley, 2019).

Many supermax prisons are located in rural areas, which often pursue prison contracts because they benefit economically from supplying and staffing the prison. Supermax prisons are typically more expensive to maintain due to the technology needed to maintain it such as high-security doors, fortified walls, and sophisticated electronic systems. Inside these facilities, the design emphasizes security and control. Supermax buildings or housing units are designed to minimize inmate movement, increase the ability of correctional officers to observe inmates, and isolate the inmates from negative prison influences. They have significant architectural and technological advancements not seen in other types of correctional facilities, such as extensive use of closed-circuit television, the provision of medical and psychological treatment services via remote technology, and the use of elements of robotics to deliver food to inmates and operate cell doors.

Federal Bureau of Prisons

The Federal Bureau of Prisons was created by Congress in 1930. It operates a system of prisons located throughout the nation. The Federal Bureau of Prisons classifies its institutions into the following (See Table 10.1):

Jails

Most Americans do not distinguish between jails and prisons. However, there is a clear administrative distinction with regard to prisons. **Jails** are the holding places of individuals who have been convicted of misdemeanor crimes. Jails are normally administered by county- or city-level officials, whereas prisons are administered by the federal government or by the state in case of state prison institutions. Jails are temporary holding cells for those who have been denied bail or those who are awaiting their audiences with the judge for preliminary hearings. A detention due to a denial of bail is also known as **preventive detention**.

TABLE 10.1   FEDERAL PRISON CLASSIFICATIONS AND THEIR CHARACTERISTICS.

Minimum	Low	Medium	High	Complexes	Administrative
Minimum security institutions, also known as Federal Prison Camps (FPCs), have dormitory housing, a relatively low staff-to-inmate ratio, and limited or no perimeter fencing. These institutions are work- and program-oriented. A number of Bureau of Prison (BOP) institutions have a small, minimum security camp adjacent to the main facility. These camps, often referred to as Satellite Prison Camps (SCPs), provide inmate labor to the main institution and to off-site work programs.	Low security Federal Correctional Institutions (FCIs) have double-fenced perimeters, mostly dormitory or cubicle housing, and strong work and program components. The staff-to-inmate ratio in these institutions is higher than in minimum security facilities.	Medium security FCIs (and United States Penitentiaries [USPs] designated to house medium security inmates) have strengthened perimeters (often double fences with electronic detection systems), mostly cell-type housing, a wide variety of work and treatment programs, an even higher staff-to-inmate ratio than low security FCIs, and even greater internal controls.	High security institutions, also known as USPs, have highly secured perimeters (featuring walls or reinforced fences), multiple- and single-occupant cell housing, the highest staff-to-inmate ratio, and close control of inmate movement.	At Federal Correctional Complexes (FCCs), institutions with different missions and security levels are located in close proximity to one another. FCCs increase efficiency through the sharing of services, enable staff to gain experience at institutions of many security levels, and enhance emergency preparedness by having additional resources within close proximity.	Administrative facilities are institutions with special missions, such as the detention of pretrial offenders; the treatment of inmates with serious or chronic medical problems; or the containment of extremely dangerous, violent, or escape-prone inmates. Administrative facilities include Metropolitan Correctional Centers (MCCs), Metropolitan Detention Centers (MDCs), Federal Detention Centers (FDCs), Federal Medical Centers (FMCs), the Federal Transfer Center (FTC), the Medical Center for Federal Prisoners (MCFP), and the Administrative-Maximum Security Penitentiary (ADX). Administrative facilities, except the ADX, are capable of holding inmates in all security categories.

Source: Federal Bureau of Prisons (2019).

According to Prison Policy Initiative (2019), there are currently 612,000 individuals are in local jails and a majority of them (462,000 or roughly 75%) are not yet convicted. The rest have been convicted and are serving their time in jail. It must be noted that recently, some counties have contracted with U.S. federal government to hold federal prisons in their facilities.

Most of these jails have very minimal rehabilitation programs and are therefore more used as holding centers for some convicted inmates. Likewise, it must be noted that most jails are much smaller, with 40% holding fewer than 50 people each.

BOX 10.1 CAREER HIGHLIGHTS: CORRECTIONAL OFFICER

The correctional career can include being in probation, parole, or correctional institutions. Correctional officers provide security, maintain order, and prevent escapes. Recently, several institutions have adopted rehabilitation programs that are sometimes managed by correctional officers. However, most rehabilitation specialists are mental and healthcare professionals. Thus, a variety of correctional careers exist for a number of disciplines.

For correctional officers at the state and county level, it is mostly required that one has a high-school diploma or equivalent, be at least 18 years of age, of good moral character, and have a stable job history. Moreover, the recruit should not have extensive criminal history and substance use disorders. Correctional workers at the federal level.

Source: Adapted from Belshaw and DeBoer (2017).

© Joseph Sohm/Shutterstock.com

Community Corrections

Community corrections refer to the spectrum of correctional alternatives that permit the convicted offender to remain in the community as opposed to serving time in a remote correctional facility (Davis, 2017, p. 59). Community corrections include probation, parole, and pretrial supervision for individuals who have been released on bail or deferred prosecutions. This form of punishment has been seen either as a "lenient" punishment, or as an ideal "alternative" to incarceration. While evidence show that remaining in the community is institutionally economical and rehabilitative, the conditions imposed on those under supervision are often so restrictive that they set people up to fail. In 2016, at least 168,000 people were incarcerated for such "technical violations" of probation or parole (Sawyer & Wagner, 2019).

A wide range of community correctional institutions, facilities, and programs exists. Most of these institutions are intended to house juveniles or women. Because of the smaller female offender population, these varieties of institutional facilities do not exist for women. Women prisons or other facilities combine the different security levels in a single facility but may be segregated by wings, levels, or pods. The level of supervision, however, might be similar to those applied in male facilities. Aside from prisons, there are different institutions for confinements, namely:

- Reformatories—Historically three kinds of facilities were especially associated with the "reformatory" label: reform schools for juveniles, institutions for women, and institutions for young adult male convicts. Today, this institution is mostly intended to rehabilitate youthful offenders or other nonserious offenders.
- Halfway houses—These facilities involve the supervision of an individual in the community. Halfway literally means that a person has served prison time and the remaining time to be served are spent in this home. These homes serve as the transitional phase in the preparation for release into the community.
- Boot camps—Boot camps are military-style facilities for youth (Davis, 2016). According to Morin (2019), they mostly focused on military-style treatment. Teens were yelled at, treated harshly, and punished with push-ups or physical discipline. Over the years, many alternative treatment programs have emerged such as those that have more focus on education and life skills, rather than harsh punishment. Some of these programs even take place in the wilderness versus jail-like settings.

Probation and Parole

Probation and parole are the generic nomenclatures for sentences that involve community corrections. **Probations** are normally applied to individuals who might be first time or nonserious offenders. Normally, probation is used as an alternative to prison. Probation is sometimes imposed in lieu of prison or as a condition for treatment and rehabilitation programs.

Paroles are normally granted to inmates who might have earned good time to be eligible for community release or have been considered for release after being determined as rehabilitated and needed to make a transition to the community. The granting of parole is normally granted under several considerations. The first is the state of rehabilitation of offenders. Normally, this is gauged through participation in and completion of prison programs. The other consideration is the "good time" behavior of the inmate. The third reason involves consideration of the contextual conditions of a person upon release such as work and family.

States vary in how they carry out the community punishments of probation, intermediate sanctions, and parole. In many states, probation and intermediate sanctions are administered by the judiciary, often by county and municipal governments. With the rise of therapeutic or accountability courts, the judiciary in collaboration with the prosecution, the police, and healthcare professionals collaboratively manage the probationer. Since parole is a conditional release granted by the executive, then the management and administration of the parolee is under the supervision of the state. Most states have either a bureau or a commission of pardon and parole also commonly known as parole boards.

Fines and Forfeitures

Fines are normally assessed for less serious offenses and have been uniformly applied to all types of offenders. They are normally assessed in combination with prison time or sometimes, in lieu of prison or jail time. Misdemeanor offenses are normally assessed fines.

Forfeitures means the confiscation of the fruits of the crime such as gain from drug deals, money laundering, and other similar profit motive offenses. Forfeitures aim to achieve two purposes. The first purpose is aimed to discourage offending by making offenders and their families not profit from the commission of the crime. The second purpose is to offset any civil damages or criminal justice expenses involved in the processing of the offender. These government actions are normally applied in serious offenses that include drug dealing, organized crime activities, or gang activities.

Accessory Penalties

Accessory penalties are those that are imposed on a convicted individual in addition to the principal punishment under the law. The principal punishments for convictions are jail or prison sentences. These additional penalties aim to achieve either the denial of the ability for the convicted individual to commit crimes in the future or to withdraw benefits that might result from the commission of a crime. For example, individuals in public service might have the accessory penalty of being disqualified to be elected for public office. In some circumstances, the retirement benefits, recognitions, and honors may be ordered to be withdrawn. In the case of sexual offenders, the offender might be barred from practicing a profession that would situate the former convict with potential victims. For this latter case, we have mechanisms such as the use of sex offender registry or restraining orders.

Forms and Application of Accessory Penalties

According to Kurti (2015), accessory penalties may operate as mitigation of punishment or the intensification of punishment to achieve the purposes of justice. In the first instance (i.e., **mitigation of punishment**), a convicted person who may have already suffered separation from a job, withdrawal of honors, and loss of parental supervision may already be considered sufficient to have satisfied the requirements for the accessory penalty that only the main punishment (e.g., imprisonment) will be the only one enforced. On the second instance (e.g., **intensification of punishment**), the court might impose additional penalties on top of the imprisonment as necessary for retribution purposes or crime prevention purposes. For example, the court might order a loss of parental authority over a child who had been abused.

Legal Constraints on Corrections

For a time, the courts have adopted the "HOP" "(hands-off policy)" involving cases of complaints by inmates against correctional facilities. HOP is the belief that judges should not interfere with the administration of correctional institutions. *Cooper v. Pate* (1964) signaled the end of the HOP. The court said that through the Civil Rights Act of 1871 state prisoners were *persons* whose rights are protected by the Constitution. The act imposes *civil liability* on any official who violates someone's constitutional rights. It allows suits against state officials to be heard in the federal courts. Most of the legal constraints are mostly found in the provisions of the U.S. Constitution.

First Amendment Rights

The First Amendment guarantees the freedom of expression and communications of citizens. Prisoners have successfully challenged many of the restrictions of prison life including access to reading materials and censorship of mail. However, the Supreme Court has also approved restrictions on access to written materials including denial of access to newspapers and magazines for prisoners housed in a disciplinary segregation unit. In addition, cases concerning the free exercise of religion have caused the judiciary some problems, especially when the religious practice may interfere with prison routine and the maintenance of order. The general rule has been to allow the exercise of religion in certain confines of the facilities. The Court, however, denies the exclusive use of that facility by any religion.

Fourth Amendment Rights

The Fourth Amendment prohibits *unreasonable* searches and seizures, but courts have not extended these protections much to prisoners. Thus, regulations viewed as reasonable to maintain security and order in an institution may be justified. Therefore, warrants are not required for the searches and seizures that are done in prison. *Hudson v. Palmer* (1984) upheld the authority of officials to search cells and confiscate any materials found.

Eighth Amendment Rights

The courts have applied four principal tests under the Eighth Amendment to determine whether conditions are unconstitutional [In re Lynch (1972) 8 Cal.3d 410, 424; In re DeBeque (1989) 212 Cal.App.3d 241, 248; *Furman v. Georgia*, 408 U.S. 238 (1972)]:

(1) Whether the punishment shocks the conscience of a civilized society
(2) Whether the punishment is unnecessarily cruel
(3) Whether the punishment goes beyond legitimate penal aims
(4) Whether the punishment is wholly arbitrary

The decisions of the Supreme Court remain inconclusive judging on the divided opinions of the Court on the matter. Also, the Court seems to have struggled with the imposition of penalties for minors and individuals with mental health issues [Atkins v Virginia, 536 U.S. 304 (2002)]. For example, the Court ruled in *Roper v. Simmons* [543 U.S. 551 (2005)] that it is a violation of the Eighth Amendment to execute individuals who are under 18 years old at the commission of a crime. This latest decision overturned the previous case of *Stanford v Kentucky* [492 U.S. 361 (1989)] where the Court upheld the execution of anyone 16 years and above. The Court has also struggled with the manner of the imposition of the death penalty and its conformity with the constitutional provision of the Eighth Amendment. These changing standards have already been by the Court in a 1958 [*Trop v Dulles*, 456 U.S. 86 (1958)] case where it was pronounced that prohibited "cruel and unusual punishments" should change over time due to society's "evolving sense of decency."

Fourteenth Amendment Rights

The Fourteenth Amendment espouses the **doctrine of incorporation**. Under this doctrine, the states are bound by the standards of due process established by the federal government. It is also known to enjoin the observance of due process. Under the due process clause of the constitution, state government officials must treat all people fairly and justly with decisions being made according to procedures prescribed by law. Thus, the Bill of Rights and the doctrines laid out in the interpretations of these rights bind the states to observe the same. Various decisions by the U.S. Supreme Court have established fundamental rules for revocations of probation and parole. Specifically, the Court has extended the fundamental fairness principle of notice and hearing prior to recommitment to prison. In addition, the right to counsel was also extended to respondents in jeopardy of being recommitted to prison due to alleged violations of the conditions of their probation or parole. In other words, the individual's Fifth and Sixth Amendment rights are also protected under these two circumstances. Likewise, assertions that prisoners have been denied equal protection of the law based on claims of racial, gender, or religious discrimination have been upheld by the Court.

On matters of prison inmate discipline, *Wolff v. McDonnell* (1974) lays down the basic elements of procedural due process that must be present when decisions are made, namely:

- To receive notice of the complaint
- To have a fair hearing
- To confront witnesses
- To get help in preparing for the hearing
- To be given a written statement of the decision
- Prisoners do not have the right to cross-examine witnesses

Corrections of the Future

The privatization of prisons in America can be traced back prior to the Civil War. In 1852, San Quentin opened in Marin County on the San Francisco Bay. More recently in the 1980s, the private prison industry began booming, fueled by the War on Drugs. Some of the detention facilities are housing individuals who have been confined to treatment for their substance use disorders under a deferred sentence program (Belenko & Spohn, 2015). As of 2016, about 19% of federal prisoners are held in private prisons. The Sentencing Project (2018) reports that the number of federal inmates confined in private prisons was over 128,000 in 2016. At the state level, Oklahoma and Texas have the highest number of inmates confined in private prison but New Mexico has the highest percentage (43.1%) of its inmates confined to private prisons. However, Arizona gained the highest percentage change (479.4%) on its reliance on private prisons.

Private prisons have grown into a multibillion-dollar industry. CoreCivic (formerly Corrections Corporation of America) is the largest operator of private prisons in the United States. With the government paying private prison operators about $23,000 per year per inmate, it has a lucrative business. In fewer than 20 years, its revenues have increased by more than 500%—from roughly $280 million in 2000, to $1.77 billion in 2017. CoreCivic reported that its 80,000-bed capacity is supported by the government to the tune of $23,000 per inmate per year and thereby American taxpayers pay these costs. If the prison beds are not fully occupied, the government has to pay for them anyway. For example, in 2011, Arizona paid Management and Training Corporation (MTC) $3 million when a 97% quota was not met.

Not only are your tax dollars funding these private prison operators, but you might also be investing in them without even knowing it. As of 2016, Wells Fargo, Bank of America, JP Morgan Chase, BNP and U.S. Bancorp, all played a role in bankrolling private prison companies. Thus, with the three main private prison companies—CoreCivic, the GEO Group, and MTC—the industry rakes in about $5 billion in revenue a year.

There is no evidence that they actually save taxpayers any money. In fact, the U.S. Bureau of Justice Statistics reported in 2016 that the cost-savings promised by private prisons have simply not materialized. Some research even indicates that private prisons often refuse to accept inmates that cost a lot to house (i.e., the violent offenders), making the statistics they report highly misleading.

In addition, a 2016 report by the U.S. DOJ said that privately operated federal facilities are less secure, less safe, and drastically more punitive than publicly operated federal prisons. Inmate on inmate assaults were almost 30% higher in private prisons, and new inmates were often automatically placed in solitary confinement due to overcrowding (Vittert, 2018).

Comprehension Check

1. Differentiate between the various goals of punishment.
2. Identify the various forms of punishment in the U.S. correctional systems.
3. Outline the different classifications of prisons.
4. Differentiate prisons from jails.
5. Identify and explain the different forms of community corrections models.
6. Explain the advantages and disadvantages of private prisons.

References

Atkins v. Virginia, 536 U.S. 304. (2002).

Belenko, S. & Spohn, C. (2015). Drugs, Crime, and Justice (2nd Edition). Los Angeles, CA: Sage.

Belshaw, S. H., & DeBoer, L. H. (2017). *Criminal justice* (2nd ed.). Dubuque, IA: Kendall Hunt.

Braithwaite, J. (1989). Crime, Shame, and Reintegration. New York, NY: Cambridge University Press.

Bronson, J., & Carson, E. A. (2019). *Prisoners in 2017.* Washington, DC: U.S. Department of Justice, Bureau of Justice Statistics.

Cochran, J. K., Chamlin, M. B., & Seth, M. (1994). Deterrence or brutalization: An impact assessment of Oklahoma's return to capital punishment. *Criminology, 32*(1): 107–134.

Cole, G. F., Smith, C. E., & DeJong, C. (2018). *Criminal justice in America*. Boston, MA: Cengage Leaning.

Collins, W. (2004). *Supermax prisons and the constitution: Liability concerns in the extended control units*. Washington, DC: U.S. Department of Justice, National Institute of Justice.

Cooper v Pate, 378 U.S. 546 (1964).

Davis v Finney, 21 Kan. App. 547 (1995).

Davis, M. S. (2016). *The concise dictionary of crime and justice* (2nd ed.). New York, NY: Sage.

Federal Bureau of Prisons. (2019). Retrieved from https://www.bop.gov/about/facilities/federal_prisons.jsp

Ford v Waignwright, 477 U.S. 399 (1986).

Furman v. Georgia, 408 U.S. 238. (1972).

Hunter, R. D., Barker, T., de Guzman, M. C. (2018). Police Community Relations and the Administration of Justice (9th edition). Pearson: New York, NY.

Hurley, M.-H. (2019) *Supermax prisons*. Retrieved from https://www.britannica.com/topic/supermax-prison

In re DeBeque. (1989). 212 Cal.App.3d 241, 248.

In re Lynch. (1972). 8 Cal.3d 410, 424

Kurki, L., & Morris, N. (2001). The purposes, practices, and problems of supermax prisons, *Crime and Justice, 28*, 385–424.

Kurti, S. (2015). Accessory penalties and their execution according to the Albanian legislation. Academic Journal of Interdisciplinary Studies, *4*(2): 505–510.

Martinson, R. (1974). "What Works?--Questions and Answers about Prison Reform." Public Interest 35(Spring): 22–54.

Morin, A. (2019). Bootcamps for troubled teens. Retrieved from https://www.verywellfamily.com/boot-camps-for-troubled-teens-1094838 on March 17, 2020.

Newman, G. (1983). *Just and painful: A case for the corporal punishment of criminals*. London, England: MacMillan Publishing Company.

Pyrooz, D. C. (2018). Using restrictive housing to manage gangs in U.S. prison. Corrections Today, (July/August): 10–13.

Roper v. Simmons, 543 U.S. 551. (2005).

Sawyer, W., & Wagner, P. (2019). *Mass incarceration: The whole pie 2019*. Retrieved from https://www.prisonpolicy.org/reports/pie2019.html

The Sentencing Project. (2018, August). *Fact sheet: Private prisons in the United States*. Washington, DC. Retrieved from https://www.sentencingproject.org/wp-content/uploads/2017/08/Private-Prisons-in-the-United-States.pdf

Sen, S. (1996). Human rights in the criminal justice system. The Police Journal, *69*(1): 51–60.

Stanford v. Kentucky, 492 U.S. 361. (1989).

Stohr, M. K., Walsh, A., & Hemmens, C. (2013). *Corrections: A text reader* (2nd ed.). New York, NY: Sage.

Trop v Dulles, 456 U.S. 86 (1958)

Vittert, L. (2018, December). *The cold hard facts about America's private prisons system*. Retrieved from https://www.foxnews.com/opinion/the-cold-hard-facts-about-americas-private-prison-system

Wolff v McDonnell, 418 U.S. 539 (1974).

Zimmerman, C. (2018). Supreme Court examines dementia, health issues in death penalty cases. *Catholic News Service*. Retrieved from https://www.catholicnews.com/services/englishnews/2018/supreme-court-examines-dementia-health-issues-in-death-penalty-cases.cfm

Endnote

[1] Ex post facto law operates retroactively when it benefits the offender.

The Corrections Process

LEARNING OBJECTIVES

After reading this chapter the student should be able to

1 Outline the correctional process from intake to release

2 Differentiate between the different forms of correctional intervention models

3 Explain recidivism and its different forms

4 Identify the challenges in the administration of persons under correctional supervision

5 Differentiate between the different forms and processes for releases of persons from correctional supervision

Introduction

According to data collected by the Bureau of Justice Statistics (Kaeble & Cowhig, 2018), the total population of adults under correctional supervision was under seven million in 2016. The trend shows declines in all categories of supervision. Probationers remain the highest number of supervised individuals, with those in jail are under one million. The study further revealed that this decline is due to decline in community supervisions and releases from incarcerations. These statistics clearly show the immense responsibility that correctional officers undertake in the criminal justice system. The major challenge for the correctional system involves the effective administration of these individuals under correctional supervisions.

This chapter identifies the processes involved in the different modalities of punishing adult criminal offenders in the United States. Punishments in the United States range from the use of civil sanctions such as fines to the most severe form of punishments such as incarcerations and death. Cole, Smith, and DeJong (2018) outlined the ladder of punishment ranging from fines all the way to the imposition of the death penalty. However, these sanctions are not mutually exclusive as these punishments could be applied in combination or may be accompanied by other accessory penalties.[1]

Starting with the sentencing stage, the different modes for correctional interventions are discussed in this chapter. The institutional supervision models will be discussed encompassing processes involved in prisons or jails. Likewise, community supervision models will be discussed. Processes involved in probation, parole, and other forms of intermediate sanctions are outlined and explained. Lastly, capital punishment in the United States is explained and various issues about the death penalty will be discussed.

Corrections Happen at Various Stages of the Criminal Justice System

The correctional process begins even before the finality of criminal convictions. Individuals that go through the criminal justice system are primarily already under correctional supervision the moment they are apprehended by the police (Lemert, 1951). The police can temporarily detain a person and may employ the supervisory power of the state through the restraint of their freedoms or the denial of access to certain amenities. In fact, the officer might start preliminary correctional interventions such as detoxification when an individual might be under the influence of substances or isolation when they are exhibiting disorderly conduct. Likewise, the police level might also involve the cooperation and intervention of healthcare and other human services professionals in order to pacify, restrain, or treat an individual. Police intervention programs, such as Crisis Intervention Teams (CIT), apply some of the immediate treatment interventions. Although these are technically not considered punishments, these interventions are, for all intents and purposes, supervision of people who have been formally placed under the custody of the state.

The current wave of therapeutic interventions has made prosecutions become the initial stage for corrections. Therapeutic intervention models do not only pertain to the treatment of substance using populations, but also with those who may need mental and psychological interventions. Primarily, the prosecution might refer some of these criminal justice clients to treatment while holding prosecution abeyance.

Finally, the drug courts place offenders under correctional supervision and treatment as a precondition for diversion or as an alternative to incarceration. Chapters 13 and 14 highlight the proliferation of these types of court in the United States.

The Sentencing Process

Under the U.S. legal system, it is acknowledged that punishments would only commence after the *final conviction*[2] of an offender. The process of punishment or corrections begins with the sentencing of an individual. There are several processes applied at the sentencing stages. However, let us also discuss the public policies that shape the sentencing process. These public policies determine the various modes and intensities of the criminal justice system's intervention at the correctional level.

There are three models that seem to be invoked in the sentencing process. The first model is an **indeterminate sentencing regime**. Under this model, the judge has the sole discretion and a whole range of options of punishment to impose from probation to death. The law normally allows the use of judges' discretion by giving a wide latitude for the judge to choose from in punishing the individual. For example, the law might provide a punishment from probation to a maximum of 10 years in incarceration. This process where the judge is given a wide latitude might be considered as **bench sentencing**. Under this regime, the judge can employ the following options (https://legaldictionary.net/determinate-sentencing/):

- **Concurrent Sentence**—A sentence that is served simultaneously with another sentence. The most common form of this concurrent sentence would be a combination of imprisonment and payment of restitution. It can also in the form of handing out a provision and some form of community service.

- **Consecutive Sentence**—A sentence that begins immediately after the completion of another sentence. Consecutive sentences are assigned for several crimes, or several counts that are assigned at the same time. This is mostly notable when a person is first confined to a prison for one type of conviction and later in a halfway house of rehabilitation center after serving the prison sentence.

- **Deferred Sentence or Suspended Sentence**—A sentence that is postponed for some reason until a later date. This type of sentencing is mostly applied in situations where an offender needs to get an incentive to remain in a treatment program. Among drug courts, the treatment is imposed while the sentence of incarceration might be suspended. A violation of the conditions, normally noncompletion of treatment, will result in the imposition of the original sentence.

- **Life Sentence**—A sentence that orders an offender to spend the rest of his or her life in jail, though in many jurisdictions there is an opportunity for parole after a certain period of time.

The second regime of sentencing process involves limiting the discretion of the judge (i.e. **determinate sentencing**). In the 1980s, it has been argued that indeterminate sentencing has led to abuse and disparity of sentencing (Newman, 1983). Under the indeterminate sentencing model, it was argued that disparities and uncertainties in sentencing are rooted in the discretion of judges. The judges were looked upon as not merely guided by laws in meting out justice. Instead, they showed the inclinations for some judges to emphasize extralegal factors including ideologies in their decisions. This has resulted in multiple unintended circumstances aside from sentencing disparity. For one, it was argued that indeterminate sentencing was considered tough on false positives[3] and lenient on false negatives.[4] On another front, it was argued that determinate sentencing does not make therapeutic sense. The uncertainties of detention results either in a stressful situation for an inmate. Arguments were also proffered that an inmate played the system by pretentious appearance of rehabilitation just to get an early release and made rehabilitation as a failed intervention model (Martinson, 1974). Since the locus of the problem was rooted in the judges' use of discretion, the natural solution would be to limit such discretion. Thus, the **determinate sentencing** model emerged. Under the determinate sentencing model, the law restricted the discretion of judges to prevent them from departing from the intended penalties under the law. The intent of determinate sentencing was for the avoidance of abuse on the part of both the judges who might make idiosyncratic punishment decisions and the abuses by correctional administration officials with respect to discipline and parole decisions. The guiding principle under this model is the administration of equal justice for all under the law. A good example of determinate sentencing was the one adopted by the state of Indiana where the judges are made to impose sentences under the law.

The third form of sentencing regime could properly be called a **hybrid regime**. Under this model, two forms of sentencing modalities emerge. First, the power of the judge to impose a sentence is either shared with some other groups or individuals. This might be called the **shared-decision model.** The second form might be called a **limited discretion model** where the law provides a range of options by which the judge will have some leeway in exercising his or her discretion. The first category (shared-decision model) involves several actors participating—sentencing juries, case workers' presentencing reports, and victim impact statements. Sentencing juries are normally assembled in capital offenses to determine whether a convicted person should receive the penalty of death or other form of sentence. The second form of shared-decision modality is the use of presentencing reports that are normally prepared by the office of probation and parole or some other commission empowered to provide recommendations to the judge. The third form of shared-decision-making involves the participation of the victims of the crime. The victims are made to declare either in open court or in writing how they feel about the offender and the damage that they suffered. This is known as victim impact statements. It is not clear how influential these statements are in the decision-making process of the judge. Sometimes, these three modalities might be applied in the courtroom to arrive at a sentence. Thus, an officer might prepare a presentence report and victims are allowed to state their feelings toward the offender even before a sentencing jury (*Payne vs Tennessee*, 1991).

The second option (i.e., limited discretion model) involves leaving the judge some discretion, but such discretion is structured by law or policies. This form of sentencing discretion has been called **presumptive sentencing**.

FIGURE 11.1 EXAMPLE OF THE MINNESOTA SENTENCING GUIDELINE.

4.A. Sentencing Guidelines Grid

Presumptive sentence lengths are in months. Italicized numbers within the grid denote the discretionary range within which a court may sentence without the sentence being deemed a departure. Offenders with stayed felony sentences may be subject to local confinement.

SEVERITY LEVEL OF CONVICTION OFFENSE (Example offenses listed in italics)		CRIMINAL HISTORY SCORE 0	1	2	3	4	5	6 or more
Murder, 2nd Degree (Intentional; Drive-By-Shootings)	**11**	306 *261-367*	326 *278-391*	346 *295-415*	366 *312-439*	386 *329-463*	406 *346-480*[2]	426 *363-480*[2]
Murder, 2nd Degree (Unintentional) Murder, 3rd Degree (Depraved Mind)	**10**	150 *128-180*	165 *141-198*	180 *153-216*	195 *166-234*	210 *179-252*	225 *192-270*	240 *204-288*
Murder, 3rd Degree (Controlled Substances) Assault, 1st Degree	**9**	86 *74-103*	98 *84-117*	110 *94-132*	122 *104-146*	134 *114-160*	146 *125-175*	158 *135-189*
Agg. Robbery, 1st Degree Burglary, 1st Degree (w/ Weapon or Assault)	**8**	48 *41-57*	58 *50-69*	68 *58-81*	78 *67-93*	88 *75-105*	98 *84-117*	108 *92-129*
Felony DWI Financial Exploitation of a Vulnerable Adult	**7**	36	42	48	54 *46-64*	60 *51-72*	66 *57-79*	72 *62-84*[2, 3]
Assault, 2nd Degree Burglary, 1st Degree (Occupied Dwelling)	**6**	21	27	33	39 *34-46*	45 *39-54*	51 *44-61*	57 *49-68*
Residential Burglary Simple Robbery	**5**	18	23	28	33 *29-39*	38 *33-45*	43 *37-51*	48 *41-57*
Nonresidential Burglary	**4**	12[1]	15	18	21	24 *21-28*	27 *23-32*	30 *26-36*
Theft Crimes (Over $5,000)	**3**	12[1]	13	15	17	19 *17-22*	21 *18-25*	23 *20-27*
Theft Crimes ($5,000 or less) Check Forgery ($251-$2,500)	**2**	12[1]	12[1]	13	15	17	19	21 *18-25*
Assault, 4th Degree Fleeing a Peace Officer	**1**	12[1]	12[1]	12[1]	13	15	17	19 *17-22*

[1] 12[1]=One year and one day

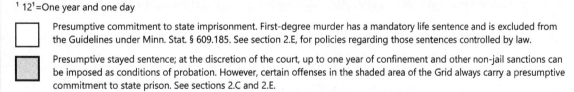

☐ Presumptive commitment to state imprisonment. First-degree murder has a mandatory life sentence and is excluded from the Guidelines under Minn. Stat. § 609.185. See section 2.E, for policies regarding those sentences controlled by law.

▩ Presumptive stayed sentence; at the discretion of the court, up to one year of confinement and other non-jail sanctions can be imposed as conditions of probation. However, certain offenses in the shaded area of the Grid always carry a presumptive commitment to state prison. See sections 2.C and 2.E.

[2] Minn. Stat. § 244.09 requires that the Guidelines provide a range for sentences that are presumptive commitment to state imprisonment of 15% lower and 20% higher than the fixed duration displayed, provided that the minimum sentence is not less than one year and one day and the maximum sentence is not more than the statutory maximum. See section 2.C.1-2.

[3] The stat. max. for Financial Exploitation of Vulnerable Adult is 240 months; the standard range of 20% higher than the fixed duration applies at CHS 6 or more. (The range is 62-86.)

Source: Minnesota Sentencing Guideline Commission (2019).

"I'm not a killer. I'm not a rapist. I'm really not a bad person once you get to know me," says Leandro Andrade, a 44-year-old convict who may make legal history. "Do I deserve to be locked up for the rest of my life, because a certain judge feels that's what he deserves?"

California's three-strikes law says that if someone commits a third felony after committing two prior similar felonies, then the sentence is a mandatory 25 years to life. In such a case, Leandro Andrade was given not one but two sentences of 25 years-to-life for stealing nine children's video-tapes, including "Snow White," "Cinderella," and "Free Willie 2." The tapes were worth $153.54, and lawyers for the state of California argue that the penalty is both correct and constitutional. But the other side argues that Andrade's punishment is cruel and unusual.

Under his sentence, Andrade will be 87 before being eligible for parole.

"I understand what I did was wrong. I knew I had to be punished. Now, you have to pay for that crime, for the mistakes that you make in life," says Andrade. "But I wasn't aware that for that little mistake I was going to receive a 25-to-life sentence."

Was it a just sentence? "For a petty theft, it carries, maximum three years," says Andrade. "That's what I believe I should be doing for petty theft . . . because I didn't kill anybody. I didn't hurt anybody."

In November 1995, Andrade, a U.S. Army veteran and lifelong heroin addict, says he wanted videotapes as Christmas gifts for his nieces. So he went to a Kmart, and a couple of weeks later, visited another Kmart store down the road. He tried to steal the videos and was caught by security guards at both stores.

"On the way out of the store, they approached me. And they asked me if I had any concealed tapes," he says. "And I said yes. I didn't argue with them. I didn't fight with them or anything else."

Andrade was sentenced to life in prison. It happened because California is the only state where a misdemeanor crime can be made into a third strike. They call it a "wobbler": So long as the first two crimes were clearly felonies, then a third crime—be it stealing a bike or a pizza, as happened to others, or videos—can send a person to prison for 25 years to life.

Andrade got the 25 years doubled for two cases of shoplifting, which became his third and fourth strikes under California's law. His first two strikes were for home burglaries that were committed back in 1983. Neither involved violence. In fact, Andrade didn't carry a weapon with him for either burglary.

Source: Excerpt from CBS News (2002).

The most popular form of presumptive sentencing guidelines is the Minnesota Sentencing Guidelines (see Figure 11.1 as example). Under the Minnesota guideline, judges are given certain range of punishment options after being given guidance on how to use seriousness of the offense and the offending history of the offender. For example, an offender who committed an assault in the first degree with a criminal history score of two would be sentenced from a minimum of 94 months to a maximum of 132 months (see the Minnesota Sentencing Guideline in Figure 11.1). Any departure from these ranges of sentences will require the judge to provide a justification from such departure.

A more stringent form of this hybrid sentencing process involves the use of mandatory sentences. **Mandatory sentence** is a specific sentence that is set by law, handed down upon committing a particular crime under specified circumstances. A judge does not have permission to alter a mandatory sentence, as it has been previously established by law. It is considered as a hybrid form because there are points where judges might have a discretion; for instance, during the first two strikes in a three-strikes law. Under the so-called three-strikes law, judges might have greater discretion on the punishment for the first two felony offenses. However, upon the third conviction, the judge will be bound to impose the maximum penalty under the law regardless of the offense and circumstances of the offender. For example, a person who commits a third offense that might only be punished for a year under ordinary circumstances will have to be imposed the penalty of 25 years in prison once convicted for that offense. (See example of such punishments in Box 11.1.)

Capital Punishment

The death penalty is an evolving issue in the U.S. penal system. As reported by the Justice Department, 34 states and the federal government have authorized the death penalty as of the end of year 2016 (Davis & Snell, 2018). It was reported that there was a total of 2,814 inmates sentenced to death with 20 executions by the end of that year. Most of the executions happened in the state of Georgia (n = 9), while 23 executions were estimated to happen in 2017. California currently has the most number of convicts sentenced to death.

Most individuals on death row are males (98%), White (55%), and were mostly between the ages of 35 and 59 years with a mean age of 49, single (55.7%), with 12th grade as their median level of education. As of 2016, 34 states have authorized lethal injection as a method of execution. In addition to lethal injection, 15 states authorized an alternative means of execution: electrocution (eight states), lethal gas (three), hanging (three), firing squad (two), and nitrogen hypoxia (one). Inmates normally have the option to select the method of execution. States that allow for multiple methods of execution would only allow these alternative methods if lethal injection is declared unconstitutional or when lethal injection could not be given (Davis & Snell, 2018).

Death Penalty Evolution

Two significant factors have contributed to the evolution of the practice of the death penalty in the United States. The first factor is the evolving nature of jurisprudence on the death penalty. The second is the ideological shift about the utility and fairness of the death penalty. In the first factor, the main legal issue about the constitutionality of the death penalty involved the interpretation of the Eighth Amendment of the U.S. Constitution.

The Eighth Amendment states that "cruel and unusual" punishment should not be imposed. The main contention hinges on the "cruel" nature of the punishment. The Supreme Court states that the death penalty is not cruel and unusual per se. Rather, it is the manner of execution that violated this constitutional requirement (*Coker vs Georgia; Furman vs Georgia*). More recently, the U.S. Supreme Court ruled that it is unconstitutional to execute juveniles (*Roper vs. Simmons*) and it has also prohibited executions of those that have mental health issues.

The ideological reason for the nonexecution hinges on the discrimination and fallibility of the criminal justice system. Although data suggest that there are more Whites on death row, it was argued that minority populations are disproportionately sentenced to the death penalty. The source of this disparity is the jury system that tends to mete out more punitive sanctions against minorities. More recently, the issue about the morality of death as a penalty is based on the argument that several of these death row inmates are wrongfully convicted. Although wrongful conviction is far less committed in the criminal justice system (Ramsey & Frank, 2007), death as a permanently incapacitating penalty is seen as unacceptable form of punishment in a fallible criminal justice system. The empirical evidence for wrongful convictions has been highlighted particularly with the development of DNA evidence and the advocacy work of such groups as the Innocence Project (see Box 11.2). The group claims that wrongful conviction is not as rare as previous research has shown (The Innocence Project, 2019).

BOX 11.2 DNA EXONERATIONS IN THE UNITED STATES

Fast Facts	Demographics of the 365	Other Facts	How DNA Makes a Difference in the Criminal Justice System
• **1989:** The first DNA exoneration took place • **365** DNA exonerates to date • **37:** States where exonerations have been won • **14:** Average number of years served	**225** (62%) African American **109** (30%) Caucasian **27** (7%) Latinx **2** (1%) Asian American **1** (<1%) Native American **1** (<1%) self-identified "other"	• 130 DNA exonerates were wrongfully convicted for murders; 40 (31%) of these cases involved eyewitness misidentifications and 81 (62%) involved false confessions (as of July 9, 2018) • 102 DNA exonerations involved false confessions; the real perp	• Since 1989, there have been tens of thousands of cases where prime suspects were identified and pursued—until DNA testing (prior to conviction) proved that they were wrongly accused.

Fast Facts	Demographics of the 365	Other Facts	How DNA Makes a Difference in the Criminal Justice System

• **5,065.5:** Total number of years served
 	
• **26.6:** Average age at the time of wrongful conviction
 	
• **43:** Average age at exoneration
 	
• **20 of 365** people served time on death row
 	
• **41 of 365** pled guilty to crimes they did not commit
 	
• **69%:** Involved eyewitness misidentification
 	
   • 42% of these cases were a cross-racial misidentification
 	
   • 32% of these cases involved multiple misidentifications of the same person
 	
• **44%:** Involved misapplication of forensic science
 	
• **28%:** Involved false confessions
 	
   • 49% of the false confessors were 21 years old or younger at the time of arrest
 	
   • 33% of the false confessors were 18 years old or younger at the time of arrest
		was identified in 76 (75%) of these cases. These 38 real perps went on to commit 48 additional crimes for which they were convicted, including 25 murders, 14 rapes, and nine other violent crimes (as of July 24, 2018)
		
		• 180 of the DNA exonerates (50%) had the real perpetrator(s) identified in their cases (as of August 22, 2018)
		
		• 137 of the DNA exonerates had the real perpetrator(s) identified through a cold database hit (as of October 19, 2018)
			• In more than 25% of cases in a National Institute of Justice study, suspects were excluded once DNA testing was conducted during the criminal investigation (the study, conducted in 1995, included 10,060 cases where testing was performed by Federal Bureau of Investigation [FBI] labs).
			
			• An Innocence Project review of our closed cases from 2004 to June 2015 revealed that 29% of cases were closed because of lost or destroyed evidence.

Fast Facts	Demographics of the 365	Other Facts	How DNA Makes a Difference in the Criminal Justice System
• 10% of the false confessors had mental health or mental capacity issues • **17%:** Involved informants • **264:** DNA exonerates compensated • **187:** DNA exonerations worked on by the Innocence Project • **160:** Actual assailants identified. Those actual perpetrators went on to be convicted of 152 additional violent crimes, including 82 sexual assaults, 35 murders, and 35 other violent crimes while the innocent sat behind bars for their earlier offenses.			

Source: *The Innocence Project (2019).*

Institutional Corrections

Intake Process

Prisons and jails have become more systematic and have been guided by evidence-based practices in their handling of individuals committed under their care. Chapter 10 provided different levels of classifications of institutions. However, those commitment orders are based on the judges' or sentencing bodies' decisions. The supervision and treatment of inmates in institutions remain in the discretion of correctional officials. It is in this light that most correctional institutions have applied certain criteria in classifying inmates during the intake process. The purposes of this intake classification process are staff safety, public safety, and effective treatment

(Brennan, 2011). The idea is to develop plans and programs that would be beneficial to the institution, society, and the inmates.

Brennan (2011) identifies several critical stages in the intake process, which he called axes.

Axis A—Descriptive Classifications of Criminal Behavior Patterns and Histories: This axis seeks to describe behavior as completely and accurately as possible—but it does not attempt to explain the behavior.

These classifications identify the types of offender that the institution is dealing with. These styles or types of offenders were applied by Brennan (2011, pp. 40–41) with respect to classification of inmates in Michigan and came up with the following prototypes:

Type 1: Nonviolent repeat drug offenders: This prototype reflects extreme substance abuse, while showing low violence. The prototype also has high affiliations with antisocial peers and boredom in leisure time.

Type 2: Multiple violence, domestic violence, and substance abuse: This prototype reflects repeat domestic violence, prior violence, high domestic violence current charges; above average.

Type 3: Serious early onset delinquency and ongoing adult violence: This prototype consists mostly of poorly educated young males with early onset of serious, often violent delinquency that is continuing into a serious adult criminal career. They typically have high crime families, antisocial peers, and live in high crime environments. Other traits include antisocial personality, antisocial attitudes, social adjustment problems, high prison misconducts, and high-risk scores for general and violent recidivism.

Type 4: Late starters with a low criminal history but with a serious current violent offense: This "late starter" prototype is well below the prisoner average for criminal and violent history, noncompliance, and delinquency, and has fewer priors or disciplinary infractions. However, many in this group have a serious current violence charge. The risk/need profile offers no obvious explanation for offending, except for low educational/vocational resources.

Type 5: Chronic serious violent offenders—early starters: This prototype reflects the classic "serious, chronic, and violent" offender, with early and substantial delinquency and a long versatile adult criminal history, including violence, noncompliance, substance abuse, domestic violence, and so on. It appears to be an older hardened version of Type 3. The risk/need profile matches this serious crime profile with multiple risk factors and the highest risk for general and violent recidivism. Some mental health issues are present.

Type 6: Lower risk, mostly nonviolent minor offenders: This late-starting prototype is well below the offender average for criminal involvement, current and prior violence, drugs, and domestic violence. It reflects a minimum-security nonviolent inmate. Criminogenic factors are also well below average with no clear risk factors.

Type 7: Nonviolent late-starting but chronic drug offenders with other criminal involvements: This late starter is a more serious version of the nonviolent drug users of type 1. It has a far longer criminal history, more chronic drug addiction, greater noncompliance, and multiple jail and prison terms. Criminogenic correlates indicate chronic drug use, poverty, residential instability, and some indications of mental health issues. Above average noncompliance and prior incarcerations cohere with above average disciplinary infractions.

Axis B—Explanatory Classifications of Criminal Behavior: Axis B attempts to explain why offenders behave the way they do. It identifies the risk factor and relates these factors to criminology theories. There remains a need in criminal justice for more comprehensive risk and need assessment to gather key explanatory factors to support more valid and informative explanatory classifications.

Axis C—Internal Classifications for Prisoner Management and Programming: Over the last decade an innovative form of "internal classification" has emerged, primarily in prisons that combine explanatory goals with management goals. Internal classifications thus aim to both explain criminal behavior and guide offender management by making databased placements to appropriate programs, work assignments, housing decisions, and security/safety requirements. This type of classification examines the need and risk of an offender to tailor the intervention to the offender. Going through these intake process enables institutions to achieve a databased approach in the handling of inmates. They can also achieve the twin purpose of maintaining safety and delivering appropriate treatment and rehabilitation programs for its inmates.

Institutional Supervision

Supervision of inmates in prisons are either indirect, direct, or hybrid. **Indirect supervision** refers to the use of institutional designs in order to control and monitor inmate behavior. This requires the crafting of an architectural design whereby inmates will be less able to commit infractions and the ability to view and react to any occurring or potential breach of rules or order in the prison. The prison designs of a panopticon or corridor design will facilitate this type of supervision.

Direct supervision uses inmate-personnel interaction and situates them in ways that they are in close proximity with each other. The higher the level of supervision need, the lower the ratio of guards to inmates. In Chapter 10, it has been noted that maximum security facilities will have a lower ratio than minimum security. In most situations, minimum and medium security prisons utilize the informal leadership of inmates in order to monitor and supervise inmate behaviors.

The **hybrid model** uses both structural designs and human interaction in order to supervise inmates (Woodruff, 2010). This type of supervision will place technology to monitor behaviors as well as maintain regular

FIGURE 11.2 INDIRECT SUPERVISION THROUGH THE USE OF TECHNOLOGY IS PORTRAYED IN THE FOLLOWING PHOTO WHERE CORRECTIONAL OFFICERS HAVE VIRTUAL SUPERVISION OF THE OFFENDERS.

personnel inspection of inmates (See Figure 11.2 as a demonstrative example). This model was used with the famous detention of Jeffrey Epstein. In Epstein's case, a closed-circuit TV was used to monitor his behavior and the guards were expected to personally check on him every 30 minutes. This type of supervision is normally applied to certain inmates or group of inmates who might need to be watched all the time and would need immediate intervention from correctional personnel.

Release Processes

Releases from prison can happen in several ways. These releases can be grouped into two—executive fiat or by operation of law. Reversals of convictions through judicial processes (appeals or writ of habeas corpus) are not included in this section as they are not per se after conviction releases. Cases that are on appeal and petitions for habeas corpus assert the presumption of innocence. Therefore, these releases cannot be technically considered as postconviction releases.

Releases by Operation of Law

Ex-post facto law operation. In general, the law can only have prospective operation. However, when laws are promulgated that favor the accused, then the laws might be applied retroactively. Thus, when a law is passed decriminalizing an act, those inmates who have been convicted for those acts will reap the benefits of decriminalization. Even a reduction of legal punishment for the acts for which an inmate has been convicted will result in the reduction of the individual's sentence. Sometimes, the operation of the law must be invoked by the inmate through a petition known *as habeas corpus*. The writ of habeas corpus is remedy of someone who claims to have been illegally detained. This petition will require government agents holding that person to produce the body of that person before the courts and explain why there should be a continuing detention of that individual.

Mandatory Releases

Mandatory releases happen for two reasons. The first is the full service of the term for which the offender has been sentenced. In this case, the offender is deemed to have maxed out. The second situation where mandatory release happens is when the offender would have earned enough good time credit that he or she becomes eligible for release deducting the actual good time credit from the mandated sentence.

Discretionary Releases

Discretionary releases are those that are granted to an inmate or offender due to the exercise of discretion by the criminal justice decision makers. The first type of discretionary releases comes from the decisions made by the chief executive of the federal or state governments. The second type of discretionary releases are those that are exercised by correctional officials such as the wardens or a group including the parole boards or in several jurisdictions, the use of reentry programs.

Releases by Executive Clemencies

These forms of releases result from the clemency of the executive whether at the federal or state level. There are certain executive agencies that could aid the executive in this process. In the federal level, the Justice Department normally advises the president on these decisions. At the state level, the governor of a state might create a board or commission that recommends dispositions of cases for executive clemencies. However, at both levels, executive clemencies are purely within the discretionary prerogative of the chief executive.

Pardon. As an executive clemency, a pardon removes the punishment that has been imposed on a convicted person. This form of clemency can only be extended after final conviction.

Reprieve. Under this form of clemency, the execution of the punishment is postponed for a later date. This is not similar to a concept known as suspended sentence in two different aspects. First, the decision is reposed with the judge. Second, the sentence is imposed upon a violation of a condition for the suspension of the sentence. These conditions are normally based on completing a treatment program or other humane considerations. A reprieve is an executive clemency that does not alter the sentence imposed except for its execution. There are normally no preconditions for this type of clemency as it is done on the wisdom of the executive.

Commutation. This type of clemency lessens or shortens the penalty that has been imposed. This has a different effect from pardon as pardon requires immediate release while a reprieve will require the inmate to serve the unexpired portion of the punishment that has not been served.

Amnesty. This type of clemency has a unique effect on the individuals. Under this form of clemency, the criminal offense is erased from the record of the offender. Also, the offender does not need to be convicted nor even arrested. So, even a fugitive or one who is still under adjudication will benefit from this type of clemency. In most circumstances, the offender needs to apply for amnesty or fulfill a condition (e.g., registration) in order to be granted the clemency. Also, all individuals under the same classification of offenders can legitimately apply. In this way, it is a form of collective pardon rather than an individual pardon.

Parole. Parole is a clemency that grants release of a person from incarceration. The person granted parole is still under the supervision of the state and the remaining punishment or recommitment might be ordered upon the violation of parole that includes reoffending or technical violations.

Community Corrections

Probation and parole are the generic names for community corrections. There are however various forms of these types of community corrections. The following list outlines these forms of supervisions and mechanics for administering these forms of punishment.

Intensive Supervision Probation (ISP)—A form of probation that involves an extra measure of supervision and control by the probation officer. ISP often is used with chronic offenders and other high-risk offenders who pose a greater probability of reoffending. One model of ISP may start with stringent monitoring in the beginning of the probationary period and such supervision becomes more relaxed as time goes on. The other model may start with less strict supervision but might become more stringent once the supervised individual starts manifesting risk factors or recidivating.

Shock Probation/Parole/Incarceration—Probation or parole following a brief period of confinement in prison designed to shock the offender with the realities of prison life. With respect to shock probation, generally, the sentencing judge imposes a term of incarceration. After a designated period of time, the inmate may then apply to the sentencing court to have a shock probation hearing. The inmate, either present or in absentia, is either granted or denied probation. If shock probation is granted, the inmate is released from prison under probation supervision for a specified period of time under certain conditions. Shock parole on the other hand is not a judge-imposed decision but rather it goes through the parole board within the executive department.

Furloughs—This form of release is temporary and is normally granted for humanitarian considerations (e.g., family illness, major life events, and so on). The inmate is given specific period of time to return to prison and may be accompanied by a supervisor during those release periods.

Work Release—This type of program varies in its duration. Some offenders are required to return to prison after work while others might be away during the work week and return to prison on the weekends or nonwork days.

Community Service—Individuals who are low-risk, low-need offenders might be assigned to this type of punishment. Oftentimes, they are imposed on misdemeanor offenders. Felony offenders might be assigned this type of punishment but for a longer period of time. The type of community service rendered may be related to the profession or expertise of the offender. Therefore, a cook might be assigned to soup kitchens for community service. Others might be required to deliver lectures in classes or even teaching vocational skills for out of school youth.

Halfway House—A community-based correctional option where offenders released from prison make the transition back to community life by living in a house with other offenders. Halfway houses operate on the premise that convicts need a period of supervised treatment after release from prison to facilitate their adjustment on the outside.

Day Reporting—This form of supervision allows offenders to stay at home but receive services at a center.

Day Fines—This is a form of financial punishment where the offender pays a portion of daily income. The amount depends of aggravating factors or seriousness of the offense.

Recidivism

Recidivism refers to the phenomenon of released individuals recommitting crimes (Davis, 2016). These offenders are also known as repeat offenders. The research literature has conceptualized recidivism in several ways. The first conceptualization involves the stage of when the crime happened. Some scholars argue that recidivism should be reckoned with at the time of arrest while others consider the prosecutorial or adjudication stage as the onset of recidivism. Others consider recidivism to have only occurred when the person has been convicted. The rationale for the last conceptualization of recidivism is due to the presumption of innocence. In most cases, a technical violation during probation or parole stages are punished with the jail time attached to the crime. If it was under a deferred prosecution, the offender might be brought to trial for the original offense that was committed. If it was a new crime, then the offender will be charged, adjudicated, and punished, if there is a conviction.

The second dimension of recidivism's conceptualization involves the type of offense committed. In some jurisdictions, a violation of probation or parole (technical violation) is considered a reoffense. In other jurisdictions, any form of crime (i.e., felony or misdemeanor) is considered a recidivism. Finally, other jurisdictions will only consider an act as recidivism if it involves a certain time frame or it is similar to the previous offense. In other words, if a crime happens after a certain reglamentary period or it involves a different offense even when it is within the reglamentary period, then the offense is considered a new offense. However, there are mandatory sentencing laws that would disregard the diversity of the offense or the interim period when the crime happened and would simply convict a person to a maximum sentence under the law.

Factors of Recidivism

Andrews and his colleagues start with the premise that it is essential to identify those deficits (criminogenic needs) that increase the likelihood that offenders will recidivate. They focus only on those causes of recidivism that can be changed, which they call "dynamic risk factors." They have now compiled eight separate meta-analyses to show empirically which factors are the strongest predictors of recidivism and thus should be targeted in treatment for change (Andrews & Bonta, 2010, p. 65).

They call these the "Central Eight," which consists of the "Big Four" and the "Moderate Four" (Andrews & Bonta, 2010, pp. 58–60). The Big Four include a history of antisocial behavior, antisocial personality patterns (weak self-control, anger management, and problem solving skills), antisocial cognition (attitudes, rationalizations, identity favorable to crime), and antisocial associates (interaction mainly with pro-criminal others). Antisocial history is included despite appearing to be a static risk factor, because even though a "history cannot be changed," it is possible to focus on "appropriate intermediate targets of change" including "building up new noncriminal behaviors in high-risk situations and building self-efficacy beliefs supporting reform ('I know what to do to avoid criminal activity and I know that I can do what is required')" (p. 58). The Moderate Four are family/marital circumstances, school/work, leisure/recreation, and substance abuse (pp. 59–60). Andrews and his colleagues use these dynamic risk factors in their assessment instrument (the Level of Service Inventory) and in their selection of modalities to address these factors (e.g., cognitive-behavioral treatment) Figure 11.3 below show the latest facts and information about released inmates' recidivism in the United States.

Reentry

Prisoner reentry program has been defined as "correctional programs . . . that focus on the transition from prison to community (prerelease, work release, halfway houses, or specific reentry programs) and programs that have initiated treatment (substance abuse, life skills, education, cognitive/

FIGURE 11.3 RECIDIVISM IN THE UNITED STATES.

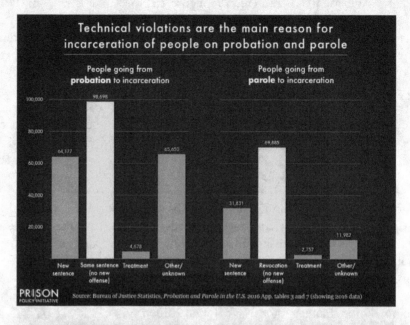

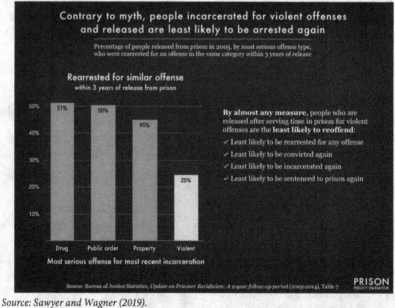

Source: Sawyer and Wagner (2019).

behavioral, sex/violent offender) in a prison setting and have linked with a community program to provide continuity of care" (Seiter & Kadela, 2003, p. 238). This definition contemplate of a continuity of treatment that starts in prison and transitions over to the community upon release. Thus, programs in prison are not only meant to reform the inmate but to prepare them for transition to community life.

Impetus for Reentry Programs

The drive to adopt reentry programs was based on several observations about the state of prison and reentry.

1. The fact that mass incarceration happened that brought about tremendous costs on the system (Glaze & Herberman, 2013; Jonson & Cullen, 2015).

2. About 700,000 of inmates are released annually from prison and into communities. This huge number of ex-inmates has to integrate with the communities they came from or in the new community from which they were placed (Travis, 2005).

3. The length of incarceration that were due to the "get tough" policies of the 1990s have significantly changed the community, culture, and technology that the released inmates will return to when they are released.

4. Many of these released offenders recidivate on the first six months at a significantly high rates (Durose, Cooper, & Snyder, 2014; Langan & Levin, 2002). In particular, offenders with substance use disorders have about 80% recidivism in much shorter period of time (Travis, 2005).

The argument for reentry programs is the realization that inmates are unprepared to transition into the communities. Several barriers to rehabilitation exist within communities that make released individuals unable to cope or adjust in their new environments. Some of these barriers include the following (Kempker, 2010):

1. Educational and employment barriers—These twin issues are primordial among inmates. Most of them are low educated with minimal work skills. This incompetence is barrier to employment. Sampson and Laub (1993) and more recently Andrews and Bonta (2010) identified having a job as key to abandoning the life of crime. Figure 11.4 depicts typical group educational program setting in prison.

2. Substance use and mental health issues—Substance use and mental health are co-occurring disorders among the inmate population. Inmates can have immediate relapse once they are released in the communities if they cannot seek health professionals who can help them overcome these disorders.

3. Survival concerns—The lack of social support presents a unique challenge for released inmates. Their needs for assistance on child care, nourishment, homes, and mobility make their transition more frustrating and challenging (Jonson & Cullen, 2015; Nelson, Deess, & Allen, 1999). For example, they need transportation to get to work. Those released inmates with physical disabilities cannot function more effectively if they are relocated to new communities that are different from where they were used to. On the other hand, some are allowed to the criminogenic environment where they came from that it was easier for them to recidivate.

FIGURE 11.4 INMATES NORMALLY UNDERGO SOME LECTURES AS A FORM OF REHABILITATION PROGRAM TO PREPARE THEM FOR COMMUNITY LIFE OUTSIDE OF THE FACILITY.

© Rebekah Zemansky/Shutterstock.com

According to Kempker (2010), the key to these challenges is to have plans in each jurisdictions aligned with the kinds of inmates they have to deal with and the specific challenges they face. He also argued that reentry preparations should happen within prison and within communities simultaneously.

As a comprehensive program, reentry programs have dramatically risen of the past decades (Garland & Wodahl, 2014; Petersilia, 2009; Rhine & Thompson, 2011). In 2006, 35 states were given grants to launch reentry programs (Kempker, 2010). In the current evaluations of the programs, it was found that service deliveries to released inmates have significantly improved although significant impact on recidivism has yet to be realized (Linquist et al., 2018). In fact, Anderson (1990) found earlier that attitudes and behaviors of ex-inmates are transmitted to those in the community on release making those communities vulnerable crimes and other social problems. Thus, a more thorough retooling of the programs has to be done in order to achieve maximum effectiveness.

Restorative Justice

Restorative justice is a new movement in the fields of victimology and criminology. The principle involves that criminal justice repair relationships and restore the losses suffered by victims and citizens. The key intervention involves the active participation in the process by all relevant parties in the crime. Restorative justice programs, therefore, enable the victim, the offender, and the affected members of the community to be directly involved in responding to the crime. The criminal justice systems serve as facilitator of a system that aims at offender accountability, reparation to the victim and full participation by the victim, offender, and community.

The restorative process of involving all parties—often in face-to-face meetings—is a powerful way of addressing not only the material and physical injuries caused by crime, but the social, psychological, and relational injuries as well. When a party is not able, or does not want, to participate in such a meeting, other approaches can be taken to achieve the restorative outcome of repairing the harm. In addressing offender accountability, these approaches can include restitution, community service, and other reparative sentences. In addressing victim and offender reintegration they can include material, emotional, and spiritual support and assistance.

Restorative justice differs from contemporary criminal justice in several ways. First, it views criminal acts as more than just a legal violation but a harmful conduct that inflicts harms to victims, the offender and members of the community. Second, it is an inclusive and collaborative process. Finally, it alters measures of success that is not only focused on punishing or servicing the needs of the offender but also includes the repair of the harms on the emotional, physical, and financial well-being of victims and society in general.

The Restorative Process

Several processes have been developed in the implementation of restorative justice models. The main idea is for the victims and the offenders to come to terms about their experiences. On the part of the offender, it involves the realization of the harm and damage that has been inflicted. The hope is for the offender to find remorse and resolve to not engage in such criminal behavior in the future. For the victims (i.e., individual and society), the process aims toward a journey for forgiveness that could be arrived perhaps in the understanding of the contexts for the occurrence of the crime (e.g., the offenders' motivations) and the healing of the emotional damage brought by crime. It is important to remember that restorative justice does not excuse criminal liability nor forego with the punishment. Instead, it aims to repair the relationship that has been disrupted by crime (Braithwaite, 1990).

Victim, Offender, and Community Meetings

Meetings between victims, their offenders, and members of the affected community are important ways to address the relational dimension of crime and justice. It is accepted that the following three methods are hallmarks of restorative justice. Each requires that the offender admit responsibility for the offense. Each is limited to parties who volunteer to participate.

Victim–Offender Mediation

This is a process that provides an interested victim the opportunity to meet his offender in a safe and structured setting, engaging in a discussion of the crime with the assistance of a trained mediator. The goals of victim–offender mediation include permitting victims to meet their offenders on a voluntary basis, encouraging the offender to learn about the crime's impact and to take responsibility for the resulting harm, and providing victim and offender the opportunity to develop a plan that addresses the harm. There are more than 300 victim–offender mediation programs in North America, and over 500 in Europe.

Research on such programs has found higher satisfaction among victims and offenders who participated in mediation, lower fear among victims, a greater likelihood that the offender will complete a restitution obligation, and fewer offenders committing new offenses, than among those who went through the normal court process.

Family or Community Group Conferencing

This process brings together the victim, offender, and family, friends, and key supporters of both in deciding how to address the aftermath of the crime. The goals of conferencing include giving the victim an opportunity to be directly involved in responding to the crime, increasing the offender's awareness of the impact of his or her behavior and providing an opportunity to take responsibility for it, engaging the offenders' support system for making amends and shaping the offender's future behavior, and allowing the offender and the victim to connect to the key community support. Conferencing was adapted from Maori traditional practices in New Zealand, where it is operated out of the social services department, and was further modified in Australia for use by police. It is now in use in North America, Europe, and southern Africa in one of those two forms. It has been used with juvenile offenders (most New Zealand juvenile cases are handled by conferencing) and with adult offenders. Research on such programs shows very high degrees of satisfaction by victims and offenders with the process and results.

Peacemaking or Sentencing Circles

This is a process designed to develop consensus among community members, victims, victim supporters, offenders, offender supporters, judges, prosecutors, defense counsel, police, and court workers on an appropriate sentencing plan that addresses the concerns of all interested parties. The goals of circles include promoting healing of all affected parties; giving the offender the opportunity to make amend; giving victims, offenders, family members, and communities a voice and shared responsibility in finding constructive resolutions; addressing underlying causes of criminal behavior; and building a sense of community around shared community values. Circles were adapted from certain Native American traditional practices, and are being used throughout North America. Repairing the Harm Caused by Crime Each of the hallmark restorative justice processes—victim offender mediation, community or family group conferencing, and peacemaking or sentencing circles—ends with an agreement on how the offender will make amends for the harm caused by the crime. Two traditional criminal justice sanctions are used in restorative responses to crime: restitution and community service.

Restitution is the payment by an offender of a sum of money to compensate the victim for the financial losses caused by the crime. It is justified in a restorative perspective as a method of holding offenders accountable for their wrongdoing, and as a method of repairing the victim's injury. Restitution can be determined in the course of mediation, conferencing, or circles; it can also be ordered by a judge. In other words, it is a potentially restorative outcome that may result from either a restorative or a conventional process. Studies have shown that restitution increases victim satisfaction with the justice process. Some studies have shown that the use of restitution was associated with reductions in recidivism. Other studies have shown that when restitution is determined during mediation, it is more likely to actually be paid than when it results from court order alone.

Community service is work performed by an offender for the benefit of the community. It is justified in a restorative perspective as a method of addressing the harm experienced by communities when a crime occurs. However, it can be used instead for retributive reasons or as a means of rehabilitating the offender. What distinguishes its use as a restorative response is the attention given to identifying the particular harm suffered by the community as a result of the offender's crime, and the effort to ensure that the offender's community service repairs that particular harm. So, for example, offenders who put graffiti on buildings in a neighborhood can be given the community service of removing graffiti from buildings in that neighborhood. Community service programs in Africa build on customary processes for making amends, thus addressing community concerns and easing the offender's reintegration into the community.

Dilemmas in Corrections

Corrections as a process are being pulled in several directions. These factors range from considerations of society, victims, offenders, and bureaucracy. These factors can be presentation of these juxtaposed positions that confront correctional institutions.

Control/Safety versus Rehabilitation/Welfare

The safety of society and victims are prime considerations of the state supervision of the individuals who are in conflict with the law. These twin goals might run counter to each other. It has been acknowledge that prison could be criminogenic and that out-of-prison intervention programs could be more beneficial to the offender. However, several examples of inmates who are released to the community commit more serious crimes while allowed to leave prison. The case of William Horton has dramatized the negative consequences of furlough. While on furlough, William Horton committed assault, robbery, and rape (https://en.wikipedia.org/wiki/Willie_Horton). This incident has brought to light the consequence of extending humanitarian considerations to inmates at the expense of danger to society. As a consequence, several jurisdictions have abolished furloughs. In fact, Feeley and Simon (1992) have noted that community supervision has transitioned from helping and counseling offenders to one of risk management and surveillance. The balancing of these twin objectives remains.

Conscience versus Convenience

Rothman (2002) brought to light the dilemma of correctional officials of maintaining balance between doing what is beneficial and what is easy to do. This presents a bureaucratic problem. Organizations are made to achieve the maximum benefit (effectiveness) with minimal resources (efficiency). In criminal justice, this is not an easy decision as these two objectives need to be met through satisficing. Satisficing is a coined term to mean that in order to meet one goal, you have to sacrifice another goal. In corrections, it is convenient to pursue a warehousing policy but it would not be beneficial to the offender and ultimately, society, who will need to live with a high-risk offender. On the other hand, rehabilitation of an offender is a long, expensive, and sometimes has uncertain outcome (inefficient), which however has a promise of long-term effects on society (effectiveness). In the study by Rothman (2002), his observation is that in correctional institutions, convenience always wins over conscience.

Restoration versus Retribution

Society expects the criminal justice as the great equalizer. When the status quo has been raptured, society expects to provide that equilibrium to bring back order. For a time, this burden of equilibrium has been placed upon the offender using the coercive power of the state. Thus, retribution has been seen as a legitimate form of punishment. However, the reality that individuals can only be restrained for time and that they need to be brought back into society has encouraged the introduction of restoration as a philosophy of punishment. In this regard, a real equilibrium can only happen if both the offender and the victim can be able to restore their relationships and live symbiotically. These two philosophies do not clash on their objective (i.e., equilibrium). The source of tension between the two philosophies is emotional rather than rational. The great moral issue is that, "Should an individual who has transgressed this equilibrium be made to continually enjoy the restored social order that he or she has ruined?" The evidence suggests that society can embrace restoration. This state of corrections is on shaky grounds in as much as the pendulum has swung from rehabilitation to just desserts or from a regime of crime control to a regime of due process (Seiter & Kadela, 2003).

Comprehension Check

1. Describe the different models and forms of sentencing offenders in the criminal justice system.

2. Explain the various inmate classification systems in the institutional facilities.

3. Identify the different instances when someone could be considered as a recidivist.

4. What are the different forms of releases?

5. What are the different forms of community corrections programs in the United States?

6. Explain the processes for the Restorative Justice Model.

7. Identify the processes involved in the reentry of offenders into the community.

References

Anderson, E. (1990). *Streetwise: Race, class, and change in an urban community.* Chicago, IL: University of Chicago Press.

Andrews, D. A., & Bonta, J. (2010). *The psychology of criminal conduct* (5th ed.). New Providence, NJ: Anderson.

Brennan, T. (2011). Better classification for better decisions: Using a "multi-axial" approach to intake, placement, programming, and reentry planning. *Corrections Managers' Report, 17*(3), 33–34, 39–44.

Cole, G. F., Smith, C. E., & DeJong, C. (2018). *Criminal justice in America.* Boston, MA: Cengage Leaning.

CBS News. (2002). *Three strikes: Penal overkill in California?* Retrieved from https://www.cbsnews.com/news/three-strikes-28-10-2002/

Davis, E., & Snell, T. L. (2018). *Capital punishment, 2016.* Washington, DC: U.S. Department of Justice, Bureau of Justice Statistics.

Davis, M. S. (2016). *The concise dictionary of crime and justice* (2nd ed.). New York, NY: Sage.

Durose, M. R., Cooper, A. D., & Snyder, H. N. (2014). *Recidivism of prisoners released in 30 states in 2005: Patterns from 2005 to 2010.* Washington, DC: Bureau of Justice Statistics, US Department of Justice.

Feeley, M. M., &Simon, J. (1992). The newpenology: Notes on the emerging strategy of corrections and its implications. *Criminology, 30*(4), 449–479.

Garland, B., & Wodahl, E. (2014). Coming to a crossroads: A critical look at the sustainability of the prisoner reentry movement. In M. S. Crow & J. O. Smykla (Eds.), *Offender reentry: Rethinking criminology and criminal justice.* Burlington, MA: Jones & Bartlett Learning.

Glaze, L. F., & Herberman, E. J. (2013). *Correctional populations in the United States, 2012*. Washington, DC: Bureau of Justice Statistics, US Department of Justice.

The Innocence Project. (2019). *DNA exonerations in the United States.* Retrieved from https://www.innocenceproject.org/dna-exonerations-in-the-united-states/

Jonson, C. L., & Cullen, F. T. (2015). *Prisoner reentry programs. Crime and justice.* Retrieved from http://www.jstor.org/stable/10.1086/681554?origin=JS TOR-pdf

Kaeble, D & Cowhic, M. (2019). *Correctional Populations in the United States, 2016*. Washington, DC: U. S. Department of Justice, Bureau of Justice Statistics.

Kempker, G. (2010). *A framework for offender reentry.* Washington, DC: U.S. Department of Justice, Bureau of Justice Assistance.

Langan, P. A., & Levin, D. J. (2002). *Recidivism of prisoners released in 1994.* Washington, DC: Bureau of Justice Statistics, US Department of Justice.

Lemert, E. M. (1951). Social pathology. New York, NY: Mcgraw-Hill.

Lindquist, C., Lattimore, P., Willison, J. B., Steffey, D., Stahl, D. H., Scaggs, S., . . . Eisenstat, J. (2018). *Cross-site evaluation of the bureau of justice assistance FY 2011 second chance act adult offender reentry demonstration projects: Final report.* Washington, DC: National Institute of Justice, Bureau of Justice Statistics.

Martinson, R. (1974). "What Works?–Questions and Answers about Prison Reform." Public Interest 35(Spring): 22–54.

Minnesota Sentencing Guideline Commission. (2019). *Standard sentencing grid 4-A.* Retrieved from http://mn.gov/msgc-stat/documents/ Guidelines/2019/StandardGrid.pdf

Nelson, M., Deess, P., & Allen, C. (1999). *The first month out: Post-incarceration experiences in New York City.* New York, NY: The Vera Institute.

Newman, G. (1983). Just and painful: *A case for the corporal punishment of criminals.* London, England. MacMillan Publishing Company.

Payne v Tennessee, 501 U.S. 808, 90–5721. (1991).

Petersilia, J. (2009). Transformation in prisoner reentry: What a difference a decade makes. In J. Petersilia (Ed.), *When prisoners come home: Parole and prisoner reentry* (Rev. ed.). New York, NY: Oxford University Press.

Ramsey, R. J. & Frank, J. F. (2007). Wrongful conviction: Perceptions of criminal justice professionals regarding wrongful convictions and extent of system errors. *Crime & Delinquency, 53* (3): 436–470.

Rhine, E. E., & Thompson, A. C. (2011). The reentry movement in corrections: Resiliency, fragility, and prospects. *Criminal Law Bulletin, 47,* 177–209.

Rothman, D. J. (2002). *Conscience and convenience: The asylum and its alternatives in progressive America.* New York, NY: Routledge-Taylor and Francis.

Sampson, R. J., & Laub, J. H. (1993). *Crime in the making: Pathways and turning points through life.* Cambridge, MA: Harvard University Press.

Sawyer, W., & Wagner, P. (2019). *Mass incarceration: The whole pie 2019.* Retrieved from https://www.prisonpolicy.org/reports/pie2019.html

Seiter, R. P., & Kadela, K. R. (2003). Prisoner reentry: What works, what does not, and what's promising. *Crime & Delinquency, 49*(3), 360–388.

Travis, J. (2005). *But they all come back: Facing the challenges of prisoner reentry.* Washington, DC: Urban Institute.

Woodruff, L. (2010). A *secondary data analysis of staff reaction to the transition from linear jail to a direct supervision model in Kane County, Illinois.* Retrieved from https://www.lexipol.com/resources/blog/the-evolution-of-prison-design-and-the-rise-of-the-direct-supervision-model/

Endnotes

[1] Accessory penalties are those sanctions that are additionally attached to the crime committed that might either be laid out in law or are determined by the judge as conditions for the legal sentence. For example, a restrain on one's mobility or practice of a profession might be imposed as additional sanction to an individual.

[2] In most circles, final conviction here means that the offender has already exhausted all the legal remedies such as appeals. The incarceration of death row inmates is not considered as the punishment but as only a means of restraint that recognizes the danger that an inmate pose to society. This is similar to preventive detentions at a pre-conviction stage of the process.

[3] False positives are those who were thought to be in need of longer incarceration and rehabilitation but in reality are do not have those risks and the need for those treatments.

[4] False negatives are those who were thought to be in less need of intervention and were seen as less risks but turned out be a high-risk and high-need individuals.

SECTION 3
SPECIAL TOPICS IN CRIMINAL JUSTICE

Chapter 12
Juvenile Justice

Chapter 13
Drugs, Terrorism, Organized Crimes, and Cybercrimes

Chapter 14
The Community Justice System

© Cheryl Casey/Shutterstock.com

CHAPTER 12

Juvenile Justice

LEARNING OBJECTIVES

At the end of the chapter, the student should be able to

1 Describe the history and development of the juvenile justice system

2 Understand the basic components of the juvenile justice system

3 Identify the differences between the juvenile justice system and the adult criminal justice system

4 Explain the transfer process and differentiate between types of judicial waivers

Introduction

So far, we have been discussing and learning about the particulars of the criminal justice system as it pertains to adults. However, it is important to understand that in the United States, we have separate systems for adults and juveniles. Individual states have the right to set age thresholds for processing youth in the adult system. Moreover, some states process any individual in the adult system, regardless of age, for specific serious offenses.

You learned earlier in Chapters 8 and 9 about our adult system and the typical court process. The juvenile justice system is separate and distinct from the adult criminal justice system. In comparing the two, one can see the many differences between them, including differing terminology and procedures. The juvenile justice system has a strong focus on individualized treatment and care, specifically taking into account the best interests of the child. This chapter is designed to provide an introduction to and an overview of the juvenile justice system. To this end, we will provide a history of the juvenile justice system and its development, and examine its basic components and concepts, as well as how it compares to the adult criminal justice system.

History of the Juvenile Justice System

In England, during the 1700s and 1800s, children were treated much the same as adults, often enduring harsh punishments and imprisoned in the same facilities as adult offenders. Additionally, children who had been abandoned or had committed delinquent acts were forced to work long hours in deplorable, abusive conditions. Others lived on the streets where they had to search for their own food and shelter.

During this same time in the United States, the 13 colonies were influenced by English common law. Children under the age of 7 were seen as incapable of forming the intent necessary for serious criminal offenses; they were deemed too young to understand their actions and consequences. Children aged 7 to 14 were held accountable for their actions if it was determined they could distinguish between right and wrong. Children over the age of 14 were treated and punished as adults, much the same as what was taking place in England at the time.

© TypoArtBS/Shutterstock.com

During the 19th and 20th centuries, the **child savers** were a group of progressive reformers who sought to improve the way juveniles were treated. These individuals believed that children were not inherently bad or evil, but were a product of their environment. The child savers were against the imprisonment of children with adults and the horrible conditions found in the workhouses, so they pushed for legislation that would make the state intervene in the care for children. This group initiated the development of institutions to rehabilitate juveniles, taking the approach that youth needed treatment, not punishment.

These **houses of refuge**, which were controlled by the state, became a place of shelter and structure for dependent, neglected, and delinquent youth. One of the first reform houses was established in New York in 1825 by the Society for the Prevention of Juvenile Delinquency, who worked to build a system of foster home placements. Thirty years later, the Chicago Reform School opened in 1855, followed by the first school for girls in Massachusetts in 1856 (Lawrence & Hemmens, 2008). Even with these efforts to help and treat children, however, the reform schools did not protect the children from harsh punishment, abuse, and unfair labor practices. It was not until over 40 years later, during what is now often referred to as the Progressive Era, that we really started to see reform take place.

In 1899, Cook County, Illinois established the first juvenile justice system through its passage of **An Act of the Treatment and Control of Dependent, Neglected, and Delinquent Children**. This act contained four main components:

1. Separate court for delinquent, dependent, and neglected children.
2. Special legal procedures that were less adversarial than those in the adult system.
3. Separation of children from adults in all parts of the justice system.
4. Programs of probation to assist the courts in deciding what the best interest of the state and the child entails.

The passage of this act sparked the juvenile court movement. Although some states had already been instituting correctional reforms and innovative court practices, Illinois was the first state to establish a truly separate juvenile court (Rothman, 1980; Watkins, 1998). Thus, any child aged 15 years or younger who committed a crime would fall under the legal responsibility of the juvenile court. As more states began to establish their own juvenile courts, this upper age limit often increased to 16 or 17. By 1927, only two states had yet to implement juvenile courts (Maine and Wyoming). By 1950, juvenile courts existed in every state, and the number of cases handled in these courts continued to increase, attempting to resolve problems rather than simply punish wrongdoing. Ultimately, the juvenile system was formed with an overall objective to focus less on punishment and more on rehabilitation of our youth.

Parens Patriae and the Child's Best Interest

Parens patriae refers to the process of when the government acts as the parent when a child's actual parents are unable to do so. It essentially becomes the government's responsibility to look after the best interests of the child. Eventually, this English law was adopted in American juvenile courts as a way to allow the government to assume the responsibility of any child who was destitute, neglected, or ill-behaved. This laid the groundwork for the development of juvenile justice.

After the first juvenile court was established, we began to recognize that youth who commit crimes should not be treated the same as adult criminals. Instead, these children are less culpable, and have a greater capacity for change. By the 1920s, every state had established a separate juvenile justice system in order to acknowledge and account for these differences.

Initially, proceedings within the juvenile court were informal, often amounting to nothing more than a conversation between the juvenile and the judge, including no legal representation for the juvenile. However, in the landmark 1967 decision *In re Gault*, the U.S. Supreme Court ruled that the Constitution guarantees many of the same due process rights to juveniles that adults are afforded (see *Important Cases*). The Court subsequently extended additional rights to juveniles, such as the standard of reasonable doubt and forbidding double jeopardy.

As we moved into the late 1980s and early 1990s, a rise in the juvenile crime rates drove legislators to take on a "get tough on crime" mentality for juvenile offenders. This new mindset led to the elimination of certain protections afforded by the juvenile justice system, and legislation to transfer youth out of the juvenile system and into the adult criminal justice system. Some of these laws even resulted in juveniles being sentenced to the harshest penalties of life without parole and the death penalty. In fact, in some states, juveniles could be sentenced to death and executed for a crime committed as a child until the ruling in *Roper v. Simmons* in 2005. This transfer to adult court and experience within the adult system ultimately exposed youth to the very same dangers experienced before the creation of a separate juvenile system over 100 years before.

Similar to the declining crime rates we have seen in adult crime, juvenile crime rates have seen a steady decline since the 1990s as well. However, many of the harsh penalties still remain. The overarching goal of the juvenile justice system—individualized care and treatment—coincides with the focus on rehabilitation, and today's juvenile justice system distinguishes itself from the adult system in several important ways.

The Juvenile Justice System

Types of Cases under the Juvenile Justice System's Jurisdiction

There are three types of cases that fall under the jurisdiction of the juvenile justice system. Juvenile **delinquency** cases involve youth who are alleged to have committed crimes. If the same crime had been committed by an adult,

© Diego Cervo/Shutterstock.com

the matter would be handled in criminal court. However, as you will soon learn, the procedures in the juvenile system vary greatly from those in the adult criminal justice system. Juvenile **dependency** cases involve children who are abused or neglected by their parents or guardians. In these cases, the juvenile court judge will ultimately decide whether the youth should be removed from the home. When a juvenile commits an offense that only applies to minors, this is known as a **status offense**. In other words, if an adult were to engage in the very same

FIGURE 12.1 JUVENILE JUSTICE FLOWCHART.

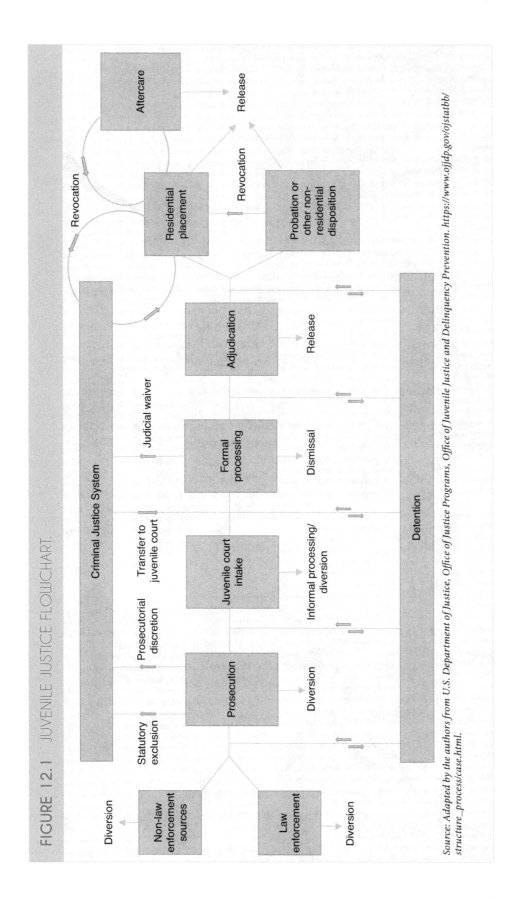

Source: Adapted by the authors from U.S. Department of Justice, Office of Justice Programs, Office of Juvenile Justice and Delinquency Prevention. https://www.ojjdp.gov/ojstatbb/structure_process/case.html.

behavior, it would not be considered a criminal matter. Some examples of status offenses include truancy, running away, underage drinking, and smoking cigarettes.

Age of Majority

To legally be considered a juvenile, the individual must fall under the **age of majority**, or the legal adult age. This age varies from state to state and ranges from 16 to 18. In the majority of states, the upper age limit to be considered a juvenile is 17, whereas some states hold it at 16, and two states (New York and North Carolina) have an upper age limit of 15 for juveniles (OJJDP, 2017). In other words, this upper age limit is the oldest age at which a juvenile court has jurisdiction over an individual for law violations. An upper age of 15 means that the juvenile court loses jurisdiction over a child when he or she turns 16; an upper age of 16 means the juvenile court loses jurisdiction when a child turns 17; and an upper age of 17 means that a juvenile court loses jurisdiction over a child when he or she turns 18. Some states have set higher upper age limits (often through age 20) for juvenile court jurisdiction in status offense, abuse, neglect, or dependency cases.

Definitions for which youth are under the original jurisdiction of the juvenile court are found within state statutes and are largely based on age. However, several states have statutory exceptions to the basic age criteria, including factors related to the age of the youth, the alleged offense, and the youth's court history. These exceptions can place certain juveniles under the jurisdiction of the adult criminal court (i.e., *statutory exclusion*). In some states, a combination of these factors can place the youth under the jurisdiction of both the juvenile and adult criminal courts, giving the prosecutor the authority to decide which court will handle the case (i.e., *concurrent jurisdiction*, *prosecutor discretion*, or *direct filing*).

Police Interaction

The juvenile justice system differs in structure, process, policy, and focus from the adult criminal justice system (see Figure 12.1), but retains some similarities as well. Most complaints against juveniles are brought about by the police, but an injured party (victim), school officials, and even the parents can also initiate complaints. Remember, the types of cases that fall under the jurisdiction of the juvenile system include delinquency cases, status offenses, neglected children, and dependent children.

Once a complaint has been initiated against a juvenile, the police must make a series of decisions:

1. Whether or not to take the child into custody
2. Whether or not to request the child be detained following apprehension
3. Whether or not to refer the child to court

However, age presents special challenges to law enforcement. In many departments, there is a juvenile officer or specialized unit that will take over a case after a patrol officer apprehends a juvenile. Police must maintain probable cause standards in order to take a juvenile into custody. Serious offenses usually result in taking the child into custody and detainment. For minor violations or status offenses, on the other hand, officers typically take the youth to the police station.

© Jan H Andersen/Shutterstock.com

Intake

When police decide to detain a juvenile, the first step in the process is **intake**. During the intake process, which is similar to an initial hearing for adults, juveniles meet with intake officers, juvenile probation officers, or prosecutors. At this point, approximately 20% of cases are dismissed, or diverted from the system. If not dismissed, one option at intake is to place the juvenile on deferred status, or informal probation, which allows for the charges to be dismissed if the youth stays out of trouble for a certain length of time. Another option is to file a petition for a court hearing, which is typically done if the intake officer believes that the juvenile's behavior calls for a more formal hearing and adjudication. In some cases, a waiver petition will be filed to transfer the youth to adult criminal court.

The Adjudication Process

If a juvenile is not released to a parent or guardian before adjudication by a judge, a **detention hearing** will be held to determine probable cause and whether the youth should be detained in a facility or released to a legal guardian. Similar to the bail hearing that takes place in adult criminal court, the judge will make a determination regarding the best interests of the child and the safety of the community.

The equivalent to the criminal court trial in the adult system is **adjudication** in the juvenile system. Although the proceedings are much less formal, an adjudicatory hearing ensures that the juvenile retains his or her due process rights, including the right to counsel, the right to confront witnesses, and protection against self-incrimination. Juveniles, however, do not have a right to a jury trial. Therefore, the judge reviews all of the evidence and information provided by law enforcement, probation officers, and attorneys, and makes a determination regarding whether the youth is delinquent and requires court supervision, or dismisses the charges. Most cases in juvenile court are delinquency cases, followed by dependent and neglected children, and status offenders.

Disposition

If a juvenile is found to be delinquent, a **disposition hearing** will take place where a judge will decide the best placement of the youth. Before this hearing, the probation department will collect and put together background and current information on the juvenile in a predisposition report. Probation officers may also make recommendations to the judge, based off factors such as history of delinquent behavior, school performance, gang involvement, psychological evaluations, and information given by parents, teachers, and school counselors. The **predisposition report** is quite similar to the presentence report presented in the adult system, as it provides detailed information regarding the juvenile, circumstances surrounding the offense, and recommendations for the appropriate disposition. The report also considers the victim's wants and needs, the community's safety, and the juvenile's needs and accountability. There are some noticeable differences between the predisposition report and the presentence report, however. For example, the predisposition report focuses on treatment options and reintegration into the community, whereas the presentence report focuses on the appropriate punishment. In the juvenile system, the judge ultimately determines whether the youth will become a ward of the state and assume the responsibility of the child, and can place them in a secure institution or a nonsecure facility in the community. Taking all of the factors into consideration, a juvenile court judge has a variety of options regarding disposition, including dismissal of the case, restitution or fines, therapy or counseling, psychiatric treatment, residential treatment facilities, house arrest and electric monitoring, probation, day treatment and reporting centers, or secure confinement.

Although probation is the most widely used disposition for juvenile delinquents, it is also likely the least effective. We see many youth reoffending, especially those sentenced to intensive supervision probation. Juveniles can also be placed in various facilities, which can be residential or nonsecure placement such as group homes or foster care, or secure detention facilities. Another disposition that is perhaps increasingly used in the juvenile system is the use of restorative justice. This process brings together the victims, the community, and the offenders, allowing all parties to work together to determine the best outcome for all involved. Through restorative justice, victims can take an active role in the healing process and offenders can take responsibility for the consequences of their actions.

Aftercare

Once juveniles have either completed their sentence or been released early, they are placed on **aftercare** (the equivalent to adult parole). Aftercare programs are meant to help prevent recidivism by supporting and monitoring juveniles through supervision. Juveniles must follow certain conditions upon release, such as obeying curfews, attending school, and staying out of trouble. Aftercare is the last phase of completing a disposition sentence.

TABLE 12.1. TERMINOLOGY COMPARISON.

Juvenile System	Adult System
Petition	Warrant
Delinquent act	Crime
Taken into custody/detained	Arrested
Detention hearing	Bail hearing
Petition for delinquency	Criminal indictment
Adjudication hearing	Trial
Respondent	Defendant
Adjudication	Conviction
Label delinquent	Find guilty
Dispositional hearing	Sentencing
Disposition	Sentence
Detention centers	Jails
Aftercare	Parole

Juvenile Courts

A Brief History

Prior to the creation of separate juvenile courts, youth typically appeared in criminal court alongside adult defendants. Judges and juries often found juveniles not guilty or even just released them, especially when they were charged with nonviolent offenses, rather than locking them up with adults. The juvenile court is one of the first organized efforts to address the needs of ill-behaved, unsupervised, and neglected children outside the orphanage or the poorhouse. What began as multipurpose social service centers due to caseloads including large numbers of non-

© cgstock/Shutterstock.com

criminal and nonserious offenders, turned into a new approach to handling young offenders and other children who were often ignored in the "crowded chaos of criminal court" (Butts & Mitchell, 2000, p. 174). The separate courts helped to ensure that more young offenders were sanctioned for their crimes, but through a flexible, informal, and personal process, allowing the legal process to attend to the unique circumstances of every youth.

Since their establishment, juvenile courts have emphasized an individualized approach. Rather than following specific standards for sentencing, or "matching" sentences to offenses, the disposition of each case was intended to address the unique circumstances of the offender. The juvenile courts sought to determine what factors seemed to lead the child to delinquent behavior, and to subsequently formulate a treatment plan to get them back on the right path. In order to help achieve this mission, juvenile laws were distinct from state criminal codes. Rather than being prosecuted for committing crimes, juveniles were brought before the court for "acts of delinquency." Conversely, adult criminal courts were focused on retribution and punishment, and emphasized due process. Adult courts sought to determine guilt or innocence as quickly and fairly as possible. Accordingly, there did not need to be any detailed investigations into the individual circumstances of the offender; instead, society showed their disapproval of criminal behavior through the court's imposition of proper punishments upon conviction. The differences observed in juvenile courts allowed for broad discretion to intervene. The judges were able to develop individual, and sometimes creative, dispositions for youthful offenders. Additionally, adult court hearings are open to the public (even if it is a juvenile who has been charged as an adult), and all files are open to the public unless sealed by court order. Information related to juvenile proceedings are much more limited. While the proceedings may be open or closed, all juvenile records, including information regarding charges and disposition, are closed.

Progression or Regression?

As more juvenile courts were developed, however, the structures and procedural approaches were altered in order to fit the overall concept of the juvenile court into each state's own legal and organizational philosophy (Rothman, 1980; Sutton, 1988). As the years went on, the juvenile court system became increasingly bureaucratic and overburdened. The profound discretion given to juvenile court judges began to be questioned. In his 1964 speech to the National Council of Juvenile Court Judges, the U.S. Supreme Court Chief Justice Earl Warren stated that controversies over due process in the juvenile court would be settled once an appropriate case came before the U.S. Supreme Court (see Box 12.1) (Manfredi, 1998).

In the following years, the discretion of juvenile court judges was significantly restricted and the juvenile court process became more formalized. There was also an increase in the number of juveniles sent directly to criminal court, essentially taking away the juvenile court's jurisdiction over a number of categories of young offenders. The juvenile justice system started to look much like the criminal justice system, especially in regard to its purposes and procedures.

BOX 12.1 DID YOU KNOW?

The case that Chief Justice Warren was referring to earlier turned out to be a 1967 decision by the U.S. Supreme Court, *In re Gault* (387 U.S. 1 [1967]). In 1964, a juvenile court judge ordered 15-year-old Gerald Gault to be detained for making a mildly obscene phone call to a female neighbor. During this call, Gerald and a friend allegedly asked the neighbor several strange questions, including, "Are your cherries ripe today?" and "Do you have big bombers?" (Bernard, 1992, p. 114). Once picked up by the local sheriff, Gerald's family was not notified that he was in custody. The court never heard testimony from the neighbor and never established whether Gerald and his friend had even made the phone call. Still, Gerald was committed to a state institution for delinquent boys until he turned 18 (three years). If this same offense had been committed by an adult, the sentence likely would have been a small fine.

Gault's appeal to the Supreme Court would turn out to be a significant stepping stone to changes to the juvenile courts. The Court ruled in his case that in any delinquency proceeding where confinement is a possible outcome, juveniles should have the right to notice of charges against them, the right to cross-examine witnesses of the prosecution, the right to assistance of counsel, and the protection against self-incrimination—due process rights that were built into the U.S. Constitution for adults accused of committing a crime.

Gault's case, along with several others decided by the U.S. Supreme Court in the 1960s and 1970s, helped to impose important procedural restrictions on U.S. juvenile courts. Although still denied the federal rights of bail, jury trial, and speedy trial, juvenile courts are now required to follow a standard of proof "beyond a reasonable doubt" instead of a "preponderance of evidence" and adjudication became equivalent to conviction in evaluating double jeopardy claims (Bernard, 1992).

Juvenile Court Waivers

Juvenile courts hold jurisdiction for any criminal (delinquent) acts committed by minors. In some cases, however, the juvenile court will transfer the case to the adult criminal court. This **waiver of jurisdiction** has traditionally been decided by a judge, but we are now seeing more prosecutors being given increasing power to request waivers (Klein, 1998). A couple of questions that have long been asked are, "At what age should children be held responsible for illegal behavior?" and "What exceptions should be allowed?" Juveniles lose any rights they have as minors, however, when they are transferred to the adult criminal justice system, and they become legally responsible for their behavior. Although transfer to criminal court usually occurs for juveniles who have committed serious and violent offenses, youth who commit lesser offenses like property and drug offenses may be transferred as well. Importantly, a defendant can only be tried in the adult system or the juvenile system, not both. In *Breed v. Jones* (1975), the Supreme Court ruled that once a juvenile has been tried in juvenile court, that juvenile cannot be transferred to adult court for the same crime, as this would be considered double jeopardy.

Transfer to adult criminal court is something that has taken place for almost a century. Throughout the 1980s and 1990s, when the crime control model prevailed, the United States saw a significant increase in the number of juvenile transfers to adult court. In fact, between 1987 and 1996, there was a 47% increase in the national number of judicially waived cases (Stahl, 1999). During this time, almost every state either enacted new waiver laws or expanded their existing waiver policies.

Types of Waivers

Discretionary Judicial Waiver

The typical method through which youth are transferred to adult court is a discretionary judicial waiver and is typically initiated by the prosecutor. These waivers allow juvenile court judges to waive the jurisdiction of the juvenile court and transfer a delinquency case to the adult criminal court if it meets the criteria necessary. The criteria usually include consideration of the offender's age, the offense, criminal history, amenability to rehabilitation, and the threat to the public.

Presumptive Judicial Waiver

As the role of the prosecutor increased in the 1980s and 1990s, the burden of proof shifted; it went from the prosecution having to demonstrate that the youth met the necessary criteria to be transferred to criminal court to becoming the responsibility of the juvenile. New policies made the judicial waiver "presumptive," requiring defense attorneys to provide proof that the youth was amenable to juvenile court disposition. In other words, the defense had to show that the youth would be responsive to treatment or rehabilitation; otherwise, he or she would be transferred to adult criminal court.

Mandatory Judicial Waiver

Whereas presumptive waiver policies provide an opportunity for the juvenile to avoid transfer to criminal court, mandatory judicial waivers do not afford this opportunity. The juvenile court's only role in mandatory waiver proceedings is to make sure the youth meets the statutory requirements for waiver. If so, the juvenile judge is required to transfer jurisdiction of the case to criminal court.

It is not known how many mandatory transfers occur or their impact, but we do know they went from being fairly uncommon in the 1970s to much more frequent in the 1990s. Criteria vary by state, with many states taking previous adjudications into account. For example, Indiana law requires juvenile court judges to transfer *any* juvenile with a prior adjudication who is charged with a felony, regardless of the juvenile's age (Griffin, Torbet, & Szymanski, 1998, p. A-28).

Statutory Exclusion

Known in some states as "automatic transfer," statutory exclusion also became widespread in the 1990s. This mechanism contributed to the blur in boundaries seen between the juvenile and adult systems during this time. Statutory exclusion laws require certain juvenile offenders to automatically be transferred to criminal court when charged with certain offenses. In other words, judicial involvement is not needed, and these cases are placed directly in the criminal court's jurisdiction, bypassing juvenile court completely. Criteria for statutory exclusion usually include a combination of age, offense, and prior record.

Direct File in Criminal Court

Another form of criminal court transfer, known as direct file, concurrent jurisdiction, or prosecutor discretion, allows prosecutors to make the decision whether to prosecute juveniles in juvenile or adult court. Because the prosecutors' charging decisions are considered an executive function, judges cannot review these actions. Essentially, prosecutors are given the power to file charges against a juvenile directly in adult criminal court, and by choosing to do so, they effectively override any juvenile court jurisdiction over the case.

In most states, a juvenile has to be at least 16 years of age to be eligible for transfer to criminal court. Some states, however, transfer youth as young as 13. Even still, a small number of states allow transfers at any age for

TABLE 12.2 ADVANTAGES AND DISADVANTAGES OF WAIVER/ TRANSFER TO CRIMINAL COURT.

Advantages	Disadvantages
Right to jury trial	Subject to more severe sentences
Juries may be more sympathetic to a minor	Fewer punishment and treatment options
In some cases, the court may be inclined to dispose of the juvenile's case more quickly (due to factors like overcrowding/case overload) and impose lighter sentences	Possibility of serving time in an adult jail or prison
	A conviction may carry greater social stigma
	More difficult to have records sealed

certain crimes (e.g., homicide). Some factors that might lead to waiver include the following:

- Seriousness of offense
- Offense history
- Age
- Unsuccessful rehabilitation efforts in the past

Juvenile cases that are subject to waiver usually involve more serious offenses or youth who have been in trouble in the past. Although the adult criminal court affords more constitutional protections and rights, it also presents some distinct disadvantages. For instance, juveniles transferred to criminal court are likely to be given harsher sentences, including serving time in adult correctional facilities.

The Court's decision in *Kent v. U.S.* gave juveniles the right to a juvenile waiver hearing, sometimes referred to as amenability hearings because the court must decide whether the juvenile will be amenable to treatment within the juvenile system or whether they should be transferred to the adult system. Before the hearing takes place, the judge is provided with a report containing pertinent information regarding the background of the juvenile defendant (e.g., criminal history, family, medical, and education). The report also includes the age of the defendant at the time of the alleged offense, the severity of the offense, and information related to the juvenile's amenability to treatment. This report allows the judge to weigh each factor and determine whether to retain the case in adult court or remand the case back to the juvenile courts.

Important U.S. Supreme Court Decisions Regarding Juveniles

© Brandon Bourdages/Shutterstock.com

In re Gault, 387 U.S. 1, (1967): A landmark U.S. Supreme Court decision in which the Court held that the due process clause of the Fourteenth Amendment applies to juvenile defendants just as it does to adult defendants. As such, juveniles accused of crimes in a delinquency proceeding must be afforded rights such as the right to counsel, the right to confront witnesses, the right against self-incrimination, and the right to maintain a record of the proceedings.

In re Winship, 397 U.S. 358, (1970): A U.S. Supreme Court decision that established the burden of proof as beyond a reasonable doubt for all criminal cases (juvenile and adult) in all states.

McKeiver v. Pennsylvania, 403 U.S. 528, (1971): The U.S. Supreme Court held that juveniles are not entitled by the Sixth or Fourteenth Amendments to a trial by jury in juvenile criminal proceedings.

Schall v. Martin, 467 U.S. 253, (1984): The U.S. Supreme Court upheld a New York statute that provided for juveniles to be held in pretrial detention if they pose a serious risk of engaging in further crime prior to their trial.

Roper v. Simmons, 543 U.S. 551, (2005): The U.S. Supreme Court ruled it unconstitutional and prohibited the execution of a juvenile offender who was under the age of 18 at the time the capital crime was committed.

Graham v. Florida, 560 U.S. 48, (2010): A decision by the U.S. Supreme Court holding that juvenile offenders cannot be sentenced to life imprisonment without parole (LWOP) for nonhomicide cases.

Miller v. Alabama, 567 U.S. 460, (2012): The U.S. Supreme Court held that sentences of LWOP are unconstitutional for juvenile offenders.

The Juvenile Justice and Delinquency Prevention Act (JJDPA) was established in 1974 with the basis that children, youth, and families who are involved with juvenile and adult criminal courts should be protected by federal standards regarding care and custody, while also maintaining the safety of the community and the prevention of victimization (Coalition for Juvenile Justice). The JJDPA provides for a national juvenile justice planning and advisory system, federal funding for delinquency prevention and improvements in programs and practices, and the operation of the Office of Juvenile Justice and Delinquency Prevention, a federal agency, to support local and state efforts (see Box 12.2).

The four core requirements of the JJDPA are the following:

- The deinstitutionalization of status offenders
- Removing juveniles from adult jails and detention facilities
- Accused and adjudicated delinquents, status offenders, and nonoffending juveniles should not be detained or confined in any institution where they may have contact with adult inmates
- Addressing and eliminating racial and ethnic disparities within the juvenile justice system

The Office of Juvenile Justice and Delinquency Prevention (OJJDP), part of the U.S. Department of Justice, Office of Justice Programs, works with individuals in a variety of areas to improve policies and practices related to juvenile justice. Through its mission, the OJJDP seeks to help and support local, state, and tribunal jurisdictions' efforts to develop and implement effective programs for juveniles.

Juvenile Corrections

The predominant aim is to avoid incarceration (custodial care). Although there certainly are some youth who commit serious offenses and ultimately need to be placed in a secure facility, research has demonstrated that a great deal of the youth in the juvenile justice system are there for relatively minor offenses, suffer from significant mental health issues, and are placed out of the home or on probation by default (Skowyra & Powell, 2006). Those who are sentenced to custodial care can be placed in either nonsecure or secure facilities. Nonsecure facilities include foster homes, group homes, camps, ranches, and schools. Secure facilities include reform schools, training schools, and juvenile detention centers.

Probation

One way to supervise offenders while also keeping them out of more formal institutions like juvenile correctional facilities is to place juveniles on **probation**. Much like adult offenders placed on probation, the intensity of juvenile probation ranges from highly intensive to essentially unsupervised.

Sometimes, probation is used following a period of confinement, but it is important to remember that judges usually have the ability to create individualized treatment plans and sentences for juvenile offenders. For example, judges can impose a straight period of confinement; a period of confinement followed by probation; a period of confinement, where either all or part has been suspended, followed by probation; or a period of straight probation.

While on probation, a probation officer is assigned to the case and will monitor the juvenile to make sure they are following the conditions of their probation. Although the duties of juvenile probation officers vary by state, they are often involved in screening juvenile or family court cases, conducting presentencing investigations of juveniles, and supervising juvenile offenders (Torbet, 1996). The frequency with which juveniles must contact or meet with their probation officers typically varies by the intensity of the probation. For instance, a juvenile under intensive probation may have to call or visit their probation officer several times a week or even every day, while a juvenile on basic probation may only have to meet with the probation officer once a month.

The monitoring of juvenile offenders by probation officers is intended to make sure they are following their probation. If the youth violates a condition of his or her probation, the probation officer will report the violation to the court. After receiving a violation report, the court will hold an evidentiary hearing to decide whether the youth is guilty of violating his or her probation. These violations can lead to serious consequences for the juvenile.

One of the most common—and serious—violations of probation is committing another offense while on probation. A juvenile can also violate probation by not following a condition of their probation (e.g., not meeting curfew, failing a drug test, etc.). If the court finds that the youth did indeed violate his or her probation, there are several options available to the judge. The judge may impose the balance of a suspended sentence if there was a split sentence, impose up to the remainder of the suspended sentence if the judge suspended all of the time, continue probation, or terminate probation.

Here, again, judges have the ability to use discretion when deciding how to handle each individual case. Sometimes, a judge will choose to give the youth a second chance and continue probation, especially if the violation was a rather minor infraction. Other times, a judge will decide to place a juvenile in a facility, believing that placing him or her on probation to begin with was already a second chance.

As part of the deinstitutionalization movement, many judges offer diversionary programs as a way of keeping nonviolent juveniles out of juvenile detention facilities. Diversionary programs were essentially developed to divert a portion of juveniles from the system. Even though these programs were developed as alternatives to more punitive options, however, the increase in ways to deal with juvenile offenders essentially created a net-widening effect by increasing the number of youth placed under supervision of the juvenile justice system. This net-widening is not specific to the juvenile system, however; it is an ongoing issue throughout the criminal justice system as well (Diversionary Programs, 1999).

Confinement

Juvenile detention facilities detain and house juvenile offenders awaiting their hearing dates and those who have already been adjudicated delinquent (similar to jails for adults). Anyone under the age of majority who has committed a criminal act can be housed in a juvenile detention center (JDC). JDCs were created to keep juvenile offenders separate from adult criminals. They were originally believed to be safer, better places for juveniles to be held. However, recent studies have shown that the problems plaguing adult facilities are afflicting JDCs as well. These problems include the inability to handle the serious health problems and mental illnesses that many of the offenders are coming in with (Prevalence of Mental Health Disorders, 2000).

BOX 12.3 CAREER HIGHLIGHTS: JUVENILE PROBATION OFFICER

Juvenile probation officers (JPOs) supervise youth who have been accused or adjudicated delinquent in the juvenile justice system and are then placed on probation or under protective supervision. JPOs often meet with the offender, their family, and other government officials from the onset of a case to determine whether a recommendation of probation should be made. The JPO's primary duty is to supervise the youth on their caseload and ensure that they are complying with court orders. They conduct regular visits to the juvenile's home, school, work, and any other places the child frequents. They help find appropriate drug, alcohol, or mental health treatment and work closely with law enforcement, social services, schools, and parents to help juveniles become successful.

JPOs typically work for the state. A minimum of a bachelor's degree (e.g., criminal justice, psychology, sociology, social work, human services) and a minimum age of 21 are usually required. Selected applicants will undergo an interview and must take and pass a drug test and background check. Once hired as a JPO, individuals must complete a state training program and pass a certification exam. Often, the newly hired JPO will work as a trainee for up to one year before becoming permanent. In order to advance to a juvenile probation supervisor or another administrative position, a minimum of a master's degree is typically required.

Comprehension Check

1. Explain the history and development of the juvenile justice system.
2. What are the main components of An Act of the Treatment and Control of Dependent, Neglected, and Delinquent Children?
3. What are some of the differences between the juvenile justice system and the adult criminal justice system?
4. What is a judicial waiver? When might these be used?

References

Bernard, T. J. (1992). *The cycle of juvenile justice.* New York, NY: Oxford University Press.

Breed v. Jones, 421 U.S. 519. (1975).

Butts, J. A., & Mitchell, O. (2000). Brick by brick: Dismantling the border between juvenile and adult justice. In C. M. Friel (Ed.), *Boundary changes in criminal justice organizations, criminal justice 2000* (Vol. 2, pp. 167–213). Rockville, MD: National Institute of Justice.

Coalition for Juvenile Justice. Retrieved from http://www.juvjustice.org/federal-policy/juvenile-justice-and-delinquency-prevention-act

Cocozza, J. J., & Skowyra, K. (2000). Youth with mental health disorders: Issues and emerging responses. Juvenile Justice, 7(1). Retrieved from https://www.ncjrs.gov/html/ojjdp/jjjnl_2000_4/youth_2.html

Griffin, P., Torbet, P., & Szymanski, L. (1998). *Trying juveniles as adults in criminal court: An analysis of state transfer provisions.* OJJDP Report, NCJ 172836. Washington, DC: U.S. Department of Justice, Office of Juvenile Justice and Delinquency Prevention.

In re Gault, 387 U.S. 1. (1967).

Klein, E. K. (1998). Dennis the menace or Billy the Kid: An analysis of the role of transfer to criminal court in juvenile justice. *American Criminal Law Review, 35,* 371–410.

Lawrence, R., & Hemmens, C. (2008). *Juvenile justice: A text/reader.* Thousand Oaks, CA: Sage.

Manfredi, C. P. (1998). *The supreme court and juvenile justice.* Lawrence, KS: University Press of Kansas.

Office of Juvenile Justice and Delinquency Prevention. (2017). *OJJDP statistical briefing book.* Retrieved from https://www.ojjdp.gov/ojstatbb/structure_process/qa04102.asp?qaDate=2016

Rothman, D. J. (1980). *Conscience and convenience: The asylum and its alternatives in progressive America.* Glenview, IL: Scott, Foresman and Company.

Skowyra, K., & Powell, S. D. (2006). *Juvenile diversion: Programs for justice-involved youth with Mental Health Disorders.* Research and Program Brief, National Center for Mental Health and Juvenile Justice. Retrieved from https://www.ncmhjj.com/wp-content/uploads/2013/07/Diversion-RPB-Final.pdf

Stahl, A. L. (1999). *Offenders in juvenile court, 1996. Juvenile justice bulletin, NCJ 175719.* Washington, DC: U.S. Department of Justice, Office of Juvenile Justice and Delinquency Prevention.

Sutton, J. R. (1988). *Stubborn children: Controlling delinquency in the United States.* Berkeley, CA: University of California Press.

The Center on Juvenile and Criminal Justice. (1999). *Diversionary programs: An overview.* Retrieved from https://www.ncjrs.gov/html/ojjdp/9909-3/div.html

Torbet, P. M. (1996). *Juvenile probation: The workhorse of the juvenile justice system.* Washington, DC: U.S. Department of Justice.

Watkins, J. C., Jr. (1998). *The juvenile justice century.* Durham, NC: Carolina Academic Press.

Drugs, Terrorism, Organized Crimes, and Cybercrimes

LEARNING OBJECTIVES

At the end of the chapter, the student should be able to

1 Explain the criminal justice problems related to drugs, terrorism, organized crimes, and cybercrimes

2 Identify the different forms of substance use, terrorism, organized crimes, and cybercrimes

3 Identify the threats associated with these different forms of crimes

4 Identify the different measures against these forms of crimes

5 Outline the interrelatedness of these crimes

Introduction

Drugs, terrorism, cybercrimes, and organized crimes are perhaps the most challenging crimes facing the criminal justice system. Although called differently, these crimes have some things in common. First, these crimes cross national boundaries and, therefore, need a more national and international approach (de Guzman, Das, & Das, 2012; Sheptycki, 1999). Second, these crimes are interlinked by sometimes forming a nexus (Mallory, 2012). It is common to see organized crimes get involved in drug trafficking and other transnational crimes such as money laundering or human trafficking. Likewise, some of these criminal enterprises form informal alliances to perpetrate their respective goals or crime objectives (Lyman & Potter, 2011). For example, terrorist groups might collaborate with organized crime groups (OCGs) to smuggle terrorist cells into another territory. Another alliance might be that terrorist groups produce or manufacture drugs as means of income and use the organized crimes' markets to be able to raise funds (Mallory, 2012). Similarly, OCGs and terrorist organizations might use the Internet as conduits for their criminal activities. They launder money using Internet commerce or conduct their attacks of the infrastructure of a country (Reichel, 2018).

It is also common to witness the linkages of these crimes with respect to victims. For example, a sex trafficking victim might be recruited through the Internet (cybercrime). Once the potential victim is enticed to meet the potential kidnapper, he or she might be abducted to be trafficked by OCGs. The victims might also be abducted by terrorist groups and indoctrinated to join a terrorist organization or criminal enterprise (e.g., Patty Hearst, Bowe Bergdahl, Boko Haram). These victims are sometimes introduced to the drug lifestyle to subdue them or they are pressured to become mules for drug trafficking activities or even suicide bombers.

Another commonality among these crimes is the multidimensional approach used in addressing these crimes. The federal and local agencies address these crimes at their levels. Likewise, the laws, strategies, and tactics to address these crimes often overlap. For instance, the Internal Revenue Code was utilized to dismantle the organized crime activities of Al Capone. Tax and business laws are also being used to break up schemes of criminal enterprises and terrorists, such as money laundering and human smuggling. Due to these characteristics and intersections in the perpetration of these crimes, these criminal justice topics are discussed collectively in this chapter. These crimes are the major challenges that practitioners face. Hence, it is imperative that students understand these criminal justice problems and how the criminal justice system currently deals with them.

The Drug Problem and the Criminal Justice System

Illicit drugs are a criminal justice problem for two main reasons. First, the trafficking and distribution of banned substances are outlawed. The criminalization of drugs requires the enforcement and adjudication powers of the criminal justice system. Since drugs are smuggled internationally into the United States, the drug problem becomes a federal enforcement concern. The United Nations Office on Drugs and Crime (UNDOC; 2018) World Report on Drugs has identified the United States as the main destination for internationally trafficked drugs, especially for cocaine, ecstasy, and to some degree methamphetamines. The Department of Homeland Security's Customs and Border Patrol (CBP) is primarily mandated to stop the influx of illicit substances into the United States (Department of Homeland Security, 2018). Likewise, the US federal government has created the Drug Enforcement Administration under the Department of Justice to enforce federal drug laws (Drug Enforcement Administration, 2018).

At the same time, drug activities (manufacturing and distribution) as well as its uses and abuses are carried out in local areas. Therefore, the prevention and control of illicit substances, including the treatment of substance use disorders, are concerns at the state and local levels. Recently, several states have adopted a decriminalized approach on marijuana (UNODC, 2018, p. 20). Considering that marijuana has been reported to be the drug of choice by most drug users in the United States (Center for Behavioral Health Statistics and Quality, 2016), local law enforcement can somewhat have a relief from marijuana law enforcement activities.

Second, there is a popular conception that drugs and crime are interrelated or correlated (Walters, 2014, 2015, 2017; Weissman, 2012).[1] The evidence seems to come from the fact that most arrestees and those who have been convicted of crimes are also addicted to drugs. The National Council on Alcoholism and Drug Dependence (NCAAD, 2018) states that about 80 percent of offenders abuse drugs or alcohol and approximately 60 percent of individuals at the time of arrest tested positive for illegal substances use.

NCADD (2018) states that "there are essentially three types of crimes related to drugs:

- Use-Related crime: These are crimes that result from or involve individuals who ingest drugs, and who commit crimes as a result of the effect the drug has on their thought processes and behavior.
- Economic-Related crime: These are crimes where an individual commits a crime in order to fund a drug habit. These include theft and prostitution.
- System-Related crime: These are crimes that result from the structure of the drug system. They include production, manufacture, transportation, and sale of drugs, as well as violence related to the production or sale of drugs, such as a turf war."

Due to the crimes committed in pursuit of the drug trade and the cooccurrence of drug use and crime, criminal justice agencies have been heavily involved in this effort to control the substance abusing population as well as the access to these substances (Tiger, 2011). Innovative practices and interventions have developed over the years that now lay the foundations for further research and development in this problem area.

Levels of Intervention with Drugs

There are three levels of intervention with substance abuses. The first level is known as the **primary level of intervention**. Prevention is the aim of this level, which is approached by addressing the supply and demand of controlled substances. First, the primary intervention aims to insulate the general population from being enticed to take illicit substances (demand side). Second, the primary intervention aims to hinder access to these illegal substances (supply side). In this level, the police are the main actors for the implementation of this level of intervention.

The **secondary level of intervention** is the detection and diversion of those that are at risk of experimenting with controlled substances. This approach seeks to address drug use once it has begun. Populations targeted at this level are the so-called "high-risk populations," including those that are prone to take these substances due to experimentation or due to their profession. The youth are particularly susceptible to influence and suggestion that they are more at risk for using illicit substances (Kandel & Faust, 1975). The adventurous and inquisitive nature of the adolescent population makes them at a high risk. However, adults who may have the potential to abuse the substances (e.g., medical and mental health patients who may have been prescribed potentially addictive substances) might have to be closely monitored for abusing some of these substances or worse, to convert these prescription drugs to purchase other illicit substances of choice.

Certain professions are also at risk of abusing illicit substances due to the pressures of the job. Medical, health, and criminal justice professionals are very much vulnerable to becoming abusers of illicit substances. Sometimes, their involvement with drugs commences due to their working conditions. These criminal justice and healthcare professionals have irregular and grueling work schedules that they might need substances to boost their energy to cope with the demands of the job. At other times, experiencing pain and witnessing human sufferings can become unbearable for some professionals that they resort to substances that help them cope with these experiences. They might also be incidentally introduced to the habit by accident. For example, police officers ingesting illicit substances during operations due to lack of protective devices or exposure to these substances. Their access to substances places them at high risk of abusing the very substance that they are trying to control.

Criminal justice seems to be in limbo with these population groups at the secondary level. The criminal justice actors can only intervene in situations where a law might have been broken, such as when an underage person drinks alcohol, someone is driving under the influence, or when a drug-taking individual engages in prostitution or steals to score a drug. In other words, they only intervene most of the time when the substance using or abusing individuals come into contact with the law.

The **third level of intervention** involves targeting the population with substance use disorders. In this level, the courts and the correctional institutions are involved. This phase is also known as the treatment phase where an individual with an identified condition of substance abuse disorder is provided treatment and efforts are made for the individual to be brought back to sober or at least a nonabusing state. Increasingly, criminal justice has been partnering with medical and mental health professionals to engage in the third level of intervention. However, due to the potential safety issues that users pose, as well as the attending criminal activities involved in the use of illicit substances, the criminal justice system remains central to the initiation and implementation of the third level of interventions. Likewise, the continued criminalization policy makes the criminal justice system the main actors in addressing the drug problem. The discussion below will center on the police, drug courts, and correctional institutions' efforts in this endeavor.

The Police and the War on Drugs

Early into the War on Drugs in the 1980s, Moore and Klein (1989b), through the National Institute of Justice (NIJ), outlined some police alternative strategies against drugs. These strategies include the following (Moore & Kleiman, 1989b, pp. 6–11):

1. *Expressive law enforcement: maximum arrests for narcotics offenses.* This strategy has been employed both on the demand and supply sides in addressing the drug problem.

2. *Mr. Big: Emphasis on high-level distributors.* This is a supply side approach that also delivers a deterrence message to the distributors.

3. *Gang strategies.* This is both a supply and demand side approach as gangs are both known consumers and peddlers of drugs.

4. *City-wide street level drug enforcement.* This strategy aims to reduce the displacement[2] of open-market drug dealing.

5. *Neighborhood crackdowns.* This strategy undertakes a grassroots approach to encourage local communities to strengthen their resistance toward drugs. This strategy is also intended to encourage cooperation by the community members with the police.

6. *Controlling drug-using dangerous offenders.* This strategy delivers the message that drugs are a menace that threaten the safety of law-abiding citizens.

7. *Protecting and insulating the youth.* The youth are vulnerable for abusing. Hence, the police perform an important social welfare function by strengthening the intervening against youth exposure to substances.

The suggestions above encompass a rigorous law enforcement approach coupled with some preventive interventions. Police interventions targeted the two ends of the spectrum, the youth who need to be shielded from gangs and illegal drugs and the adults who deal and use gangs to peddle their drugs in the neighborhoods.

The police officers became involved in a major way in the "War against Drugs" by becoming the face of the most expansive and aggressive drug education program in the country, the Drug Abuse Resistance Education (D.A.R.E.) program. However, the primary level intervention[3] role of the police did not diminish their secondary level intervention role of aggressive law enforcement against substance abusers and dealers. They just added being use educators as part of their role.

In the 1990s, the police found themselves engaged in the tertiary level of interventions. During this period, the police became the initial impetus for the introduction of treatment as options for substance abusers. It is now sometimes a protocol for police officers to be able to administer some antagonist drugs to overdosed individuals. They have also been trained to check for sobriety on the road as part of their public safety services. Due to these roles, the police are placed in the forefront of the treatment intervention as they are the first to come into contact with substance abusers and dealers. Thus, the police have now become the first line of intervention on all levels against illegal drugs and substance abusers.

Police Operations against Illicit Substances

The police operate using the philosophies of deterrence, interdiction, and control. More recently, some police departments have included rehabilitation and restoration in their intervention efforts (Frabutt, Hefner, Di Luca, Shelton, & Harvey, 2010). They conduct activities that prevent the general population from accessing and marketing the product. They also come into contact with the abusers and dealers in the drug trade and initiate some rehabilitation and restoration initiatives.

The fight of the police on drugs is a two-pronged approach. On the one hand, they need to address the **demand side of illegal drugs**.[4] The demand side refers to controlling the abuse of illegal drugs by the substance abusers. It is hoped that the decrease in addicted users will address the other side of intervention—the supply side—using the basic econometric approach of lessening demands to suppress the suppliers of illegal substance. On the other hand, the police also have addressed the problem from a supply side. The **supply side of illegal drugs** refers to the eradication of the illegal trafficking and sale of drugs outside of the legitimate markets. The supply side approach addresses drugs in the open air and closed spaces and all the way to the stoppage of entry of these illegal substances into the country. It is hoped that the two-pronged approach will alleviate the drug problem.

Levels of Interventions by the Police

With reference to substance abusers, police interventions have primarily evolved to correspond to the three levels of drug interventions. The first level of intervention is the prevention stage known as "**walling**" (i.e., creating effective barriers to the commission of the offense). This intervention phase is primarily proactive and preventative, as it is targeting potential targets before they get involved in substance abuse. The second level of police interventions refer to "**watching**" (i.e., trying to intervene on those that have been identified as high-risk abusers of illegal substances). This level of intervention can consist of both proactive and reactive measures. In this level, the delinquent and troubled youth are primary targets of the police. The third group is the "**catching**," where substance abusers are targeted and some form of intervention to rehabilitate offenders is introduced. Lately, the police have also partnered with healthcare services providers to address clients who may be showing signs of the cooccurring disorders of substance abuse, mental health disorders, and crime commission.

Primary Level Intervention of the Police (Walling)

Two major strategic intervention models at the primary level are deterrence and education. Both models are intended to target the general population to prevent them from abusing substances. These two police intervention models were intended to control potential users of illegal drugs. These interventions attack the demand side of substance abuse by trying to influence the choice of the potential consumers.

Although both models aim to achieve the same objective of providing a barrier toward drug abuse, the same models appeal to the individuals on different levels. To influence their choices, the primary levels of intervention appeals to the individuals' sense of fear (deterrence) and altruism. Deterrence appeals to an individual's sense of shame and fear. Among school youth, deterrence is achieved using fear arousal techniques, such as lecturing about the negative consequences of drug taking (Brown, D'Emidio-Caston, & Pollard, 1997). Education appeals to the individual's sense of altruism about making a "wise" choice. This wise choice consists of one's conviction that abusing and dealing illegal drugs is morally wrong. This choice is formed by the education that one receives. The other form of education is the enhancement of skills to resist influences toward drugs.

Drug Abuse Resistance Education

One of the biggest programs that the police implemented was the Drug Abuse Resistance Education Program (D.A.R.E.). Started in 1983, D.A.R.E. first targeted elementary and middle school–age kids. Today, under its Keepin' It REAL curricula, the program caters to different school groups, namely, elementary school, middle school, and high school students. It has also integrated modern technology into the delivery of its lessons. For example, the high school curriculum is now a hybrid model where face-to-face instructions are mixed with independent online modules (https://www.dare.org/d-a-r-e-educational-courses/). Likewise, athletes have special modules, as they might be susceptible to the abuse of performance enhancing drugs. Similarly, junior and senior high school kids are specially targeted to make wise decisions during drug consumption tempting events such as the prom (Figure 13.1).

D.A.R.E. Curricula

Merrill, Pinsky, Killeya-Jones, Sloboda, and Dilascio (2006) observed that D.A.R.E. created a great model of infrastructure to deliver a drug prevention education program. They have noted that the curricula are solid and instructors have credibility and expertise to deliver the program (Donnermeyer & Wurschmidt, 1997; Dukes, Stein, & Ullman, 1997; Hansen & McNeal, 1997). Most school-based drug prevention curricula seem to pursue the following categories of strategies (Rosenbaum, Flewelling, Bailey, Ringwalt, & Wilkinson, 1994):

FIGURE 13.1 THE MOST FAMOUS SLOGAN ON THE WAR ON DRUGS.

© StacieStauffSmith Photos/Shutterstock.com.

Cognitive strategies: Designed to increase knowledge about the nature and effects of alcohol, tobacco, and other drugs.

Affective or intrapersonal strategies: Designed to enhance personal growth through improved self-esteem, self-awareness, and/or values clarification without reference to drugs.

Social and influence strategies: Designed to strengthen interpersonal skills and equip youth with the behavioral strategies needed to resist peer pressure to use drugs.

Comprehensive programs: Designed to enhance cognitive, affective, and social skills through the provision of comprehensive curricula.

Under its current "Keepin' it REAL" curricula, these same intervention categories are still being tapped. The REAL acronym stands for Refuse, Explain, Avoid, and Leave. These are the strategies and skills that are being pursued through the new D.A.R.E program. The elementary school curriculum consists of ten lessons that aim to develop the skills of students to make good choices inculcating responsibility and decision-making. The middle school curriculum involves a ten-lesson curriculum that is highly interactive, involves multiple media materials that youth find engaging, and, like the elementary school curriculum, is based on Social Emotional Learning (SEL) principles that fit well with current research and practice in teaching middle-school youth (https://www.dare.org/keepin-it-real-middle-school-curriculum/). The high school curriculum consists of three modules that are hybrid and target specific. Module 1 can be used for the general student population. Module 2 targets athletes specifically, but it was also being promoted as a module applicable to all. Module 3 is specific to the junior and senior levels who might have the greatest pressure to consume alcohol during prom nights as well as engage in other risky behaviors. Compared to the previous curriculum, the roles of the police officers under the Keepin' It REAL modules are minimal as the students are required to complete some of the materials online.

Secondary Level of Intervention Functions of the Police (Watching and Catching)

The primary policies of local, state, and federal policies against illegal substances have been to use law enforcement to aggressively enforce the laws (Moore & Klieman, 1989a; Rosenbaum et al., 1994). There are two types of secondary intervention models that the police can do. First is intervention with the drug dealers. The second is intervention with populations at risk or those that are suspected to be abusers of substances. In terms of establishing priorities, the decision should be hinged on which produces the most impact. Reviewing the drug enforcement literature, Mazerolle, Sole, and Rombouts (2007) concluded that addressing the drug-involved individuals (demand side) seems to produce the bigger returns in substance abuses. In particular, they found the elements of wide spectrum collaborations and community empowerment as effective. They also noted that using the criminal justice powers to divert and make referrals tends to have better results.

Two approaches used by police officers are through the use of the deterrent approach and the harm reduction approach. These two secondary level approaches may be pursued alongside each other. However, due to role incompatibilities that these two philosophies present, the police might not be comfortable in pursuing both at the same time. Under these philosophies, the police take on two role orientations, social worker versus law enforcement, which have been found to be more often viewed by police officers as inconsistent with each other (Worrall & Schmalleger, 2018). Therefore, we examine the processes and effectiveness of these two models.

The Deterrence Model

Drug enforcement relies heavily on deterrence (Fader, 2016; Jacobs, 2010). Poret (2009) observed that about three-fourths of total expenditures against drugs are for supply side to the detriment of demand side (Stevenson, 2001). For deterrence to work, certainty, severity, and swiftness of enforcement should be undertaken by the police (Nagin, 2003). In his analysis of the effectiveness of deterrence, Nagin (2003) stressed the critical role that police play in the certainty and swiftness of punishment. As the gatekeeper of the criminal justice system, the ability of the police to detect and arrest offenders is the ultimate cause for the imposition of punishment. In the same article, Nagin adds that severity of punishment does not have a major role in deterrence. Indeed, in some circumstances, severity of punishment has a brutalizing effect.

Warner, Fischer, Albanese, and Amitay (1998) conducted an extensive focus group using 279 adolescents to determine the belief of high school students about enforcement of marijuana. Their data suggest that non-adherence to the three elements of deterrence by the police had negative consequences on the belief and drug-taking behaviors of their subjects. First, the researchers found that marijuana smoking is unlikely to attract attention from the police. This means the certainty and swiftness of punishment are not implemented with youth drug offenders. Second, the offenders described the punitiveness of the police as merely "slaps on the wrist." The offenders narrated that they knew they would be merely reprimanded or their drugs would be confiscated. At most, they would get several hours of detention. In a more recent study by Fader (2016), she found that drug dealers experience no sanctions at all. In other words, the police were perceived as not practicing the second element of deterrence—severity. Interestingly, the other findings were dysfunctional in the study of Warner et al. (Fader, 2016) as the police use the confiscated marijuana themselves. This act severely undermines the police stance as being role models in the community. Finally, there were perceptions of discrimination where the marijuana use was disproportionately enforced along racial and class considerations by the police. This discrimination against disadvantaged groups was also observed in the harm reduction law enforcement implementation in Vancouver where the frequent targets of police arrests are homeless individuals (Werb et al., 2007). Again, these law enforcement biases do not only undermine the deterrence effects of police actions but also undermine the legitimacy of the police (Tyler, 1990).

Restorative Model of Drug Enforcement

Western Salem and High Point (North Carolina) Police Departments embarked on an intervention model targeting drug dealers. They applied the principle of restorative justice in this intervention model. This approach is now officially labeled "focused deterrence" as it targets a specific population and crime to deter (Braga & Weisburd, 2012). However, the intervention has elements of restoration and repair as contained in restorative literature that we would argue that focused deterrence intervention as police a restorative justice model.

The process of restoration at the High Point and Western Salem models has the following stages (Frabutt et al., 2010):

Identification stage—The identification of the target for intervention is a product of a multistage and triangulated model of data collection. It included surveillance of suspected drug dealers, gathering of intelligence from multiple sources in the community, and crime analyses of police data using problem-solving techniques and geographic information systems (GIS) mapping. The main objective is to determine with certainty the target and the related activities of the target. This is intended to convey to the offender that they have developed enough evidence to guarantee certainty of arrest and perhaps punishment due to the quantum of evidence gathered.

Notification stage—Once the target is identified, three forms of notifications are undertaken. The first is the notification to the community about the identities of drug dealers in the community. The second is the notification to the offender's family about the involvement of their family member in drugs. Third, is the formal notification to the offender about his or her drug dealing activities, including a warning about desistance from further drug dealing activities and the immediate police action where severe punishments might ensue. However, such notice is accompanied by some promise of rehabilitation and support.

Resource delivery and community support stage—Community stakeholders are mobilized at this stage to provide the needed support for the offender. It was also in this stage where communities are mobilized to report crimes in the area more aggressively to the police and the police would need to act with immediacy and consistency.

Table 13.1 summarizes these key stages in the process. However, a close examination of the program reveals that the key stages run parallel to the reintegrative shaming model by Braithwaite (1989)

1. Crime Identification—Braithwaite suggest that the most important stage in the shaming process is to identify the offender and the act. This was carried out exhaustively and with precision by the North

TABLE 13.1 STAGES AND OPERATIONAL STEPS OF THE WESTERN SALEM AND HIGH POINT MODELS OF DRUG INTERVENTION STRATEGIES.

Stages	Operational Steps
Identification	Identifying the target area through crime mapping
	Engaging the community
	Engaging the police department internally
	Identification of street drug offenders
	Reviewing street drug incidents to refine the list
	Conduction the undercover operation
Notification	Establishing contact with the offender's family
	Conducting the notification
Resource delivery and community support	Setting a deadline
	Strict enforcement
	Follow-up

Source: Frabutt et al. (2010).

Carolina models. They used various information to clearly identify the offender and the acts of the offender.

2. Shaming—The process of shaming starts with gathering solid evidence about the involvement of the offender with drugs. For this strategy to work, the offender must be confronted with evidence about their guilt. The process also exposes the offender to shame by revealing these offender activities to the family members and the community.

3. Reintegration—Perhaps because very little help was provided by the police department in terms of reintegration that this model of policing is not considered as restorative but instead acquired the moniker of "focused deterrence." There were efforts to find alternative means of employment, but the last stage of the intervention was more about efforts toward crime prevention through incapacitation and surveillance.

The Harm Reduction Model

International guidelines issued by agencies of the United Nations recommend a public health approach to problematic substance abuse. Despite such appeal to harm reduction, vigorous drug law enforcement activities continued (Hayashi et al., 2013). "Harm reduction refers to policies, programmes, and practices that aim primarily to reduce the adverse health, social, and economic consequences of the use of legal and illegal drugs without necessarily reducing drug consumption" (Trace, 2012). Does this policy make sense considering the fact that it does not lead to the ultimate goal of reducing, if not totally eradicating, illegal substance uses/abuses? To understand the logic of harm reduction for law enforcement, the development should be examined in its proper context. At around this time, the emerging consensus is that substance abuse is incurable (Tiger, 2011, 2013) and therefore, society would be best served by pursuing the next most utilitarian objective of reducing harm. After examining the extant literature on the effects of drug prohibition policies, Haden became convinced that "giving dependent users controlled access to stimulants has the potential to reduce risky and illegal behaviours and therefore improve health and social functioning." He further commented that due to the high costs of enforcement, treatment and prevention measures only receive less than a fourth of the total budget against substance abuse. Therefore, as the focus started shifting to harm reduction, the law enforcement community has to reshape its focus in order to follow the money, which would eventually happen once harm reduction becomes a mainstream philosophy of substance abuse. As a result, the police became involved in such programs as emergency first aid providers, crisis interventionists, and implementers of syringe exchange programs (SEPs).

Blumenthal, Lorvick, Kral, Erringer, and Kahn (1999) conducted series evaluations about SEPs. They found that SEPs are effective strategies for reducing risky behaviors of users, but law enforcement actions have been shown to negate the effects of these programs on avoiding needle sharing practices. Those that are more likely to engage in needle sharing are likewise the population more subjected to police scrutiny and interventions (Blumenthal, Kral, Erringer, & Edlin, 1999; Wagner, Simon-Freeman, & Bluthenthal, 2013). In cases of needle harm reduction programs for those that are highly at risk, the police have untoward effects on harmful drug practices.

Tertiary Intervention Functions of the Police

The tertiary intervention functions of the police involve those that are granted parole or probation. Two important programs for this police level of intervention have been noted as innovative. The first is one is the Seattle, Washington intervention called Project Law Enforcement Assisted Diversion (LEAD). The other is the Crisis Intervention Team (CIT) that was originally initiated in Memphis, Tennessee. These approaches are considered tertiary level interventions because the police are now involved with the treatment of substance abusers. Although police are merely on the treatment initiation stage, it is still an important role in the delivery of tertiary level interventions.

LEAD Program

Project LEAD is known to be a pre-booking intervention model (Clifasefi, Lonczak, & Collins, 2017; Collins, Lonczak, & Clifasefi, 2017). As a secondary and tertiary prevention model, this model allows the police (LEAD officers) to decide who among its arrestees should be sent to a diversionary treatment program. This intervention would allow immediate entry into treatment, provided the offenders meet certain criteria. Under this program, offenders who have committed serious felonies are ineligible. In addition, offenders that have intent to distribute drugs or try to exploit minors or facilitate prostitution are also ineligible. Likewise, those that are deemed not amenable to treatment due to mental and health conditions are not admitted (Collins et al., 2017).

> Once an arrestee has been deemed eligible and showed willingness and ability to undergo the program, the individual is referred to a LEAD case manager who will tailor a plan of action. Thus, the program seeks to force the user/addict into a treatment program. The program also involved a close monitoring of the arrestee and engages the criminal justice system should the arrestee discontinue treatment.

LEAD consisted of three primary components (Collins et al., 2017, p. 49):

1. "an initial program entry process, which includes diversion from the criminal justice and legal systems;
2. harm reduction case management (i.e., low-barrier counseling and connection to social and clinical services that is offered with neither requirement of nor pressure towards substance-use treatment or abstinence); and
3. higher-level coordination of legal system involvement."

Included in the program offered to LEAD participants are those that would support the offender's basic needs such as housing, job, education, and enrollment in alcohol and drug treatment programs. Collins et al (2017). conducted a study comparing LEAD participants and arrestees who were processed as usual. The results indicated that LEAD participants have lower recidivism rates both in the short and long terms. They also fared better than their non-LEAD comparison group in their offending patterns. LEAD participants tend to commit less serious offenses upon rearrest compared to their counterparts. In the analysis of the program's impact on the participants' capacity for improvement on their housing, jobs, and income/benefits, Clifasefi et al. (2017) found them to have substantially improved their chances for accomplishing these goals after participation in LEAD. Ultimately, these factors have had a significant impact on the participants' non-reoffending (Clifasefi et al., 2017). Thus, these findings show that not only is the program having a direct effect on their drug and criminal behaviors, but it also shows that the mediating variables being addressed by LEAD are the right services needed by recovering substance abusers.

CIT Program

The CIT model trains responders to identify and intervene in crisis events involving individuals with emotional and behavioral problems. It is an on-the-scene decision-making about dispositions of the arrestee—jail versus diversion to healthcare system.

Components of CIT

Dupont, Cochran, and Pillsbury (2007) underlined the basic goals of CIT to include officer safety and divert mentally ill individuals that have come in contact with the police away from the regular justice system and into a mental health facility. Although it specifically targets mentally ill individuals, the program inevitably included those that are suffering from substance abuse disorders as they are co-occurring with mental health disorders (Substance Abuse and Mental Health Services Administration, 2014).

Advantages of the CIT Model

1. Excellent immediacy of response (Deane, Steadman, Borum, Veysey, & Morrissey, 1999)
2. Changes the nature of interaction from confrontational to helping
3. Reduces injuries and lessens the use of force (Dupont & Cochran, 2000)
4. Changes in attitudes and perceptions (Borum, Deane, Steadman, & Morrissey, 1998)
5. Decreases arrest rates (Steadman, Deane, Borum, & Morrissey, 2000)

6. Increases healthcare utilization
7. Clarifies lines of responsibility immediately

Despite encouraging results from CIT, Compton et al. (2010) have found three major challenges that CIT faces for its full implementation. The first among these challenges is the inclusion of dispatchers in the team. They noted that dispatchers have critical roles in the mobilization of police resources. In the end, they noted that implementers of the program have already included the dispatchers as part of its key personnel and started training them for this specific purpose. The second challenge they noted was the lack of available medical facilities that have ongoing collaboration with the police. The police become frustrated with their work if they could not place a person in crisis to a receiving facility (Borum et al., 1998; Deane, Steadman, Borum, Veysey, & Morrissey, 1999; Gillig, Dumaine, Stammer, & Grubb, 1990; Green, 1997). Police officers prefer to use their time more efficiently if they could immediately place a person in crisis (Wells & Schafer, 2006). The third challenge is one of service expansion. They noted that rural areas are hardly served, or if they are served at all, it becomes very inconvenient for the police due to the distance that needs to be traversed to place a person in a facility. They noted that several alternatives could be desirable, but might be prohibitively costly, such as the construction of regional, mobile, or satellite facilities. They concluded that the program could be enhanced should these challenges be addressed. It would lead to an intervention that is ongoing, operational, and sustainable.

Courts and the Drug Problem

The War on Drugs has increased the dockets of regular courts (Huddleston, Freeman-Wilson, & Boone, 2004; Tiger, 2011). Criminal prosecutions have increased due to the stringent penalties that have been associated with drug crimes (Mauer, 2001). Moreover, there is evidence to show that the War on Drugs and the succeeding creation of drug courts have increased arrests and punishments of minor drug offenses (Lilley, 2017). Although only a minimum number of cases go to trial, which is approximately 5 percent of all known offenses (Cole, Smith, & DeJong, 2018), the pretrial processes that courts spend on drug cases can take its toll on the judiciary. The petitions and motions that are associated with drug cases have increased, such as asset forfeiture decisions and pretrial detention hearings, because most of these cases are nonbailable (Lilley, 2017; Spohn, Kim, Belenko, & Brennan, 2014). These conditions have exacerbated the perceived menace of drugs and the preoccupation of the criminal justice system with the drug problem. The National Association of Drug Court Professionals reports that 3,057 drug courts are in operation in all fifty states and US territories. However, the National Institute of Justice (NIJ; 2017) states that 3,124 drug courts have been established in the United States.

The Drug Court Model

Although drug courts vary in target population, program design, and service resources, they are generally based on a comprehensive model involving:

- offender screening and assessment of risks, needs, and responsivity
- judicial interaction
- monitoring (e.g., drug testing) and supervision
- graduated sanctions and incentives
- treatment and rehabilitation services

Drug courts are usually managed by a nonadversarial and multidisciplinary team including judges, prosecutors, defense attorneys, community corrections, social workers, and treatment service professionals. Support from stakeholders representing law enforcement, the family, and the community is encouraged through participation in hearings, programming, and events like graduation. The judge is the formal authority in the court system that directs the other members of the therapeutic teams. The judge is also the communicator of the court to the offenders regarding the actions and decisions of the supervisors of the substance abusing participants. Tiger (2011, 2013) narrates that the ritual normally involves the judge asking information from the offender about his or her progress or infractions and communicates the consequences that the offender has already been previously communicated by the treatment provider.

Drug Courts Philosophy

According to Roper (2007), drug courts operate on seven principles.

1. Retaining the participant in treatment through the pain of withdrawal.
2. Helping the participant overcome fear, craving, and shame.
3. Providing modulated and immediate sanctions.
4. Discriminating between behavior and addiction symptoms.
5. Providing a system of rewards.
6. Understanding that whether an act constitutes a punishment or a reward depends on the perception of the recipient.
7. Dismissing of charges as a reward.

Ten Key Components of Drug Courts

In 1997, the National Association of Drug Court Professionals (1997) produced a document defining the key component of drug courts. The following are the key components of drug courts (Bureau of Justice Assistance, 2004).

Key Component No. 1: Drug courts integrate alcohol and other drug treatment services with justice system case processing.

Key Component No. 2: Using a nonadversarial approach, prosecution and defense counsel promote public safety while protecting participants' due process rights.

Key Component No. 3: Eligible participants are identified early and promptly placed in the drug court program.

Key Component No. 4: Drug courts provide access to a continuum of alcohol, drug, and other related treatment and rehabilitation services.

Key Component No. 5: Abstinence is monitored by frequent alcohol and other drug testing.

Key Component No. 6: A coordinated strategy governs drug court responses to participants' compliance.

Key Component No. 7: Ongoing judicial interaction with each drug court participant is essential.

Key Component No. 8: Monitoring and evaluation measure the achievement of program goals and gauge effectiveness.

Key Component No. 9: Continuing interdisciplinary education promotes effective drug court planning, implementation, and operations.

Key Component No. 10: Forging partnerships among drug courts, public agencies, and community-based organizations generate local support and enhances drug court program effectiveness.

Drug Court Intervention Models

System-wide drug courts follow two types of client processing. These processes involved the determination of the person's guilt or innocence.

Deferred Prosecution Program

Defendants are diverted to drug court prior to pleading to a charge. Defendants are referred without entering a plea. Furthermore, their completion of the program results in the nonprosecution of their offense. This process has become questionable as a violation of a due process clause. This process is also susceptible for prosecutorial abuse as individuals might be arbitrarily sent to drug court on cases which otherwise might not have been prosecutable or constitute a criminal offense.

Post Adjudication Program

Defendants plead guilty to a charge, but their sentences are suspended or deferred while they participate in the program and successful completion results in a waived sentence or expungement of the offense. Most drug courts have now adopted this mode of processing.

Correctional Interventions on Drugs

Correctional institutions have diverse programs in addressing drugs. During incarceration, correctional institutions provide counselling and therapy group programs. Cognitive behavioral therapy has been mainly used and focuses on some positive coping strategies. There are even treatment programs that use acupuncture and recreational therapy to address the craving for substances (Berman, Lundberg, Krook, & Gyllenhammar, 2004). Several treatment programs included the use of methadone and lofexidine (Howells et al., 2002). Some inmate programs included providing community support (Brown, O'Grady, Battjes, & Katz, 2004). Likewise, the correctional institutions and treatment providers have collaborated with the drug courts in the implementation of these treatment programs. These correctional treatment programs provide inconsistent results as evidenced by high rates of recidivism among substance abusing population.

Terrorism and the Criminal Justice System

Terrorism became a more pronounced problem in the US criminal justice system after the attacks that happened in New York City on September 11, 2001. Before such events, however, the United States had already been encountering problems with terrorism. It had experienced both home-grown terrorism as well as international terrorism. The establishment of the Homeland Security Department in the US federal government and the subsequent emergences of antiterrorism initiatives and the creation of counterterrorism units and activities have brought to the forefront the concerns about terrorism (Figure 13.2).

Terrorism Defined

Defining terrorism is a very important endeavor. The key to successful prevention of a terrorist attack is the assessment of risks and threats that uses terror as a way of achieving goals. In this chapter, we adopt the government definition of terrorism. The way government defines terrorism is important for prevention and intervention purposes, as various definitions can be found in different laws.

The following are several definitions:

- Premeditated, politically motivated violence perpetuated against noncombatant targets by subnational groups or clandestine agents.[5]
- The unlawful use of force and violence against persons or property to intimidate or coerce a government, the civilian population, or any segment thereof, in furtherance of political or social objectives.[6]
- The unlawful use of—or threatened use of—force or violence against individuals or property to coerce or intimidate governments or societies often to achieve political, religious, or ideological objectives.[7]

FIGURE 13.2 GLOBAL WORLDWIDE TERRORISM EXPLOSIONS ON MAP.

© Mikko Lemola/Shutterstock.com

From these definitions, we can get a glimpse of the elements of terrorism from government perspectives. The first element refers to the unlawful use of force and violence. Government sanctioned acts of violence are not terrorist acts per se. Thus, when an army of a nation is mobilized to invade another territory, or even the use of covert operations against a government, this would not be considered an act of terrorism. In other words, only nongovernmental actions are covered by the definitions. The second element refers to the target. Deliberately directing the violence toward noncombatant targets is an outlawed use of violence. The Geneva Convention on the Rules of War and the Rome Statute have specifically considered this particular act as an international and war crime. The Geneva Convention aims to protect noncombatants from armed conflict. It even excludes the targeting of personnel that may be delivering services (e.g., doctors, nurses, and so on) to combatants as well as those that have ceased to engaged in active conflict (e.g., wounded, sick, and shipwrecked troops or prisoners of war) against further atrocities. The Rome Statute considers targeting of civilians as a crime against humanity. The third element is the intent, which could be political, religious, ideological, or combinations of these motives. Random acts of violence or instrumental acts of violence (e.g., for financial gain or personal revenge) are not considered terrorist acts.

Different Types of Terrorism

Typologies of terrorism abound. Sometimes they might overlap in some of these categories. For instance, dissent terrorism might also have a tinge of separatism. There are also inconsistencies on labeling certain groups.

Revolutionary groups might be called terrorist organizations. A mass shooter is sometimes suspected of terrorism when in fact it was just a random act of violence and was not in support of or promotion of a certain ideology. Some of the labels are based on the means of conducting their terrorist activities, such as bioterrorism. Still others classify terrorism based on their harm, such as the environment or abortion clinics. The different forms are presented as a laundry list instead of organizing them. Students can very well add to this list, as the forms of terrorism are constantly evolving (e.g., cyberterrorism).

The following have been advanced as the major classifications of terrorism (White, 2012).

- **State-sponsored terrorism**, which consists of terrorist acts on a state or government by a state or government. Some nations and states often resort to violence to influence segments of their population, or rely on coercive aspects of state institutions. National governments can become involved in terrorism or utilize terror to accomplish the objectives of governments or individual rulers. Most often, terrorism is equated with nonstate actors or groups that are not responsible to a sovereign government. However, internal security forces can use terror to aid in repressing dissent, and intelligence or military organizations can perform acts of terror designed to further a state's policy or diplomatic efforts abroad.
- **Dissent terrorism**, which are terrorist groups that have rebelled against their government.
- **Terrorists and the left and right**, which are groups rooted in political ideology.
- **Religious terrorism**, which are terrorist groups that are extremely religiously motivated.
- **Criminal terrorism**, which are terrorists acts used to aid in crime and criminal profit.

Combatting Terrorism

The primary means of addressing terrorism was through the legislation involving the creation of antiterrorism or counterterrorism forces. At the federal level, the Department of Homeland Security was created to consolidate multiagency efforts in addressing terrorism. The operational functions of the department included the screening at US international borders for entry of terrorists and other instruments of terror such as dirty bombs, anthrax, and so on. The FBI also performs counterterrorism efforts in the detection and investigation of terrorist suspects. The intelligence agencies of the United States are also involved in counterterrorism efforts by providing actionable intelligence to prevent a terrorist attack. At the local level, several initiatives are in place, such as the Intelligence Centers or the Joint Terrorism

Task Forces (JTTF). In other words, there is a widespread effort to address terrorist attacks. In addition, the United States has also actively lobbied for countries to come up with their own antiterrorism and counterterrorism laws. This is an acknowledgement of the danger that international terrorism poses to the United States and that efforts against terrorism should include global collaboration toward this effort.

How the US conducts surveillance and investigation of electronic communication media—particularly the Internet—is largely shaped by three pieces of legislation:

- Uniting and Strengthening America by Providing Appropriate Tools Required to Intercept and Obstruct Terrorism Act (USA PATRIOT Act)
- Uniting and Strengthening America by Fulfilling Rights and Ending Eavesdropping, Dragnet-collection and Online Monitoring Act (USA FREEDOM Act)
- Foreign Intelligence Surveillance Act (FISA)

The Uniting and Strengthening America by Providing Appropriate Tools Required to Intercept and Obstruct Terrorism Act (USA PATRIOT)

The law covers a broad range of subjects including border security, detention of immigrants, funding for counterterrorism, and, of course, surveillance.

Title II of the PATRIOT Act amended FISA and greatly expanded the scope of surveillance allowed under US law. Foreign intelligence information could be gathered from both Americans and foreigners. Government agencies no longer needed to prove that a target is an agent of a foreign power. The maximum duration of surveillance and investigations were lengthened. Any district judge in the United States could issue surveillance orders and warrants for terrorism investigations. The FBI gained access to stored voicemail through search warrants. The definition of wiretapping expanded to include communication over the Internet and other electronic "packet switching" networks.

Sneak and peak warrants came into existence with the passing of the PATRIOT Act, which allowed law enforcement to break and enter a premise without the owner's consent and stealthily search the premises. Law enforcement can notify the receiver of the warrant after the fact. **Roving wiretaps** were implemented. A roving wiretap removes the need for a new surveillance order if a suspect throws away their phone or moves to a new address, for instance. It could also expand the scope of an investigation so that anyone who comes into casual contact with a suspected terrorist can be wiretapped.

Under the PATRIOT Act, the FBI can order a person to produce documents to protect against terrorists or foreign spies without a court order. These documents range from business records to library registers.

Intelligence agencies could conduct investigations on **lone wolves**. A lone wolf is a person suspected of engaging in terrorism-related activities, but without any ties to terrorist groups.

The USA FREEDOM Act

Many of the most controversial parts of the PATRIOT Act listed above were set to expire in 2015. The USA FREEDOM Act renewed many of those expiring provisions through 2019, albeit with some new limits concerning bulk interception on telecommunication metadata about US citizens. The act reauthorized roving wiretaps and tracking of lone wolf terrorists.

The Foreign Intelligence Surveillance Act (FISA)

FISA, passed by Congress in 1978, lays out the procedures for physical and electronic surveillance of foreign powers and agents; that includes US citizens and permanent residents suspected of espionage or terrorism. The act provided judicial and congressional oversight of spying activities by intelligence agencies on foreign entities and US citizens suspected of working with them. Perhaps most importantly, it officially removed the need for a court order to spy on foreign powers. Judicial authorization *is* required to spy on a US citizen, but only within seventy-two hours *after* such spying has already begun. To use FISA, a government entity must have probable cause that the subject is a foreign power or an agent of a foreign power.

FISA Section 702. Updated on February 1, 2018, Section 702 is part of FISA added as an amendment in 2008. It allows intelligence agencies to collect foreign intelligence from non-Americans located outside the United States. But, under the surveillance authority set up under this section, many Americans also have their communications swept up by surveillance programs operated by the FBI and National Security Agency (NSA). Section 702 is not bulk collection, and by law it can only target non-US citizens outside of the United States. However, Americans' data can be gathered as part of "incidental collection." To put it simply, if an American is communicating with any non-US citizen outside of the United States, their conversations can be monitored and recorded. This incidental collection is the major sticking point among privacy advocates.

The FISA court (FISC). The US Foreign Intelligence Surveillance Court (FISC) is a federal US court set up under FISA. The court oversees law enforcement and intelligence agency surveillance and issues warrants to track and monitor foreign spies. Requests are most often made by the NSA and FBI, the bulk of which are kept secret. The nature of the court's business makes it a secret court, acting without anyone other than the government and judge present. This lack of transparency has led to heavy criticism about the court's lack of oversight. It has been known to rubber stamp warrant requests, though supporters deny that accusation.

Organized Crime and the Criminal Justice System

Organized crimes are a primordial concern for the criminal justice system because of the combination of criminal motives and criminal means. The concept of organized crime was popularized by Donald Cressey (1969, 1972) when he unraveled that criminal groups have some sort of organization involved. Although the organization does not have a concrete formal structure, it follows a certain level of hierarchy in their operations.

Definitions of Organized Crime

In 2002, the United Nations Office on Drugs and Crime (UNODC) gathered law enforcement officials and academics to establish a working definition of organized crime. The group failed to arrive at a consensus on the definition. Even among scholars, the definition of organized crime abound and lack in consensus (Albanese, 1985). Klaus von Lampe (2018) compiled various definitions of the term and he came up with more than 150 definitions that included legal and scholarly definitions. The United States has generated the most number and varied definitions of organized crime (von Lampe, 2018).

Several approaches to the definitions have accumulated over the years. The first is the activity approach. The second is the organization approach. The third is the means approach.

Liddick (in press) identifies the three main attributes of organized crime:

1. **A continuous, organized hierarchy**. Organized crime is characterized by levels of command structure and accountability. There is also a semblance of bureaucracy where division of labor is observed. Some scholars, however, argue that the structures of organized crime are more loosely coupled than envisioned (Albini, 1971). It involves a whole host of cabal that are corrupted or coopted by the criminal group in order to perpetuate their criminal activities. Furthermore, it has been observed that OCG's can sometimes disintegrate, merge, split, or regroup, which negates the idea that OCs are continuous in nature (Block, 1979).

2. **Profit motive, criminal method.** These attributes clearly isolate OCGs from terrorists, ordinary criminals, and legitimate businessmen. Surely, terrorists use criminal methods, but their motives are not to gain profit but to promote a political, ideological, or religious agenda. Likewise, ordinary criminals such as thieves, robbers, or

frauds aim to profit from the act through criminal means, but they normally do outside of a group. Finally, legitimate businesses aim for profit, but do so within the bounds of law. Hence, OCGs are motivated by money and use the advantage of organization to engage in a criminal act.

3. **The use of violence and coercion.** Violence is the means to protect the illegal enterprise. Although more recent research suggests that violence is rarely used, the threat of violence is more used to project a reputation of the ability and willingness of the group to inflict physical harm (Block, 1983; Reuter, 1983; Reuter, Rubinstein, & Simon, 1982). However, there are some criminal enterprises (e.g., drug trafficking and human trafficking) where OCGs may have engaged in more violence in the conduct of their business (Reuter, 1985).

Hagan (1983) added several more attributes, including the ones mentioned above, namely:

1. Corruption of public officials
2. Public demand for the illicit services
3. Monopolized control of illegal markets
4. Restricted membership
5. Nonideological
6. Specialization of work tasks
7. Secrecy
8. Extensive planning

Toward a Working Definition

Several definitions developed and propounded by various scholars and agencies over the years. Liddick's (in press) forthcoming book laid out the major definitions of organized crime and came up with this definition:

> *Organized crime is the provision of illegal goods and services, various forms of theft and fraud, and the restraint of trade in both licit and illicit market sectors, perpetuated by informal and changing networks of "upper-world" and "under-world" societal participants who are bound together in complex webs of patron-client relationships.*

This definition incorporates the essential attributes of organized crime and its main actors, including the means and relationships involved in the phenomenon. This definition is comprehensive, as it includes the actors in the licit business including those in power, the upperworld who could serve as conduits for the existence of OCGs, as well as the facilitators of their activities.

Types of Organized Crimes

Block (1991) classified organized crime by dividing the phenomenon into two subtypes: enterprise syndicates and power syndicates.

Enterprise syndicates, as a subcategory of organized crime, involve those activities related to the management and coordination of various illegal distribution systems, including but not limited to the supply of illicit drugs, alcohol, and untaxed cigarettes; the fencing of stolen property; the smuggling of various commodities; the traffic in human beings; the provision of illegal gambling, sex, and money-lending services; and the laundering of ill-gained revenue. Essentially, this facet of organized crime involves the provision of illegal goods and services. Enterprise syndicates are distinguished by the fact that this type of organized crime would not exist without willing and demanding **customers**. If one adheres to this classification, the main focus would be the regulation of these goods and services.

Power syndicates, on the other hand, are characterized by the acts of theft and **extortion.** These types of syndicates would like to eliminate their competition so they could monopolize profits. In other words, wealth is illicitly appropriated and societal resources are channeled to criminals through the use of private violence and threats. This type of organized crime is manifested most prominently in the realm of business and labor racketeering, where legitimate commercial activity is distorted by criminals who, through illicit force, shape and restrain trade to their economic advantage. Specific actions by power syndicates include the infiltration of trade unions and legitimate businesses, the manipulation of employer trade associations, pension fund rip-offs, healthcare fraud, and large-scale thefts (e.g., the hijacking of trucks and piracy on the high seas).

Anti-organized Crime Measures

Measures against organized crime are mostly in the promulgation of enabling acts in order to investigate and prosecute OCGs. It operates on the deterrence and incapacitation models. Through these measures, the criminal justice approach is to toughen laws against the OCGs and set up barriers for the conduct of their enterprises. The laws also intended to increase the certainty of getting caught and convicted by establishing rules that would allow for easier apprehension and conviction of organized crime members.

The following are some of the important legal measures to address organized crime.

Hobbs Act (18 U.S.C. 1951–1955)

The Hobbs Act prohibits actual or attempted robbery or extortion affecting interstate or foreign commerce. The US Attorney's Office (2018) lays out the elements of the violation of this Act as follows:

In order to prove a violation of Hobbs Act extortion by the wrongful use of actual or threatened force, violence, or fear, the following questions must be answered affirmatively:

1. Did the defendant induce or attempt to induce the victim to give up property or property rights?
2. Did the defendant use or attempt to use the victim's reasonable fear of physical injury or economic harm in order to induce the victim's consent to give up property?
3. Did the defendant's conduct actually or potentially obstruct, delay, or affect interstate or foreign commerce in any (realistic) way or degree?
4. Was the defendant's actual or threatened use of force, violence, or fear wrongful?

Because OCGs' mode of operation is the use of intimidation and violence, this law has become instrumental in prosecuting OCGs. Behaviors punished under this law are not merely the illegal taking of property, but that the act obstructs the operation of interstate commerce. This element distinguishes the crime from ordinary theft or robbery. Mallory (2012) observed that this law is rarely used, as the Racketeering Influence and Corrupt Organizations (RICO) Act is more utilized.

RICO Act (18 U.S.C. 1961–1965)

The RICO Act was passed by Congress with the declared purpose of seeking to eradicate organized crime in the United States through the disruption of the entire organization instead of just the underlings. A violation of Section 1962(c) of the Act requires (1) conduct (2) of an enterprise (3) through a pattern (4) of racketeering activity. A more expansive view holds that in order to be found guilty of violating the RICO statute, the government must prove beyond a reasonable doubt: (1) that an enterprise[8] existed; (2) that the enterprise affected interstate commerce; (3) that the defendant was associated with or employed by the enterprise; (4) that the defendant engaged in a pattern of racketeering activity[9]; and (5) that the defendant conducted or participated in the conduct of the enterprise through that pattern of racketeering activity through the commission of at least two acts of racketeering activity as set forth in the indictment (*U. S v. Phillips*, 1982).

The RICO statute expressly states that it is unlawful for any person to conspire to violate any of the subsections of 18 U.S.C.A. § 1962. The government need not prove that the defendant agreed with every other conspirator, knew all of the other conspirators, or had full knowledge of all the details of the conspiracy (*U.S. v. Delano*, 1993/1995). All that must be shown is (1) that the defendant agreed to commit the substantive racketeering offense through agreeing to participate in two racketeering acts; (2) that he knew the general status of the conspiracy; and (3) that he knew the conspiracy extended beyond his individual role (*U.S. v. Rastelli*, 1989).

In conjunction with the Hobbs Act, RICO is normally used to prosecute for the following acts:

1. Using income received from a pattern of racketeering activity or through collection of an unlawful debt to acquire an interest in an enterprise affecting interstate commerce
2. Acquiring or maintaining, through a pattern of racketeering activity or through collection of unlawful debt, an interest in an enterprise affecting interstate commerce
3. Conducting or participating, through a pattern of racketeering, racketeering activity, or collection of an unlawful debt, the affairs of an enterprise affecting interstate commerce
4. Conspiring to participate in any of these activities

On top of these direct acts, racketeering can be proven by commission of predicate acts[10] listed under the law and a pattern exists if committed within a specific span of time.

Asset Forfeiture Laws

Asset forfeiture laws are meant to disable the perpetrators from enjoying the fruits of their crime. Any assets that are shown to be the products of the criminal enterprise are going to be seized from the offender. Two forms of asset forfeiture have been utilized for this purpose.

> *Civil forfeiture—a legal proceeding against property that is purchased with profits from illegal activities. Under this approach, the conveyance of property or the use of dummies to purchase assets are not allowed. For example, assets that are purchased by a family member using the proceeds of the illegal activity will be confiscated for the state. No criminal act will ensue against the cover unless there is a showing of conspiracy.*

> *Criminal forfeiture—a legal proceeding against an offender arising from a conviction or a commission of a crime. Any property that an offender has acquired through his or her criminal acts will be confiscated by the state.*

Conspiracy Statutes

Definitions of conspiracy and its penalties are found in 18 U.S. Code § 371. The advantage of prosecuting organized crime under a conspiracy statute is that you do not need to charge different offenders with multiple charges. The perpetrators can all be charged with a similar offense because the "act of one is the act of all." Evidence against the offenders is collectively applied and it requires no bounds as regards to proving the elements of each crime charged against the individual participants. Likewise, the defendants must present an affirmative defense of withdrawal from the conspiracy. Thus, the burden of evidence of desistance rests on the defense. Likewise, inchoate offenses[11] could be charged. By using conspiracy as a charge, the government is hitting two birds with one stone by charging all participants and destroying the organized crime network.

Tax Evasion Law

This tax law became a popular means of prosecuting and disrupting organized crime with the famous apprehension and successful prosecution of Al Capone. Under this statute, unexplained wealth and undeclared income in order to evade the payment of taxes can be used to control the proceeds of organized crime activities. After the use of this strategy, organized crime turned into other diversion or covers, such as the use of dummies and money laundering.

Money Laundering Laws

All organized crime activities are "designed to conceal the existence, nature, and final disposition of funds gained from illicit activities (Mallory, 2012, p. 229)." This is a more proactive means of addressing organized crime. This law punishes third parties who might be participating in the activities of OCGs by using the financial institutions as conduits for laundering money. Certain measures include the reporting of certain transactions (e.g., cash transactions of more than $10,000). Thus, financial institutions are required to report suspicious transactions in order to escape criminal liability under the Annunzio-Wylie Money Laundering Act of 1992 and the Money Laundering Suppression Act of 1994. Some OCGs try to evade the law by transferring smaller amounts (smurfing), but the Anti-Drug Abuse Act of 1986 (§ 5324) penalizes such acts. In order to curb evasion, financial institutions are required to provide the identity of the suspected launderer and the associated documents in the transactions (Anti-Drug Abuse Act, 1986, § 5325–5326).

Classification of Anti-organized Crime Measures

After examining the various criminal justice means to address organized crime, we present a classification of these efforts into three:

Head-Hunting Strategies

This strategy assumes that the life of the organization is the head or heads of the criminal enterprise. Thus, the objective is to target the head of the organization in order to topple it. This strategy seemed to have worked in several instances, such as when the FBI targeted Al Capone and put him in jail. This strategy, however, might not be more applicable among networked crime organizations.

Domino Strategies

This strategy demands the attack of the weakest link in the organized crime structure. If it is the single or closed ethnic structure, the strategy is to find someone who can be attacked to provide information and become state witnesses for the government. In the fight against the mafia, the government concentrated on the cooperation of mid-level organization members. To address government corruption, whistleblower programs have been created so that corrupt or irregular government practices, especially those that have connections to organized crime, can be disrupted. Michael Dowd of the New York Police Department was made a witness to disrupt the drug trade and corruption in New York.

Market Strategies

This strategy involves making the provision of illicit goods and services unprofitable. Three substrategies seem to be employed by means of disrupting the market for organized crime. The first substrategy is street level intervention where the direct consumers and providers are addressed in order to control the proliferation of the illegal market of these services and goods. Several notable strategies that address illegal commerce on the ground are employed. There are various interdiction strategies that target illegal drugs to neutralize drug cartels and divert their business to more legitimate ones. The second substrategy is to target the enablers. This involves the monitoring and control of legal businesses that may facilitate the enjoyment of the fruits of illicit activities. Banks, lawyers, and politicians are targeted for this approach as they serve as conduits for the enjoyment of the proceeds from illegal activities and protection for the organization. The third substrategy is to collaborate with governments across the world in order to address different activities of organized crime that are outside the jurisdiction of states acting independently.

Cybercrimes and the Criminal Justice System

The Internet has now become the lifeblood of society (Koops, 2016). Koops observed that the Internet has become the infrastructure for everything from commerce to the management of individual lives. People move around in physical space and cyberspace at the same time (e.g., communicating in a meeting and looking up information on the web) and they manage their affairs both physically and virtually. People would feel cut-off from life if you take away their Internet access. Because the Internet has gained tremendous value for society and it, likewise, has the potential to increase one's value, it has become the target of attacks. Attacking someone's computer or online access could bring enormous harm. Thus, controlling and preventing cybercrimes have come under the domain of the criminal justice system.

Cybercrime Defined

Several definitions of cybercrime have been advanced primarily from both the law and scholars. From the academe, the following definitions are proposed:

1. Cybercrime is a crime related to technology, computers, and the Internet (Schell & Martin, 2004)
2. Unlawful acts wherein the computer is either a tool or a target or both (Chawki, Darwish, Khan, & Tyagi, 2015)
3. A crime that involves computers and computer networks (Hill & Marion, 2016)

From these definitions, it can be stated that cybercrime involves both an instrument and target elements. When either one of these are present, the crime becomes a cybercrime. The current definitions need a bit more refinement. Black (1985) suggests that criteria for a good definition should be comprehensive, mutually exclusive, and unbiased. All of the definitions provided above are very generic and not mutually exclusive. The definitions are too broad in that any form of crime where computing technology is involved either as a target or an instrument of crime becomes a cybercrime. If this is the case, would a bank employee who violates the computing system's breach be committing a cybercrime or a white-collar crime? In another instance, would someone who used the telephone to detonate bombs be committing a cybercrime or terrorism? Could you treat someone who used the Internet to victimize targets a cybercrime? For example, is a person who posed a fictitious product for sale online committing a cybercrime? Right now, crime classifications are still tied up to their traditional definitions. For example, someone is still charged with child prostitution even when the crime is committed over the Internet. Very few crimes are truly cybercrimes, such as identity theft, point of service denial of service, hacking, and phishing, among others (Figure 13.3).

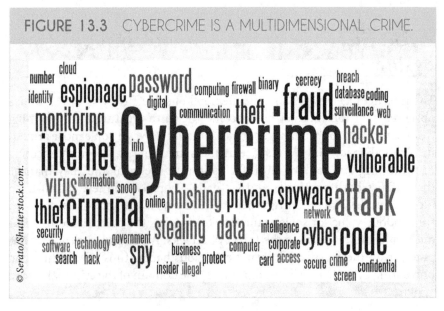

FIGURE 13.3 CYBERCRIME IS A MULTIDIMENSIONAL CRIME.

© Serato/Shutterstock.com.

Classifications of Cybercrime

Hill and Marion (2016, p. 9) provide a classification of cybercrime. The first classification includes the traditional forms of crime committed with the use of electronic communications networks and information systems. This means that crime formerly committed without the use of computing technology is now being used to commit the crime. For example, forgeries, counterfeiting, and fraud are now being perpetrated through the Internet. This classification will also include such crimes as identify theft. The second classification involves the publication of illegal content over electronic media. For example, child sexual abuse materials and incitement to foment a rebellion or racial hatred are perpetrated through the Internet rather than through the print or broadcast media. The third classification involves crimes that are unique to the electronic networks. These forms of crimes include cracking, attacks against information system, or denial of service, among others.

The Evolution of Cybercrime

The first generation of low-end cybercrime concerned traditional crimes in which computers were used as a mere tool, for example, in computer-related fraud or forgery. The second generation, of hybrid cybercrime still consisted of classic crimes, but were facilitated by computer networks to the extent that the scale and scope started to make important differences. The third generation of high-end cybercrime concerns crimes targeted at computers or computer networks themselves, such as hacking or denial-of-service attacks. The fourth generation will involve attacks of infrastructure through the Internet and the attack on people through their biological implants or enhancements.

Strategies Versus Cybercrimes

Strategies against cybercrimes are rooted in multiple levels. The range of prevention and control can be located from the individual all the way to the government level.

Individual Level Control

The individual level prevention and control consists mostly of target hardening measures. Several target hardening strategies can be employed at the individual level. Among these strategies are the following:

1. Equipment Identity Registers. This refers to a list of all eligible computers that are allowed to use a network. It also contains a list of banned equipment from the network because they have been lost or stolen.
2. Use of software protection. The use of antivirus or antimalware software including a firewall.

3. Password mobile device lock. These safeguards normally disable access to the device if passwords are not entered correctly. Normally, it requires an administrator to reset the password. In some devices a multifactor authentication is required to enter a website or reset a password.

4. Remote lock of mobile devices and remote wipe of mobile devise. Mobile devices that have been lost or stolen might be locked through a connected device or the data from the device are erased once the person trying to have unauthorized access fails to authenticate the login requirements.

5. Encryption of data at rest and in transit. Sensitive information in transactions, whether they are sitting in the digital equipment or being transferred to another network, cannot be captured. These encryptions are necessary to protect sensitive information.

6. Authentication and identity management. Financial institutions normally employ strict authentication requirements such as multifactor authentication or biometric authentication. Financial institutions normally employ capturing devices to detect unauthorized access to their network or sensitive data. They also have strict exit protocols such as exiting the website whenever they are away from their computer or automatic logout for a certain period of inactivity.

The security measures for computing and mobile devices are continually evolving. The need for individuals and business to safeguard personal and business information has been particularly highlighted with recent breaches of major commercial entities as well as recent unauthorized use of data gathered from social media apps.

Government Level Approaches

The prevention and control of cybercrimes at the government level are also multifarious. Primarily, criminalization is the major way of trying to address cybercrime. In this regard, several legislative acts in the use of the Internet and mobile technology are criminalized, including texting and driving. Several of these legislations include anticyberbullying law, antichild pornography, and phishing.

On the one hand, government uses the Internet for investigations and prevention of certain crimes. For example, law enforcement agencies could use social media for reporting crimes or providing crime tips. Law enforcement agencies have increased their social media presence over the last ten years (de Guzman & Hunter, 2015). Recently, social media are being used by citizens to publicize anomalies and misconduct committed by government officials, particularly with the police. So far, social media have not been used to monitor court proceedings and correctional institutions, as recording devices are not allowed in their operational areas.

Several of these practices by criminal justice are worth noting here.

Collection of Metadata

Metadata is information about the use of technology, but not the contents of the data itself. When it comes to the PATRIOT Act, metadata often refers to information gathered through the NSA's bulk surveillance program, most notably call records. The NSA insists that it does not collect or analyze the calls themselves, but only the call metadata. That means it is not listening in on a call, but the agency does record the time, location, callers, devices, and other information on the general public, whether or not they have ties to terrorist groups.

Investigative Operations

Several strategies along this line are for government to set up websites intended to catch those that are already engaging in illegal activities using the Internet. For example, the FBI may set up a website to monitor who is engaging in sexual predation. Another might be to set up an online trading site to capture individuals who are selling counterfeit or stolen goods. As an information gathering tool, the police use social media for crime reporting or they examine the social media postings and activities of individuals suspected of crimes.

GIS and GPS

GIS are being used by several police departments to analyze crime patterns and come up with actionable intelligence. The Geographic Positioning Systems (GPS) has been used by probation and parole agencies for electronic monitoring of clients under their supervision. GPS is used for those that are subject to limited mobility such as those under house arrests or sexual predators who are not allowed to be within a certain distance from schools or daycare facilities.

Comprehension Check

1. Describe the various approaches used by the criminal justice system against drugs and other substances in the United States.
2. What are the major strategies of the United States in combating terrorism?
3. Explain the various forms of terrorism.
4. Define organized crime and describe its different forms.
5. How has the criminal justice system been addressing the problems associated with organized crime groups?
6. What is the meaning of cybercrime and identify the various means of confronting this new form of criminal activity.

References

Albanese, J. (1985). *Organized crime in America*. Cincinnati, OH: Anderson Publishing Company.

Albini, J. (1971). *The American Mafia: Genesis of a legend*. New York, NY: Appleton-Century Crofts.

Anti-Drug Abuse Act of 1986 (31 U.S.C. 5324).

Berman, A. H., Lundberg, U., Krook, A. L., & Gyllenhammar, C. (2004). "Treating drug using prison inmates with auricular acupuncture: A randomized controlled trial." *Journal of Substance Abuse Treatment, 26*(2), 95–102.

Black, D. (1985). *The idea of police*. Beverly Hills, CA: Sage.

Block, A. A. (1979). "The snowman cometh: Coke in progressive New York." *Criminology, 17*(1), 75–99.

Block, A. A. (1983). *East-side west-side: Organizing crime in New York, 1930–1950*. New Brunswick, NJ: Transaction Publishers.

Block, A. A. (1991). *Master's of paradise*. New Brunswick, NJ: Transaction.

Blumenthal, R. N., Kral, A. H., Erringer, E. A., & Edlin, B. R. (1999). Drug paraphernalia laws and injection-related infectious disease risk among drug injectors. *Journal of Drug Issues, 29*(1), 1–16.

Bluthenthal, R. N., Lorvick, J., Kral, A. H., Erringer, E. A., & Kahn, J. G. (1999). Collateral damage in the war on drugs: HIV risk behaviors among injection drug users." *International Journal of Drug Policy, 10*, 25–38.

Borum, R., Deane, M. W., Steadman, H. J., & Morrissey, J. (1998). "Police perspectives on responding to mentally ill people in crisis: Perceptions of program effectiveness." *Behavioral Sciences and the Law, 16*, 393–405.

Braga, A. A., & Weisburd, D. L. (2012). "The effects of focused deterrence strategies on crime: A systematic review and meta-analysis of the empirical evidence." *Journal of Research in Crime and Delinquency, 49* (3), 323–358.

Braithwaite, J. (1989). *Crime, shame, and reintegration*. Cambridge, UK: Cambridge University Press.

Brown, B. S., O'Grady, K. E., Battjes, R. J., & Katz, E. C. (2004). "The community assessment inventory client views of supports to drug abuse treatment." *Journal of Substance Abuse Treatment, 27*(3), 241–251.

Brown, J. H., D'Emidio-Caston, M., & Pollard, J. A. (1997). "Students and substances: Social power in drug education." *Educational Evaluation and Policy Analysis, 19*(1), 65–82.

Bureau of Justice Assistance. (2004). *Defining drug courts: The key components*. Washington, DC: U.S. Department of Justice, Office of Justice Programs.

Center for Behavioral Health Statistics and Quality. (2016). *2015 national survey on drug use and health: Detailed tables*. Rockville, MD: Substance Abuse and Mental Health Services Administration.

Chawki, M., Darwish, A., Khan, M. A., & Tyagi, S. (2015). *Cybercrime, digital forensics, and jurisdiction*. Cham, Switzerland: Springer Publishing.

Clifasefi, S. L., Lonczak, H. S., & Collins, S. E. (2017). "Seattle's Law Enforcement Assisted Diversion (LEAD) program: Within subjects changes of housing, employment, and income/benefits outcomes and associations with recidivism." *Crime & Delinquency, 63*(4), 429–445.

Cochran, J., & Chamlin, M. B. (2000). "Deterrence and brutalization: The dual effects of executions." *Justice Quarterly, 17,* 685–706.

Cole, G. F., Smith, C. E., & DeJong, C. (2018). *Criminal justice in America* (9th ed.). Boston, MA: Cengage Learning.

Collins, S. E., Lonczak, H. S., & Clifasefi, S. L. (2017). "Seattle's Law Enforcement Assisted Diversion (LEAD): Program effects on recidivism outcomes." *Evaluation and Program Planning, 64,* 49–56.

Compton, M. T., Broussard, B., Hankerson-Dyson, D., Krishan, S., Stewart, T., Oliva, J. R., & Watson, A. C. (2010). "System- and policy-level challenges to full implementation of the Crisis Intervention Team (CIT) model." *Journal of Police Crisis Negotiations, 10*(1–2),72–85.

Cressey, D. R. (1969). *Theft of the nation: The structure and operations of organized crime in America.* New York, NY: Harper and Row.

Cressey, D. R. (1972). *Criminal organization: Its elementary forms.* New York, NY: Harper and Row.

Deane, M. W., Steadman, H. J., Borum, R., Veysey, B. M., & Morrissey, J. P. (1999). "Emerging partnerships between mental health and law enforcement." *Psychiatric Services, 50*(1), 99–101.

de Guzman, M. C., Das, D. K., & Das, A. M. (2012). *The evolution of policing: Worldwide innovations and insights.* Boca Raton, FL: CRC Press/ Taylor & Francis.

de Guzman, M. C., & Hunter, R. D. (2015). *Social media and police: Technology uses and challenges.* Research Presentation during the Annual Conference of the Criminal Justice Association of Georgia, Morrow, GA. Retrieved from http://cjag.us/conference-presentations/

Department of Homeland Security. (2018). *Border security overview.* Retrieved from https://www.dhs.gov/border-security-overview

Donnermeyer, J. F., & Wurschmidt, T. N. (1997). Educators' perceptions of the D.A.R.E. program. *Journal of Drug Education, 27*(3), 259–276.

Drug Enforcement Administration. (2018). *DEA mission statement.* Retrieved from https://www.dea.gov/about/mission.shtml

Dukes, R. L., Stein, J. A., & Ullman, J. B. (1997). "Long-term impact of Drug Abuse Resistance Education (D.A.R.E.). Results of a 6-year follow-up." *Evaluation Review, 21*(4), 483–500.

Dupont, R., & Cochran, S. (2000). Police response to mental health emergencies— barriers to change. *Journal of American Academy of Psychiatry and the Law, 28*(3), 338–344.

Dupont, R., Cochran, S., & Pillsbury, S. (2007). *Crisis intervention team core elements.* Memphis, TN: The University of Memphis School of Urban Affairs and Public Policy, Department of Criminology and Criminal Justice, CIT Center. Retrieved from http://cit.memphis.edu/CoreElements.pdf

Fader, J. J. (2016). ""Selling smarter, not harder": Life course effects on drug sellers' risk perceptions and management." *International Journal of Drug Policy, 36,* 120–129.

Frabutt, J. M., Hefner, M. K., Di Luca, K. L., Shelton, T. L., & Harvey, L. K. (2010). "A street-drug elimination initiative: The law enforcement perspective." *Policing: An International Journal of Police Strategies & Management, 33*(3), 452–472.

Gillig, P. M., Dumaine, M., Stammer, J. W., & Grubb, P. (1990). "What do police officers really want from the mental health system?" *Hospital and Community Psychiatry, 41,* 663–665.

Green, T. (1997). "Police as frontline mental health workers: The decision to arrest or refer to mental health agencies." *International Journal of Law and Psychiatry, 20,* 469–486.

Hagan, F. (1983). "The organized crime continuum: A further specification of a new conceptual model." *Criminal Justice Review, 8,* 52–57.

Hansen, W. B., & McNeal, R. B. (1997). "How D.A.R.E works: An examination of the program effects on mediating variables." *Health Education and Behavior, 24*(2), 165–176.

Hayashi, K., Ti, L., Kaplan, K., Suwannawong, P, Wook, E., & Kerr, T. (2013). "Drug-related harm among people who inject drugs in Thailand: Summary findings from the Mitsampan Community Research project." *Harm Reduction Journal, 10,* 21. doi:10.1186/1477-7517-10-21

Hill, J. B., & Marion, N. E. (2016). *Introduction to cybercrime: Computer crimes, laws, and policing in the 21st century* (Praeger Security International). Santa Barbara, CA: ABC-CLIO.

Howells, C., Allen, S., Gupta, J., Stillwell, G., Marsden, J., & Farrell, M. (2002). "Prison based detoxification for opioid dependence: A randomised double blind controlled trial of lofexidine and methadone." *Drug and Alcohol Dependence, 67*(2), 169–176.

Huddleston, C., Freeman-Wilson, K., & Boone, D. (2004). *Painting the current picture: A national report card on drug courts and other problem solving court programs in the U.S.* Alexandria, VA: National Drug Court Institute.

Jacobs, B. A. (2010). "Deterrence and deterrability." *Criminology, 48,* 417–441.

Kandel, D., & Faust, R. (1975). "Stages and patterns in adolescent drug use." *Archive of General Psychiatry, 33*(7), 923–932.

Koops, B. J. (2016). "Megatrends and grand challenges of cybercrime and cyberterrorism policy and research." In B. Akhgar & B. Brewster (Eds.), *Combatting cybercrime and cyberterrorism. Advanced sciences and technologies for security applications* (pp. 3–15). Cham, Switzerland: Springer Publishing.

Liddick, D. (2018). *Organized crime: The essentials.* San Diego, CA: Cognella.

Lilley, D. (2017). "Did drug courts lead to increased arrest and punishment of minor drug offense?" *Justice Quarterly, 34*(4), 674–698.

Lyman, M. D., & Potter, G. W. (2011). *Organized crime* (5th ed.). Upper Saddle River, NJ: Prentice Hall.

Mallory, S. L. (2012). *Understanding organized crime* (2nd ed.). Burlington, MA: Jones and Bartlett.

Mauer, M. (2001). "The causes and consequences of prison in the United States." In D. Garland (Ed.), *Mass imprisonment: Social causes and consequences* (pp. 4–14). Thousand Oaks, CA: Sage.

Mazerolle, L., Sole, D., & Rombouts, S. (2007). "Drug law enforcement: A review of the evaluation literature." *Police Quarterly, 10*(2), 115–153.

Merrill, J. C., Pinsky, I., Killeya-Jones, L. A., Sloboda, Z., & Dilascio, T. (2006). "Substance abuse prevention infrastructure: A survey-based study of the organizational structure and function of the D.A.R.E. program. *Substance Abuse Treatment, Prevention, & Policy, 1*(25), 1–13. doi:10.1186/1747-597X-1-25

Moore, M. H., & Klieman, M. A. R. (1989a, September). *Perspectives on policing: The police and drugs* (No. 11). Washington, DC: National Institute of Justice and the John F. Kennedy School of Government, Harvard University.

Moore, M. H., & Kleiman, M. A. R. (1989b). *The police and drugs.* Washington, DC: U.S. Department of Justice, National Institute of Justice.

Nagin, D. S. (2003). "Editorial introduction: Drug law enforcement." *Criminology & Public Policy, 10*(3), 541–542.

National Association of Drug Court Professionals. (1997). *Defining drug courts: The ten key components.* Washington, DC: U.S. Department of Justice, Office of Justice Programs, Drug Court Program Office.

National Council on Alcoholism and Drug Dependence. (2018). *Alcohol, drugs and crime.* Retrieved from https://www. ncadd.org/about-addiction/alcohol-drugs-and-crime

National Institute of Justice. (2017). *Drug courts.* Retrieved from https:// www.nij. gov/topics/courts/drug-courts/Pages/welcome.aspx#note1

Poret, S. (2009). "An optimal anti-drug law enforcement policy." *International Review of Law and Economics, 29*, 221–228.

Reichel, P. L. (2018). *Comparative criminal justice systems: A topical approach* (7th ed.). New York, NY: Pearson.

Reuter, P. (1983). *Disorganized crime: The economics of the visible hand.* Cambridge, MA: MIT Press.

Reuter, P. (1985). *The organization of illegal markets: An economic analysis.* Washington, DC: U.S. Government Printing Office.

Reuter, P., Rubinstein, J., & Simon, W. (1982). *Racketeering in legitimate industries: Two case studies.* Washington, DC: National Institute of Justice.

Roper, G. F. (2007). "Introduction to drug courts." In J. E. Lessenger & G. F. Roper (Eds.), *Drug courts: A new approach to treatment and rehabilitation* (pp. 1–22). New York, NY: Springer.

Rosenbaum, D. P., Flewelling, R. L., Bailey, S. L., Ringwalt, C. L., & Wilkinson, D. L. (1994). "Cops in the classroom: A longitudinal evaluation of Drug Abuse Resistance Education (DARE)." *Journal of Research in Crime and Delinquency, 31*(1), 3–31.

Schell, B. H., & Martin, C. (2004). *Cybercrime: A reference handbook* (p. 2). Santa Barbara, CA: ABC-CLIO.

Sheptycki, J. (1999). "Policing, postmodernism and transnationalization." In R. Smandych (Ed.), *Governable places: Readings on governmentality and crime control* (pp. 215–238). Brookfield, VT: Ashgate.

Spohn, C. C., Kim, B., Belenko, S., & Brennan, P. K. (2014). "The direct and indirect effects of offender drug use on federal sentencing outcomes." *Journal of Quantitative Criminology, 30*(3), 549–576.

Steadman, H., Deane, M., Borum, R., & Morrissey, J. (2000). "Comparing outcomes of major models of police responses to mental health emergencies." *Psychiatric Services, 51,* 645–649.

Stevenson, R. (2001, April). *Costs of the war on drugs. In sensible solutions to the urban drug problem.* Vancouver, BC: Frazier Institute Digital Publication.

Substance Abuse and Mental Health Services Administration. (2014). *Results from the 2013 national survey on drug use and health: Summary of national findings* (NSDUH Series H-48, HHS Publication No. (SMA) 14-4863). Rockville, MD: Substance Abuse and Mental Health Services Administration.

Tiger, R. (2011). "Drug courts and the logic of coerced treatment." *Sociological Forum, 26*(1), 169–182.

Tiger, R. (2013). *Judging addicts: Drug courts and coercion in the criminal justice system.* New York, NY: New York University Press.

Trace, M. (2012). "Measuring drug law enforcement—from process to outcomes." *International Journal of Drug Policy, 23,* 16–23.

Tyler, T. (1990). *Why people obey the law.* New Haven, CT: Yale University Press.

United Nations Office on Drugs and Crime. (2018). *World drug report 2017.* Vienna, Austria, United Nations Publication.

The U.S. Attorney's Office. (2018). *2403. Hobbs Act—extortion by force, violence, or fear.* Retrieved from https://www.justice.gov/usam/criminal-resource-manual-2403-hobbs-act-extortion-force-violence-or-fear

U. S v. Phillips, 664 F. 2d 971, 1011 (5th Cir. Unit B Dec. 1981), *cert. denied,* 457 U.S. 1136, 102 S. Ct. 1265, 73 L. Ed. 2d 1354. (1982)

U.S. v. Rastelli, 870 F. 2d 822, 828 (2d Cir.), *cert. denied,* 493 U.S. 982, 110 S. Ct. 515, 107 L. Ed. 2d 516 (1989).

von Lampe, K. (2018). *What is organized crime: Definitions of organized crime.* Retrieved from http://www.organized-crime.de/OCDEF1.htm

Wagner, K. D., Simon-Freeman, R., & Bluthenthal, R. N (2013). The association between law enforcement encounters and syringe sharing among IDUs on skid row: A mixed methods analysis. *AIDS Behavior, 17*(8), 2637–2643.

Walters, G. D. (2014). *Drugs, crime and their relationships: Theory, research, practice and policy.* Burlington, MA: Jones and Bartlett.

Walters, G. D. (2015). "Recidivism and the worst of both worlds hypothesis: Do substance misuse and crime interact of cumulate?" *Criminal Justice and Behavior, 42,* 435–451.

Walters, G. D. (2017). "The drug-crime connection in adolescent and adult respondents: Interaction versus addition." *Journal of Drug Issues, 47*(2), 205–216.

Warner, J., Fischer, B., Albanese, R., & Amitay, O. (1998). "Marijuana, Juveniles, and the police: What high-school students believe about detection and enforcement." *Canadian Journal of Criminology, 40,* 401–420.

Weissman, J. C. (2012). "Understanding the drugs and crime connection: A systematic examination of drugs and crime relationships." *Journal of Psychedelic Drugs, 10*(3), 171–192.

Wells, W., & Schafer, J. A. (2006). "Officer perceptions of police responses to persons with a mental illness." *Policing: An International Journal of Police Strategies and Management, 29,* 578–601.

Werb, D., Wood, E., Small, E., Strathdee, S., Li, K., Montaner, J., & Kerr, T. (2007). "Effects of police confiscation of illicit drugs and syringes among drug users in Vancouver." *International Journal of Drug Policy, 19,* 332–338.

White, J. R. (2012). *Terrorism and homeland security* (7th ed.). Belmont, CA: Wadsworth, Cengage Learning.

Worrall, J. L., & Schmalleger, F. (2018). *Policing* (3rd ed.). New York, NY: Pearson.

Endnote

[1]   See Walter's (2017) latest study for a more extensive literature review and a more refined examination of the drugs-crime relationship.

[2]   Displacement is a phenomenon where crime is transferred over another area or jurisdiction due to the intervention.

[3]   Drug interventions have been operationalized on three levels. The first level of intervention is the prevention aspect. The second level of intervention targets those that are most highly at risk of engaging in substance abuse, such as those that live in certain families or go to school where drug use is rampant. The third level of drug intervention model concerns the treatment of those that have acquired the drug disorders.

[5]   Title 22, Chapter 38, Section 2656f.

[6]   28, C.F.R. Section 0.85.

[7]   US Department of Defense as quoted in Hoffman, 2006, 19.

[8]   An "enterprise" is defined as including any individual, partnership, corporation, association, or other legal entity, and any union or group of individuals associated in fact although not a legal entity. 18 U.S.C.A. § 1961(4) (West 1984). Many courts have noted that Congress mandated a liberal construction of the RICO statute in order to effectuate its remedial purposes by holding that the term "enterprise" has an expansive statutory definition. *United States v. Delano,* 825 F. Supp. 534, 538-39 (W.D.N.Y. 1993), *aff'd in part rev'd in part,* 55 F. 3d 720 (2d Cir. 1995), cases cited therein.

[9]   "Pattern of racketeering activity" requires at least two acts of racketeering activity committed within ten years of each other. 18 U.S.C.A. § 1961(5) (West 1984). Congress intended a fairly flexible concept of a pattern in mind. *H.J., Inc. v. Northwestern Bell Tel. Co.,* 492 U.S. 229, 239, 109 S. Ct. 2893, 2900, 106 L. Ed. 2d 195 (1989). The government must show that the racketeering predicates are related, and that they amount to or pose a threat of continued criminal activity. *Id.* Racketeering predicates are related if they have the same or similar purposes, results, participants, victims, or methods of commission, or otherwise are interrelated by distinguishing characteristics and are not isolated events. *Id.* at 240, 109 S. Ct. at 2901; *Ticor Title Ins. Co. v. Florida,* 937 F. 2d 447, 450 (9th Cir. 1991). Furthermore, the degree in which these factors establish a pattern

may depend on the degree of proximity, or any similarities in goals or methodology, or the number of repetitions. *United States v. Indelicato*, 865 F. 2d 1370, 1382 (2d Cir.), *cert. denied*, 493 U.S. 811, 110 S. Ct. 56, 107 L. Ed. 2d 24 (1989).

[10] Under RICO two or more related acts of racketeering can be used to establish a pattern. A predicate offense is committed for the purpose of committing the greater crime. Predicate acts are related to the ultimate crime if they have the same or similar purposes, results, participants, victims, or methods of commission, or otherwise are interrelated by distinguishing characteristics and are not isolated events. Extortion and blackmail are examples of RICO predicate acts.

[11] Inchoate offenses are those acts preparatory to or connected with the commission of an offense. For instance, the hiring of thugs to extort money from businesses.

© Lightspring/Shutterstock.com

The Community Justice System

LEARNING OBJECTIVES

After reading this chapter, the student should be able to

1 Define community justice and identify its various elements

2 Explain the different principles involved in the implementation of a community justice system

3 Explain the different forms of community justice within the criminal justice system

4 Explain restorative justice as a holistic approach in the administration of justice

5 Define the challenges that community justice confronts

Introduction

Bayley and Shearing (2001) observed that public safety services have been restructured. Hunter, Barker, and de Guzman (2018) have particularly noted that one of the modes of providing public safety is responsibilization—the participation of the community in the definition of safety and their personal involvement in the achievement of that safety level (de Guzman & Kim, 2017). This achievement of this ideal community safety level through the participation of community is a hallmark of a truly democratic society – meaningful participation and self-determination.

This model of participating in the administration of justice is not novel. Starting with the feudal societies where policing was a form of self-help (Lundman, 1980; Travis & Langworthy, 2008), this form has evolved into the modern concept of self-help in community policing (Hunter et al., 2018; Karp & Clear, 2000; Travis & Langworthy, 2008). In penology, Braithwaite (1989) has documented how the process of punishing offenders was communal. Even in the adjudication and prosecution of crimes, citizen participation is very evident. The use of the grand jury for felony indictments, the use of petit juries for trials, and recently, the use of sentencing juries for convicted criminals are features of the adjudication process in the United States. Indeed, community justice is a model that comes and goes and has undergone several reiterations in the US justice system.

This chapter expounds on the ideas of Karp and Clear (2000) on the conceptual framework of community justice. We discuss the basic principles, goals, and forms of community justice at different levels of the justice system. Likewise, the chapter provides more up-to-date examples or ideas on how to implement the model. Finally, the chapter closes with the identification of the challenges that the community justice model may encounter.

What Is Community Justice?

Community justice broadly refers to all variants of crime prevention and justice activities that explicitly include the community in their processes and set the enhancement of community quality of life as a goal (Karp & Clear, 2000, p. 323). The definition connotes two essential components of community justice. The first component is the need for meaningful participation of the community in the business of administering justice. The second component is that the model will redound to the benefits of the local community. The second component particularly identifies the benefits of community justice as those that will result in the improvement of the quality of life for local community members and more importantly, the prevention of crime. These outcomes seem to be simultaneous undertakings, but as will be shown later in the chapter, the restoration of order comes ahead of participation in crime prevention that will ultimately lead to better quality of life. In other words, the relationship of these components is linear rather than circular.

Participation in the justice system is not a new phenomenon. Every discussion in the chapters of this book includes community participation as part of the justice system. For example, in the criminalization process, the people can voice their preferences through elections or sometimes through direct legislations in terms of voting for certain initiatives and referenda. In several states, drugs and gun laws are criminalized or decriminalized based on the votes of the citizens. Crime prevention also involves the active participation of the public. Through the diligent reporting of crime and the undertaking of social actions to address disorders in society, crime can be prevented. The courts have used citizens in its adjudication through the jury processes from indictments (through the use of grand juries) to conviction (through the use of petit juries). Lately, communities have also been more involved in corrections through probation and parole participation. What makes the new movement of community justice different is the local focus of its benefit. It is a locality-relevant benefit that gives new flavor to the citizen participation component.

FIGURE 14.1 COMMUNITY PARTICIPATION IN POLICING TOOK SHAPE THROUGH THE NEIGHBORHOOD WATCH PROGRAMS.

© Kent Sievers/Shutterstock.com

Community Justice Goals

Community justice primarily consists of two major goals: (1) the promotion of well-being and quality of life and (2) the restoration, maintenance, and enhancement of social order or public safety.

Promotion of Well-Being

Crime brings harm to the victims as primary victims and the community members as secondary victims (Taylor & Auerhan, 2015). The well-being of these victims has to be restored. This condition of having a deteriorated sense of well-being, if allowed to persist, undermines the efficacy of the justice system (Kirk & Matsuda, 2011).

Restoration, Maintenance, and Enhancement of Social Order

Lambertus and Yakimchuck (2007) argued that communities have several ideal needs. The first is the restoration of order that has been disturbed by crime. The second is the maintenance of that order that has been restored. The third need is to achieve an enhanced order that they ultimately want to achieve. These ideals of order are hierarchical community safety needs.

The primary need of every community is to have social order restored that has been broken by crime. It has been argued that the institutional agencies that are primarily tasked with establishing order (the criminal justice system) should be the most appropriate agency to perform this task. Community members will be reluctant to participate in a state of disorder. Once community members see that safety and order have been restored, only then will they aspire to become more involved and begin to participate in the maintenance and enhancement of social order in society. Lambertus and Yakimchuck noted that this hierarchy is linear; that is, the aspirations for safety and participation move in this particular order (see Figure 14.1). They also argued that most communities really have the basic desire of restoring order. That is the basic need for them to remain as members of the community. A community that is plagued by disorder is normally abandoned. A community that has order will be more attractive for other people to occupy. The members of the community will have the greater desire to maintain such order and would devise ways to enhance the present order. In a study by de Guzman and Kim (2017), highly disorganized communities could hardly implement community policing.

Elements of Community Justice

Karp and Clear (2000) identified five elements of community justice. These elements operate simultaneously. Whether or not these elements are all essential remains unconfirmed.

Community Justice Operates at the Neighborhood Level

This element refers to the geographic locus of the intervention. Crime tends to be concentrated in a certain geographic spot known as hotspots (Sherman, 1997). The concentration of crime in particular areas makes sense to concentrate crime prevention and control efforts in neighborhoods.

Community Justice is Problem-Solving

The search for the ultimate cause of crime incidences has been touted as the more effective way of addressing crimes (Eck & Spelman, 1987).

Problem-solving can be an internal process with only the agency involved. However, community involvement has been shown to have improved the capability of communities and agencies to arrive at a more effective solution (Eck, 1997).

Community Justice Decentralizes Authority and Accountability

The New York Police experience with CompStat (McDonald, 2002) demonstrates that when you make local precinct commanders analyze and implement intervention against crime and disorder, a more effective outcome happens. The approach becomes more relevant and focused on the source of the problem. This relevance and focus are also true when autonomy is given to probation officers to exercise an appropriate level of supervision of their probationers. The implementation of Megan's Law where citizens are alerted about the presence of sex offenders in their neighborhoods has increased guardianship among households.

Community Justice Gives Priority to Community's Quality of Life

Wilson and Kelling (1982) proposed that crime prevention can be achieved by attending to quality of life issues, particularly the repair of disorders in society. Earlier, Wilson (1962) argued that a zone of indifference, that is, a situation where no one cares, precipitates the commission of more serious offenses in the neighborhood. Thus, addressing seemingly minor issues in the community tends to be a more viable crime prevention method.

Community Justice Involves Citizens in the Justice Process

Perhaps, this element is sometimes the most difficult to implement. The twin elements of incentives and infrastructures are necessary for meaningful community involvement to happen. Incentives for participation must be carefully thought out. It is not an "if you build it, they'll come" situation. Community members should clearly see the benefits of the contribution that they are about to make. The other issue is the establishment of the right infrastructure to achieve participation. In the Cincinnati Initiative to Reduce Violence (CIRV) (Engel, Tillyer, & Corsaro, 2011), community members were active participants in the planning and intervention phases of the program, and it has become a model for success in reducing gang and gun violence. The Chicago Alternative Police Strategy (CAPS) experienced a lack of participation by community members in community policing initiatives (Skogan & Hartnett, 1997). This lack of participation led the authors to declare that communities that need community policing the most are also those that have minimal participation in the program.

Principles in Community Justice

Democratic Principles

These principles address the need for civic participation in the justice process.

Norm Affirmation

Behavioral expectations should be communicated to the offender and would be offenders. Pronouncement from community members is a strong affirmation of these expected norms in society. Community decisions are expressions of the prevailing values of the time. Legislations are presumably the formal expression of the will of the citizens and constitute as reference for the wrongful conduct. However, community values are dynamic. These values can change over time or sometimes very suddenly. When change happens, the current law sometimes becomes inadequate in addressing the recent change. The process of legal amendment takes some time. Meanwhile, further observance of the law in the interim might offend current sensibilities as well as fail to address community exigencies. Having a community justice system would be able to address these changes that laws cannot immediately address. In some jurisdictions, an illegal conduct may be tolerated because of the prevailing consensus about nonenforcement of such law. For instance, there are certain areas where curfew violations by the youth may not be enforced because the community might not approve of such formal intervention to a behavior that might be considered benign. In other areas, vagrancy or homelessness may be treated with benign neglect. Benign neglect is a situation where law enforcement or government may not enforce the law out of compassion for the individual or group (Travis & Langworthy, 2008).

Marijuana arrest enforcement sometimes presents a dilemma for law enforcement officers. It is equally a dilemma for the courts and correctional institutions where communities have a consensus regarding the benign effects of such controlled substances in society. Thus, it will not be unusual for the decriminalization of an act to be preceded by the tolerance of legal violation. The opposite can also be true. The legal mandate might promote a more benign punishment for such act of truancy or vagrancy. However, when communities encourage the aggressive and punitive response toward these population groups, the police were forced to implement zero-tolerance policing. Therefore, the community is the barometer of the crime and order climate.

Restoration

The emphasis is problem-solving in terms of repairing the harm that a crime has inflicted on the offender, the victim, and the community. Restoration involves the imposition of formal sanctions, but more importantly, it provides a resolution for the restoration of damaged relationships caused by crime

(Braithwaite, 1989). Community justice can effectively promote restoration (Karp & Clear, 2000; Wood, 2015). This broken bond should be repaired by providing some restoration of relationships that has been disturbed by crime (Brathwaite, 1989). Offenders need to be restored back to their families and communities. Likewise, communities must overcome the trauma of the crime that has been committed. Their actual participation on some of the justice process brings them closer to the cognitive and emotional aspects of crime. The process would enable them to understand the needs of all the parties concerned. Thereby, restoration can be more smoothly attained.

Several documented experiences have shown that when the victim and community members are part of the restorative meetings, a more positive resolution and understanding could be reached (Gal, 2016). The offender still suffers the penalty. Likewise, the victim still receives justice and compensation. However, the more important outcome of the process could be the reconciliation of the parties involved.

Public Safety

This principle means the provision of assurances that the offender will not cause additional harm to community members. These assurances are necessary for the healing of the victim and for reducing the fear of community about crime. Justice efforts should be focused on individuals at risk and those that are the sources of crimes and disorders. A sense of safety for the victims is an important component as well as indicator of healing.

Egalitarian Principles

These principles address the criminogenic conditions that precipitate offending.

Equality

This principle demands the heralding of resources to address the crime problems in communities that lack social capital. Community resources are pooled to increase such capacity to address crime.

Inclusion

This principle involves the provision of opportunity to benefit from the community justice model. It means that special needs must be given the appropriate intervention that they need.

Mutuality

This principle demands cooperation among different sectors that are mutually beneficial to everyone. It provides incentives for participation and disincentives for wrongdoing.

This call on all citizens to be responsible for the welfare of the larger community. It also includes resource building ideas to serve collective good.

Processses of Community Justice

System Accessibility

For participation to happen, the agency should be accessible and transparent. Several innovations have been made to bring the justice system closer to the citizens. Karp and Clear (2000) identified three domains by which accessibility could be achieved: (1) physically accessible locations, (2) flexibility in delivery of services, and (3) relaxed formality.

In policing, the precinct system has considerably improved the access of citizens for police services. Despite such efforts, there are other systems to bring the police closer to the community. The foot and bike patrol programs have accomplished part of that objective. However, we can learn more about these accessibility programs from other countries such as Japan, where the koban system is strategically located within neighborhood blocks.

The use of social media has enhanced the second aspect of flexibility and formality. Over 90 percent of police departments now use social media as a communication tool (IACP and Urban Institute, 2017). Citizens can report crimes and provide information to the police through these media (IACP, 2015). The Internet presence of the police has been enhanced where citizens can receive information about their complaints or download their case reports online (de Guzman & Hunter, 2015).

The access to the courts have made some strides through some of its informalities in processing of drug offenders and other special cases. However, the judges' courtrooms remain centralized and its buildings are heavily guarded like a fortress. In some countries, they have justice on wheels (e.g., Philippines), where court processes are handled in satellite offices. There has been some strides in providing information such as the resident-driven search warrants in Portland (Boland, 1998) and the youth court in Brooklyn (Atherton, 2015) where problem-solving and dialogues were done to process juveniles.

The geographic access to correctional facilities is far worse among the justice agencies. Due to the Not in My Backyard (NIMBY) mentality, correctional institutions are remotely located. This provides hardships for family and inmate service providers to have frequent contacts and productive meetings. In the study by Sampson and Laub (1993), they found that a healthy marriage is a significant factor in changing the course of one's criminality. Such fostering of a healthy marriage is difficult to maintain with the remote locations of prisons.

Providing incentives to community members to participate is critical, but sometimes almost nonexistent. Serving on a jury sometimes brings on financial hardships. Involvement with community policing is tiresome due to their out of business hours scheduled meetings. Likewise, safety concerns prevent some of them from participating. In a study by de Guzman and Kim (2017), they found that police departments are more able to implement community policing in communities that have lower crime rates. This means that there should be a semblance of order before communities can be enjoined to enhance the state of public order in society through their participation in community-oriented policing (COP).

Community involvement is also the key in prosecution and trial of cases. Most of the time, cases are not prosecuted or trials are dismissed due to the lack of willingness of witnesses to provide information or to testify. Again, this fact shows that incentives to participate and safety are apparently lacking.

According to Gal (2016), there are community members who are involved and can represent the community in the processes. They can also serve as facilitators where they take a leadership role in explaining the social contexts in which the crime has occurred. The facilitator also establishes the norm in the process and identifies the mutual interests and shared values of the parties involved. In addition, participants in these models can identify the social support and provide connections to the social network available to the parties. At times, the community members might be the direct stakeholders in the process. They are the victims and are, therefore, the most needed element in the process.

Reparative Process

Community justice does not negate punishment or retribution. The administration of justice is still the central concern of community justice. It should not be perceived as soft on criminals or that it is nonpunitive. It should also not be so barbaric that it leads to the brutalization effect. The brutalization effect happens when individuals are more emboldened to commit crimes due to the extreme harshness of punishment. This phenomenon was discovered in the examination of the death penalty in Oklahoma (Cochran, Chamlin, & Seth, 1994).

There are some notable strides in this aspect. Karp and Clear (2000) identified two categories for this process: (1) the identification of reparative tasks and (2) the implementation process that facilitates the completion of these tasks. These processes are normally done through mediation proceedings or meetings. Central to these meetings are the concrete expressions of the harm and the acknowledgement of fault by the offender. This is not a punitive-seeking process, but instead a problem-solving process to provide a solution to repair the relationships and harm.

Reintegrative Process

This is where the victim and the community are restored and the offender who has become a marginal member of the community is reintegrated back into the community. The reintegration process is the affirmation of the norm that was violated. In other words, the offender is made to understand the behavior expectation that was violated. The process also involves the assessment of risk before an individual is released into the community. It is important that community fear is not affected and that necessary support networks are available for the offender. The final phase of reintegration is the development of programs for competency development for both the offender and the victim. For example, job training and drug treatment programs may be included in the rehabilitation program of the offender. In the case of the victim, some strategies for self-protection or counselling programs may be offered.

Outcomes of Community Justice

Restoration

Two entities need to be restored: the victim and the community. If damages are incurred, then compensation must be arranged. The victim traumatized by crime should be given the necessary support to recover from the trauma of crime—medical, mental health, and other services. Communities also need to be restored by repairing the harm that was inflicted on that community and to address the criminogenic conditions of that community.

Integration

This refers to the return of the offender into communal life. The barriers to participation in community life must be removed. On the part of the victim, the hindrance to their normal community interaction should be addressed. Both victims and offenders have to develop their competencies to become functional and productive members of the community.

Community Empowerment

This refers to the community capacity to solve its problems particularly in relation to crime. This empowerment can also be indicated by the active participation of the community members in justice processes. This refers to their willingness to volunteer their time and energy.

Community Satisfaction

A basic sense of safety is an outcome that is indicative of safety satisfaction. In the thesis of Lambertus and Yakimchuck (2007), the basic need of any community is the repair of the social order that was broken by crime. They argue that a social order repair is necessary before communities can be inspired to aspire for maintenance and enhancement of order. They argue that participation in the justice system is possible only after the satisfaction of the basic social order need. Figure 14.2 depicts this hierarchy of community needs developed by Lambertus and Yakimchuck (2007, p. 13).

FIGURE 14.2 COMMUNITY HIERARCHY OF SAFETY NEEDS.

Source: Lambertus and Yakimchuck (2007).

Practices in Community Justice

There are varieties where community justice can be brought to fruition in practice. After all, democracy is the government by the people. As stated earlier in the chapter, the essence of community justice is to give meaningful roles to the community in defining their safety needs and the ability to effectively contribute to the provision of that need. Below are discussions of some of the major innovations and trends in the practice of community justice in various arenas of the criminal justice system.

Community Justice in Policy Formulation

Policy formulation is the first contribution that community can provide to community justice. The will of the community can be given a concrete expression in the formulation of policies. The first major effort whereby the community can effect policy is of course voting in initiatives and referenda. For example, the current move to legalize marijuana either as a medical or recreational endeavor has come to fruition due to the participation of the electorate in casting their votes to legalize it.

Community Justice in Policing

Policing has been revolutionized due to the concept of COP that was propounded by Herman Goldstein (1990). The idea of an autocratic, detached, bureaucratic police has been replaced by an informal, personalized, and dynamic response to crime and disorders. Although community policing has been broadly implemented (Peak & Glensor, 1996; Wilson, 2006), its conceptualization and implementation are hardly uniform (Shilston, 2015). In fact, Travis and Langworthy (2008) identify COP as one of the forces that diversifies policing. This diversity in police services delivery is really the outcome of being responsive to community needs. Different communities have different needs, which would therefore require a unique model of public safety service delivery. In their study of the constraining effect of the community's needs, de Guzman and Kim (2017) have argued for this dynamic model of police services delivery that would match these needs. In their perspectives, traditional policing might be more appropriate to initiate the restoration of order in society. They believe that the restoration of order is a precursor to the participation of citizens to community policing initiatives. If communities are afraid or do not see clear returns on the investments of their time and effort, they will not participate. They argued that community members are needed to maintain and enhance higher levels of order, but community members cannot be expected to participate unless order is restored. Hence, although several practices are discussed below, it is really a condition where the police have already maintained an atmosphere of order that community members are comfortable and feel safe in participating in the administration of justice by becoming active coproducers of safety under the community policing model (Bayley & Skolnick, 1986).

Community Policing Programs

Several community policing and crime prevention programs have recently included community participation as key to their effectiveness. A cursory description of these programs is presented below.

CompStat

The Police Research Executive Forum (2013) describes CompStat as "a performance management system that is used to reduce crime and achieve other police department goals. CompStat emphasizes information-sharing, responsibility and accountability, and improving effectiveness. It includes four generally recognized core components: (1) Timely and accurate information or intelligence; (2) Rapid deployment of resources; (3) Effective tactics; and (4) Relentless follow-up." These core elements, however, are difficult to achieve without the active participation of the citizens. They are the primary source of information and they are the ultimate barometer of how well police are performing their job.

CompStat, as practiced by the New York City Police Department (NYPD), was department centric despite the decentralization and grant of autonomy to ground commanders. Problem-solving was primarily department led instead of being collaboratively done. The origin of CompStat at the New York's subway police was a more grassroots approach with the riding community and different stakeholders more involved in the process. For this reason, CompStat can be considered a community justice model.

Focused Deterrence

Focused deterrence is another problem-solving approach to crime. The basic idea for focused deterrence is to certain individual or groups that are highly responsible for crime in the community. The program aims to deliver a strong message of intolerance about certain problematic activities to the targets (i.e., criminal actors) and that the targets are asked to cease from committing such activities. In all of the publicized implementation of this program, the most important component of such approach is not only the police department that vigorously communicates these demands and alternatives (i.e., deterrence) to offenders, but more importantly, the participation of the community in the their collective pronouncement about the unacceptability of the disavowed behavior (i.e., shaming) and the mobilization of community resources to provide alternatives to the individual's or group's criminal life (i.e., restoration and social support). The original implementation of focused deterrence at High Point, North Carolina (Frabutt, Hefner, Di Luca, Shelton, & Harvey, 2010) shows that community members were involved from the intelligence and information gathering and the provision of services to those who chose to amend their lives. The application of focused deterrence has become more widespread and has demonstrated a huge deal of success (Braga & Weisburd, 2012). The same factors were observed by the Cincinnati Police Department in its implementation of CIRV. Communities and businesses were active participants in this crime prevention initiative (Engel et al., 2011).

Third-Party Policing

Third-party policing is defined as police efforts to persuade or coerce other regulators or nonoffending persons, such as health and building inspectors, housing agencies, property owners, parents, and business owners, to take some responsibility for preventing crime or reducing crime problems (Buerger & Mazerolle, 1998). In third-party policing, the police create or enhance crime control through guardians in locations or situations where crime control guardianship was previously absent or noneffective. Sometimes the police use cooperative consultation with community members to encourage and convince third parties to take more crime control or prevention responsibility. At other times, the police use coercive threats, with the backing of a range of civil and regulatory laws, to engage third parties into taking some crime control responsibility.

A key defining feature of third-party policing is the presence of some type of third person (or third collectivity) that is directed by the police to enforce laws particularly involving maintenance of order in their establishments. The list of potential third parties can include property owners, parents, bar owners, shop owners, local and state governments, insurance companies, business owners, inspectors, and private security guards. Indeed, any person or entity that is engaged by the police to take on some type of role in controlling or preventing crime could potentially be identified as a third party or what Buerger and Mazerolle (1998) refer to as "proximate targets" and what Mazerolle and Roehl (1998) have referred to as "burden-bearers." These are the people or entities that are coerced by the police and who carry the burden for initiating some type of action that is expected to alter the conditions that allow crime activity to grow or exist.

These are but some of the efforts that police are using to encourage communities to become active participants in the provisions of safety. There are others that have been used under the umbrella of community policing and problem-oriented policing. Some of these traditional methods are neighborhood watches, citizen's academy, volunteers in policing, among others. Indeed, ever since the emergence of community policing as an overarching philosophy in policing, the multiplicity of roles and forms that communities participate in the provision of safety continues to evolve. Lately, citizen participation in policing has become virtual through the use of social media and the ability to file complaints through the Internet (de Guzman & Hunter, 2015).

Community Justice in Prosecution and Adjudication

The Jury System

The underlying assumption of community courts is that communities are deeply affected by the sentencing process, yet are rarely consulted and involved in judicial outcomes. The jury system is a direct manifestation of the participation of the community in the prosecution, adjudication, and sentencing of the individuals in the criminal justice system. The use of jury is enshrined in the US Constitution (Sixth Amendment) and is perhaps the most direct form of participation by citizens in the justice system. There are now three forms of jury that are participated in by the citizens. The first is the grand jury wherein ordinary citizens are assembled by the prosecution to decide whether a case should be heard in a trial or dismissed through a "no bill." Another form of jury is the petit jury where again a panel of six to twelve jurors are made to decide on the guilt or innocence of a person charged with a criminal offense. The latest form of jury is sentencing juries or sentencing panels. In certain cases, sentencing ceremonies give a voice to citizens through the victim impact statements that are sometimes openly given in courtrooms. These sentencing groups assist in the determination of the proper punishment to be imposed on a person. Thus, courts have given meaningful voice to the community in the prosecution and adjudication of cases.

Community Prosecution Programs

Community prosecution is a grassroots approach to law enforcement involving both traditional and nontraditional prosecutorial initiatives. It invites citizens to participate in establishing crime-fighting priorities and collaborating with prosecutors. By clearly defining an area in which to implement community-based programs, committing resources for the long term, and being sensitive to residents' concerns, prosecutors can target key problems identified by residents (Weinstein, 1998). Several of these initiatives were established in New York and have been viewed as successes.

Third-Party Enforcement through Prosecution

Just like third-party policing, the prosecutor's office may use third parties to control or prevent crime and disorders through the threats of citation or prosecution for contributory negligence (Mazerolle & Ransley, 2004).

Teen Courts and Community Centers

Teen courts are sometimes called youth courts or peer courts. The peer-run court establishes a system where a juvenile faces the ordeal of undergoing an analogous process of adult courts, but are done by his or her peers. The program is conducted by youth who are trained in court protocols and processes. These processes are sometimes supervised and coached by adult volunteer coaches. Only intermediate sanctions are imposed on these sentences. These courts are also known as community justice centers. Teen courts do not only provide the shock treatment of adjudication (Anderson, 1999), but they are also the means to access local community support that might be available to the youthful offender (Llewelyn-Thomas & Prior, 2007).

Therapeutic Courts

These courts involve the participation of various agents of change, both formal and informal, in order to address the criminogenic needs of individuals who might have special needs. This movement started with the drug court, but as of recently, there are more than a dozen therapeutic or accountability courts that operate, dealing with various populations, such as veterans, family, and other special needs population.

Community Justice in Corrections

Several notable programs have emerged within the last ten years that are aligned with the community justice system. These programs are intended to achieve the goals of repair and restoration of the offenders and the victims including the community. Most of these programs are aligned with the restorative justice perspective. As conceptualized by McCold (2004), communities are secondary victims of crime. They are the ones who might be affected by crime through its impact on their quality of life and fear of crime. However, they are also considered as secondary perpetrators of crime as they fail to prevent the occurrence of crime through their lack of exercise of informal controls (McCold, 2004).

The following are some of the notable programs that have been happening in corrections, including probation and parole.

Reentry Programs

Reentry programs are one of the most widespread efforts in helping former inmates transition into the community. Prior to release into the community, the inmates are rehabilitated through cognitive and skills development programs. These reentry programs are carefully planned so that inmates are given services during their incarceration to address their criminogenic needs. The strength of the reentry program lies in its ability to partner with community members and businesses who would be able to provide the necessary support and aftercare for the released inmate's transition back into the community. The released inmates are provided access to employment and education and other assistance that they might need in order to resume their lives after incarceration.

Restorative Justice through Community Service

The Clark County Juvenile Court (CCJC) in Seattle, Washington is one of the notable programs in the aspect of fostering an effective citizen participation in restorative justice model. The novelty and innovativeness in the program is its ability to gain wide community support from the community through the nonprofit and business organizations volunteerism in the program. In the CCJC, the juvenile delinquents were not simply made to render "community service to" the community, but rather to render "community service with" the community. The ingredients for success in this program were clearly the enthusiastic support that communities extended to the program (Wood, 2015).

Challenges to Community Justice

Despite the allure and mysticism surrounding community justice, certain challenges need to be outlined (Taylor & Auerhahn, 2015). There are sometimes situations where good intentions do not always produce good results. At the same token, there is always a price to be paid for any program. These challenges need to be raised in order not to line up community justice as one of those failed reforms in the administration of justice.

Vague Goals

Quality of life has been floated as the desirable outcome of community justice. However, this concept seems to admit of arbitrary and subjective conceptualization. In several quarters, quality of life policing has been decried as discriminatory and coercive (Katz, Webb, & Schaefer, 2001). Quality of life in overincarceration or overenforcement can actually produce more crimes (Taylor & Auerhahn, 2015). Community justice claims to address all parties' well-being in the process. However, this can be easily lost in the process as different stakeholders might advance their own points of view.

Even its seemingly more concrete objective of crime prevention is hard to determine. In the context of crime, we are not really sure if the lower rates of crime are the direct effect of the intervention or the by-product of other social factors. For instance, higher crime rates or arrest rates might indicate that crime is not being prevented. However, such increase in crime rate is not at all related to the capacity of the model to prevent crime. Instead, it is indicative of how the justice system became more productive in identifying offenders and crimes in society, particularly with the involvement of citizens in the detection, apprehension, and resolutions of crime.

In light of these controversies about goals, community justice should strive to have clearer concepts with which to measure its successes.

Legal Cynicism

Legal cynicism is a cultural frame in which the law and the agents of its enforcement are viewed as **illegitimate**, **unresponsive**, and **ill equipped** to ensure public safety (Kirk & Papachristos, 2011). Kirk and Matsuda (2011, 444) "argue that the controlling influence of the law carries little weight when people view the law and its agents negatively. Thus, more crime will occur in neighborhoods characterized by legal cynicism." Community justice in these neighborhoods where legal cynicism is high becomes community vigilantism, which Black (1985) calls self-help. It is in this context that Kirk and Papachistos (2011) found high crime rates in Chicago neighborhoods despite the increasing economic activities in the city. This condition of anomic state in community is borne by the inability of the very institutions who desire for communities to participate in the administration of justice. This becomes a tautological situation where formal criminal justice reforms must first be achieved in order for community justice to thrive.

Infrastructure Reforms

Perhaps the most important factor for facilitation community participation is the lack of infrastructure for this to happen. Meaningful participation can only happen if there is an empowerment of citizens to direct the actors of the justice system. One of these factors should be the power to hire and fire their officials. In the justice system, this power is available only to the citizens when they elect prosecutors and judges. However, some prosecutors, judges, and all other criminal justice officials, this power and participation of citizens seem miniscule. There is hardly any input from citizens when it comes to the hiring of correctional and police officers. There are some systems where citizens participate in the hiring process, but this is few and far between. Likewise, the officers have very little direct accountability to citizens. In the case of police officers, a civilian review would have been effective in this process. One of the more pressing questions about the participation of the public is in controlling the police through the civilian review board. As we read earlier in the chapter, civilian review boards have very rocky relationships with the police. Federal judges and prosecutors are not directly subject to recall by the electorate. Their control and accountability are reposed to a government bureaucracy. In other words, the citizens through their collective actions and wills are not directly responsible for defining their own sense of justice system and have no effective means of participation in realizing those ideals of justice.

The other challenge for participation is the lack of incentives and avenues for participation. One of the laments of community policing is the lack of participation from the citizens in attending the meetings. Community obligations become tedious requirements for those that have economic and family hardships. The infrastructure of community bringing themselves over to the venues of justice so that they can participate is a constraint. The justice machinery should instead bring the justice to them. For example, perhaps there should be more training and meetings of community in their workplaces with companies compensating for those times. In this regard, community members will not find extra time and lose income by participating in the process. This can also be done with some court processes.

Specificity of Rights, Roles, and Responsibilities

The other challenge is the lack of specificity in the roles that citizens should perform. In policing, for example, to what extent are the policing duties of citizens being exercised, especially in the use of compliance technique?. Over the years, the empirical results suggest that the clear organization and specificity of rights, roles, and responsibilities are keys to effective community justice models. Two of the programs noted for this clarity in organization are the Washington State's Restorative Community Service (RCS) and the CIRV. In both programs, clear delineations of the roles and responsibilities of all the stakeholders have been instrumental to its success. In the case of the Washington program, the presence of a liaison officer has clarified the intent and goals of the programs to the community members. Thus, massive participation happened because of the clarifications of these expectations and roles (Wood, 2015). In the case of the CIRV, the clear functions of law enforcement and the services teams have created a smooth working relationship in the implementation of the program (Engel et al., 2011). These experiences illustrate how the program can become effective and efficient with clear communications and expectations.

Sidestepping the Unintended Consequences

Coercive Compliance

Third-party policing (Worrall & Schmalleger, 2018) and prosecution have been somewhat viewed with skepticism because of the coercive nature of the programs. A threat of sanctions to engage participation in a crime prevention program negates the ideals of volunteerism. This can become problematic as it transfers complete accountability to third parties. This practice might also result in a situation where third parties may become more aggressive in their performance of their roles (Mazerolle & Ransley, 2004; Mazerolle & Roehl, 1998).

Disruption of Informal Social Networks

Taylor and Auerhahn (2015, p. .01) claim that community justice "inhibit communities abilities to exert information social control by disrupting social networks and reducing collective efficacy." Their contention is that the state, by not being able to maintain safety effectively, has not met its obligations under the social contract arrangement. In the outcomes, we have identified that community empowerment was one of the outcomes of community justice. The effectiveness of the justice system without the corresponding achievement of the other goals might result in increased arrests and also greater incarceration. These measures of effectiveness impact the disruption of family and the diminution of informal social control due to the strains associated with such punitive sanctions. Offenders who also cycle back and forth to the communities might erode the social capital that has been established. As a proponent of community justice, Clear (2007) cautions that increasing levels of incarceration and reentry will increase rather than decrease crime rates. As a result, community members might be disillusioned with the program. In Baltimore, it was reported that neighborhoods with high concentrations of released prisoners were more likely to report high levels of anomie, incivilities, and crime. There has to be deeper thoughts involving the true outcomes that community justice needs to achieve.

Comprehension Check

1. Define community justice and identify its goals, principles, and processes.
2. What are the various ways by which police can implement community justice?
3. How do the prosecutors and courts practice community justice?
4. Explain how corrections implement community justice.
5. What are the challenges and controversies in the practice of community justice?

References

Anderson, D. C. (1999). *Kids, courts, and communities: Lessons from the Red Hook youth court.* New York, NY: Center for Court Innovation.

Atherton, S. (2015). "Community courts to address youth offending: A lost opportunity?" *British Journal of Community Justice, 13*(2), 111–123.

Bayley, D. H., & Shearing, C. D. (2001). *The new structure of policing: Description, conceptualization, and research agenda.* Washington, DC: Office of Justice Programs, National Institute of Justice.

Bayley, D. H., & Skolnick J. R. (1986). *The new blue line: Police innovation in six American cities.* New York, NY: Free Press.

Black, D. J. (1985). *The idea of police.* Beverly Hills, CA: Sage.

Boland, B. (1998). "Community prosecution: Portland's experience." In D. R. Karp (Ed.), *Community justice: An emerging field.* Lanham, MA: Rowman & Littlefield.

Braga, A. A., & Weisburd, D. L. (2012). "The effects of focused deterrence strategies on crime: A systematic review and meta-analysis of the empirical evidence." *Journal of Research in Crime and Delinquency, 49*(3), 323–358.

Braithwaite, J. (1989). *Crime, shame, and reintegration.* Cambridge, UK: Cambridge University Press.

Buerger, M. E., & Mazerolle, L. G. (1998). "Third party policing: A theoretical analysis of an emerging trend." *Justice Quarterly, 15*(2), 301–328.

Clear, T. (2007). *Imprisoning communities: How mass incarceration makes disadvantaged neighborhoods worse.* New York, NY: Oxford University Press.

Cochran, J. K., Chamlin, M. B., & Seth, M. (1994). Deterrence or brutalization: An impact assessment of Oklahoma's return to capital punishment. *Criminology, 32*(1), 107–134.

de Guzman, M., & Hunter, R. (2015). *Social media and police: Technology uses and challenges.* Research Presentation during the Annual Conference of the Criminal Justice Association of Georgia, Morrow, GA. Retrieved from http://cjag.us/conference-presentations/

de Guzman, M. C., & Kim, M. (2017). "Community hierarchy of need and policing: Toward a new theory of police organizational behavior." *Police Practice & Research: An International Journal, 17*(4), 352–365.

Eck, J. (1997). "Preventing crime at places." In L. W. Sherman (Ed.), *Preventing crime: What works, what doesn't, what's promising: A report to the United States congress.* Washington, DC: National Institute of Justice.

Eck, J., & Spelman, W. (1987). "Who you gonna call? The police as problem busters." *Crime and Delinquency, 33*, 31–52.

Engel, R. S., Tillyer, M. S., & Corsaro, N. (2011). "Reducing gang violence using focused deterrence: Evaluating the Cincinnati Initiative to Reduce Violence (CIRV)." *Justice Quarterly, 30 (1)*, 403–439. doi:10.1080/07418825.2011.619559

Frabutt, J. M., Hefner, M. K., Di Luca, K., Shelton, T. L., & Harvey, L. K. (2010). "A street-drug elimination initiative: The law enforcement perspective." *Policing: An International Journal of Police Strategies and Management, 33*(3), 452–472.

Gal, T. (2016). "The conflict is ours": Community involvement in restorative justice." *Contemporary Justice Review, 19*(3), 289–306.

Goldstein, H. (1990). *Problem-oriented policing.* New York, NY: McGraw-Hill.

Hunter, R. D., Barker, T., & de Guzman, M. C. (2018). *Police community relations and the administration of justice* (9th ed.). New York, NY: Pearson.

IACP. (2015). *2015 social media survey results*. Retrieved from http://www. iacpsocialmedia.org/wp-content/uploads/2017/01/FULL-2015-SocialMedia-Survey-Results.compressed.pdf

IACP and Urban Institute. (2017). *2016 law enforcement use of social media survey*. Retrieved from http://www.theiacp.org/Portals/0/documents/ pdfs/2016-law-enforcement-use-of-social-media-survey.pdf

Karp, D. R., & Clear, T. R. (2000). "Community justice: A conceptual framework." *Criminal Justice, 2*, 323–368.

Katz, C. M., Webb, V. J., & Schaefer, D. R. (2001). "An assessment of the impact of quality of life policing on crime and disorder." *Justice Quarterly, 18*(4), 825–876.

Kirk, D. S., & Matsuda, M. (2011). "Legal cynicism, collective efficacy, and the ecology of arrest." *Criminology, 49*(2), 443–472.

Kirk, D. S., & Papachristos, A. V. (2011). "Cultural mechanisms and the persistence of neighborhood violence." *American Journal of Sociology, 116*, 1190–233.

Lambertus, S., & Yakimchuk, R. (2007). *Future of policing in Alberta: International trends and case studies* (A discussion paper). Alberta, Canada: Alberta Solicitor General and Public Security Office Research Unit.

Llewelyn-Thomas, S., & Prior, G. (2007). *North Liverpool community justice centre: Surveys of local residents* (Ministry of justice series). London, England: Lord Chancellor's Department.

Lundman, R. J. (1980). *Police and policing: An introduction*. New York, NY: Holt, Rinehart, & Winston.

Mazerolle, L. G., & Ransley, J. (2004). Third party policing: Prospects, challenges, and implications for regulators. *Research and Public Policy Series*. Retrieved from https://research-repository.griffith.edu.au/bitstream/ handle/10072/5027/27003_1.pdf;jsessionid=09C2A2D0D75 F77F00DC319F D638DA26B?sequence=1

Mazerolle, L. G., & Roehl, J. (1998). "Civil remedies and crime prevention: An introduction." In L. Mazerolle & J. Roehl (Eds.), *Civil remedies and crime prevention: Crime prevention studies* (Vol. 9, pp. 1–20). Monsey, NY: Criminal Justice Press.

McCold, P. (2004). "Paradigm muddle: The threat to restorative justice posed by its merger with community justice." *Contemporary Justice Review: Issues in Criminal, Social, and Restorative Justice, 7*, 3–35.

McDonald, P. P. (2002). *Managing police operations: Implementing the New York crime control model—CompStat*. Belmont, CA: Wadsworth.

Peak, K. J., & Glensor, R. W. (1996). *Community policing and problem solving*. Upper Saddle River, NJ: Prentice Hall.

Police Research Executive Forum. (2013). *COMPSTAT: Its origins, evolution, and future in law enforcement*. Washington, DC: Bureau of Justice Assistance.

Sampson, R. J., & Laub, J. H. (1993). *Crime in the making: Pathways and turning points through life*. Cambridge, MA: Harvard University Press.

Sherman, L. W. (1997). "Family-based crime prevention." In L. W. Sherman (ed.), *Preventing crime: What works, what doesn't, what's promising: A report to the United States congress*. Washington, DC: National Insitute of Justice.

Shilston, T. (2015). "Democratic policing, community policing, and the fallacy of conflation in international development missions." *International Journal of Police Science & Management, 17*(4), 207–215.

Skogan, W., & Hartnett, S. (1997). *Community policing, Chicago style*. Chicago, IL: University of Chicago Press.

Taylor, C. J., & Auerhan, K. (2015). "Community justice and public safety: Assessing criminal justice policy through the lens of the social contract." *Criminology & Criminal Justice, 15*(3), 300–320.

Travis, L. F., & Langworthy, R. H. (2008). *Policing in America: A balance of forces* (4th ed.). Cincinnati, OH: Prentice Hall.

Wilson, J. M. (2006). *Community policing in America*. New York, NY: Taylor & Francis.

Wilson, J. Q. (1962). *Varieties of police behavior*. Boston, MA: Cambridge University Press.

Wilson, J. Q., & Kelling, G. L. (1982). "Broken windows." *Atlantic Monthly, 211*, 29–38.

Wood, W. R. (2015). "Soliciting community involvement and support for restorative justice through community service." *Criminal Justice Policy Review, 26*(2), 131–155.

Worrall, J. L., & Schmalleger, F. (2018). *Policing* (3rd ed.). New York, NY: Pearson.

CPSIA information can be obtained
at www.ICGtesting.com
Printed in the USA
JSHW011144170822
29381JS00001B/1